I0764853

Edited by
Astrid Ohletz

BEYOND THE EPILOGUE

New Stories of
Beloved Sapphic
Couples

Table of Contents

Foreword

As readers of romance, we cherish that moment when the curtain falls on two people who have found their way to each other. But if you are like me, you have often wondered what happens after the happily ever after. In *Beyond the Epilogue,* we invite you to step back into these beloved worlds, this time beyond the final page.

What makes this anthology so special to me is the chance to revisit the couples we have grown to love. Each of these short stories picks up after the original novel's close. We find out how life unfolds for them after the grand declarations, after the last kiss on the final page.

As the editor of this collection, I found it deeply rewarding to witness these glimpses of what comes next. I have always felt that love stories, especially sapphic ones, do not end when the book does. They continue with all the joys and challenges that life brings. In times like these, when the real world feels especially heavy, it is all the more important to have stories that give us a moment of reprieve and remind us of hope. I hope you will enjoy these second acts as much as I did, because every love story, even after the epilogue, still has so much to give.

Astrid Ohletz
Editor

Caitlyn's Got Talent

by Quinn Ivins

"Ow! Fuck!" Caitlyn shook her finger. A fat drop of blood appeared where she'd lost the battle with the staple remover.

"What's wrong?" Her coworker Nina appeared at her office door. "You're bleeding!"

"I'm okay." Caitlyn reached for a tissue and dabbed at the wound. "The screen in the conference room is broken again, so I made handouts for senior staff, and our crappy printer put the staple in the wrong place."

Nina inspected the pile of documents. "Uh, I don't see a problem. This is the title page, right? *Fall Semester Enrollment Update*? The staple is in the top left corner."

"Yes, I know, but it's too high. See how the staple hangs off the page? It's unprofessional."

Nina chuckled. "Your work is always excellent. No one will care about the staple." She flipped through the pages of the packet on top. "Just as I suspected, these charts are gorgeous. You're the best researcher we've ever had."

Caitlyn couldn't suppress her smile or the warm glow of pride in her chest. "Thanks. But I'm still going to fix it."

"No time. Unless you want to be late." Nina tapped her wristwatch, a dainty oval on a silver band.

"It's time to go already?" Caitlyn grabbed her phone. "Oh no, you're right. We only have two minutes." She had never been late to senior staff, and she wasn't about to break her streak.

"Come on, then." Nina moved toward the door.

"I guess I'll have to distribute these as they are." Caitlyn ruefully picked up the pile. She'd only managed to fix about half of the staples. "Wait. This one has blood on it."

"Give that one to me." Nina winked. "I won't faint."

They crossed the administrative building's lobby, Nina's high heels clicking on the tiled floor while Caitlyn's sensible loafers stepped silently beside her.

I should dress up more. Then again, Nina was a dean, several levels above Caitlyn, and her sleek pantsuit fit her role. Caitlyn's dress pants and button-down shirt were professional enough for the director of research. Weren't they?

"I hope they fix the screen before you end up in the hospital," Nina said lightly. "Or, better yet, replace the thing. All of the technology in that room is ancient."

"I'm sure they don't have money for a new one," Caitlyn said. "But that's life at community college. We make it work."

"Indeed. And that attitude is why you fit in here."

I hope so. Caitlyn's first ten months had gone well, but as her one-year performance review approached, she couldn't help feeling more anxious.

They slipped into the conference room, where their colleagues were gathered around the massive table.

"Welcome." Dr. Tomin, Caitlyn's boss, gestured to a stack of paper agendas.

Caitlyn's presentation was eighth on the list. *Great. More time to obsess*. She crossed and uncrossed her legs, half-listening to the meeting while she mentally revised her prepared comments.

"Our next agenda item is a fun one," Dr. Tomlin said. "It's time for Linvale's Got Talent!"

"Oh no," Nina whispered.

What? Caitlyn mouthed back, but Nina pressed her lips together.

Dr. Tomlin smiled, but most people averted their eyes.

How odd. A student talent show sounded like fun, so what was the problem?

"For those of you who weren't here last year," Dr. Tomlin said, "we have a faculty/staff talent show every year to raise money for the scholarship program. We've been asked for at least one representative from the management team to participate. Any takers?"

Definitely not me. Caitlyn studied her lap.

"Belinda does a great comedy routine, but, of course, she's on maternity leave. Walter, any interest in playing your trombone?"

"Can't," Walter said. "Finger injury. No trombone for me. Doctor's orders."

Caitlyn snuck a glance at Walter, whose fingers appeared perfectly fine. *Please. My finger is in worse shape from the staple remover. Is Dr. Tomlin buying this?* She glanced at their boss, only to see him look right back at her.

Shit! She'd inadvertently made eye contact.

"Caitlyn, you're relatively new. It would be great if you could participate."

No no no no no. "Oh gosh, I don't think—"

"It's a great opportunity because you could get to know some of the faculty." Dr. Tomlin sounded entirely too pleased with himself. "Leah Schulman is in charge—you know, the chair of the Theater Department?—and you'll need to work with her next year on accreditation. This will get you on her good side."

Caitlyn had the sensation of struggling in deep water, desperate to reach the surface, where she could breathe. "Of course I always want to help out. The thing is..." *I've got a clinically diagnosed anxiety disorder and epic stage fright.* "I don't have any talents. Wait. That came out wrong. I'm good at research and data, but I don't have the sort of talent that works onstage. I'm sure someone else would do a much better job. Anyone else." Caitlyn searched her colleagues' faces and found a mix of smug amusement and careful avoidance of her gaze.

No one would bail her out, not if it meant volunteering in Caitlyn's place.

"Oh, it doesn't have to be anything fancy." Dr. Tomlin waved his hand. "I'm sure you can think of something. Did you ever play a musical instrument?"

"Well, I do play a little guitar, but—"

"Why didn't you say so?" He broke into a wide smile. "I knew you had a hidden talent."

Damn it. Why had she said that? "No, wait. It's more like a private hobby. I don't perform, and I haven't seriously practiced in years. My repertoire is limited to some old pop songs, and my voice..." Caitlyn's brain caught up to her mouth before she confessed to singing. "I don't have a vocalist, so the music wouldn't really translate."

"That's our Caitlyn, always overthinking." Dr. Tomlin nodded with terrifying finality and scribbled something in his notebook. "You'll be great. I'll let Leah know."

Beside her, Nina couldn't hide a *sucks-to-be-you* smirk.

"Next up," Dr. Tomlin said, "we need to prepare for midterm tutoring outreach..."

As her boss droned on, Caitlyn's head swam with images of the looming catastrophe: bright stage lights, a huge audience, and Caitlyn there in the center, struggling to play her guitar.

Sure, it wasn't a top-ten nightmare. Her most frequent stress dreams involved academic failures, such as her PhD getting revoked because she'd never finished high school. Dreams where she'd forgotten to study for an exam were also in heavy rotation. Public performing was a less salient fear, but only because she'd spent her life avoiding scenarios where she'd have to sing, play music, or do anything artistic in front of a crowd.

Caitlyn looked down at the handouts that had been her biggest source of stress until a few minutes ago. *I'm a researcher, not a performer.* She worked so hard at her job, the one involving her actual qualifications and training. Why wasn't it enough?

Hi Dr. Tomlin, I appreciate you thinking of me for the LCC talent show! As you know, I strive to be a team player. Unfortunately—

Caitlyn swiveled in her chair, brainstorming and discarding excuses before her fingers could type them.

However, due to a medical condition—

Unfortunately, I checked my schedule and discovered a conflict.

What if Dr. Tomlin asked her to explain the so-called conflict? She'd have to come up with a plausible lie and keep the story straight for the next two weeks, and she'd probably panic and mess up.

Still, she had once impersonated her twin sister Chloe for an entire summer. Surely she could manage a tiny white lie? A simple fake conflict. People made up excuses all the time.

Then again, the fallout from her stint as Chloe should teach her to never lie at work. Caitlyn backspaced the sentence. But the alternative…

No. She'd just lie.

Unfortunately,

A sharp knock on the door frame caused Caitlyn to jump in her seat.

"Hey-o!" Leah Schulman stood in the doorway, her LCC lanyard swinging over her fitted T-shirt and jeans. Her wavy black bob was even more chaotic than usual, as if she'd been running. "I hear you're joining us for the talent show!"

Damn, Dr. Tomlin was fast. Almost as if he knew Caitlyn would try to bail. She swiveled her chair to face Leah. "Oh, hi. Um, Dr. Tomlin did suggest it, but I'm not sure it's a good idea."

Leah threw back her head and laughed, a hearty barking sound. "Don't be scared! We don't bite!"

"No, I know! And I love spending time with the faculty." She swiveled back and forth in her chair. "It's just… I'm not really sure…"

"What questions do you have?"

The issue wasn't that Caitlyn had questions, but pinned by Leah's intense gaze, she felt compelled to come up with some. "How many people come to the show?"

"Oh, everyone comes! It's a great time. Students love seeing their professors in a new light. And administrators too, of course."

"Great." *Oops, did that sound sarcastic?* "I mean it's great that so many people support the scholarship fund." She swallowed. "What kinds of things do people do?"

"Whatever they want! Derek reads his slam poetry. Jeanette sings, and our Shakespeare professors perform a scene from one of his plays. Oscar does a magic show that's always a hit."

"That sounds fun." *Fun to watch.*

"Oh, and donations decide the winner. People vote with their money, and the act that brings in the most wins!"

"That's…a neat idea." Unlike the faculty, Caitlyn was unknown to the students. She'd be surprised if anyone voted for her at all, compounding the humiliation of a lackluster performance. There had to be a way out. "It sounds like the talent show is very popular, and you probably have a lot of people wanting to participate. Instead of taking up a whole slot by myself, I wonder if I could join another group. Maybe they need extras in the background of the Shakespeare skit? I'd make a great townsperson."

"Oh no, don't worry—we have plenty of room. You'll get your own spot for sure!" Leah beamed. "Dr. Tomlin already told me you're a whiz on the guitar!"

"Wonderful. So nice of him."

"I'll send an email with the details! See you there!" Leah walked off before Caitlyn could respond.

She sank back in her chair. *Why me?* Now her chances of getting out of the talent show seemed worse than ever.

Why does this feel like a giant conspiracy?

Caitlyn shouldn't assume she could barge into Pulaski College whenever she pleased simply because she happened to date the college president. But the truth was, she could—and she desperately needed to talk to Ruth. So she didn't bother to text before driving across town after work.

After a quick stop at the campus coffee shop, she arrived at the president's suite with an iced latte in each hand. Thankfully, the door to the suite was propped.

Bernice, the receptionist, was dressed in her coat and packing up her purse. "She's still in there. No sign of stopping anytime soon."

That's my workaholic president. "I had no doubt."

Caitlyn nudged the door with her butt and slid through. "Surprise."

Ruth looked up from the computer. Her blonde hair was mussed with frizzy ends, her shoulders bare, and her blazer slung over the back of her chair. The sight made Caitlyn want to straddle her and do naughty things. *Damn those big, clear windows.*

"Oh! Bless you." Ruth jumped up and grabbed one of the drinks as if lifting the holy grail.

"They're both decaf."

Ruth's exultant expression soured into a petulant scowl. "Again?"

"We both know you don't need more caffeine, especially not in the evening."

"Fine. I'll take what I can get. Thank you for the drink." She kissed Caitlyn on the lips, then sat on the edge of her desk and took a sip. Her lips left rosy prints on the straw. "How did you know I'd still be at work?"

"Lucky guess." Caitlyn gave her a meaningful look.

"Okay, I've been working late. It's just that with midterms—"

"Hey, it's okay." Caitlyn squeezed Ruth's shoulder. "I know how much you care about your college."

"Thanks. You get it because we're the same. I know how much you care about LCC."

"Right." A hard knot in Caitlyn's stomach reminded her of what she'd been asked to do on behalf of said college.

"What's wrong? Did something happen at work?"

Caitlyn pushed a pile of papers aside and sat on the desk next to Ruth. "Dr. Tomlin volunteered me for something, and I'm afraid it's too late to say no." She quickly recapped her day, the senior staff meeting, and Leah's visit. You're a president. You know how these politics work better than anyone. How bad would it be to drop out?"

"Hmmm. I'm not exactly Dr. Popularity at Pulaski. Things have improved in recent months, but we both know I'm not an expert in charming the faculty." Ruth swirled her finger in the condensation on her cup. "Still, any college administrator will tell you this stuff is huge. Participating in college events shows you care. It's especially important for someone like you, a data person who might at times be perceived as adversarial."

"It's true. The faculty are suspicious of metrics and data. They worry the administration wants to use numbers against them, even though..." Caitlyn shrugged. "Well, okay, it's a little bit true."

"Exactly." Ruth sighed ruefully. "You can't improve the college without looking at instruction, whether it's enrollment, passing rates, retention rates. All of it shines a spotlight on underperforming programs, and some faculty will be threatened by your work. Ideally, you need to make as many friends in instruction as possible, and building relationships in a fun setting can help. But I take it the talent show isn't your idea of fun."

Caitlyn shook her head. "I can't perform in front of people. You know I have anxiety. And you know what it's like."

"I do," Ruth said. "But when you were...well, here with me"—Caitlyn appreciated the gentle euphemism for the time she'd impersonated her twin sister and worked as Ruth's assistant—"I remember you presenting data at a meeting, and you did great. You seemed comfortable enough."

"Yes, I can present my research. Because it's essentially teaching, and I've had a lot of experience in academia. But this is completely different. They're expecting me to do something entertaining, in front of a huge auditorium full of people." She rubbed her forehead. "God, I wish I'd never told them I play guitar. It just slipped out."

Ruth entwined her fingers with Caitlyn's. "Your playing is lovely."

"Thanks. But do you remember the first time I played for you? My face was so hot. It must have been bright red. I could barely get through one song, and we'd already slept together."

"Of course I remember. I thought it was cute." Ruth brushed a strand of Caitlyn's hair from her face.

"Yes, but you always think my anxiety is cute."

"I do." Ruth leaned in, and their lips met in a soft kiss. "But I didn't realize how you felt about performing in front of crowds, and I'm sorry it's like that for you."

Caitlyn sat back. "So, what do I do? I want to make a good impression, and barfing all over the stage—or freezing, or trembling and screwing up in front of everyone—isn't going to help my image at LCC."

"Okay, slow down. When is the show?'

"Next Friday. Sadly, it's not enough time to find a new job or flee the country."

"Hey, there's no need to be drastic. We've got some time. I can come to your place this weekend. You can practice a few songs for me and see how you feel?"

"Well, of course it won't be hard when it's just you. I feel safe with you."

Ruth smiled. "I'm really glad."

"It's true. But that means you can't help with my stage fright."

"Hmmm. I can make my unimpressed administrator face, if that helps?"

Caitlyn's cheeks warmed. "Okay, that might help." It wouldn't, actually, but she'd never turn down the stern looks Ruth gave her subordinates. "In fact, maybe if I can see it right now?"

Ruth chuckled and then narrowed her eyes in a disdainful scowl.

Windows be damned, Caitlyn shoved her drink aside, pushed forward and captured Ruth's mouth in a long, juicy kiss.

Caitlyn gave herself until the end of the weekend to pick a song, which is how she found herself on her sofa on Sunday afternoon, sheet music spread out all over the table. But instead of looking through it, she absently played a few notes of a familiar tune.

Ruth walked in, carrying a glass of wine. "Oh, 'Fast Car'!" She perched on the other side of the couch. "I love Tracy Chapman. Is that what you're going to perform?"

"It's one of my favorite songs ever. But I can't play 'Fast Car.' Everyone will expect me to sing."

"You have a beautiful…" Whatever Ruth saw on Caitlyn's face made her stop and hold up her hands. "Okay, no singing. Got it."

"Yeah, I can't sing in front of an audience. That's even worse than playing guitar. My voice will shake, and everyone will know I'm nervous, and then my stage fright will spiral into a full-on nervous breakdown."

"And we can't have that. So, what are you thinking of playing?"

Caitlyn shuffled her sheet music. "Something similar to this." She launched into the piece, a contemporary instrumental song by Devendra Banhart.

When she finished, Ruth applauded. "I like that one!"

"Thanks, but it's just to give you an idea of what I'm thinking. I can't play this specific song because it has an offensive name."

Ruth raised an eyebrow as Caitlyn passed her the relevant page. She held it up to read. "'Tit Smoking in the Temple of Artisan Mimicry.' Ah. I see your point."

"I need something like this. Short, not too difficult, works without vocals—but without *tit* in the name."

"What is tit smoking, exactly?" Ruth tilted her head as if contemplating a deep philosophical question. "I assume it involves the mouth."

"Stop, you're distracting me." Caitlyn shifted and clenched the neck of her guitar. "I need to focus."

"First, you need to relax." Ruth moved closer and gently lifted the guitar out of Caitlyn's hands. She set it on the table and wrapped her arms around Caitlyn's shoulders in a secure embrace.

Caitlyn's tension eased as she melted into Ruth's warm body. *Safe. I feel safe.* If only Ruth could hold her during the performance.

A rhythmic knock sounded on the door, followed by the jiggling of the doorknob, then more knocking.

They broke apart.

"Chloe?" Ruth raised her eyebrows.

"Oh, right." Caitlyn remembered their text exchange. "She wanted to borrow an outfit. Something about a job interview. I said she could come over."

"Okay." Ruth pushed to her feet and answered the door. "Come in," she said to Chloe. "Your sister is under a bit of stress."

Chloe walked in, clutching a whipped drink in one hand and her phone in the other. "What's wrong?"

"My boss is making me perform in a talent show. It's a fundraiser for the college."

"Oh shit." Chloe sat on the other couch and crisscrossed her legs. "You're terrible onstage!"

Ruth glared. "Not helpful."

"I just mean because of her nerves. Uh, but I'm sure you'll be fine?" Chloe attempted a lopsided smile. "What are you going to do?"

"Regrettably, I told them I play guitar. Of course they jumped on it, and now that's what everyone expects. It's not too late to switch to something else, but what else could I do?"

"Hmmm, okay. Let's think. What are your talents?" Chloe took a long, thoughtful sip of her drink. "Um, you could analyze data? Like, project it on the screen and do some calculations."

"You can't be serious," Caitlyn said.

"That's the worst idea I've ever heard," Ruth said.

"No, but that's the point—it would be funny. The worst talent ever!" Chloe giggled.

"A new dimension of cringe," Caitlyn said. "I'm not going to do math for my talent."

"Okay, so we're back to guitar," Chloe said. "Are you going to sing?"

Caitlyn shook her head frantically. "No! No way."

"It's too bad, because your voice is fine—I mean it should be, since I'm a great singer and we're twins." Chloe's eyes widened. "Hey, there's an idea! What if I performed in your place?"

"Huh?" Caitlyn processed the words. "You mean...you would pretend to be me at the talent show?"

"Yeah, just think about it. I can't play guitar, but I can sing! And I don't have stage fright. I'd be happy to perform for an audience. It would be fun."

God help her, Caitlyn was tempted. It would work. They were identical twins, after all, and Leah didn't know her well enough to—

"Absolutely not," Ruth said. "Haven't you learned anything from your twin-switch escapades last year?"

Chloe had the decency to look sheepish. "Okay, yes, that was bad. But you have to admit it worked out." She gestured between Ruth and Caitlyn.

"Yes, but first, I fired both of you." Ruth said. "You cannot impersonate Caitlyn at work."

"Technically, it would be an after-work event," Caitlyn said. "It's in the evening, so..."

Ruth's sharp gaze caused the rest of Caitlyn's words to die in her throat.

"Right. Never mind." The prospect of an escape had scrambled her good sense. She couldn't let Chloe impersonate her, no matter how much she longed to get out of this. "I'll just have to power through it."

"Maybe you can take extra Zoloft?" Chloe said.

"That's not how it works," Caitlyn said.

"Okay. Well, I wish I could help," Chloe said, swishing the ice in her drink, "But I'll come to cheer you on."

"You will?" Caitlyn had hoped to minimize the number of witnesses to her humiliation, but at the same time, it would be nice to have some guaranteed applause.

"Of course! It's the least I can do after everything you've..." Chloe looked at Ruth and trailed off, probably because *everything you've done for me* included certain twin-switch activities that Ruth had condemned. "What are sisters for?"

"I'll be there too, obviously." Ruth said. "So you'll get some votes."

"Oh, there's voting?" Chloe said. "I'll definitely vote for you."

"You have to donate to vote," Caitlyn said.

Chloe made a face. "Oh."

Caitlyn sighed. "I'll give you the money in advance."

"Thanks!" Chloe said. "You're the best sister ever."

"Believe me, I know."

Ruth surveyed the Linvale Community College auditorium, glad to see most of the chairs empty. Caitlyn was already worried about rehearsal; at least she wouldn't have to contend with a crowd.

There was no sign of Caitlyn, though, so Ruth inspected the decor. The room was clean, but the carpet was faded, and the seating cushions were decades out of date. As much as Ruth complained about her college's lack of funding, she had to admit, community colleges had a fraction of the funds.

Onstage, someone juggled a set of bowling pins with a distinct lack of confidence. One dropped to the floor and rolled behind him.

If this is the standard, whatever Caitlyn does will be fine.

"Are you here for rehearsal?" A chipper voice interrupted Ruth's thoughts. A woman with an asymmetrical black bob and a lanyard that said LCC Theater Department appeared beside her, wielding a clipboard. "You need to sign in."

"Ah. No. I'm here to see Caitlyn."

"And you are...?"

"I'm her...." Ruth had been loath to say *girlfriend* lately. It seemed too casual to describe their relationship. "I'm here to support her."

"Did you check in with security? You need a visitor's pass."

Ruth stretched to her full height. "I am actually the *president* of Pulaski College."

The woman's eyes widened.

Oops. Faculty and administration had strained relationships at every college; Caitlyn didn't need Ruth to make enemies on her behalf, especially when the whole point of Caitlyn subjecting herself to the talent show was to win favor with faculty. "Sorry—"

"You came!" Caitlyn's voice came from behind her.

"Of course." Ruth squeezed Caitlyn's shoulder and gave her a quick kiss on the lips.

Caitlyn clutched Ruth's arm as if holding on for her life. "It's *really* good to see you. Um, do you know Leah?"

Leah's mouth hung open. "You two are a couple?"

"Yes," Ruth said firmly. Caitlyn's association with a college president wouldn't help her with faculty relations, especially after Ruth had just pulled the *don't you know who I am* routine. But there was no other answer. They were together. Caitlyn was hers.

Leah turned to Caitlyn with sparkling eyes. "That's so cool! I had no idea!"

That was odd. Leah seemed...excited for Caitlyn? Maybe Ruth hadn't made a bad impression after all.

"I'm the Vice Chair of the LGBTQ Council here! We'd love to have you as a member! If you—I mean, not to make assumptions about how you identify." Leah waved her hands in fluttery circles. "But our group is open to everyone!"

Oh. That was the exciting part.

"Thanks so much for the invitation." Caitlyn gripped Ruth's arm even harder. "I'll definitely think about that. But they said I'm up next, so"—she cast an apprehensive gaze at the stage—"I should get ready."

"Sure thing! You're going to be great!" Leah waved them off with a wide grin.

"I can't believe it." Caitlyn huffed as they walked toward the stage. "I'm torturing myself with a public performance just to get Leah to like me, when I could have joined her club instead. Joining clubs is easy! This is 99 percent more stressful."

"You could do both?'

"Yeah, I guess. If this talent show doesn't kill me first."

"Hey, it'll be okay. It's just rehearsal and..." Ruth grasped for words of encouragement. She knew better than to say, *There's no reason to worry*. Anxiety didn't work like that. "I'm here."

Caitlyn nodded grimly and climbed the steps to the stage with Ruth close behind her.

A guitar case sat on the table, covered in stickers that marked it as Caitlyn's. The stickers represented Caitlyn's true personality—colorful, fun. Ruth wished she was more comfortable showing it. *But then she'd be a different person.*

Caitlyn unsnapped the latches and pulled out the instrument. "They said this is mainly a sound check. I don't have to play right now."

"But you can play if you want, right?" Ruth didn't want to push Caitlyn, but avoidance was often a bad strategy. "If you practice now, with just a few people watching, it might help you relax for the show?"

"Yeah, sure." Caitlyn didn't look convinced.

"Caitlyn! There you are." A scruffy-looking man holding a radio walked up to them. "Come on out. I have a mic that should work..." Their voices faded as Caitlyn followed him to center stage.

Ruth settled onto a folding chair to watch, doing her best to transmit good vibes telepathically. *It's okay. You got this.*

After the mic was secured, Caitlyn hesitantly strummed her guitar. A soft, melodic chord rang out over the speakers. They conversed for a moment, and the man adjusted something.

Caitlyn played a few more notes, then stopped.

The man turned toward the sound booth and gave two thumbs up.

Caitlyn lifted her guitar strap over her head, abruptly pushed to her feet, and hurried off stage, cheeks flushed with embarrassment. "Sorry you came all the way here just to see me choke."

"Nonsense. I'm always glad to see you." Ruth gave her a peck on the cheek.

"I just couldn't...." Caitlyn knelt next to her guitar case. As she moved to place the guitar in it, her fingers trembled, and she dropped the guitar on the ground. "Oops." She picked up the guitar and inspected it. "Nothing's broken. It's okay."

Ruth ached for Caitlyn. Thanks to her own struggles with anxiety, she knew how recalcitrant it could be. Caitlyn's stage fright might not be rational to anyone else, but it was real to Caitlyn. No amount of talking would make it go away.

Caitlyn looked up. "Will you come over for dinner?"

"Of course." Ruth held out her hand to help Caitlyn up, then declined to let go. They walked out of the auditorium and into the parking lot still holding hands.

"I'm parked on the other side, in the visitors' section," Ruth said. "I'll see you at your place?"

"Perfect. Thanks again for being here." After one last kiss, Ruth turned and walked toward her car.

"Ruth!" Eli Tomlin strode toward her, his oversized suit flapping as he walked. "What brings you to our humble college?"

He already knew of their relationship, so Ruth decided to tell the truth. "I came to see Caitlyn at rehearsal."

"Oh, for the talent show! Excellent. We're so pleased that Caitlyn decided to participate."

The amusement in his voice was too much. "Really? I had the impression you forced her to do it."

Eli took a step back. "Well, yes. I advised her that it would be a good opportunity."

I should stop. But Ruth couldn't. "Generally, I don't ask my employees to do things far outside their duties, particularly when they've explicitly said they aren't comfortable doing so. But other managers have different styles, I suppose."

He opened his mouth to respond, but Ruth was done with him. "Have a nice evening." She turned and marched to her car without looking back.

Ruth spent the drive ruminating on what she'd like to do to Eli Tomlin. LCC was smaller than her college. Perhaps she could annex it and demote Eli to a clerical role, promoting Caitlyn in his place. While not realistic, it was a pleasing dream.

As the hour of the talent show approached, Caitlyn's coping strategies changed by the minute. First, she played her song over and over, the quality degraded with each rendition. Then she switched to changing outfits and fussing over her makeup. Now she was locked in her bathroom, obsessing over her hairstyle.

Ruth tapped on the door.

"I'm almost ready," Caitlyn said.

"I know. Just letting you know Chloe's here. Apparently, she wants to ride over with us." Ruth's tone was light and neutral.

"Okay, thanks." Caitlyn was grateful that Ruth tolerated Chloe's frequent presence in their lives, despite a rocky history. "I'll be out in a minute."

She pushed a bobby pin further into the nest of hair that she'd hoped would pass as a stylish twist. It scraped her scalp.

Shit, this is useless. Caitlyn tore out the bobby pins and the two elastics, throwing them onto the sink counter in disgust. There was no time to salvage it. Instead, she sprayed her hair with styling spritz and aggressively brushed it straight.

Her stomach twisted as she emerged from the bathroom. *This is it.*

Chloe, of course, was resplendent in a sapphire sequin dress that hugged her chest and hips. Her eye makeup was dark—even by Chloe's standards—with thick black eyeliner, smoky eyeshadow, and extra-long false lashes.

"Whoa. You look like you're ready for the club," Caitlyn said. "You know this isn't going to be fancy, right? It's a community college auditorium."

"I just dressed up for fun." Chloe tossed her hair.

Typical Chloe. Caitlyn's dress, charcoal gray in a waffle-knit fabric, was drab by comparison. "Do you think this outfit is okay? I changed three times already, but I don't know. It's too plain, right? Maybe I should wear my magenta dress instead?"

"Nah, you look great."

"Really?" Caitlyn hadn't expected Chloe to approve. "Are you just saying that because it's hopeless, and you know this is going to be a humiliating disaster no matter what I wear?"

"It's not going to be a disaster, I promise. In fact, I got you something."

"Oh? It's not drugs, is it?"

Chloe rolled her eyes. "No, it's not drugs. You think so little of me!"

A tiny part of Caitlyn had hoped that it was drugs. "Then what is it?"

"I want to show Ruth at the same time."

Ruth appeared behind them. "Show me what?"

"It's in the closet," Chloe said. "The one in the hall. Come here, both of you."

"Um, okay." Caitlyn walked over to the closet, Ruth following behind. "You put something in the coat closet for me?"

"Way in the back. I want you both to see it at the exact same time."

What is she up to? Caitlyn pushed her heavy winter coats aside. "I don't see anything."

"Nothing's here," Ruth agreed. "What are you—hey!" Ruth fell forward and landed on Caitlyn. They both fell into the mass of coats as closet door slammed shut behind them.

"What the hell?" Caitlyn steadied herself. They were in near-total darkness.

"You can thank me later!" Chloe said in a sing-song voice.

"What are you doing?" Ruth thumped at the door. "Chloe! Get back here." There was a furious jiggling sound, followed by pounding. "She locked us in!"

"That's impossible. The closet doesn't even have a lock."

"She jammed it somehow. The handle won't budge." Ruth banged at the door with her palm. "Chloe! Get back here! Open the door."

While Ruth worked the handle, Caitlyn's phone buzzed in the pocket of her leggings. She fished it out and fumbled it. "Shit." She tried to crouch down, guided by the glow of the lock screen, but the closet was too small. "Can you reach my phone? It's closer to you."

Ruth nudged it with her foot and managed to pick it up. "Here." She passed the phone to Caitlyn.

There was a text from Chloe:

Don't worry, I've got you covered! You bailed me out for an entire summer, so I'm returning the favor tonight!

Ruth peered over Caitlyn's shoulder. "I can't believe her. Well, I can. But this is too much." She gave the door another shove.

Caitlyn's thumbs flew over the keypad.

You need to come back and let me out. Please. I don't want to get in trouble.

You won't get in trouble. You didn't even know, so you're totally innocent! The only person who could get in trouble is me...but I won't because nobody will know the difference!

Before Caitlyn could respond, another text appeared:

Gtg drive

Caitlyn looked up at Ruth. "What do I do?"

The glow from the phone screen cast a pale-blue light on Ruth's frown. "Is there someone you can call? Who has a key to your apartment?"

"Well, you, of course. And Chloe."

"Shit." Ruth banged her fists on the door. "I don't suppose you store a chainsaw in here somewhere?"

"No, just coats. My fall coat, my winter coat, my super-warm winter coat for subzero temperatures. My spring jackets. There isn't room for anything else."

"Illinois does require a lot of coats." Ruth reached for the shelf above them. "What about up here?"

"My hats, gloves, and scarves."

"What about a tool box? Or at least a screwdriver?"

"No. I just call the landlord for that stuff."

Ruth was silent.

"I know what you're thinking. You're thinking that I'm a bad feminist and I should learn to use tools."

"No. I was thinking that we really are stuck."

"Which means I'm going to miss the talent show." Caitlyn couldn't help but laugh. Then she laughed again, and soon she was half doubled-over and giggling.

"What?" Ruth asked. "What's so funny?"

"Nothing. It's not funny. But part of me feels...relieved? I'm worried about what Chloe is going to do tonight. But I don't have to perform, because I literally can't. We're stuck! It's impossible. And I can't help it, but I'm glad. Hell, maybe Chloe really did me a favor." Another giggle escaped. "Shit, I think the lack of oxygen is affecting my brain."

"And it's hot in here." Ruth pushed against the door a few more times, but her efforts seemed halfhearted; she used less force than before. Still, she kept up a steady rhythm, her ass nudging Caitlyn's crotch every time she moved back to try again.

"Um." The heat in the closet was nothing compared to what was happening beneath Caitlyn's dress. She squeezed her thighs together.

"What?"

"You keep bumping into me." Caitlyn's voice was hoarse.

Ruth turned around. "And?" A slow smile spread across her face. "Ohhh. I see. You like that?"

"Like I said, lack of oxygen. Otherwise I'd be laser-focused on the, uh, situation. Getting out of the closet and all. Top priority."

"No doubt." Ruth moved closer, pressing their bodies together, and ran her hands through Caitlyn's hair. "You're missing your work event, which is very unfortunate. But since we don't have a choice..." She leaned in and captured Caitlyn's lips in a hot, wet kiss.

Caitlyn sank into Ruth's body, her core pulsing with need as Ruth kissed her senseless.

Ruth stroked down Caitlyn's back, then teased her thighs and ass as she kissed harder and deeper.

God, I need this. More than oxygen, more than getting out of the closet, or dealing with Chloe, or dealing with work. *I just need Ruth.* Her worries faded to noise as her body succumbed to sensation.

The temperature soared as the heat between them filled the small closet. Under Caitlyn's dress, beads of sweat rolled down her back. Her legs wobbled. "Fuck. We need a bed."

"Mmmm. That sounds nice." Ruth kissed Caitlyn's neck. "But as you may have noticed…" She reached under Caitlyn's dress and slipped her hand between Caitlyn's legs.

"Oh my God." The touch hit like rum on an empty stomach, straight to her bloodstream. Caitlyn shivered, coming undone in spite of herself.

"As you may have noticed, we're thoroughly stuck."

Caitlyn's panties were already soaked. She leaned back against a crush of coats and arched into Ruth's touch.

While Ruth's fingers worked Caitlyn's sex through her panties, she placed searing kisses up and down Caitlyn's neck.

Caitlyn breathed hard, now sweating from everywhere, as the heat and pleasure unwound her. "You're wrecking me," she gasped into Ruth's hair. "I'm falling apart."

"Good." Ruth rasped into her ear. "Let go for me. Let go."

As Caitlyn's orgasm ripped through her, she lost balance with nowhere to fall. Her head bumped into the rod and several hangers, but she didn't care.

Ruth caught her and held her steady. "Are you okay?"

Still out of breath, Caitlyn could only nod. She clutched Ruth's shoulders. "I… I can't believe I just came in my closet."

"You've never had sex in a closet before?" Ruth asked.

"No! Have you?"

"No. Not even in the metaphorical sense, since I came out before I ever had a girlfriend."

"Yeah, same. God."

"Still, I wish we could get out of here. It's hard to breathe." She reached around Ruth and pushed hard on the handle in frustration. There was a creaky sound from whatever the handle was pressing against.

Caitlyn tried it again. "Wait. I think it's getting looser?" She pushed with all of her weight. "There! Something moved. Here, you try."

Ruth pushed, and there was a ripping sound as the handle gave way. She stumbled through the door, and Caitlyn followed, inhaling a face full of cool open air.

"Oh my God. Oxygen." Caitlyn dropped to her knees. After a few deep breaths, she looked up at the closet door handle. A plastic contraption hung from a strip of wood and paint.

Ruth examined it. "Looks like a safety device. For childproofing. It sticks to the door and blocks the handle from moving up or down."

"Ugh. She does babysit sometimes." Caitlyn stood up and smoothed her dress. "Well, I guess we need to get to the college. I'll fix my hair on the way." They had lost valuable time, but there might be time to stop Chloe. She was halfway toward the door when she realized Ruth hadn't followed. "What?"

Ruth shook her head. "Nothing. You're right. Let's go."

As Ruth drove her to LCC, Caitlyn wondered what Chloe planned to do in her place. Chloe didn't play guitar. Presumably she planned to sing something, but what? Caitlyn shuddered to imagine.

Security was lax, as usual, and students lounged and chatted behind the ticket counter. They didn't react as Caitlyn and Ruth swept through the lobby without buying tickets, but Caitlyn supposed she looked like a performer with her guitar strapped to her back.

"We need to get backstage," Caitlyn said. But as she spoke, the auditorium doors swung open, and she glimpsed sapphire sequins onstage. "Oh no."

"What?" Ruth followed her gaze. "Oh. We're too late." The doors swung closed.

"Fuck. What should I do?" Caitlyn's first instinct was to run before anyone saw her, but the strains of recorded music stopped her. "Wait. Is that...?"

Ruth stepped up to the door and opened it. "Come on."

Caitlyn followed Ruth through the doors. They stood together in the back of the dark auditorium.

"Why does this sound familiar?" Ruth asked.

Caitlyn wanted to sink through the floor and die. "It's 'Hero.' By Mariah Carey."

"Oh. That's…an ambitious choice."

Chloe spread her arms as she sang the opening phrase. Her skin glowed under the stage lights. Clearly in her element, she sang with a proud, strong voice, undeniably pulling it off.

The applause started after the first long note, and it never fully stopped. The cheers intensified as Chloe built up to the song's climax. At the final note, the crowd jumped to their feet for a sustained standing ovation.

Chloe beamed, soaking it in, before taking an exaggerated bow. She walked off the stage with her head held high.

"There's no way they think that's me," Caitlyn said. "Do they really think that's me?"

Ruth shrugged helplessly.

Chloe had disappeared from sight; the Shakespeare professors were making their way onto the stage.

"Ruth?" An all-too familiar voice sounded from behind them.

Caitlyn froze, her fight and flight instincts at war with each other as her boss stepped in front of them.

"Eli." Ruth's voice was tight.

Dr. Tomlin fixed his gaze on Caitlyn. "And we just saw Caitlyn perform, so you must be…?"

"I'm her twin sister." *It's not a lie*. Caitlyn was, technically, the twin sister of the woman who had just performed.

"That's right. Caitlyn told me she had a twin." Dr. Tomlin looked her up and down, his gaze pausing on the guitar. A shrewd glint appeared in his eyes. "Your twin is very talented. Smart too. Always thinking of creative solutions to problems."

"That's, um, good. Nice to hear." *Does he know? Fuck, I think he knows.* Caitlyn's heart thumped against her ribs.

"I'll let you enjoy the rest of the show. Be sure to congratulate your sister for me." He winked before walking off.

"Oh my God." Caitlyn thought she might faint. "He knows. He totally knows."

The audience went silent as the Shakespeare professors began their scene.

Ruth nodded toward the exit and mouthed, *Let's go.*

Caitlyn practically ran for the door.

"The scene of the crime," Caitlyn muttered as she hung her coat. "I'll never look at this closet the same way again."

Ruth came up behind her and straightened some of the jackets. "You mean because we were locked in or because we..."

"Both, I suppose. A disaster, and a nice orgasm."

"But it worked out in the end, didn't it?" Ruth ran a soothing hand over her shoulder. "It's over, and your boss isn't mad. That's all that really matters."

Caitlyn narrowed her eyes, flashing back to a spark of suspicion she'd felt earlier, before Ruth had thoroughly distracted her with sex. "Are you..."

"What?"

Caitlyn faced Ruth. "Look, I know you didn't conspire with Chloe. You specifically told her not to do this. And I know you tried to break us out of the closet...at first."

Ruth's eyes darted back and forth, something she often did when she felt guilty.

"But then it seemed like you weren't pushing as hard. I would have thought that you, of all people, would be desperate to stop Chloe from going through with this. You were so angry when you found out I'd been impersonating her at Pulaski, and now she's done the same thing at my job. But you don't seem upset about it. Or am I reading you wrong?"

Ruth took a deep breath. "No, you're not wrong. Of course I didn't plan to get locked in a closet. But you were so relieved when you realized we'd miss the show, and I just thought, well—how bad can it be? It's not your real job. It's a talent show. And, frankly, your boss shouldn't have pressured you into this in the first place. You're a researcher. You don't like to perform onstage, and that's okay. This world isn't lacking people who do enjoy it. You don't need to face every fear."

"So you stopped trying so hard on the door. And you distracted me with hot closet sex." Caitlyn smiled and brushed Ruth's cheek with her fingers. "Thank you."

"For the closet sex?"

"For just being you." Caitlyn embraced her and held on. "You know," she said into Ruth's shoulder, "I wouldn't mind getting into *your* pants in the closet. Just to see what it's like."

As Ruth started to respond, the front door flew open and Chloe burst into the apartment.

They broke apart, as Caitlyn once again cursed Chloe's timing.

Chloe's eyes widened as she took in the scene—the childproofing device on the floor and Ruth and Caitlyn decidedly not in the closet. She held up her palms. "Look, I know you're probably mad."

"Chloe…"

"But I took care of everything for you, and it was a huge success! I sang Mariah Carey, and everyone loved it. And you got a ton of votes. You should have seen the jar with your name on it. There was so much money!"

In all the chaos, Caitlyn had forgotten about the voting portion of the event.

"Seriously, I think you might have won. But I didn't stay until the end, of course. I came home *right away* to let you out." Chloe paused to catch her breath. "So, are you mad? How mad are you? Just tell me."

Ruth simply stood back, arms crossed and mouth twitching with suppressed amusement.

"Look. First of all, you can't just lock people in closets. What if there had been a fire? We'd have burned alive."

"Oops," Chloe said. "I didn't think about that."

"And don't ever impersonate me again without asking, especially at my job."

Chloe winced. "Okay. I'm sorry."

"But…as it so happens, we managed to get out of the closet after a brief delay, and we got there in time to see you sing."

"Really?" Chloe perked up. "You saw my performance? What do you think?"

Caitlyn managed her stern face for a few more seconds, and then a smile broke through. "Honestly, you were great. Your singing was perfect. Everyone loved it, and while you did *not* fool my boss, he's not mad."

Relief spread over Chloe's face. "Oh, wow, that's amazing. I'm so glad."

"So I won't stay mad if you promise to never, ever lock me in a closet again."

"I promise!" Chloe couldn't stop grinning. "So, since it worked and you're not mad, that means I'm like… your 'Hero'?"

Ruth rolled her eyes, and Caitlyn groaned. "Let's not get carried away."

"But I saved the day, right? You have to admit it." Now she glowed with triumph.

"Let's say, we all saved the day in our own way." Caitlyn shared a private smile with Ruth. "And it's over now, thank God, so we can sit down and have a drink." She started toward the kitchen and wobbled, catching herself on the wall. "Actually, I need to start with some food. I think I'm experiencing some combination of an adrenaline and blood-sugar crash."

"And I can stay too?" Chloe said. "Since you're not mad?"

"Yes," Caitlyn said, "you can stay for some food."

"Awesome." Chloe shrugged off her coat and moved toward the closet.

"Wait, don't—"

Chloe stopped. "What? What's wrong?"

Behind Chloe, Ruth raised her eyebrows, looking far too amused.

"The closet is a mess from when we were, um, trying to get out," Caitlyn said, heat creeping up her neck. "Just keep your coat with you, okay?"

"Okay." Chloe shrugged and headed for the living room.

"We can clean it up tomorrow," Caitlyn whispered to Ruth. "Unless you still want to try a few things?"

"I prefer spaces with more airflow, to be honest. I didn't want to admit this at the time, but I'm slightly claustrophobic."

"Oh shit, really?" Caitlyn squeezed Ruth's arm. "I'm sorry. You must have been miserable."

"Nah." Ruth gave her a kiss on the lips. "It was stuffy and hot but also…hot. If I had to be trapped in a closet, I'm glad it was with you."

Enjoyed this glimpse into their life after the happy ending? Discover how their story began in *Something's Different.*

Rumors

by Rachael Sommers

"Have you heard about Dr. Thomas?"

At the sound of her name, Eva held out a hand to stop Alisha in her tracks. They were walking back from an early morning staff meeting, and the students around the corner had no idea the subject of their gossip could hear every word.

"No," said a different student. "What about her?"

"Apparently her and Miss Cross are *dating*!" Thinly veiled excitement laced the student's voice.

A smattering of disbelief met the words. How many teenagers were in the group?

"That can't be true," said another voice. "Miss Cross would never go for someone so—"

Eva chose that moment to make her move, stalking around the corner in her three-inch heels. Silence fell, as the student who had been speaking—Denny Marshall—snapped his mouth closed.

Six pale faces looked toward her.

"Oh, do go on." Eva folded her arms across her chest and quirked an eyebrow. "I'd *love* to know what you were about to say. I'm so...?"

"Um." Denny shuffled his weight from one foot to the other. "I-I wasn't going to say anything."

"No?"

He shook his head fast enough to rattle his brain.

"Hm." Eva's gaze flicked over the rest of the group. "Anyone else have anything to add?"

One brave soul raised their hand.

Eva didn't recognize them; they hadn't been in any of her classes. "Yes?"

"Is it true? Are you and Miss Cross together?"

The other five students sucked in a breath.

Eva had had enough. "I am not going to dignify that with a response. Get out of here, all of you. Now."

The group dispersed, quick as lightning. Amused laughter reached Eva's ears, and she turned to Alisha.

"What?" Eva said. "You can't expect me to let them get away with that."

"Oh, I don't." Alisha's smile widened. "I thought you went easy on them; Lily's rubbing off on you."

With an indignant huff, Eva continued on toward her classroom. "She has done nothing of the sort."

"How many detentions did you give out on the first day of school this year?" Alisha hurried to catch up. Her longer legs made it easy. "Six, was it? Half of last year."

"That doesn't necessarily mean anything. Perhaps the students were better behaved."

"Or you were in a better mood."

Grumbling, Eva didn't dignify Alisha with a response.

At least she hadn't had a problem when Eva had told her she was dating the science department's newest hire. It wasn't against any written rule, but workplace relationships weren't always the easiest thing to navigate. To her credit, Alisha had managed to disguise her shock at the news. And considering Eva's icy, standoffish nature, and Lily's sunny and cheerful disposition, a *shock* might be downplaying how unexpected Eva's revelation had been.

They reached the science department, and Eva couldn't help but slow her stride outside of Lily's classroom. Through the glass window in the door, Eva watched her grade papers, head bobbing along to the beat of the music playing through her AirPods. Some pop nonsense, if Eva had to guess. Her hair was scraped back into a ponytail, revealing the sapphire earrings Eva had bought her for their first Christmas together.

Her blouse was white, dotted with flowers; Eva had watched her button it earlier that morning with hungry eyes.

"Careful," Alisha said, a teasing lilt to her voice. "If the students catch you looking at her like that, there'll be no denying the rumors."

"I don't know what you're talking about." Eva turned away. "I look at her like I do any other colleague."

Alisha snorted. "Whatever helps you sleep at night."

Two students whispered at the back of Lily's final class of the day.

It was cute how they thought she couldn't hear them, despite standing only a few feet away, arms folded across her chest as she watched her class complete the worksheet she'd set for them. Maybe they were hoping they'd be drowned out by the rest of the chatter. Lily had never liked ordering them to work in silence.

Normally, she ignored the gossip of teenagers, but the glances Becca and Hannah kept throwing Lily's way made her suspicious they might be talking about *her*. She watched them out the corner of her eye.

"I can't believe they said it to her face," Becca said, leaning close to her co-conspirator. "I'm surprised Dr. Thomas didn't throw them all in detention."

Lily's interest piqued further. What, exactly, had someone said to Eva's face? Something unwise, by the sounds of it. Eva hadn't been as quick to anger, lately, but that didn't mean she'd gone soft.

"Me too." Hannah shook her head. "Do you think it's true?" Her eyes darted toward Lily once again.

Keeping her gaze focused on the front of the room, Lily hoped she was doing a good job pretending she wasn't listening to Becca and Hannah's every word.

Becca shrugged. "Shauna is adamant she saw them together last weekend. And they were holding hands."

"I don't know..." Hannah tapped her pencil against the worksheet she hadn't written a single answer on. "Is she sure they were holding hands? Maybe they were just out as friends."

"Friends? Come on, Hannah. Do you think Dr. Thomas is the type to hang out with another teacher on the weekend?"

Ice slid down Lily's spine.

Oh.

Oh *no*.

Oblivious to Lily's eavesdropping—or her sudden discomfort—Becca bundled on. "Shauna said they were holding hands, and they were laughing, and they got into the same car and drove away together. They were on a *date*, Hannah. Dr. Thomas and Miss Cross."

Both sets of eyes glanced at Lily.

It was getting harder and harder for her not to react. Because whoever Shauna was, she was right—last weekend, Lily *had* gone on a date with Eva. They'd gotten dinner at a cute Japanese place in High Grove before retiring to Eva's place for the night.

With High Grove being forty-five minutes away from the high school, they'd always assumed it would be relatively safe for them to go out together in public. Few of their students lived so far away.

But apparently some of them visited the town on the weekends.

It wasn't a problem in itself, of course. Lily and Eva were grown adults, and their relationship had been cleared with both Alisha, their head of department, and the headteacher of Greenfield High. It was no one else's business if they were dating. Certainly not their students.

And yet… Eva was so viciously private. It had taken Lily months to pry anything personal out of her, and most of what she *had* learned had been unwittingly through a dating app when she hadn't known it was Eva on the other end of it.

To have students talking about her—*gossiping* about her, about them—well.

Lily was sure she wouldn't like that at all.

She hadn't seen Eva since they'd parted earlier that morning. In school, they rarely spent time together. Their lunch duties didn't align like they had the previous year, and they both spent their free periods working so they could snatch some precious time together in the evenings.

But Lily would need to seek her out once school was over.

She had a feeling they'd have a few things to discuss.

Knuckles tapped lightly on Eva's classroom door.

She raised her head from the grading she was doing—she had ten more essays to go—and smiled when she saw Lily.

"You don't have to knock," Eva said.

"I wouldn't come in without permission." Lily closed the door behind her. "You might give me detention."

"The look in your eye suggests you wouldn't be opposed to that." Setting down her pen, Eva leaned back in her chair, letting her gaze run over Lily's body. The top two buttons of her blouse had been popped open, no doubt as soon as the last of her students had left for the day. Wisps of blonde hair had escaped her pony, and black ink was smudged all over her hands from a day of drawing on the whiteboard.

Even so, she was beautiful. Fondness spread through her as Lily came to a stop at the front row of desks, perching on the edge of one and swinging her legs.

"I'm never opposed to spending more time with you."

"You weren't saying that a year ago."

Lily grinned. "On the contrary, I would've loved to spend more time with you back then. I think you'll find it was *you* who couldn't stand being around me."

"Actually, I liked being around you too much. That was the problem." Eva was glad she'd finally come to her senses. The last few months had been the best of her life.

Lily smiled, but it didn't reach her eyes.

Tilting her head, Eva studied her girlfriend's face. "What's wrong? Bad day?"

"Um, not really." Lily wrapped her hands around the edge of the desk, her fingers tapping against the wood. "I wanted to talk to you about something."

A flutter of panic erupted in Eva's chest. She didn't like the look on Lily's face—uncertain and wary. It made her uneasy, mind whirling with endless possibilities of what she might say. Had Eva done something to upset her? Had someone else? Was she—

"I overheard a conversation in one of my classes today," Lily said. She spoke slowly, like she was choosing her words carefully. "Two sophomores."

"Okay...?" Eva had no idea where this was going.

"They were talking about, uh, us. You and I. Being together. Romantically."

"Is that all?"

Lily blinked, an adorable frown between her eyebrows. "What do you mean is that all? Doesn't it bother you? People talking about us?"

"No. I overheard something similar this morning. One of them had the gall to ask me if we were together." Eva rolled her eyes. "It must be doing the rounds, but I'm sure it'll all blow over soon enough. They're speculating, though I don't know why."

"I do. Someone saw us out together last weekend. Must've been when we went to the Japanese place."

Ah. So it wasn't mere speculation, after all. "Well, I suppose it was bound to come out sooner rather than later."

Lily's head snapped up. "You're not upset?"

Pursing her lips, Eva considered the question. "Do I wish we hadn't been seen? That our business wasn't going to spread around the school like wildfire? Of course I do." Eva rose from her chair and rounded her desk, reaching out to take Lily's hands between her own. "But we've never hidden this. It was always a possibility that someone found out."

"I thought you'd freak out when I told you."

"Well, it's not like I'm a stranger to having people gossip about me. Everyone does it." Eva raised an eyebrow. "I bet you've been a part of it, too. I know what the rest of the department used to say about me. They were all desperate to know why I left Georgetown and came here. And the students... That's what they do. At least them talking about my love life is a break from them calling me every colorful name under the sun."

"Maybe if you weren't such a closed book, people wouldn't have to speculate."

"Hm." Eva squeezed Lily's hand, a smile pulling at her lips. "Or maybe people shouldn't be so nosy."

Lily laughed, a sparkle in her eye. "Please. You love that about me."

"I do. I love a great many things about you." The temptation to pull Lily close and kiss her was strong, but there were some lines Eva wouldn't cross within the walls of her classroom. It was one thing for people to know they were together—it was another thing entirely for a student to see them kissing. "Does it bother *you*? People knowing?"

Lily shook her head. "I would like to stop hearing about it, though."

"Sadly, darling, I think this is only the start. Wait until it spreads through the whole student body."

Lily was the last one into the staff meeting, hurrying through the door of Alisha's classroom and dropping into her usual seat next to Eva. Stupid parent phone call. She *hated* being berated for daring to discipline a child.

Sensing her annoyance, Eva dropped her hand onto Lily's knee beneath the desk. Her thumb rubbed the bare skin where her skirt ended, and Lily relaxed into the touch, glad it was Friday.

"It'll be a quick one today," Alisha said. "We need to go through the budget and iron out the details for the trip to the Museum of Science and Industry next month."

Knowing neither of those things had much to do with her, Lily tuned in and out of the meeting. She was much more focused on thoughts of the weekend. Friday evenings—after the staff meeting finished—were spent having a few drinks with the rest of the science department in a nearby bar.

Well, almost all of the department. Eva rarely joined them, and that suited everyone. Eva much preferred going home to check on her mom, and Lily's colleagues still didn't know how to act when Eva was around. Which was fair enough. After all, until Lily came along, Eva had barely spoken a word to anyone outside of a professional capacity.

Once after-work drinks were finished, Lily usually stayed over at Eva's. Her role as carer to her mother, who had MS, meant Eva couldn't spend much time away, but Lily didn't mind. She got along well with Eleanor.

And the chance to play with Eva's adorable Spaniel, Franklin, was always welcome.

"I think that's all for today," Alisha said, flashing them a smile.

Lily brushed off her guilt for not paying as much attention as she probably should have. It *was* Friday. And she was exhausted.

"I'll see you all at the bar."

With the meeting adjourned, Lily and the others gathered their things. Mei, the earth and physical sciences teacher, caught Lily's eye.

"Do you two know you're the talk of the school?" The way Mei glanced between Lily and Eva made clear who she was talking about.

"Don't. I'm sick of hearing about it." All week, the rumors had dogged Lily's heels. Whispers and stares had followed her along every hallway. It was like her days in high school all over again, when she'd been outed by her ex-best friend, and Lily wished it would stop. "Like, do they not have anything better to talk about?" Lily ran a frustrated hand through her hair. "Is no one pregnant? No major breakups? No cheating scandals?"

Mei gave Lily's arm a sympathetic pat. "Sorry, but I don't think it's going away any time soon."

"No." Eva appeared at Lily's elbow. "I can't help but think if it were any teacher other than me, it wouldn't be of such interest."

Eva had a point. She was mysterious, an untouchable enigma to almost everyone around her—students included. The knowledge she was not only queer but in a relationship with another teacher must have spread like wildfire.

"Well, I, for one, am glad it's not anyone else," Lily said. "I only want you."

"God, you two are so disgustingly in love." Mei's lip curled, but she was smiling.

A smile that widened when Eva stiffened.

While Mei hadn't been thrilled to discover Eva and Lily were dating, it hadn't taken her long to get over it. Mei liked teasing Eva—and, despite protesting she hated it, Eva secretly liked having another person to talk to.

"Are you coming to the bar, Eva?" It was a question Mei asked every week, despite being able to count on one hand the number of times Eva had said yes.

"Not today." Eva brushed her fingers over Lily's elbow, drawing her attention. "But I'll see you tonight?"

Like Eva needed to ask. "Of course. I'll let you know when I'm on my way."

With a curt nod, and a small smile, Eva left the room. Falling into step beside Mei, Lily followed her into the hall.

"Seriously, though, do you have any idea how many kids have asked me if you and Eva are together?"

"I don't think I want to know." No one had been brave enough to ask Lily—no doubt cowed by how Eva had reacted. "Is it such a big deal?"

"Yes," Mei said. "Sorry. If you confirmed it, it might die down quicker. Right now, it's so interesting to them because no one *really* knows."

"What do you want us to do? Make an announcement over the tannoy?"

Mei snorted. "Oh, yes, please. But only if Eva does it."

"I'll bring it up later tonight when I see her. And I'll make sure I mention it was your idea."

Mei's step faltered. "I don't know about that."

"What's the matter?" Outside her classroom door, Lily turned and raised an eyebrow. "Thought you weren't scared of her anymore."

"Are you kidding? She still terrifies me. Now I just know you'll be able to talk her out of killing me."

Lily laughed. "That's where you're mistaken—if Eva wants to do something, not even I'd be able to stop her."

The thump of Franklin's tail on the wooden floor alerted Eva to Lily's arrival a few seconds before her bedroom door opened. He scampered out from beneath Eva's desk, where he'd been keeping her feet warm, his claws pitter-patting on the floor as he bounded over.

"You're early." Eva discarded her pen and rolled her neck from side to side. Long periods of grading always wreaked hell on her muscles. She wasn't built for spending hours behind her desk with her head bent over endless papers. Back when she'd been a professor at Georgetown University, she'd tried to limit the amount of coursework she'd set, preferring to judge her biology students on their practical laboratory work instead.

Unfortunately, teaching high school biology didn't afford her the same luxury.

"Early?" A frown creased Lily's eyebrows. "Eva, it's nearly eight o'clock."

"What?" Surely she hadn't been sat at her desk for three hours. But a glance at the clock on her bedside table confirmed she had. "I must've gotten carried away."

"Mm." Lily padded across the room and stood behind Eva, draping her arms over her shoulders and pressing a kiss to her cheek. "Your mother said you'd been holed up in here for too long. She told me to tell you that you work too hard, and you should be enjoying your Friday night instead."

"I'll bet."

Warm lips kissed the skin beneath Eva's ear, and she sighed, tilting her head to one side to grant Lily more access. Taking full advantage, Lily kissed her way down Eva's neck. Lily paused at the spot where Eva's neck met her shoulder, teeth grazing teasingly.

Eva wished she'd press harder, wished she'd bite until her skin was tender, but Lily would never dare leave a mark.

Still, the pressure was enough for heat to ignite in Eva's stomach, for goosebumps to erupt on her flesh, and for a low moan to catch at the back of her throat. Want flooded through her, and she arched further into the press of Lily's mouth.

"I love how sensitive you are here," Lily said, her voice husky enough to make Eva shiver. "Do you think I could make you come just from kissing you?"

"I'm always happy to experiment." Eva gasped when Lily flicked her tongue against her skin. "Though I'm not sure this is what my mother had in mind when she said I should be enjoying my evening."

Laughing, Lily leaned away. "On the contrary, I think it's exactly what she had in mind. Considering she told me that as she was on her way out the door. She said she's spending the weekend at Angela's so we can—and I quote—finally spend some time alone together."

Eva frowned. "She didn't mention that to me."

"Probably thought you'd talk her out of it."

"It has been a while since we had the place to ourselves..." Nights at Lily's home had been few and far between, lately. Her mother's MS had ups and downs, and the past few months her symptoms had been worse than usual. It hadn't left Eva much in the way of spare time.

Lily spun Eva's desk chair around and straddled her lap. "And think about how nice it will be to not have to be quiet."

Eva settled her hands on Lily's thighs. She'd changed out of the skirt and blouse she'd been wearing when they'd parted ways earlier at the school. Now she wore a pair of soft slacks and a worn Georgetown sweatshirt she'd stolen from Eva's closet.

"Did you have fun with the others at the bar?"

"Yes." Lily wrapped her arms around Eva's neck, fingers playing with the hair at the back of her neck. "I stayed later than usual, sorry. You know what it's like when we get chatting."

Eva did, from the handful of times she'd joined Lily. "You don't need to apologize. I'm glad you had fun."

"Missed you, though."

Eva chuckled. "You saw me a few hours ago."

"But not like this." Lily shifted closer, warm in Eva's lap. "I think Alisha would disapprove if I pounced on you in your classroom."

"We'd definitely get a written warning." Eva slid her hands up Lily's thighs and beneath the hem of the sweatshirt. She wasn't wearing anything underneath, her skin blisteringly hot beneath Eva's fingertips. "Though I have been tempted to chance it before."

Lily grinned. "Oh really? When?"

"That would be telling." Eva dragged the back of her hand along the notches of Lily's spine, gratified when she shivered. When she discovered Lily had forgone a bra as well as a shirt, she curved her hands around Lily's sides to cup her breasts. "What do you want to do with our unexpectedly free weekend?"

"I have a few ideas," Lily said, breathing growing labored as Eva brushed her thumbs over her nipples. "Most involve not leaving this room."

"I think Franklin might have a few things to say about that. And Hades." While Lily's adorable cat was fiercely independent, a full weekend alone was asking a bit much.

"I brought her with me. She's made herself at home in the lounge. Franklin is probably glaring at her as we speak."

Eva chuckled. The pair of them pretended they hated one another, and yet they were never far apart when they were in the same house. Amusingly, it was rather like her and Lily's relationship had begun.

"Before we get too carried away, I have an important question to ask you." Lily's eyes sparkled in the light, at odds with the serious tone of her voice.

It was enough for Eva to pause, hands falling back to Lily's waist. "Oh?" A dozen thoughts flickered through Eva's head. Lily wasn't going to do something crazy like propose, was she? They'd only been together for six months. They didn't even live together—despite the increasingly obvious hints from Eva's mother to the both of them that she would be fine if Lily moved in.

"Yes," Lily said, voice solemn as she cupped Eva's jaw between her hands, tilting Eva's head so their eyes met. "Eva Thomas, will you—" Lily paused, drawing it out.

Eva's heart raced, her throat dry.

"—be my date to the Winter Formal dance next week?"

Disbelief flooded through Eva, quickly followed by mortification.

"Look at your face!" Lily swiped a thumb along Eva's cheek. "What's wrong?"

"Nothing."

Blue eyes scrutinized Eva's face. "Something. Wait... you didn't think I was proposing, did you?"

Eva raised an eyebrow. "Wasn't that what you were trying to imply?"

"I mean, yes, but..." Lily worried her bottom lip with her teeth. "I didn't for a second think you'd think I was being *serious*."

"I didn't."

"You did!"

Lily had always been able to tell when she was lying. It was terribly irritating.

"Fine. Maybe I did. For a second."

"I'm sorry." Lily leaned back, eyes never leaving Eva's face. "I didn't mean to."

Eva smoothed her hands over Lily's back. "It's okay. I shouldn't have thought you were serious—we haven't even discussed marriage. Why would you ask me when we haven't talked about it?" Eva hated the frown that took over Lily's face, knowing she was the cause.

"Do you think we *should* talk about it?"

"I... suppose. I wouldn't be opposed to marriage, if that's what you're asking."

"Wouldn't be opposed? Wow, Eva, you're so romantic."

Eva narrowed her eyes into a signature Thomas glare.

Other than causing a grin to cross Lily's face, it had little effect. "Well, for the record I wouldn't be opposed either."

"Okay. I'm glad that's settled." Eva shifted her weight, uneasy at the turn their evening had taken. Talking about her feelings or doing a deep dive into the state of their relationship wasn't something she was comfortable with; she doubted she ever would be, no matter how deeply she cared for Lily.

It wasn't something she did.

"You haven't answered my original question."

"About Winter Formal?" Eva raised an eyebrow. "We're already going. Or have you forgotten we're chaperoning it together?"

"Of course I haven't forgotten. But I thought I should officially ask you to be my date. It's a serious tradition, you know."

With a roll of her eyes, Eva slid her hands into the back pockets of Lily's slacks and used her grip to urge her closer, lessening the distance between them. "Is it?"

"Mhmm." Lily ducked, her hair curtaining their faces. "So, will you come with me?"

"I suppose. So long as you make it worth my while."

"And how would you like me to do that?" Lily leaned close, lips brushing against Eva's once, twice, and then pulling away. "Should we recreate what happened last year?"

At the memory of pressing Lily against a wall and sliding her fingers beneath her dress, Eva shuddered. It had been stupid and reckless but oh so worth it to feel Lily shatter beneath her touch.

"I wouldn't be opposed."

Lily laughed into her mouth as Eva kissed her breathless.

Lily smiled as she watched Eva settle Emma into a swing at the park. Babysitting her niece wasn't her idea of a perfect Saturday, but it ranked highly, considering her family had been one of the main reasons she'd left Miami and moved back home.

Eva's nose wrinkled in distaste as Emma wrapped her hands around the plastic seat that kept her safely enclosed. "I'm not sure this is such a good idea," Eva said to Lily. "Do you know how many germs are on this thing?"

"Probably no more than she encounters on a daily basis. She's in daycare, Eva. She's surrounded by germs every day."

"That doesn't mean I have to be."

"Please. You spend eight hours a day around teenagers."

"At least they know how to wash their hands." Despite her reticence, Eva pushed Emma gently on the swing.

She babbled happily, a gigantic grin on her face when she twisted her head around to look at Eva.

Lily didn't know who had been more surprised at the way Emma had taken to Eva—Lily or Eva herself. Eva didn't exactly give out comforting, motherly vibes, yet from the first time they'd met, Emma had been obsessed, toddling around after her every time Eva attended one of the Cross family gatherings.

And on days like today, when Daisy and Alex needed a babysitter—in the form of Aunt Lily and her girlfriend—oh, they were Emma's favorite.

Secretly, Lily suspected they were Eva's favorites, too.

"No child of ours will be spending time in a playground like this." Eva muttered the words under her breath, and Lily wondered if she was supposed to hear them.

But she *did*, and stared, astonished, at the side of Eva's head.

Last weekend they'd talked about marriage—awkwardly, both aware it was far too early to make any permanent decisions—and now Eva was talking about children?

Eva? The woman who was allergic to commitment? Who Lily had practically had to force to admit she had feelings for her? That a relationship wasn't an awful, terrible idea that would all end in tears?

Eva was talking about their future hypothetical children?

Seeming to realize what she'd said—or noticing Lily's sudden stiffening—Eva raised her head, her eyes widening at the look on Lily's face.

"I—"

"Dr. Thomas? Miss Cross?"

The interruption was unexpected—and unwelcome—and Lily spun around to see one of her students from last year standing a few feet away. Carly was clasping the hand of a toddler in her own.

Carly glanced between Eva and Lily, her gaze lingering on Emma. "What are you doing here?"

Eva was the first to recover. "We're babysitting."

Lily was too busy replaying *no children of ours* in her head in a loop to think about the wider implications of being seen out and about by one of Greenfield High's students.

"This is Miss Cross's niece," Eva continued, still pushing Emma on the swing. She had a tightness to her eyes, a tension in the set of her shoulders, though she was trying hard not to let it show. "What are *you* doing here?"

"Hanging out with my cousin." Carly raised the arm of the toddler still held fast in her grip. Her eyes flicked again between Lily and Eva. "It's true, isn't it? You're together? Someone said it to me and I said it was bullshit, but—"

"Language, Carly." The admonishment leapt quickly to Eva's lips. "We might not be at school, but we're still your teachers."

Carly made a face. "Not this year."

"And there are little ears present." Eva glanced meaningfully at the two children.

"Right. Sorry. I just... can't believe it." Carly shook her head. "You're so..." She trailed off, clearly looking for the right word, heedless of Eva's warning look. "Different."

Well, it wasn't the worst word she could have used.

Lily was content to let Eva take the lead on this. After all, she knew Carly best. She was in her homeroom, and Eva had a soft spot for her.

"Yes, well." Eva shifted her weight from one foot to the other. "Sometimes that works out."

For the fourth time, Carly glanced between them. "I guess. Everyone at school is talking about it you know."

Eva puffed out her cheeks as she sighed. "Yes, we're well aware."

"Well, don't worry," Carly said cheerfully. "I won't tell anyone I saw you both here. It's no one else's business, right?"

"Right. Thank you, Carly."

"Bye." With that, she pulled the toddler away.

Lily watched her walk him toward the nearby slide, and let out a breath. "Looks like nowhere around here is safe from our students."

"Sure seems like it."

At least it was only Carly. Next time they might not be so lucky, but Lily supposed that was the risk they were taking.

"Look," Eva said, seeming more uncomfortable than she had when she'd been talking to Carly, "about what I said—"

"About our future children?"

Eva winced. "Yes."

"Last weekend you were uncomfortable talking about marriage." Lily tilted her head to one side, trying to read Eva's face. "And now you're talking about kids?"

"Maybe that conversation made me think about the future." Eva's eyes darted to Lily's face then away again. "Maybe it made me realize I want to experience a lot of things with you."

Warmth flooded through Lily's chest. Watching Eva with Emma had always filled her with longing, wondering what Eva would be like with a baby of their own one day, but she'd never seriously considered it as a possibility because they'd never talked about it.

And watching her now, uncertain look in her green eyes, lit by the rays of the February sun, Lily had never been more certain she was where she was supposed to be.

"I'd like that, too."

Lily smoothed the skirt of her dress as she stepped out of Eva's Mercedes.

Chaperoning a high school dance wasn't high on her agenda when it came to fun date ideas, but there were worse places to spend a Friday night. One that didn't have free food and drinks—though admittedly, the drinks on offer were all of the non-alcoholic variety.

Eva had donned a suit for the evening, and she looked magnificent. The black pinstripe pants were tight, and the blazer was cut in a way to reveal the matching waistcoat beneath, molded to her curves.

Already, Lily couldn't wait to pluck the buttons of that waistcoat undone, and kiss every inch of skin beneath.

Eva had made it clear she appreciated Lily's dress in return, running her gaze from Lily's collarbones, left bare by the dainty straps of the black dress, over the swell of her breasts, to where the dress cinched at her waist before falling to below her knee.

The heat in those eyes made Lily shiver as Eva fell into step beside her. "It's going to be a long night, isn't it?"

"A long night?" A smile played around the edges of Eva's full lips. "What gives you that impression? You aren't eager to stand in the corner of a room and watch awkward teenagers grind on one another?"

"I must confess it's not my idea of a perfect Friday night. That would involve you, me, and curling up on the couch in front of a movie with Franklin." Lily couldn't keep the wistful note from her voice.

"Mine too." Eva steered Lily through the doors of the golf club with a hand low on Lily's back. "I'd much rather be at home in my sweats right now."

Even through her dress, the heat of those fingers set a low fire burning in Lily's stomach. Would there ever come a day when she wasn't so affected by Eva's touch? She hoped not. "Oh, no, the suit can stay." Lily didn't want it going anywhere. Eva's dress from the last Winter Formal was burned into her mind, thanks to how they'd ended the night, but this suit was going to feature in some of her fantasies, too.

"You're a fan?"

"Of that?" Lily took a step back, once they were inside the ballroom, to better admire the lines of Eva's body. "I might never let you take it off."

Eva's laughter rang in her ears, loud enough for them to garner some interested looks from the few members of faculty already in attendance, plus the smattering of dance committee students who were still setting up.

But Lily didn't care if they stared. And neither, it seemed, did Eva, who ignored everyone else in favor of pulling Lily toward the makeshift bar running along the back wall of the ballroom.

Behind it, Greenfield High's history teacher, Paige, watched them with raised eyebrows. "You're in a chipper mood tonight, Eva."

"Well, I have to laugh or I'll cry." Eva reached for a red solo cup of fruit punch. "Plus, it could be worse—at least I'm not on drinks duty. How'd you draw that short straw?"

Paige sighed. "I'm still not sure. But hey, if I do it now, at least I'm off the hook for the next few dances. The two of you are more than welcome to join me if you like."

"Tempting," Eva said, dryly enough for Lily to elbow her in the side, "but I think I'll have to pass." She handed Lily a second cup before stalking away toward the nearest shadowy corner.

"Lily?" Paige peered at her with hopeful eyes.

"Sorry, Paige. But I promised I'd keep her company." Before Lily could follow after Eva, Paige's voice stopped her in her tracks.

"Is it true?" she said. "What everyone's saying?"

"What's everyone saying?" Lily kept her voice bright, playing dumb even though she knew exactly what Paige was asking her.

"You must know."

"Enlighten me."

Paige shifted her weight from one foot to the other. Apparently nosiness didn't come with confidence. "That you and Eva are… in a relationship."

"Who told you that?" Did Lily care? No, but it sure was fun to watch people squirm.

Paige blanched. "N-no-one. I just… heard it. Around. You know what? Forget it. It's none of my business, anyway."

"Yeah, it's not." Without another word, Lily sought out Eva, slipping into the shadows beside her. She surveyed the room. Lily had to give the dance committee credit—they'd managed to transform the place into an ice castle. Blue and white balloons lined the ceiling, white trees were dotted around the room, the walls covered with snowflakes, and the tables surrounded with white gauze made to give it the appearance of piles of snow.

Everything was white, the low blue lighting managing to make everything look like it was made of ice.

"Are you okay?" Eva tilted her head as she glanced at Lily. "You have your "I'm annoyed at something" eyebrow crease right here." Eva brushed her thumb over the offending frown line.

Some of the tension seeped out of Lily at the touch, fleeting as it was. "I wish people would mind their own business."

"Ah. Paige inquired about your relationship status, did she?"

Lily shook her head. "I'm getting tired of it. Why does everyone think they can ask?"

"Because we never truly leave high school. And the teachers are bigger gossips than the children." Eva winced when the music started up, shuffling closer so she could hear Lily's reply.

The bass thudded through her chest, making her brain rattle. "I know. But do they have to keep asking me directly?"

"I imagine they will until they get an answer," Eva said.

"Mei suggested we break the news over the tannoy during morning announcements."

Eva laughed. "Well, it's certainly an option. I'm not sure it'll make the buzz die down as much as you want, though."

"No, probably not."

Around them, the room filled as more and more of their students arrived. For a while, they entertained themselves by watching their deputy headteacher follow around some of the girls who wore dresses that flirted with the dress code, squawking at them to tug their skirts down to cover more of their thighs, or their necklines up to reveal less cleavage.

"Last year was a lot more fun." Eva leaned close to say the words into Lily's ear. "I bet the balcony's free..."

"Don't tempt me." Lily would love nothing more than to steal away and get her hands beneath Eva's waistcoat, but it had been risky enough last year. This year, with people already watching them curiously, they wouldn't be able to slip away together undetected.

And no way they'd keep their jobs if they were discovered.

"Well, if I stand here for another minute I think I might die of boredom. I'm going to do a lap," Eva said. "See how many students I can scare into dancing two feet apart."

Lily stayed where she was, watching Eva stalk around the room. She moved, like always, with an easy grace, her long legs making quick work of the dancefloor. One look from Eva made a few students quail, and when a slow song came on, and couples began swaying together, Eva flitted amongst them, a few well-placed stares putting an extra few inches of space between the teenagers' bodies.

By the time Eva returned to Lily's side, the music had changed to something livelier, but many couples still danced close together around the room.

Eva extended a hand toward her. "Can I have this dance?"

Lily stared at her. "What?"

"You want people to stop asking you if we're together? They will if they know we are. And sure, this isn't as obvious as a school-wide announcement, but I think it'll do the trick all the same."

Still, Lily remained rooted to the spot. "Are you sure?"

Eva shrugged. "We're not the only ones."

A few of the other teachers who were chaperoning were indeed on the dancefloor. Most were decidedly not couples, though, and the sight of Eva doing anything other than slinking around the perimeter would raise eyebrows.

Eva let her hand drop to her side. "We don't have to."

"No! No, I-I want to." With a deep breath, Lily took Eva's hand and allowed herself to be pulled a few steps forward, onto the corner of the dancefloor. Looping her arms around Eva's neck was the most natural thing in the world, though she made sure to keep some distance between their bodies as they swayed along to the song.

Stares turned their way before long, but Lily blocked them out, content to drown in Eva's eyes. Their intensity had used to thrill her, and now, they felt like home. Eva's hand sat low on her back, grounding her.

"You know, this is the first time I've ever had a date at a school dance." Lily never would have had the guts to ask out any girls when she'd been a teenager—and her high school hadn't exactly been the most welcoming environment. She was glad Greenfield High's student body were more accepting. That wasn't to say it didn't have its issues. Lily had had to curb homophobic or transphobic comments on more than one occasion in her one and a half years as a teacher there. But around them, people of all genders danced together and no one batted an eye.

"Me too," Eva said. "Shockingly, I was never asked."

"Their loss." Lily tightened her hold on Eva's neck. "And my gain."

They swayed for a while longer, until the song changed, and they retreated back into the shadows. Eyes followed them, whispers breaking out amongst the teenagers of Greenfield High, but Lily didn't care.

How could she, when Eva was by her side? When the look on Eva's face, as their eyes met, was filled with so much love and adoration it made her want to tremble?

"Why are you looking at me like that?" Eva peered at Lily over the rim of her glasses.

"Just thinking about how much I love you."

"I love you, too, but let's not get too soppy in front of the student body, hm?"

With a laugh, Lily turned away, leaning her shoulder against the wall behind her. "Deal. As long as you let me show you how much I love you when we get home."

Beside her, Eva tensed. "Home?"

Oh, shit. Lily had let that slip out. But to her, Eva's house felt more and more like home with each passing week. She spent more time there than her own home, often staying for the weekend, watching *Jeopardy!* with Eva's mom and taking long walks with Eva and Franklin. "I… sorry." Lily didn't know why she was apologizing. But she wanted Eva to relax. They'd never talked about moving in together, and clearly, it wasn't a conversation Eva was ready for. "When we get back to yours."

"It could be," Eva said, her voice quiet.

Lily had to strain her ears to hear her over the music. She turned to face Eva, and found her staring out across the dancefloor. "It could be what?"

Eva met Lily's gaze. "Your home. If you wanted."

Heart beating fast in her chest, and her palms growing sweaty, Lily couldn't believe they were having this conversation at Winter Formal. "Are you asking me to move in with you?"

This time, Eva caught and held her gaze as she answered. "Yes."

"But what about your mom?" This wasn't a decision affecting only Eva. "Would she be okay with it?"

"She would love to have you live with us. And I can say that with confidence, because we've discussed it. And she keeps dropping increasingly obvious hints. Like how much more often you can see your own family if you were in High Grove—"

"I thought she meant like, in general."

"—and how we could convert the guest bedroom into an office for you."

"I thought she meant for when I come to stay!"

Eva's lips twitched. "She also took you to get a key cut two weeks ago."

"So I can let myself in." Lily cast her mind back over the last few weeks. "I've been oblivious, haven't I?"

"Yes, but that's okay. I could've asked you sooner, but the moment never seemed right."

"And this did?" Lily gestured around them.

"Perhaps not. But you gave me a good opening." Eva brushed her fingertips along the small of Lily's back. "You also haven't given me an answer."

"I'd love to move in with you," Lily said, breaking into a smile so wide her cheeks ached. "And I really want to kiss you right now."

"Later." The look in her eyes held a promise. She glanced at her watch. "We only have to suffer through another hour."

"And then we can go home."

Eva smiled, her eyes bright in the low lighting. "Yes. Then we can go home. Together."

Want to know how their love story began? Read *Chemistry,* where these two first meet.

No Place Like Home

by E. J. Noyes

Though it pained me to do it, because Rebecca Keane in her wedding dress was one of the most incredible things I'd ever set eyes on, the promise of naked Rebecca underneath made the decision to remove the dress easier.

I undid the pearl buttons hiding the zipper, then slid the zipper down and held the garment as she stepped out of it. The lacy off-the-shoulder dress with its curve-hugging bodice and elegant flowing skirt falling to a short tulle train had been wowing me all afternoon. Now we were in my childhood bedroom—all embarrassing teen-idol posters thankfully removed—I no longer had to contain my staring.

Bec placed a hand on my shoulder to steady herself. "Thank you, darling," she murmured. She took the dress from me and I helped her place it in its bag.

"I feel like I should be thanking you." If Rebecca in her wedding dress was one of the most incredible things I'd seen, then the lingerie she had on underneath was a very close second. I often undressed her to find lingerie, but this? This was something special—a very light blue satin bra and thong edged in lace, with a suspender belt adding both a touch of class and fuck-me-now sexiness.

Her mouth quirked into a smile, dimples creasing her cheeks. "And why is that?"

"For the way you looked in this dress. For the way you look out of it. And for marrying me." Wrinkling my nose, I amended, "Or...almost marrying me."

"We'll make it official in a few days," Bec gently reminded me, not that I needed the reminder.

"I know. I just want it now." It felt like a petulant whine. Especially because I'd just participated in one of the happiest events of my life—a "pretend" wedding ceremony at my parents' ranch in Ohio for my aging grandparents' benefit—and the bittersweet feeling of it not being real hung over me. But Bec was right, and it was only another few days before we got married back in DC where it was actually legal.

Her dark-blue eyes softened, as did her voice. "We've waited this long. We can wait a couple more days."

Bec's pragmatism was one of the many things I loved about her, and in this instance I was grateful for the instant calm it brought me. She'd always been able to do that, almost from the moment I'd first met her at Forward Operating Base Atlantis Military Hospital in Afghanistan. Back then I called her Lieutenant Colonel Rebecca Keane, my superior officer. She somehow made even the most heinous circumstances, the worst casualties, the scariest of live-fire drills seem bearable. Of course, the fact she was the hottest woman I'd ever seen, in and out of scrubs, didn't hurt.

"You're right. Of course you're right. What's another few days?" I swept away the blonde curls brushing her shoulders so I could kiss her neck. I kissed my way up until I found her mouth, and Bec responded with enthusiasm. When we broke for air, I asked, "When will the car get here?"

Bec arched an eyebrow. "Too soon for us to do what you're suggesting." Her gaze moved downward, lingering at my breasts before coming back up to my face. "Especially because you're still dressed."

She made a good point, but it wasn't like we'd never had a quickie before. And those wandering eyes didn't exactly help her gentle discouragement. But I didn't want to keep people waiting, and there was plenty of time for something not-quick when we got to the hotel. The curl of anticipation had heat rushing into my belly.

"Fine," I said, unable to keep the sigh from that one word. The hotel felt too far away. I turned slightly so she could unzip me. "Do you think it's too much to wear these dresses to the courthouse when we get married for real?"

Bec paused, her fingers tracing the lacy edge of the racerback along my right scapular before she slid the zipper down. "No, we can wear whatever we want. But I thought we'd already decided on outfits?"

"We did," I said as I carefully stepped out of the off-white dress, which was a body-hugging mix of lace-cutout bodice and an airy chiffon skirt that my younger sister, Jana, had described as "ethereal." I laid the dress on the bed. "But you just look so hot in your wedding dress that I want to see you in it again."

The dresses we'd wear for our courthouse wedding were perfectly suitable, nice even, but *that* dress? That dress was sublime and Bec looked sublime in it.

"There's no reason I can't put it on again in the future," she pointed out, a touch a coyness sliding into her tone.

"That's very true," I mused. I bit my lip as thoughts of her in the dress, pinned against a wall while I fucked her, settled in my brain. "Is that a promise?"

She took a step closer. "Do you want it to be?" she asked, her voice heavy with desire.

"Bec," I complained as I unzipped the garment bag. "You can't tell me we don't have time for sex before we leave, and then say something like that, in that voice."

Bec exhaled loudly. "You're right," she agreed. "I'm sorry. No more innuendo until…later." She gestured to my dress. "Do you need help with that? What about your hair?"

"Dress, yes. Hair, no." I'd already decided to leave my hair up in its chignon—it was going to take some time to get Grandma's borrowed diamond hairpiece and all the pins out—until we were at the hotel later. Together we got my fragile gown into the bag and hung it with Bec's.

Bec opened her arms to me. "Come here."

I stepped into the hug, and the moment her arms stole around my waist, she ducked her head under my chin, nestling herself into the spot against my shoulder—*her* spot.

Today had been everything I'd hoped for, and some things I hadn't even dared dream about, but it'd also been stressful. Not stressful enough to take the shine from the day, but having Bec's quiet comfort now eased the tension that I hadn't been able to let go of.

I hugged Bec tightly, my cheek resting against her hair. The tips of her fingers pressed into the small of my back, lightly massaging either side of my spine. We stood like that for a minute or so, just being together away from everyone else, away from everything else. Bec's fingers stilled. "Are you ready to get dressed and go to the hotel?"

I wasn't really. I wanted to stay like this with her for the rest of the evening, safe in her arms. Reluctantly, I disengaged myself from her embrace. "Mhmm."

Bec gave me a knowing look, kissed me, then stepped away to the other side of the room.

I kept myself facing away from her as I put on dark-gray slacks and a pale-blue silk blouse. If I looked at her I was going to break the loose no-sex-right-now rule we'd just agreed upon. I slipped my feet into leather loafers and turned back, glad to see she was already dressed. Bec's expression made me think of the way she'd looked at me during the ceremony—with unwavering love and pride and desire.

"I'm sorry I laughed during my vows," I blurted. Laughing when nervous was one of my more annoying traits, and of all the bad times to do it, professing my love and commitment to my would-be wife could quite possibly be the worst. "I really hope it doesn't happen at the courthouse."

Bec gently cupped my face in her hands. "Darling, you don't need to apologize for that." She smiled, the laugh lines at the edges of her eyes creasing a moment before her dimples flashed. "It was very *you*. And I love you." She kissed me softly, though I could feel the desire emanating from her.

I gently grasped her wrists as her warm, strong, steady hands held my face. "I love you too." When I leaned down to kiss her again, Bec arched up into me, her hands coming to my shoulders. Car and hotel be damned. I wrapped my arms around her waist, pulled her into me, and began to maneuver us to the twin bed. Need curled through me, and I pushed my hands under her blouse to cup her breasts.

Bec pressed into my hands, a quiet groan escaping against my lips. Then her body stilled. "Sabine..." Her conflict was clear, and I paused too. "We shouldn't. There's no time," she said weakly. "I want you, but I don't want to rush or be interrupted."

"Goddammit," I whispered. I knew she was right, but my libido was *not* getting the message.

As if they knew now was the time to splash water on the fire of my desire, someone knocked on the closed door.

"Sabs?" Jana's voice preceded more pounding on the door. "Bec?" The knocking stopped. Jana's voice did not. "You'd both better be in some stage of dressed, because I'm coming in."

After a ten-second pause—who could get dressed in ten seconds?—my sister opened the door. "Phew. I was worried you guys might be consummating things." She stared, the edges of her mouth quirking. "Seems like you're very close by the look of...this."

"Unfortunately not," Bec said wryly, taking a step back.

Jana grinned. "Shame." She made a sweeping gesture. "Your chariot is here. So you can go consummate somewhere other than your childhood bedroom, Sabs. Everyone's downstairs waiting. Oma and Opa, and Grandma and Grandpa are tired and ready to go home. It's been a long day. You two got your overnight bags?"

"Okay," I said, my libido stepping aside for more important things like my grandparents' comfort. "And yeah, we do."

Jana nodded. "Good. I'll tell everyone you'll be down in a minute." She left the room, deliberately pushing the door wide open.

Bec took my hand, squeezing gently. "Ready to go?"

I squeezed back. "As I'll ever be."

Downstairs, there were tears, hugs and kisses, and thrown grains of rice—far too many of which hit me in the face. It was basically the usual send-off of a happy (not-yet) newlywed couple, before Bec and I were whisked away to spend the night in a hotel.

After another day with family and friends tomorrow, we'd fly back to DC to officially get married in a quick courthouse ceremony before beginning our honeymoon.

Technically, we'd begin our honeymoon after a six-hour flight from DC to Los Angeles, and then a thirteen-hour flight to Auckland, New Zealand, and *then* the flight down to Queenstown where we'd base ourselves to enjoy the Southern Hemisphere winter.

We'd tossed up dozens of ideas, including Europe, a tropical paradise like Bora Bora, a road trip around the States to hike national parks, and Australia. But we'd settled on Queenstown with its proximity to wineries, ski fields, hiking, natural wonders, and more wineries to spend the two weeks of our honeymoon.

Jana, in her official role as maid of honor had organized the hotel and thankfully the driver seemed to know where he was going, because I sure as fuck didn't. And I was surprisingly okay with that. He pulled up outside a charming Victorian-style hotel and cut the engine so he could rush to open the door and collect our bags from the trunk.

I had a sudden irrational urge to laugh when I spotted myself in the ornate mirror in the entryway. Full hair and make-up worthy of a wedding ceremony paired with a nice, but not fancy, outfit. Probably a good thing Bec gently insisted I shouldn't go completely jeans-and-sneakers casual for our relocation to our evening's accommodation.

When I opened the door to the aptly named honeymoon suite I realized Jana had gone above and beyond. It wasn't quite "red rose petals strewn over every surface" romantic (she knew Bec and I well enough to know that wasn't our vibe), but it was exactly what we needed—a bottle of Veuve Clicquot chilling in an ice bucket, a small platter of delicate chocolates, and vases of beautiful flowers adorning the space.

"Oh wow," I murmured.

Bec echoed my awe. "Oh wow indeed." She closed and locked the door behind us then slipped her hand into mine. We did a quick hand-in-hand tour of the room, pausing near the California King bed.

I inhaled a deep breath. "That is a very big bed. We could do a lot of things in that bed."

"Yes, we could. But let's get comfortable first," suggested Bec, ever the voice of reason. "I don't know about you, but I really want to get these pins out of my hair and take a shower."

She pulled me closer and stretched up to kiss me, lingering long enough to make it clear that these things were only temporary distractions from us taking advantage of the bed. Or anywhere else in this hotel suite.

"Sure." I'd been kind of dreading pausing, fearing if I stopped then I'd never start again. After the high energy of the day, and the months leading up to today, I was afraid I'd crash as soon as I let my hair down—literally—and took a shower to wash off my make-up.

Bec seemed to know exactly how I felt, and she rested her hands on my hips, twisting me side to side. "Come on. Let's get ourselves undone and then we can…relax."

After undressing, again, we pulled on the plush hotel robes, and took each other's hair down. Hers was easier, so I worked the pins and hair-holding gadgets free from her hair first. She was careful with my hair, slowly pulling the pins, her fingertips brushing through my scalp as she dismantled the fancy updo. She finger-combed my hair, placing light kisses on my neck.

"No sleeping," Bec said, laughing lightly—she knew running hands through my hair always lulled me to sleep.

"No chance," I said thickly.

I put the diamond-crusted hairpiece into its box and collected all the pins and funny little hair-holding devices into a baggie, though who knew what we'd do with them because I had no intention of dressing up like this anytime soon, though it had been well worth it.

I looked up to find Bec running her hands through her hair, trying to tame the waviness that had turned to curliness with all the product that had been put in it. "Ready for a shower?" I asked.

She smiled, her ocean-blue eyes creasing at the edges. "You go first, darling. Are you hungry? You hardly ate today."

"Neither did you. And yeah, I am."

"I'll open this bottle and take a look at the room service menu." Bec paused. "Or would you prefer we went out for dinner and drinks? We can go down to the hotel restaurant to eat, or explore the town?"

I knew Bec well enough that I could tell by her tone that she didn't want to leave this room until morning, and I was totally on board with that. "I don't want to go out," I confirmed.

I'd hoped she'd join me in the shower, but she probably knew we'd never actually wash ourselves, and after the huge day, I wanted to clean up properly. Get clean before you get dirty, a juvenile part of my brain chimed in.

"How hungry are you?" she asked.

I shrugged. "Not enough for a full dinner. Hungry enough for more than just snacks."

Bec's dimples deepened. And she knew me well enough by now to figure out exactly what I meant, even though I wasn't actually sure what I meant myself. "Got it. Leave it to me."

The hotel shower was huge, certainly big enough for a pair of newly married women. I stuck a hand under the spray to test the water. While it heated more, I leaned out of the bathroom door.

Bec was now reclined on the plush sofa, a flute of Champagne in one hand and her phone in the other. Whatever was on the phone made her smile, and I hated to interrupt, but… I kept thinking of the way she looked in her wedding dress earlier.

I called, "Honey? Could you please come in here?"

Bec glanced up and brought both phone and Champagne into the bathroom. "What's wrong?"

"Nothing's wrong." I pointed to the phone and flute in her hands. "Do you *need* either of these things right now?"

"I don't need them, no." She smiled. "But I am enjoying both. The photographer sent through some shots from today, and you know I love Veuve." Bec offered me the flute and I drank a large mouthful while looking at the picture on her phone, which she'd held up for me.

I loved Veuve too. And the picture—an unposed shot of us by the fence bordering the back pasture, Bec smiling up at me while I looked down at her like I'd just seen the most incredible thing of my life—was gorgeous. *She* was gorgeous. And she was here, with me.

Bec was my life partner, the woman who had been with me during some of the worst and darkest moments of my life and hadn't run away. I lightly stroked my fingers along her exposed collarbone. "If you don't need them right now, I have something else that could occupy your time."

"You think I need something to occupy my time?" she quietly asked. She'd been sneaking peeks at my naked body, making her appreciation clear, but now she openly stared, letting her gaze slide slowly up and down.

"I think you and I should be spending our time together. Or at least a little time right now."

She made a face as though she was pretending to consider it. After a few seconds she said, "I think you're right." Bec set her phone and the glass on the bathroom sink, then quickly removed her contacts. She pulled the knot at her waist free, and slipped the robe from her shoulders, letting it fall to the tiled floor. "Is the water warm yet?"

"Yes," I said hoarsely, eliciting something between a smirk and a grin from her. I'd seen her naked more times than I could recall, but the sight of her bared for me still thrilled me to my core. The excitement spread slowly through me, bringing heat with it until it settled low in my belly.

"Good." She opened the glass door and pushed me backward into the marble-tiled shower. She gripped my hips, keeping me in place as she stretched up to kiss me. The water cascaded upon us, sluicing down our bodies, but it was clear that neither of us were interested in showering for cleanliness.

There was no space for words as we kissed, our hands roaming to familiar places. Not that I'd really doubted it, but I knew her desperation truly matched mine when she slicked her tongue along my lips until I parted them for her.

Despite the passion in the kiss, Bec's hands moved slowly, a counterpoint to the intensity of her lips and tongue, until one hand hovered over my pubic hair. Every cell in my body was screaming for her hand to move lower, but Bec kept that hand maddeningly still.

When I cupped her breasts, she moaned and when I thumbed her nipples, Bec inhaled sharply. She broke the kiss to ask breathlessly, "Do you want to stay here?"

I didn't want to move, but as much as I loved shower sex, it was often loaded with slippery danger. A concussion or injured limbs were not on my agenda for tonight. With a groan of frustration, I removed my hands from her body. "Let's shower, then I want to see how much of that huge bed we can mess up."

We rushed through showering, washing off our make-up and helping soap each other clean, which only heightened my arousal and anticipation. The devilish grin Bec gave me as she ran the bar of soap over my breasts and between my thighs made me certain she knew exactly the effect her touch had on me.

When I was as clean as my impatience would allow, I made sure we were both rinsed, and shut off the rainfall showerhead. We dried off perfunctorily. I took Bec's towel and tossed it haphazardly over the towel rack with mine before I took her hand to lead her out of the bathroom. We fell onto the bed, tangled up in each other.

Her breasts, so full and delicious were too tempting to resist. So I didn't. I sucked on a plump nipple and Bec arched her back, pressing her breast into my mouth. Our foreplay was long and delicious, winding my arousal so tightly that I knew I would uncoil furiously into climax when she touched me. But for now, I kept all my focus on Bec, on her pleasure and the way it fed my pleasure.

I loved the way she unraveled with me, the way she opened herself to my touch, how the calm, confident, used-to-being-in-control-at-work woman melted away to leave nothing more than her desire and trust. Those things, and her love, were all I needed. Everything else I was, everything I did, was made possible by that love.

When I settled my shoulders between her spread thighs, Bec whimpered. That was all the encouragement I needed. There would be countless other times to draw out her climax, but right now I just wanted to make her come. So I thrust my fingers deeply into her wet, slick heat and worked her clit with my tongue in exactly the way I knew would bring her to a shattering climax.

Bec gripped a handful of my hair, encouraging me to keep going exactly as I was, and it felt like barely a minute passed before she came in a sudden rush. Her body, tense and tight with the buildup of her pleasure, relaxed as if someone had deflated a balloon.

The entire time I'd fucked her she'd barely said a word, except to hoarsely whisper my name. But she'd vocalized plenty—moans, groans, throaty little exhalations—and those sounds were enough to send my arousal spiralling into a place where I thought I might not be able to contain it.

Bec, again, seemed to know the exact thoughts and sensations rushing through me. She gripped my biceps, tugging until I shifted and crawled up her body. She hooked a leg around the back of mine and rolled us so she was on top.

The press of her body was exquisite and I let myself sink into the mattress, surrendering myself to her. And Bec made sure I surrendered. There was nothing I could do except for submit—willingly—to the thorough attention she paid to every part of my body.

She licked and sucked. Stroked and caressed. And when I thought I couldn't get any more aroused, that I might *actually* cry from the desperation, Bec roughly pushed my legs apart and put her mouth on my clit.

"Fuck," I hissed.

I felt her chuckle against my wet, swollen flesh. "Yes, exactly." Her fingers paused at my entrance. "Is that what you want?"

"Yes," I gasped. I gasped again, sharply, when she entered me. It felt so, *so* good.

As Bec's tongue stroked my clit, her fingers stroked inside me. She alternated her thrusts—deep, hard, fast, shallow, and my climax built as a molten-hot ball of pleasure that hovered right on the edge. My entire body felt tight, desperate, and I gripped a fistful of the sheets, trying to focus on the intensity of the love Bec was showing me.

I had a sudden, irrational fear that she wasn't going to let me finish, that she was going to tease me until I couldn't stand it any longer, broke down, and begged her. She loved when I begged, and I loved giving her what she wanted, but I didn't think I could wait right now. I wanted to come so badly that I almost felt as if I were coming apart.

"Bec...I want...please, I—"

"I know exactly what you want," she murmured, her lips moving against the skin of my inner thigh. She bit lightly. "Can you be patient for me, darling?"

I inhaled shakily, and let the breath out on a long exhale that calmed the pointless fear, along with a tight, "Yes..." For her I'd be anything.

"Good girl." Her voice was deliciously throaty. "I promise it'll be worth it."

Oh, I had no doubt. But the waiting was still beyond torturous.

Bec's expert touch held me right on the edge until she hit exactly the right spots to send me tumbling over the edge, and my orgasm came upon me with explosive intensity. I didn't even try to suppress my cries of pleasure, didn't care if the rooms either side of us heard me expressing my love for this woman who fulfilled me in every single way.

Bec waited until the twitchy reactiveness of my orgasm had abated, then made her way back up my body, bestowing gentle kisses along the way, until we lay pressed together. I pulled her to me, held her close.

"I love you, Bec. I *love* being married to you." My throat felt tight, and I forced the rest of the words out. "I know it's only just happened, and we're not one hundred percent official, but...I love you, so much I don't even know how to express the enormity of it." I had to stop talking before I started crying.

She kissed me sweetly and when she pulled back, the edges of her mouth trembled. Bec blinked hard, but the tears still leaked from the corners of eyes shining with love. "I love you too."

The next day of continued nuptial celebrations with family and friends passed in a blur. The flight home to DC passed in a blur. The actual getting married for real legally this time passed in a blur. I felt as though I should be trying to remember everything, to imprint the memory of our actual wedding into my mind. But now it was here, I realized it didn't really matter. I already felt joined to Rebecca in every possible way, and this was simply a legal formality now.

The only things that really registered about the actual ceremony was Bec's hands in mine, warm and comforting, and then signing papers. Jana and her (very new) girlfriend, Brooke, and my best friend, Mitch, and his boyfriend, Mike, were present and taking photos like they'd all changed careers to paparazzi. We all cried, some more than others (cough, cough, Mitch) and after we were officially married, the six of us went to a steak restaurant to celebrate.

Bec and I begged off the celebrations early because we had a disgraceful amount of hours of flying the next day. Of course that led to a round of teasing from everyone about newlyweds going home to consummate their marriage.

Which we did.

I slept more deeply than I had in months, and woke refreshed, ready, and excited for our honeymoon. Bec showered first while I double-checked my suitcases, then came into the bedroom naked, playfully patting my butt to get me into the shower.

When I came out of the shower to get dressed, I stopped short by the bed when I saw Bec. Instead of contacts, she wore her black-framed glasses. Before Bec, glasses were just...a thing. Some people wore them, some didn't. But now, I was a glasses-ophile. But only for her. To stop myself from dragging my hot wife into bed when we had literally *no* time for detours, I asked for what was probably—no exaggeration—the tenth time in the past two hours, "Got your passport?"

Bec smiled, but I could tell she was holding back an eye roll. "Now you're just being facetious." But she pulled out her passport and wordlessly held up it, as she'd done every single time I'd asked her if she had her passport.

I grinned. "Thanks. I know I'm not the only person who thinks passports can somehow become sentient and grow arms to unzip the compartment they're in and run away."

Bec secured it back into her carry-on bag. "Oh no, I'm pretty sure you are the only person who thinks that. Come on, darling, you need to get dressed. Our ride to the airport will be here soon."

Our flight to LA was uneventful, and after a couple of hours in the airline's lounge, we boarded the plane for Auckland. I'd joked to Bec that I tried to get us a space on a C17 military plane, the way we used to travel long haul to and from deployments when we worked together as Army surgeons, but none were available, so it was business class instead. And she'd looked at me, raised an eyebrow, and drawled, "And thank fuck for that."

The lie-flat business class seats were arranged in single file, diagonally. We both had window seats, with me seated in front of her. The amount of space and promise of being able to sleep comfortably on a long flight (my benchmark of comfort was anything above a yoga mat on the floor of a cargo plane) only *just* negated not having her next to me.

Once we were settled in our seats, and given a drink—Champagne for Bec, a gin and tonic for me—I fussed with my things to make the space ready for a long flight.

I'd traveled business for short-haul flights, but the last time I'd been on a long-haul flight that wasn't to or from a deployment to Afghanistan, I was back in coach. This was far more preferable, and not just because I was traveling with my wife.

My wife.

I swallowed hard, blinking rapidly to push away the sudden press of tears.

Just two words. A new way to describe my soulmate. Nothing more than a legal formality, really. But those two words felt like the most important words I'd ever have in my life. I didn't think I'd actually stopped to let it sink in until just now, now that I was still and able to relax. I raised my left hand to study my engagement ring—a band of white gold with a double row of inset diamonds—and the unadorned wedding ring nestled behind it.

Bec popped up over my right shoulder, and I turned to face her. "Making sure it hasn't fallen off?" she asked quietly.

"Maybe."

"Are wedding rings like passports?" she teased. "Somehow turning sentient and slipping off your finger, even though your engagement ring has stayed on just fine all this time?"

I raised my chin, trying to affect an imperious air, but I probably just looked deranged. "I've never worn one before, so I need to be cautious..."

I didn't want to admit it, but I *had* worried about losing my engagement ring, though perhaps not about it spontaneously jettisoning itself from my finger. It had almost killed me to take it off for surgery, and I kept wanting to check it was still on the sturdy chain around my neck, nestled under my scrubs.

Bec's dimples creased her cheeks. "Nothing wrong with a little caution," she said diplomatically.

"Exactly. Because this ring is one thing I *never* want to lose."

Sabine's voice, always low and husky but now with the added gravelly roughness that always crept in when she was tired, spoke close to my ear. "Bec? Honey? Time to wake up. They'll serve breakfast soon, then we'll be landing."

As surgeons who'd deployed to combat areas, both of us could sleep through almost anything, yet we were tuned to wake up at the smallest prodding, and her quiet voice was enough to drag me from my surprisingly deep sleep.

I rolled over, blinking to adjust my eyes to the cabin lighting which was warming up. She was leaning across the lie-flat seat, bracing herself on her right hand, her left gently stroking my arm. "What time is it?" I asked.

Sabine tucked some of my hair behind my ear and after a quick glance around, gave me a soft kiss. "Almost nine a.m. in Auckland."

"Did you sleep?"

"About three hours. Mostly I watched movies, snacked, and wandered around the plane." Sabine grinned. "Chatted with the flight attendants in the galley. And I made some other-passenger friends, I passed them so often. They're from New Zealand and gave me some great tips for our trip."

She was terrible at being still and I wasn't surprised to hear that she'd wandered the entire plane front to back, repeatedly.

The landing was smooth, and New Zealand Customs and Immigration just as smooth, and after a few hours where I had some of the best coffee of my life in the Auckland airport (what Antipodeans call a long black is an Americano, Sabine had said, information courtesy of her plane friends), we boarded our flight to Queenstown.

Sabine and I were both seasoned international travelers who knew how to beat jet lag—sleeping well on the flight to match your destination's time, arriving refreshed and with our bodies adapted to the new time zone. She'd hardly slept so I was worried about her crashing early, but the excitement seemed to be fueling her awakeness.

If Sabine's repetitive question was about passports, mine was about her willingness to drive all over New Zealand. Once we'd stowed our luggage in the roomy cargo compartment of the Nissan X-Trail SUV, I asked, "Are you certain you're comfortable driving?"

Sabine grinned as she opened the driver's side door. "As comfortable as you'll be."

"That's true," I mused, and got in the passenger side.

"How hard can it be? And look"—she pointed to the upper righthand corner of the windshield—"it says it right here. Keep left."

Once she'd adjusted everything in her careful way and familiarized herself with the car's controls, she set the GPS for our Airbnb, which was about ten minutes' drive away. The traffic leaving the airport and moving toward Queenstown was a steady stream of cars, and Sabine slotted into the line effortlessly. Except...

"Sabine," I said calmly. "You're drifting."

"I am?" She squinted at the road markings to our right. "No I'm not?"

"Not to the middle of the road over the line, but off to the side."

"Oh." Sabine laughed sheepishly. She carefully corrected the car. "Maybe I *am* a little worried about that whole 'keep left' thing." She remained firmly in her lane for the rest of the short drive.

Our accommodation was a modern two-bedroom house within walking distance of the town center, with views of both the lake and mountains. I'd had some input into where we'd stay, but had mostly trusted Sabine to find a place that suited both of us. The exterior was mountain-cottage chic, and once we'd parked in the one-car garage I leaned over to kiss Sabine. "This is gorgeous, darling."

"I thought so."

As soon as we'd exited the car, Sabine rushed around to the back. "Let me get those, Bec." She hoisted our larger bags from the back of the SUV. "Can you grab the carry-ons?"

"Sure," I agreed. Of course I was perfectly capable of dealing with my own luggage, just as I was perfectly capable of opening doors and lifting heavy things. But Sabine was, by nature, a helper, and I had to admit that having her want to do things for me had pushed aside my natural inclination toward independence.

I loved her mix of chivalry with femininity. I'd spent so many years alone, or in vapid relationships, and I still marveled at how easy it had been to transition to this life with Sabine.

The Airbnb host had left a bottle of New Zealand sauvignon blanc, a box of chocolates, and a vase of fresh flowers on the small kitchen table. The house wasn't huge, but it was new, clean, and cozy—everything we both wanted as a home base for our honeymoon. We unpacked, showered, and agreed to open the bottle of wine while we decided what to do with our first evening in New Zealand.

Sabine was perusing the "Helpful Hints" folder the host had left for us, turning the pages slowly as she took in the information. Every now and then she'd impart some information on me about local recommendations for places to eat and things to do. I knew she was absorbing what she read, but there was something in her expression—almost absent—and her body language—not relaxed—that made me ask, "Are you okay?"

Sabine's head snapped up, her thoughtful expression transforming into a smile I only ever saw her direct toward me. Instead of one of her usual amused, teasing, facetious, or cheeky smiles, it was gentle and trusting, conveying every ounce of love she had for me. "Yeah. I was just thinking."

Before I could ask what she was thinking about, Sabine continued, "The last time we were overseas together was Afghanistan on deployment. FOB Invicta."

She said those last two words as if I'd ever forget the Forward Operating Base where we'd finally given in to the attraction that had been building between us for years. It was a place where I'd broken all the rules, mine and the Army's, and fallen in love with a subordinate.

"That's right," I agreed, carefully keeping my tone neutral though my heart had started thudding. It was partly my body's automatic response to thinking about what had happened on my final deployment at Invicta, when we'd given in to our desire, and part fear of what she might be about to say, that she might bring up the horrible, gut-wrenching events that had followed.

She grinned. It was like a warm summer's breeze, and even now after all these years, I still felt the same rush of pleasure as I had the first time she'd directed one of her grins at me. "So I was just thinking, it's a little different this time. And we deserve no drama. Especially on our honeymoon."

"Maybe no drama ever again," I said dryly. I'd had enough trauma and drama for many lifetimes.

She smiled knowingly, then moved swiftly past her previous musings. "Do you want to explore the town before dinner? Some mental stimulation will help keep us awake."

It was on the tip of my tongue to tell her other forms of stimulation might also keep us awake, but I could tell by her expression that she'd had the same thought. Even so, we pulled on coats, scarves, and woolen hats and made our way into town.

The Queenstown city center was situated on a lake—Lake Wakatipu was one hundred and twelve square miles, fifty miles long and had a depth of one thousand three hundred and eighty feet, according to Sabine who reeled off facts from memory—and was quite possibly one of the most scenic towns I'd visited. Snow-smothered mountains surrounded us, rising jagged and beautiful into the sky. I took photographs that I knew would never adequately capture the vista, nor the exact feeling I had as I looked at them.

We strolled around the lake, dodging runners and cyclists, and sidestepping people strolling even slower than us, which was a miracle. Not so much a miracle as Sabine strolling instead of hurrying along. She was high energy, perpetually in motion, and this calm, gentle walk was so unlike her usual pace.

I knew she was deliberately slowing down for me, who wanted to indulge and observe and enjoy, and if I weren't already utterly in love with her, this thoughtfulness might push me over the edge.

I'd never thought I could find so much bliss with one person, but Sabine fulfilled me in a way nothing or nobody had before. Being here together was undoubtedly exciting, relaxing, interesting, and fun, but it was Sabine that made it all the more special for me.

Our Thai food was delicious, and after dinner we moved on to a bar. We spent a few hours sampling local wines while overlooking the lake, watching the rising moon reflecting on the water. We confirmed our solid plans, and solidified some of our looser ones for how we were going to spend our honeymoon. I didn't need to go over plans to know our days were going to be jam-packed.

And they were.

During the days we walked miles, fitting in as many activities as we could. Some nights we went out, discovering a new restaurant every evening. Other nights we ordered in or cooked something simple, accompanying the meal with one of the bottles of wine from our winery tours. We worked on the jigsaw puzzles left in the house, played card games, or watched television. In spite of Sabine's feelings on yoga—she'd pooh-poohed it after a therapist had suggested it as a way to help with her PTSD—she joined me for yoga on the patio each morning before we left for our day's adventures.

On our sixth day, we hiked to the Flats Hut on the Routeburn Track—an easy, mostly forested trail about an hour out of Queenstown that followed a river (the Route Burn, Sabine informed me, "burn" being a Scottish word for small river or large creek) through to a valley. I'd never seen water this color; a kind of slate blue mixed with an almost aquamarine in places, and so clear I could see every pebble in the riverbed.

"It's the fine silt in the water that makes it that color," Sabine told me, slipping her hand into mine as we stood on the bank of the river at Forge Flat—the small inlet that had been a quick detour off the track. "Glacial flour they call it. I think because the water is moving, it doesn't look like a thick, solid blue, it's clear instead."

"It's beautiful," I said. "Such a bright, clear blue."

"It is," Sabine agreed. "But I like the dark blue of your eyes better. Ocean blue."

I stretched up to kiss her. "Do you want to stay here and have a snack and some hot tea, or keep going to the hut?"

"I do want to stay here. But there's sandflies…"

"And they're already making a meal of you," I finished for her. She was a magnet for any blood-sucking insect, even in winter it seemed.

"Yeah," she said ruefully.

"Then let's keep moving. I don't want you getting eaten."

Sabine's mouth quirked, and it took approximately two seconds for her to take my unintended bait. "Except by you, you mean."

I raised my eyebrows. "Exactly."

She ensured I made good on my promise when we got back to the house.

On our eighth day in Queenstown, Sabine insisted she wanted to try bungy jumping. "This is the place that invented it for commercial fun, Bec, so it feels like one of us should do it. And if they started it, then their safety record must be great."

"I'm up for it," I enthused.

Sabine smirked. "Thought you might be, thrill-rider." She was right—I was an adventure-park ride lover. The scarier and more nausea-inducing a ride was, the better I loved it.

"Do you *really* want to bungy jump?" I asked, slightly dubious at her declaration.

"I'm…about eighty percent sure. I mean, it looks kind of fun? In a slightly terrifying way."

I couldn't believe she'd just said that. "It really does."

"And if I can't step out of my comfort zone on my honeymoon, when I'm safe with you, then when can I do that?"

"That's a great point. Do they have a tandem option?"

She reached for her phone and after scrolling, said, "They do." Sabine looked up, eyes bright with excitement.

I smiled, enjoying her enthusiasm. "Let's book it in."

We did our tandem bungy, which was as fun as I'd expected, and almost as soon as we were done, Sabine was burbling about our next honeymoon adventure-seeking activity. To be fair, she was burbling through a shocked expression, but it seemed the adrenaline was overriding her usual misgivings about thrill-seeking.

The next day, we tandem-paraglided from the top of a mountain overlooking the town, taking in the incredible views as we floated down. She booked us in for a jetboating ride through the Shotover Canyon, and, as seemed to be the rule for any tourist attraction, we were given a talk on features of the area and how the jetboats worked. Sabine lapped it up, drinking in the knowledge and regurgitating it at random times. I loved it. And I loved her so much I felt like I couldn't contain the depth of the emotion.

And so it continued, our honeymoon filled with a mix of activities and relaxing. Sabine had told me that the days between the ceremony in Ohio and our courthouse ceremony in DC were a blur, even though now when she looked back she realized she'd felt every wonderful moment. I understood what she meant—every day was passing by in a wonderful rush of new adventures, and yet I could recall every detail of doing these things with Sabine.

After a soothing hour in the onsen hot tubs just outside of town to cap off a busy day of walking and more winery tours, Sabine practically dragged me home and into bed. It had been like that every night, as if we couldn't get enough of touching each other, of tasting, of enjoying intimate places we already knew so well.

On one of our last days in the country, we drove the very scenic and very winding New Zealand roads to the west coast for a night boat tour through a glowworm cave. The next day we continued to Milford Sound for a cruise. The crystal-clear water looked so enticing, but as we found out when the boat deliberately took us right up to a waterfall flowing from the top of the mountain to be sprayed—it was freezing. Glacial waters indeed.

I stood pressed against Sabine at the bow of the large boat, braving the brisk wind and occasional freezing spray, not wanting to miss a moment of the cruise. The mountainous walls of the sound—partly forested and partly snow-covered—loomed above us as Sabine listened intently to the guides explaining how the feature had been formed by volcanic activity millions of years ago. I tuned in and out, more intent on watching Sabine's expression of delight in response to learning about the formation of this UNESCO site.

"So, the black coral," Sabine began, and I knew I was in for Some Information, "is not actually black. It's white. But their skeletons are black, hence the name."

"I see."

"And I'm sure you know, but corals aren't 'plants,' they're actually animals. A whole lot of them, living in symbiosis."

"I did know that, but I definitely hadn't thought about it."

Her eyes brightened. "Do you want to go down into the viewing chamber?"

"Yes," I said immediately.

She held my hand as we made our way down the steep stairs to the underwater viewing chamber, and we spent a little time studying the life underneath the surface until it was time to finish up the cruise.

The drive back to our Airbnb took almost four hours, with us stopping at every scenic spot we found to take in the sights, and we arrived well after dark. With our marathon of flights back to DC looming the next morning, we agreed staying in was prudent.

Sabine beelined for the shower and after checking she didn't want wine, I poured myself the remainder of the last open bottle of pinot noir and ordered dinner.

I'd finished almost half my glass by the time she came out of the bathroom. Sabine leaned over the back of the couch to kiss my neck, enveloping me in the lemony scent of her shampoo. After a playful, gentle bite to my ear she murmured, "How long until dinner? And what is dinner?"

"Twenty minutes. Indian." I'd ordered from one of the places the folder recommended. I turned slightly to kiss her, then carefully extricated myself before there was no shower and no dinner in favor of taking her to bed.

"Perfect. I'll finish packing." Her gaze moved to my mouth then away again. Sabine bit her lower lip, then seemed to muster a heroic effort and straightened again, putting a tiny amount of space between us. Thankfully she had some self-control because mine was wafer thin at that moment.

Dinner was quieter than usual, not silent at all but definitely without the almost manic excitement of all our other meals where we were either discussing what we were going to do that day, or what we'd done. We cleaned up after dinner, and I'd barely started the dishwasher when Sabine turned, pinning me gently against the kitchen counter.

That simple movement always meant one thing, and had from the very first time we'd slept together when we'd indulged in delicious foreplay in her kitchen. She held eye contact, and having seen no reticence in my expression, Sabine drew my hand to her chest. After briefly pressing it against her left breast, she pulled it to her mouth and slowly sucked my fingers.

The languid movement of her tongue sent arousal flooding through me. She bit teasingly, then guided my hand down the front of her sweatpants. Given the naked desire in her eyes, I wasn't surprised to find her wet and wanting.

"You want me to fuck you in this kitchen?" I asked, sliding my fingers through her wetness. The sensation of her arousal made my own peak.

"I want you to fuck me anywhere," she breathed. A beat passed before she kissed me, her arm snaking around my waist. Sabine turned us and guided me toward the master bedroom where she undressed me with the same careful attention she allocated to everything she did.

She shed her own clothing before I could help, as if she were as desperate as I was to make love, and we tumbled onto the bed together. Our kisses grew heated, our touches frantic. By now we knew each other so well that our intimacy was as natural as breathing.

I loved her small, neat breasts and the way they fit so perfectly in my hands. I thumbed a tight nipple, delighting in Sabine's quick inhalation. When I replaced a hand with my mouth, she gasped again. I kissed and licked my way down her body, lingering at my favorite places which were the places that elicited the loudest moans from her throat.

Making love to Sabine had always felt revelatory, from the very first time we'd fallen into bed. And now, after three years together, there was so much trust and love between us that made our intimacy all the more pleasurable. I'd never had a lover like Sabine, and I marveled that I'd ever been without her—in or out of bed.

Her hand tangled in my hair, guiding my mouth down toward her spread thighs. "Please, Bec." It was a quiet, desperate plea.

When I gripped her thighs, the muscle underneath my hands tensed. Sabine's barely audible, second "Please" was even more desperate.

I slicked my tongue through her arousal, pausing at her clit. She exhaled loudly, pressing herself up into my mouth. The hand in my hair tightened, and I needed no more encouragement. I kissed and licked and sucked her toward her climax, accompanied by Sabine's breathless urging.

I could feel the tension in her body, the tight coiling of muscles begging to release with her orgasm. Her breathing hitched and in the next breath she came hard, her arousal hot and wet against my tongue. Sabine propped herself up on an elbow, looking down the length of her body at me. Her eyes were soft, almost unfocused with the remnants of her pleasure. "Come up here."

I couldn't help pausing to kiss her hipbones, her belly, her breasts, as I crawled back up the length of her. I straddled her hips, not bothering to suppress my gasp at the sensation of her skin against my arousal.

Sabine's mouth quirked, clearly knowing the reason I'd just made that sound. "God, I love the way you fuck me," she said thickly. She gripped the back of my neck and pulled me down for a kiss.

"And I love fucking you," I managed when she finished thoroughly exploring my mouth with her lips and tongue. Even if I'd been able to think of a more articulate response around the overwhelming tease of pleasure throbbing through me, Sabine's kiss would have cut it off.

She sat up, wrapping an arm around my waist to pull me closer. As she kissed me, her other hand pressed insistently between my thighs and I raised myself up so she could enter me.

I slung my arm around her shoulders to steady myself, my other hand gripping the bed frame as I rode her toward my climax. I was so aroused, so wet, so desperate. Our sweat-slick torsos pressed together as Sabine's thumb stroked my clit with every thrust. I rocked my hips in time with her, grinding onto her fingers, and when I came it was hard and fast, a molten rush of pleasure that made my whole body tremble.

I buried my face in her shoulder, trying to catch my breath.

Sabine pulled slightly back so she could press her forehead to mine. "I love you," she said, her voice rough with the emotion of her statement.

"I love you too," I whispered hoarsely. "I'll never stop loving you."

When I woke early the next day, the final morning of our honeymoon, I confirmed Sabine was still sleeping soundly then slipped out of bed to watch the sunrise.

Sitting on the deck with my coffee, staring out over the lake and a town just waking up, I had to admit my honeymoon-soaked brain wasn't particularly enamored with the idea of returning to my job running a busy level-one surgical trauma unit. But existing in a perpetual honeymoon wasn't realistic and, honestly, as long as I was with Sabine, it didn't matter that we were back home in our "regular" lives.

I turned at the sound of the glass sliding door opening. A smile spread over my lips without conscious thought. "Morning. How'd you sleep?"

"Like I was in a coma. I wonder why?" Sabine's mouth quirked. She set her coffee on the table beside mine and leaned over me from behind to wrap me in her arms. She kissed my neck, then my lips when I turned my head. "I can't believe it's over. I've had the best time." She laughed. "That sounds lame. It's been better than the best."

I exhaled loudly. "This has been amazing, but…it's time to go home."

"Yeah," she quietly agreed. There was a tinge of something I couldn't quite place in that single word, and I hated to think it could be regret, though I understood why she wouldn't want to leave our honeymoon destination to go home and back to work.

I twisted around fully to look at my wife. "Are you sad, darling?"

"Why would I be sad?"

I thought carefully about what I wanted to say, because spoiling the mood at the end of our honeymoon was not on my agenda. "You seem a little unsettled."

She was quiet for a few long moments, nodding slowly. "Yeah…"

"Do you want to talk about it?"

This pause was even longer, and I gave her the time she needed to put form to her thoughts. Sabine sighed deeply, and her words came out in a rush on the exhalation. "I think I've been feeling a little aimless? Now the wedding is over and there's nothing to plan for. And…I'm almost done with the Army and I'm trying to wrap my head around no more deployments and what all that means for me. Plus we've been away for a few weeks." She shrugged. "I think I'm maybe just not sure where I fit now."

I knew exactly where she fit, but before I could verbalize it, Sabine's gaze found mine and my words died in my throat. Her dark-brown eyes shone with love, with pride, with contentment.

"Actually, no, Bec. I know where I fit. I fit with you, and that's always been home to me."

Enjoyed this glimpse into their life after the happy ending? Discover how their story began in the *Ask, Tell* series.

Northern Lights

by Liz Arncliffe

"It's a cotton candy sunrise." Sloane stretched her legs out and pointed her toes toward the rising sun before letting them dangle again from the end of the ferry dock on K'gari, an island in the Coral Sea, just off the Fraser Coast of Queensland. It would be their vacation spot for the next several days. "It's a fairy floss sunset."

Ava smiled at Sloane's correction, leaned her head on Sloane's shoulder, and looked down at their intertwined fingers. Her heart swelled with a quiet joy and she turned her head to kiss Sloane's bare shoulder, just below the edge of her singlet.

"Look at the way the sand reflects the blue and pink back up into the sky. Fucking magical," Sloane added.

"The pink will begin edging toward orange any second now."

"You think?" This had become routine for them, a nearly scripted conversation about sunsets and sunrises since Sloane had made her permanent home with Ava and Grace more than a year earlier. They had happily settled and watched the changing colour of the sky morning and night ever since.

"Just wait." Ava recited her lines to perfection.

Sloane wiggled closer to Ava. "Happy to."

They sat quietly, bare feet swinging from the edge of the dock, and watched dawn turn from grey-blues and delicate purples to soft pinks and finally to the mandarin oranges Ava promised.

Ava sighed her contentment at the stillness of it all—these quiet moments had become her favourite. But she knew she had to tell Sloane her news and she was anxious for Sloane's reaction, even more so because Sloane had seemed introspective in the days leading up to the big family trip to K'gari.

"Hey. Hi," Ava whispered. "Before we head back for breakfast…"

"Yeah?"

"Thank you for last night." She hadn't meant to say that, but now that she had, she was glad.

"Last night?"

"Last night. You don't remember last night?" Heat rose in her cheeks, and she knew Sloane had seen it.

"Oh, I remember last night." Sloane smiled, a softness in her eyes. And maybe mischief too.

"Thank you for last night. And all the nights before last night."

"And all the nights yet to come?" Ava asked.

"Yes, my heart. And all the nights yet to come."

"Sloane, I have something I need to tell you," Ava said simply and quietly.

"Tell me." Ava noted Sloane's nonreaction and pushed on.

"I auditioned for a principal role in a big series."

Sloane ducked her head toward Ava, as if waiting for an answer. "And?"

"And I got the part."

"That's fantastic! Tell me all about it. And then tell me why this is the first I'm hearing of it." Sloane turned to fully face Ava, her expression one of excitement and pride.

"Well, um, it's going to be a massive production—probably three series. That's what they're hoping for. It's already getting lots of buzz in the US. It'll be big. Worldwide, they say." Ava's stomach knotted with nerves—she was only getting her career back on track and this could prove to be a massive step in that direction. She knew Sloane supported her, but she also knew that the impending separation would be difficult.

"Oh, wow. Ava this is wonderful! Wait...where will you film?" Sloane's breathing slowed, and she creased her brow.

Ava recognized the expression and braced herself.

"That's what we need to discuss. We'll shoot entirely on location. In Iceland." Ava held her breath.

Sloane said nothing but worry passed over her face, and Ava winced.

"I didn't think I'd get it. It's a major studio. The producers and the directors have—"

"How long? You said three seasons—but how long for each? And how long in between?"

The questions were fast and asked flatly, in a tone that Ava also recognized and didn't like.

"Six to eight months, probably. For each series. I'm not sure about time off in between. It'll depend on—"

"Eight months! In Iceland! Ava! What about us? Will Grace go with you? She's more involved in school now, Ava. What will we do? Ava, why didn't we talk about it? Have you accepted? Does your mother know—does Ellen know? Ava…" Sloane covered her face with her hands.

Ava wondered if Sloane might cry. "I didn't think I'd get it," Ava repeated.

"Then why didn't you tell me? You tell me about all the tests. Why not this one?" Sloane looked at her and there were no tears, but there was confusion. And fear, maybe.

"Maybe I did think I'd get it." Doubt sparked and then, guilt. Embarrassment, even. Her own. Why hadn't she told Sloane?

"What? Ava, that makes no sense. Will you take Grace? Ava, have you signed the contract?" There was panic in her voice.

"No, I haven't. Not yet anyway. But I think I should. Sloane, this could make up for—"

"Does Ellen know? What about us? What will happen to us?"

"No, Mum doesn't know. You think I'd tell her before you? Sloane, we'll work it out. I just can't turn this down. I can't. Actors and their families manage this kind of thing. We'll manage."

Sloane turned and looked toward the sun, floating well above the horizon now. She grew quiet again. And very still. "We missed the orangest of oranges."

Ava turned from Sloane's worried and sad expression to look at the morning light reflecting on the surface of the sea.

"Iceland." Sloane sighed.

"Iceland."

Ava's phone buzzed next to her, and she turned it over knowing that it would be Grace calling from the resort as it was nearing the time she normally woke in a buzz of renewed vim and vigor.

"Mum! Mimi says that y'all have to come back now. We have to eat brekky and get to the bus by 8 o'clock sharp!" Her daughter was in quite the excited state and, from the sound of it, so was Ellen.

Ava smiled every time her daughter spoke the word *y'all* even though it had been common for many months now. "We're on our way, Gracie. We'll meet you in the breakfast line."

Sloane stood and began the walk back before Ava even ended the call, and Ava had to rush to catch up to her. She took Sloane's hand and kissed her palm.

Sloane smiled weakly back at Ava. "We'll talk about it later?"

"We will. It'll get sorted, I promise."

"I will not fall for it, Traci. Your daughter has been trying for ages. I will not put that salty sludge in my mouth." Sloane turned her nose up in defiance at the offer and then turned to her best mate. "Mo, I see where you get your persistence."

"Calling it persistence is generous, Sloane. I'm not so sure I'd manage such equanimity." Leota shook her head and sipped her tea.

"As Mo's wife, I'm sure your experience of her bullheadedness isn't nearly as endearing as it is for me." Sloane smiled at Mo, and they raised their mugs in solidarity.

"It's a rite of passage, hon," Traci tried again. Since having returned from the States, Traci had more or less adopted Sloane as her second daughter and Sloane cherished her found family. "Just a little with a good smear of butter on toast. It's the done thing."

But try as they might, Sloane remained adamant in her refusal to try Vegemite. Mo had tried to convince Sloane to try it her entire first year teaching, and again when she returned for good. And now Traci. Sloane refused it then and now, and every time it was offered.

Ava and Leota both laughed at the exchange. But Ellen just rolled her eyes.

"It's gross." Grace wrinkled her nose.

"Thanks, bug. You're the truest mate I have at this table." Sloane pulled Grace close and handed the child the second half of a passionfruit from her plate, which Grace happily spooned up. Sloane noticed the slight side-eye from Ava and maybe a small expression of frustration or hurt. But the news of Ava not telling her about the role had been a shock. And Sloane was very much feeling a small sting of betrayal still.

"I do wonder if it would be good in a big ol' pot of collard greens," Sloane distracted herself and picked up the small pot of goo from the table.

"Blasphemy," Traci said flatly.

"Sacrilege," Mo added.

"Simply un-Australian." Traci's smirk betrayed her mock disappointment as the mother and daughter commentary bounced from one to the other like a ping-pong match.

They often united forces in ribbing Sloane, and this time, Sloane chuckled at their efforts.

"I know a woman who puts it in the best stew I've ever had," Ellen said evenly, eyeing both Mo and Traci as if challenging them. When she got no argument from either of the women, she added, "We're going to be late. Let's make a move."

She stood, gathered her shoulder bag and hat, and began walking toward the exit, not waiting for the others. Ava collected Grace and their things and followed behind Ellen.

"Tense morning with the better half and her mum, mate," Mo whispered, as much as Mo whispered, to Sloane as they followed Ellen, Ava, and Grace from the resort dining hall.

"Everything alright?" Leota asked, looking genuinely worried.

"No worries." Sloane smiled and tried to reassure her mates that all was well. "Not sure what's up with Ellen though. She seems to be in a bit of a snit."

"In her defence, Mo and Traci together are a lot," Leota offered.

"Hey!" Mo and Traci responded in unison.

Sloane and Leota both laughed as they all made their way through a maze of tracks toward the meeting place for the tour bus, scheduled to leave at eight o'clock AM sharp.

Grace chattered with exuberance in Ava's direction about the tour. She hoped to see a dingo. Did her mum think there were ghosts at the shipwreck? Could she ride in Mo's tube when they floated the creek? Where would they eat lunch? Where would they go to the toilet? Would the dingoes eat their lunches? All before they reached the end of carpark where the bus sat.

Sloane loved moments like this, watching Ava and Grace together. Listening to Grace's endless questions and hearing Ava respond with immense patience and care. There was a pang deep in her chest at the thought of being away from them for six months. Or more. Much more if the series was multiple seasons. She tried to push away the mild panic and focused on the moment.

"This is a weird bus," Grace exclaimed. "Why are the tyres so big?"

"In you go now. And I'll tell you all about it." The guide stood proudly next to the vehicle and gestured for the group to begin boarding. "Got your towels? Your water? Aerogard? Salt for the leeches? Your dingo safety stick?"

"This is not the vacation I would have planned." Ellen's dissatisfaction was apparent, as she turned and eyed Sloane and Mo before boarding the bus.

"Just kidding with you. I've got a safety stick on the bus. But you did bring your towel, sunscreen, and water, yeah?" He was tall and lanky and looked like he was playing a role in a 1980s movie about the outback with his khaki shorts, wide-brimmed hat, and leather boots.

The group settled in two rows near the front of the bus, Ellen and Ava sat together. Sloane and Grace across the aisle from them. Mo behind Sloane and Grace and across the aisle from her sat Traci and Leota, directly behind Ava and Ellen. They piled all the bags and towels in the empty seat beside Mo. A dozen or so other tourists filled the seats around them.

"Welcome, mates. How're we going? My name's Joel and I'm happy to show you 'round K'gari on this beautiful summer day. How many first-timers do I have?" He clapped his hands together and looked out over his charges, counting them all.

Everyone on the bus raised their hands that they were all on the tour for the first time.

"Right! Well, this will be exciting! Everyone settle down and buckle up while I get this rig on the road, and I'll tell you about the bus and why we need such big puffy tyres. We're on an all-sand island here—the biggest in the world. The only bitumen is right around the few resorts on the place, like this one. No conventional roads or highways. Our bus here has got to make it over the sand tracks. Sometimes the sand gets pretty soft, other times it holds enough moisture and compression to give us a little more traction. Pretty dry this month, so the sand is gonna be soft. This bus was converted from a German-designed vehicle meant to travel in extreme conditions and over tropical islands. It'll get us where we need to go." Joel patted the back of his seat as if cajoling the bus and went on to explain vehicle safety, toilet stops, and what to expect along the tour.

Sloane was as mesmerized as Grace, maybe more so. She thought it wild that an all-sand island could support the thick vegetation and infrastructure she'd seen thus far. "I've got plenty of questions of my own, bug. Like, how does a rain forest grow out of sand? What a thing! And are these tracks actual roads? Whatever that means." She and Grace chatted excitedly about their surroundings as they pulled out of the car park.

They soon turned on a road that took them away from the resort and further inland. The bitumen ended up ahead, and as they approached, Joel put the bus into a lower gear. The ground underneath them shifted. Sand roads, Sloane thought to herself. Up and up they climbed, the road narrowed, and the thick, green forest crept right to the edges of the road.

"What happens if we meet another vehicle?" she asked Joel as he navigated the precarious curves and hills of their route.

"One of us will reverse until there's a passing bay or enough room to move over. We're bigger, so they'll reverse." He smiled broadly into the mirror above his head at Sloane.

"I haven't seen a passing bay; they'd have to reverse quite a ways." She looked all around and saw nothing but forest.

"Nah yeah, we've already passed several of them," Joel said. "I'll show you."

And sure enough, not long after Sloane's question, they passed a bay—or rather a vehicle that had been abandoned in a tiny spot barely off the road. Joel squeezed by without much effort, but Sloane held her breath. She'd hardly call that a suitable place to pull off the road.

"Bloke was inexperienced. There's loads of them visit and think they can make it around here in their rented four-wheel drives. Expensive mistake to make." Joel shook his head and drove on.

The first stop was Lake McKenzie with the clearest water Sloane had ever seen. She learned that all the water on the island was from rainwater and that it was incredibly clean. Joel told her it was so pure, she could drink it, but Sloane wasn't willing to risk it. She splashed around with Grace, Mo, and Traci while Ava smiled and laughed with Leota and Ellen on a blanket on the shore. Sloane was sure to keep herself and Grace on the opposite side of the lake from the musk ducks as Joel had warned them that while beautiful, the ducks always seemed angry at intrusions into their territory and could be aggressive.

"That Joel is a stunner." Traci looked longingly toward shore where Joel prepared a morning tea break for the tour-goers.

"Mum fancies younger men," Mo explained matter-of-factly. "Often, they fancy her in return."

"Let's see if I've still got it." Traci winked at the group and started back toward the shore.

Grace looked from Mo to Sloane. "Still got what? Did she leave something on the bus?"

"No, little tiny tasseltop. What she's looking for isn't on the bus. Let's go and have a snack." Sloane chuckled and the trio followed Traci toward the shoreline.

Ava knew what Sloane was thinking before the woman even spoke. She had heard the same argument many times over since all the way back in Sloane's early days on the farm in the Hinterlands of the Gold Coast.

"I do understand that much of Australian culture is British-adjacent, but the one thing I don't understand holding so strongly to is hot tea in hot weather." Sloane drank water and bikkies while everyone else sipped English Breakfast and Earl Grey.

"You're not still going on about missing iced sweet tea?" Ava asked over her mug, self-satisfied that she'd been correct about Sloane's thoughts. "Maybe you should make some when we're home."

"Sounds just awful." Mo popped a ginger biscuit in her mouth.

"Don't knock it 'til you've tried it. It's refreshing in the summer—" Sloane stopped mid-sentence and slowly stood, mouth hanging open. She wordlessly pointed over Ava's left shoulder.

Ava turned to find a goanna slinking slowly through the sand and into an opening in the ground under a tree fern eight or nine metres away.

Before she could reassure Sloane that it was harmless, Ellen took Sloane's hand and guided her back into her seat. "It's not dangerous, dear. Just a tree goanna."

"But if it's running at you, better get flat to the ground. They're known to run right up you if they think you're a tree. Nasty claws. Tear you right up." Mo sipped her tea nonchalantly, but Ava saw the hint of a smirk.

"Whaa...wha...what?" Sloane stammered.

"Mo—" Ava started and then leaned back on the bench, unable to quell her laughter.

Traci looked over Ava's shoulder toward the tracks that the goanna had left in the sand. "That's a big one. Real nasty claws."

"It'll think I'm a tree?" Sloane asked, still wide-eyed.

"Thank the gods your Grace is on the short side," Traci turned to Ava, wearing the same smirk as Mo.

"Oh, stop scaring her!" Ellen side-eyed Mo and Traci and turned to Sloane. "They're tree monitors. They eat eggs from nests in the trees. I assure you it wants nothing to do with us."

"But seriously, if it's running at you, lie down," Traci insisted.

"Is that true though? Really?" Sloane asked and turned to Ava for confirmation.

"It's true actually," Ava said gently.

Ellen nodded in quiet assent.

"That's what they told us in science class." Grace stood on her tippy toes to see where the goanna had slipped off to.

Sloane looked at Grace like she'd been betrayed, looked back to Ava, and gasped. "Why in the world would it think I'm a tree? Do they have poor vision?"

"It doesn't think you're a tree. Mo is being melodramatic. But if it's being chased by a predator, it looks for height. And any height will do." Ava bumped her shoulder to Sloane's trying to comfort her.

Ellen sighed her exasperation. "Sloane, I assure you that lizard is no threat to us."

"Unless it's chasing you." Mo said, and she didn't bother trying to hide the smirk this time.

"Mo!" Ava and Ellen yelled in unison as Leota sidled up to the table and slipped into the chair next to her partner, having just come back from the toilet.

"What mischief are you getting into now?" she asked Mo and leaned in to kiss her on the cheek. "Telling tales about the goannas again?"

"I'm just trying to educate. I'm an educator. It's what I do." Mo smiled broadly at Sloane and then shrank slightly when Ellen groaned.

"Maybe Grace and I should go back to the bus." Sloane made to stand up, clearly not finding reassurance in their words at all.

"We're all fine. Pay no mind to my wife and her mother." Leota tried to assuage Sloane's worry. "They're just up to their typical shenanigans."

"Um...I think I would feel better if we just moved away a bit." Sloane eased out of her chair, scooped up Grace, and moved to the other side of the pavilion. She looked over her shoulder twice as she walked.

Ava was sure she did it to see that the goanna wasn't following.

Traci and Mo laughed, and Ellen scowled in their direction.

"Just so that I understand, you came all this way to frighten your best mate with stories of violent lizards?" Ellen asked, clearly irritated.

"Well, yeah," Traci answered for her daughter. "All in good fun."

"They're marshmallows, Ellen. But wily ones." Leota chose a biscuit from Sloane's abandoned plate.

"We're complex and layered women, Ellen. Who like to have a little fun." Traci draped her arm around Mo, pulled her close, and dropped a kiss on her forehead, as if Mo were a child.

The gesture made Ava smile. Ellen rolled her eyes, not for the first time that day.

They stopped next at the area where the Eli Creek emptied itself onto the beach in a large, shallow pool perfect for wading and cooling off. It was crowded with families splashing in the clear water and relaxing at the water's edge. Joel had said earlier that this was the likeliest place to see dingoes and, as they were unloading, he spotted one lurking at the base of the dunes, spying all the food the humans had delivered to its doorstep. Joel used his safety stick to chase off the lone creature and explained that it wouldn't have gone far away from the possibility of easy loot. After Grace asked a million questions about the K'gari dingoes, he told a story about camping and waking up to find a litter of pups had made off with his boots. He had followed the tracks until he found the pups and his not-so-gently gnawed upon boots.

Joel pointed the way up the boardwalk along the creek and told them he'd meet them back at the bus at the appointed time after their float. The track up was gently sloped and Ava knew the float would be slow and easy. At the top, they put their tubes in the water, climbed on, and started back down the cool, calm, soothing stream. The cool water felt both refreshing and invigorating on Ava's skin, still warm from the sunny walk up the track.

She pulled herself over to a pouting Sloane. She took hold of Sloane's hand, so they floated side by side for as long as the creek was wide enough.

"Do you plan to pout with me all day?" she asked.

"Maybe. No. But, probably a little."

Ava laughed quietly. "I appreciate the honesty."

"I guess I should have expected this, especially after the big award. But it's just so far away and for so long and we just settled into our lives here. And what will I do without you here for so long?" Sloane stared up into the tree canopy above them.

Ava leaned her head back as well and watched the vibrant green as the stream carried them gently through the forest. "We'll work it out. Facetime, digital movie dates..."

"With that time difference?"

"Do you really want me to turn it down?" She rolled her head to look at Sloane and took off her sunnies, wanting to see her with no filter.

Sloane took off her own sunglasses in response, and now there was nothing between them to screen the eye contact. "No, of course not. But why didn't you tell me about the role to begin with? Because you knew it would upset me? That it would upset us?" There was worry in Sloane's eyes.

A pang of guilt and doubt rippled through Ava's chest. "Maybe. No. But, probably a little."

"I would have appreciated your honesty weeks ago when you sent an audition video."

A slight movement distracted Ava just as Grace crashed into Sloane's float, and the girl let out a peal of giggles. "We caught you two! Mo, they were holding hands! Being *romaaaantic*!"

"Busted! Being *romaaaantic!*" Mo's voice boomed from behind them, and Leota's laughter drifted along after.

Sloane turned herself around to face them and grabbed Grace's feet for a tickle. "Mo, where's Traci? Bickering with Ellen about the best route to the top of the creek?"

"Nah, Mum stayed back to flirt with Joel and Ellen was chatting with the German couple about their travel plans after K'gari. And schnitzel recipes."

"I like schnitzel!" added Grace as she grabbed the edge of Ava's float and pulled herself close, bouncing and twisting as she did. "Mum, can I have schnitzel for dinner?"

"I bet there's some at the lunch buffet." Leota offered, as a swifter current pushed her even with Mo and just behind Ava, Sloane, and Grace.

"That's next right? I'm bloody starving!" Mo said, and her stomach loudly seconded the sentiment.

"How far away is lunch? I'm pretty hungry myself." Sloane trailed her fingers along the water's surface, watching the ripples on the surface of the crystal-clear creek.

"I think we have to take the beach highway to a different resort," Leota said and pulled herself closer to Mo, wrapping her ankle around her partner's so that they too floated side by side.

"Will we see the shipwreck and the coloured rocks?" Grace rolled around on the floatie, so she lay on her stomach, her nose skimming the surface of the water. She giggled and Ava smiled at her daughter's squirmy delight.

"After lunch, I think," Ava answered.

"Oh, thank god! I'm bloody starving!" Mo whinged.

"We know!" They all answered in unison. Even Grace.

There was indeed schnitzel. It was the most eclectic buffet Sloane had ever seen. Schnitzel, lo mein, spaghetti, fish, overcooked vegetables, meat pies of undisclosed flavours, chips, roasted potatoes, crispy kipfler potatoes, rolls, salad that had gone questionably limp in the heat, and an assortment of puddings that was sure to have Grace on a sugar high all afternoon.

"I think I'll go with roast potatoes and veg." Ava picked out the firmest of the vegetables and Sloane and Ellen followed suit.

"Yeah nah, a little of everything for me. Maybe a lot of everything." Mo announced but Sloane noticed she skipped the vegetables.

Grace held her plate for Ava to help with the serving. "I would like schnitzel and spaghetti, please."

"Righto! Brilliant! Bloody legend, you are! Very nearly chicken parm, mate!" Traci filled her plate to match Grace's, and the group made their way to a table near the open doors of the large dining room.

"Mind if I join you, ladies?" Sloane looked over to find Joel. And then chuckled as Traci dramatically welcomed him to sit beside her.

The two proceeded to swap stories of time on the road— his, the sand roads of K'gari and hers, driving trucks around Western Australia and the top end decades earlier. Dust storms, floods, crossing rivers teeming with crocs. Mo shared her own stories too, from her youth and from when she was driving on her own before finishing university to teach.

Sloane loved these stories of Mo's life before the classroom, and she often wondered if Mo sometimes felt nostalgic for the open road.

The best story though, came from Joel, and had nothing to do with transporting goods or tourists. And it ended lunch with a crash of laughter. "I was riding a dirt bike my uncle had given me when I was ten. I was coming back home from having a swim in the creek. Barefoot, of course. Ran that bike right into a red gum. Lost three toes." And for dramatic effect, he had removed his boot and sock and threw his foot onto the table for everyone to see. "Only got the two remaining on this foot." And he howled with laughter, and Traci and Mo along with him.

Sloane was stunned. Ava looked concerned, Grace fascinated, and Ellen scandalized.

"On the table?" Ellen asked incredulously, clearly more concerned about eating a sanitary lunch than Joel's missing toes. Sloane and Ava joined the laughter, and Grace walked around the table to get a better look—curiosity clearly getting the better of the girl.

When the laughter began to die down, recognition tugged at the edges of Sloane's consciousness and she changed the subject from Joel's bare foot to the restaurant playlist. "Are they really playing Groove Armada at a family buffet?"

Mo, Leota, and Ava paused to listen and then burst into another round of laughter as they all began singing along to "I See You Baby." When they got to the lyrics about gyrating body parts, Traci and Joel joined in the singing and Sloane thought it the most entertaining and memorable family buffet she'd ever been to. Ellen looked even more scandalized and decided she and Grace needed ice cream at the shop across the car park immediately. She took the girl's hand and stormed out.

As they were scurrying from the dining room, Grace told Ellen that she liked the song.

Sloane laughed even harder at the girl's innocent cheek.

They cruised the beach highway—also the island's airstrip—toward the Maheno shipwreck and the rainbow-coloured sands of the Pinnacles, and Sloane marvelled at the ancient colours. They concluded the tour with a walk through a rainforest that pulsed with the sound of cicadas and bee-eaters, and they were surrounded by hundreds of vibrant greens and the lush, clean scent of hoop pines, satinays, and strangler figs. They strolled along a boardwalk set well above a creek so clear that Sloane thought it empty of water until the sun streaming through the tree canopy caught a ripple in the water and made it glimmer and sparkle.

At an opening in the tree canopy where the water slowed to nearly standing, they learned that the space had been a sacred birthing place to the Butchulla people, the Traditional Owners of K'gari.

Sloane breathed in deeply and breathed out a silent apology for their trespass before she sombrely followed the others back to the bus and Joel steered them back onto the sand roads that crisscrossed the island.

Sloane was tuckered out and ready for a shower, dinner, and rest. She knew she and Ava desperately needed to talk about the shoot in Iceland, but she wasn't sure she had the energy and focus the conversation rightly required. She looked around at her family to see how everyone was faring after a very long day full of adventure and laughter. Grace had fallen asleep lying across Ava's lap. Leota dozed, her legs draped over Mo's thighs. Traci chatted uncharacteristically quietly with Joel about what Sloane couldn't fathom. Ellen talked more with the German tourists about her favourite places to visit in Brisbane, Melbourne, and Sydney. The other bus riders looked weary and had grown quiet.

After climbing a steep hill and hurling the bus down the other side to a low point in the track, they began to lose speed at the next incline and Sloane noticed both Joel and Traci stiffen.

"Ah, mate, I don't think you're gonna make it," Traci said with apprehension in her voice.

Joel didn't respond.

The bus momentarily lurched as if he'd tried to accelerate. Then it slowly ground to a halt and all riders sat up to attention.

"I'll back her up and give her another go," he said without worry.

"That's the spirit. This sand is soft. You'll have to build some real speed here." Traci slapped him on the shoulder and gave him a little squeeze.

He backed up as far as he could to the curved hill behind them and eased the bus into forward and accelerated. They got no further on the second attempt.

"We need to let some air from the tyres. Mo, let's help him get the air pressure down." Traci stood and Mo along with her.

"They're already low—I don't think we can go lower," he said. "I'll try her again."

Mo and Traci sat back down.

"What happens if we're stuck?" someone asked from the back of the bus.

"We'll call for rescue if it comes to it. They'll bring us some mats to put under the tyres for traction." Joel said as he took a long drink from the water bottle he'd carried all day. "But we're a long ways from needing to do that."

"But it's getting rather late." Sloane heard another voice from behind them. And the light was beginning to wane ever so slightly.

Joel threw the bus into reverse and backed up until they heard tree branches scratch along the back and sides of the bus. He plunged forward once more. And still got no further than the first and second times.

"Mum, I'm scared." Grace squirmed, wide-eyed and worried. The girl wrapped herself around Ava.

"It's ok, Gracie. Joel's a pro. He'll have us back to the resort in no time." Ava put both her arms around Grace and cuddled her close.

Sloane rubbed Grace's back and scooted even closer to them.

"All right, I'll go and have a look. Open the door, Joel." Traci stood and moved to the door of the bus.

He complied without hesitation.

Traci, Joel, and Mo all exited and walked around the bus twice before climbing back aboard. Traci sat down behind the wheel, with Joel standing behind her. Mo walked to the back of the bus and peered out the back window.

"Traci, what on earth are you doing? You can't drive this bus. Let Joel do his job or go ahead and call us a rescue." Ellen stood and exclaimed.

Everyone turned to look.

"Ellen, I've been driving double D's through god knows how much bull dust since before this boy lost those toes to a dirt bike and a red gum. Sit down and let me get us unbogged."

And she did. She backed up until Mo told her she could go no further. She put the bus in drive and turned sharply to the right and then straight again, pulling the vehicle to within centimetres of several large tree trunks.

The bus tilted sharply to the left and several people called out in surprise or maybe fear, Sloane wasn't sure. But Traci was able to gain purchase on the edge of the track where low vegetation held the sand together a bit. It was just enough to pull the tyres on the other side of the bus through the deep sand and up the hill.

Everyone cheered.

Joel looked proud as punch. Mo too. Ellen simply looked relieved.

"Mo's mum is a badass," Grace said quietly.

Ava and Ellen looked at her in shock, and Sloane wasn't sure if it was the child's use of the word *ass* or because she'd used Sloane's American version of the word *ass*.

"Language!" Ellen announced.

"Well, she's not wrong." Sloane smiled and settled in her seat.

Traci stopped at the top of the next hill to give the wheel back to Joel and the rest of the ride was mercifully uneventful.

"Hey, wake up." Ava shook Sloane's shoulder gently. "Wake up. I think we should go and apologize to Traci."

Sloane rolled over and creaked one eye open. "Why are we apologizing to Traci?"

"For mum. She was, um, not very nice to her yesterday."

"Yeah, I noticed. What's going on with your mum?" Sloane stretched and tried to pull Ava back to her.

Ava had intended that they talk about the new series as Grace had spent the night with Mo and Leota, but Sloane had fallen asleep as soon as they returned to their room after dinner. Ava hadn't slept much at all—she worried about the conversation that awaited them and about her mum's foul mood all night.

"I don't know. But I've been awake all night, feeling badly about it. Let's go and apologize." Ava rolled out of bed and pulled the curtains apart to let the barely there light in.

"How did you not sleep last night, after the day we had? I slept like the dead. I'd like to be sleeping still." Sloane propped herself on one elbow and rubbed her eyes. "But why are we apologizing for Ellen being a b—"

"Careful, my heart. And I noticed how well you slept last night. I think I'll make her a tea. I'll make Traci a tea. A mea culpa. A tea culpa. A mea cuppa." Ava smiled in pleasure at what she thought a clever joke for so early in the morning.

"Oh, wow. That was, um, wow. It's a bit early for Latin puns." Sloane pulled the covers back and sat on the edge of the bed. "You're serious, aren't you?"

"Yes." Ava went about the business of preparing tea.

"You know what we'll actually be apologizing for? Waking her up. That's what we'll be apologizing for."

Ava slipped on lounge pants and a light cardigan as she waited for the water to heat. "Something just feels off and I want to apologize and check that she's ok."

"Should we ask Ellen what's going on first?"

"You want to ask my mother why she behaved badly yesterday?"

"Well, no. But you could. And I could go back to sleep."

Ava gave Sloane her best don't-try-me look and Sloane dropped her shoulders in obvious surrender.

"You know, this was supposed to be a relaxing weekend with the family. But nope. Instead, you drop a bomb on me, Ellen's being weird, we're up early on a morning Grace is staying with Mo and Leota, which is unthinkable, and Mo has me positively terrified of rampaging goannas."

"I did not drop a bomb on you. This is the life of a working actor. The tea is ready. And you may want to put some clothes on." Ava looked at Sloane, wearing only a tight singlet and tight shorts and a zing of arousal coursed from her chest into her belly and lower. She pushed it aside. "Let's go make amends."

Sloane sighed deeply and slipped on some trackies and a tee. "You know you can't make amends for someone else, right?"

Ava opened the door onto the corridor and led them toward Traci's door only a few rooms down.

They arrived at Traci's door just as Mo approached from the other direction, smiling and carrying steaming cups of coffee. "What's this? Thought you two would be sleeping in this fine morning."

"So did I." Sloane yawned her disapproval.

"We decided to check on your mum. My mum was, um, unpleasant yesterday."

"Unpleasant? She was a real c—"

"Whoa, there, mate. Let's not get carried away. I think Ellen was just tired and worried yesterday, and Traci took the brunt of that." Sloane held up her hands to stop Mo saying the worst. "Grace with Leota?"

"They're getting dressed for brekky. Early riser, that Grace. And no worries, mate, you know I love Ellen. She's family. Family can be a real pain in the arse. Speaking of pains in the arse, let's check on Mum. Sul, hold the coffees." She keyed them in with a spare card Traci must have given her and announced their presence, "Mornin', Mum, brought coffees and to wake you for brekky."

There was a rustling as they eased into the dark room and Ava felt around for the light switch on the wall where it would be in hers and Sloane's suite. She finally found it and pushed it on. Light filled the room, and Ava nearly dropped the tea on the floor.

Traci jumped and pulled the covers up around her naked torso.

Lying next to her, was Ellen James. Who stretched and then yawned.

Mum! Apparently also naked!

Ava's feet stuck to the floor. She realized that her mouth hung open, slack and wide, but she couldn't bring herself to close it.

Finally, Ellen broke the silent stand-off. "Well, children. Perhaps you should knock the next time."

"Sloane, is that coffee you're holding, mate?" Traci asked, sitting a little straighter now that Ellen had answered seemingly without regret or embarrassment.

Ava forced her mouth closed.

"Wha—" Mo started and suddenly stopped, also gawping.

"Um, yes, coffee and Ava has tea. I'll just put these here." Sloane crept further into the room, staring intently at her own feet and set the coffees on the low table nearest her. She turned to the wall and stared away from the tableau facing them all from the bed. Then she turned and took the mug of tea from Ava's hand and placed it next to the coffees, all while training her eyes opposite Ellen and Traci.

"Mum, I—Mum, how?" Mo tried again.

Traci and Ellen looked at one another and giggled.

Giggled. They giggled. Ava couldn't process what was happening. She forced her mouth closed, *again*.

"Well, darlings, I came to apologize to Traci last night for my behaviour yesterday and we shared some beers. We were talking about how the three of you—and Leota—seem to know something about relationships and sex that we don't know. So, we decided to find out."

"And that's what we did. We found out." Traci added, and covered Ellen's hand with her own. They giggled again.

"Oh. My." It was all Ava could manage, and her mouth went slack again.

"Mum! You're awake! We're on our way to brekky!"

Ava turned to see Grace and Leota step just inside the still open door of the suite.

"Stop!" she called out and turned to block the child's view, raising and waving her hands at the two newcomers.

"Is everything all right?" Leota looked worried as Ava, followed by Mo and Sloane, ushered them into the corridor.

"Everything is great. We're just gonna let everyone get dressed."

"Everyone?" Leota asked, confusion on her face. "Ah, Joel. Right."

"Um, no. See you at brekky, Mum!" Mo called out over her shoulder before closing the door. "Let's just walk. Can we just walk? Let's just walk. Maybe a run. Should we run?" Mo looked confused and lost.

"Darling, what's happening?" Leota asked, real worry in her voice.

They drifted slowly along the corridor, Grace and Leota asking a million questions. And Mo, Sloane, and Ava too stunned to answer. Suddenly, an older, well-dressed man crossed in front of them from an adjoining boardwalk corridor. He whistled a little tune to himself, oblivious to their presence. After passing them and continuing merrily on his path, he stopped and announced to no one in particular, "Sound the trumpets!!" He then enthusiastically farted.

Grace and Mo were the first to burst into laughter, nearly falling to the boardwalk in a fit of giggles.

The man turned and momentarily seemed embarrassed, then simply winked and walked on.

Ava, Leota, and Sloane joined in the laughter and the absurdity of the entire weekend came into full relief. They laughed all the way to breakfast.

"Traci and Ellen!" Leota's shock was apparent. "Not Joel?" So was her confusion.

Sloane couldn't stop laughing about it now that she'd had a half hour or so to process, but she couldn't quite pin down Ava's and Mo's thoughts on the matter. She paused long enough to ask, "So all that bluster and eye rolling yesterday was just…sexual tension on Ellen's part?"

Ava groaned. Mo rubbed her forehead as if trying to solve some great problem. Sloane laughed again.

"Traci and Ellen…" Leota repeated.

"What about Mimi and Auntie Traci? Are they still cross with each other?" Grace chased a blueberry around her plate with her fork before surrendering and pinching it between her finger and thumb. She popped it in her mouth.

"No, I don't believe they're cross anymore, Gracie." Ava sighed and sipped her tea.

Everyone sat in silence, watching Grace chase her blueberries around the plate.

Sloane really couldn't control the smirk—she was beginning to think she'd be smirking and belly laughing at the Great Mum Sex Scandal all her days.

"Well. Fine. Whatever. Fine. Now that those two lovebirds have sorted themselves, what's going on with you two?" Mo looked at Sloane and Ava.

"I'm being a bad partner," Sloane looked down at her hands which she had wrapped around her mug of coffee, long gone cold.

"I never said that!" Ava said adamantly.

Grace startled and a blueberry went flying. "Wait, are you cross with each other?"

"No, bug, we're not. And I know you didn't say that, Ava. But I am. You should tell them. Tell them your news."

"Tell us what?" Ellen sidled up to the table, having finally joined everyone in the dining room.

She carried a breakfast the likes of which Sloane had never seen her eat before. Traci followed closely behind, and they sat across the table from one another and smiled over their plates and mugs.

No one said anything for what felt like long minutes.

Ava looked at her mother as if she were really seeing her for the first time in some while.

"Tell us what, darling? You have news?" Ellen asked again and patted Ava's hand.

Finally, Ava wrapped her hand around her mum's forearm. "I've been offered a role in a new project. A big project. Big Hollywood studio. It's, um, a big role for me. It's expected to draw a big box office. It's big..." Ava's jumbled and repeated words trailed off.

Sloane suddenly recognized the doubt and the reluctance on Ava's face and heard it in her words. She put her hand reassuringly on Ava's thigh, underneath the table.

Everyone erupted into cheers and claps and congratulations to the point that other diners turned to look.

"I knew it was a matter of time! After the AACTA, I knew it was just a matter of time." Mo was positively elated.

"Why do you seem so glum, dear? Are you having second thoughts?" Ellen clasped her free hand over Ava's and furrowed her brow.

"No, Mum. I absolutely want it. It's just that it'll film on location."

"Well, of course it will. And where will that be?"

"Iceland."

The table went silent. Everyone looked from Ava to Sloane to Ellen.

"Sounds cold." Grace broke the ice.

Leota chuckled and Mo looked at Sloane with worry.

"For how long?" Ellen asked without emotion. She turned her attention to her breakfast, forking mushrooms onto a piece of toast.

"Eight months."

There was a slight twitch of Ellen's left eyebrow. "Eight months? Well, we'll make it work. We'll figure it all out." Ellen halved a roasted tomato, looking undeterred. She raised her face to look at Ava. "We'll be fine, dear. Do you want to leave Grace with me? Or will you take her?"

"Damn, Sullivan. I'm gonna miss you. Hey, can we visit?"

"I've always wanted to visit the hot springs in Iceland," Leota looked keen.

"I can't go. I have a job here," Sloane protested, the thought having never occurred to her.

"Why wouldn't you and Grace both go along?" Leota asked. "Is that not allowed?" She turned to Ava.

"No, it's certainly allowed."

The table went silent again.

Sloane watched Ava's restlessness grow.

"Mum, I want to take Grace with me. I can't bear the thought of being away from her for so long. And Sloane. I am making enough now that you wouldn't have to teach. You could come along, and you could keep Grace on level in school. We can hire help to keep her on level. Can we at least consider this? I know you're only newly settled here, but is it even an option for you?"

"But it sounds cold. And what about Mimi and our doggie and the horses?" Grace rose to her knees and put one hand on Ava's shoulder pleadingly.

Ellen put her knife and fork carefully on the plate. "I'll care for Charlie and the horses. The three of you should be together for as long as Grace is little enough that she can easily go without missing too many school obligations. I'll take care of things here. Ava, I'll support you no matter what you decide. But I suspect you'll not be turning this down."

"I'm retired and have a strong back and the freedom to be where I want. Ellen, didn't you mention a cottage on the property? I'd be happy to stay around and help," Traci offered sheepishly. Sloane had never noticed her looking sheepish before.

"Oh, I'm sure you'd love to stay on and help out. Take one for the team, eh, Mum?" Mo leaned back and looked at her mother with exasperation.

More silence.

Sloane absentmindedly toyed with the foil cover from a honey packet Ava had opened to put in her tea. "I could go with you? You and Grace? We could go as a family…" Sloane hesitantly tried the words.

"We could go as a family, yes," Ava said. "I'd like to do this as a family. Will you go with me? You and Grace?" Ava fully faced Sloane and cupped her hands around Sloane's.

"You know, I have always wanted to see the aurora borealis."

Ava laughed softly and nodded. "Of course you have."

"Aurora bor…borls? There are lights? In Iceland?" Grace climbed over Ava's lap and between them, excited now. "Coloured ones? Like the ones we saw in Tasmania?"

"Yes, Gracie, there are lights—coloured ones." Ava pushed the girl's wild straying hair behind her ear and leaned to kiss her forehead. She looked back to Sloane, expectation and hope in her eyes.

And Sloane answered. "Well, then, let's go see those northern lights."

Curious about how their story started before this epilogue? Read *Southern Lights*.

Marry (Me on) Christmas

by Chris Zett

The phone rang just as Maia left the hospital's parking lot—perfect timing. She pushed the answer button without looking. No one ever called except Rowan. "Hi!"

"Maia?" The voice didn't belong to her partner, and, for a second, Maia had a hard time placing it.

"Yes. Debra?" Why was Rowan's mom calling her? "Is everything okay with you and Susan?" Rowan's mom moved to Florida to be with her sister last year, and she usually talked with Rowan, not Maia.

"We're fine. I'm calling because I wanted to organize something. I'd like to surprise Rowan with a visit over Christmas. Do you think we can stay at your place?"

"Of course. We'd love to have you over. We just finished renovating the guest room, and it'll be perfect for you two. Should I pick you up from the airport?"

"No need. We want to get a rental car anyway. So, how are you two doing?"

The twenty-minute drive home after work passed quickly while they chatted. The sun hung low on the horizon, coloring the sky pink as she turned into their long driveway through the forest surrounding their house.

Maia ended the call to concentrate on the last stretch. Since that night almost one and a half years ago, when she'd driven for the first time in years during a storm, she'd gained much more experience during her commute, but she still wasn't overconfident.

Rowan had repaired the worst of the potholes, but it was still far from comparable to a regular paved road. She sighed with relief when the familiar gray house with white trim came into view. As always, Rowan had parked on the far side and left her the easiest spot to get out of.

Maia smiled. Nothing beat coming home to her partner and their dog after a long day at work.

Rowan heard the low purr of Maia's car a moment before she saw the headlights shining through their kitchen window. "I need to hang up now, Maia's coming home. Let me know when I should pick you up from the airport."

"Thanks. We'll talk soon. Bye." Bess hung up.

Rowan smiled. It would be fun to surprise Maia with an extended visit from her mom over Christmas, and she looked forward to meeting Bess in person. They'd only talked before over the phone or on video chat.

She stirred the soup, switched off the stove, removed her headphones, and went to the front door.

Jasper beat her there and waited with a wagging tail for her to open it. He almost ran Maia over as she approached the porch.

Rowan leaned against the doorframe and watched Maia greet him with cuddles. Two years ago, she'd never expected to live this perfect, peaceful life with a loving partner and a cute dog in their own house. Or to be working her dream job making furniture.

When Jasper had calmed down, Maia looked up with a broad smile and stepped into Rowan's arms for another enthusiastic greeting.

After they stopped kissing, Rowan leaned back. "Welcome home. You want to eat first or go on a walk with Jasper?"

"If the food can wait, let's go to the lake while there's still some light outside. I want to see how far it's frozen." Maia placed her work bag into the hall and picked up Jasper's leash and a thick woolen beanie.

"It's only soup." Rowan quickly dressed for the walk and led the way to the back door.

"I love your soups. Almost as much as your creative sandwiches." Maia inhaled deeply as she passed the kitchen door. "And it smells delicious. So, what have you been up to today?"

As usual, they discussed their day during the short walk to the lake while Jasper ran circles around them. By now, they trusted him to come when they called and only took the leash as a backup.

Frozen leaves crackled under their feet, and the last rays of sunshine glittered over the gray lake. Rowan sighed. It would be at least four to five months until she could swim outdoors again.

"Miss the water?" Maia slipped her hand into Rowan's and leaned into her.

"Mm-hmm. Swimming in a pool is not the same." She deeply breathed in the clear air, relishing the slight pain of the cold in her lungs. "But I don't need as much alone time to think and brood anymore as I did before we met."

Swimming was still her favorite form of exercise, but she no longer needed it to escape from a life in which she felt trapped.

After dinner, Maia sank on the couch while Rowan started a fire in her newest home-improvement project. She'd restored the old fireplace, and now they could watch the flames in the evening while listening to audiobooks together instead of spending too much time in front of a TV.

She pulled out her phone to open *Enemies by Nature*, the paranormal romance that had them at the edge of their seats this week, when an email notification popped up. It was from her dad. What did he want?

Maia quickly scanned the mail. "My dad wants to visit us for Christmas."

Rowan stopped poking the emerging flames and half turned around. "Does he want to stay here?"

"Yeah. He hates Airbnb and small hotels. Would that be okay with you?" Maia frowned. Did Rowan have a problem with that? They had only met once and would probably never be best friends, but she'd thought they'd got on well enough to spend a couple of days together.

"Sure, it's just..." Rowan turned back to the fire. "I don't want to spoil the surprise, but..."

What surprise? "Oh, did your mom tell you?" Maia couldn't think of any other surprise.

"My mom? What does she have to do with it?" Rowan closed the safety glass protecting the fireplace and stood. Her expression was hard to read in the flickering light.

"Who are you talking about if not her?" Maia was as confused as Rowan sounded.

"I got a call from *your* mom today. She wants to surprise you with a long visit." Rowan sank onto the couch and put her hand on Maia's thigh. "Would that be weird having both your mom and your dad over? Have they ever stayed at the same place since their divorce?"

"I don't think they've ever talked again, except at my graduations, and both are far from over their breakup. I stopped mentioning them to each other." Maia groaned. This was shaping up to be the least peaceful holiday she could imagine. "I don't know if the house is big enough for them both."

"We have a guest room and the home office with the sofa bed. But I guess you're not talking about actual space." Rowan grinned wryly. "And what were you saying about my mom?"

"No, I suppose a palace wouldn't be big enough for the two of them." Maia massaged her own temple. "Well, I got a call from your mom, also about a Christmas surprise visit."

"Really? And what about Aunt Susan?" Rowan gently pushed Maia's hand aside and took over the massage.

"She wants to come too. Something about missing snow in Florida. I don't think we can host my mom and dad as well as your mom and aunt, even if we give up our bedroom and stay here on the couch—it doesn't even turn into a bed."

Rowan chuckled. "I don't know. We sleep well in confined spaces."

"I remember." Maia snuggled into her shoulder, and Rowan put her arm around her. They had fit well enough on a couple of deck chair cushions on their first night together.

"I'll never forget it either." Rowan kissed her deeply.

For a long moment, nothing mattered but Rowan's soft lips and firm embrace. When she finally pulled back with a sigh, Maia's tension had receded.

Rowan leaned against the backrest but kept her arm around Maia and played with her hair. "So maybe we should just ask everyone what they think."

"That's probably the wisest decision. I'd feel bad disinviting anyone."

"I haven't been this popular since high school, when our swim team won the state championship." Rowan grinned. "Maybe we should open a hotel."

It was already dark when Rowan parked in front of the house. The kitchen window was brightly lit, and her stomach grumbled in anticipation. She climbed out of her truck and groaned as her tired muscles protested against the hard ground and cold wind. A hot meal and an even hotter shower before bed would go a long way to restoring her strength, as would some long-overdue snuggling with Maia.

The last thought propelled her up the steps and to her front door in two long strides. Jasper barked from the other side of the door, so she opened it much more carefully than she wanted to. "Honey, I'm home!"

She squeezed herself past Jasper and tried to greet him but at the same time keep him from running outside.

Maia leaned through the kitchen door and smiled widely. "I'll never get enough of how happy you two are to see each other."

"When I said 'honey,' I meant you, not him." Rowan slipped off her work boots and jacket before kissing Maia hello.

"Mmh. Sure you did." Maia slid her hands over Rowan's flannel shirt, which was probably dusty and crinkly. "You look tired. All done?"

"Yep. All the furniture is finished and delivered. I don't have any more work obligations for the next two weeks. I can concentrate on getting everything ready for our visitors." She sniffed the air. Something spicy she couldn't identify wafted over from the kitchen. "That smells great. New recipe?"

Maia nodded. "I was in the mood for chili and found a new vegetarian recipe. It's almost ready. Maybe another ten minutes."

"Then let me take a shower first." Rowan would rather join Maia in the warm kitchen and listen to her talk about her day, but she knew she could enjoy the evening more if she got rid of the sweat and loosened up her muscles.

"Take your time. The food can wait." Maia looked up to her in a way that instantly let her forget her fatigue.

"Or you could join me?" Rowan raised her eyebrows. She was pretty certain what the answer would be.

"Let me switch off the stove so it won't burn."

With a sigh, Maia crossed out half of what she'd written and ripped the page off her notepad. This wouldn't work at all.

Suddenly, Jasper leaped up and ran to the kitchen door.

A second later, soft footsteps came down the stairs.

Maia left her window seat and poured coffee into Rowan's favorite mug before she reached the kitchen door.

"Morning." For the first time in weeks, Rowan didn't have dark rings under her eyes. The ten hours of sleep had done her good.

After a long shower and a late dinner, Rowan had fallen asleep on the sofa before they'd even finished the next chapter of their audiobook, and it had taken all of Maia's charm to persuade her to move upstairs. This morning, she'd been extra quiet when she slipped out of bed at dawn.

Rowan bent down to greet Jasper, then gave Maia a quick kiss. "Been up for long?"

"Yeah. Couldn't sleep and didn't want to wake you with my constant tossing and turning." Maia pointed to the stack of crumpled paper on the kitchen table. "I'm trying to divide our time between all our family members. But Christmas Day doesn't have enough hours."

Rowan nodded. "I know. I've been thinking about it all last week while driving around delivering furniture. How can we be fair to everyone? And as Mom and Susan will stay with Martha, we must also consider her plans."

"And Ann and Gabby's as they'll host my mom. Only one more week to come up with a schedule that fits everyone." Maia sighed and handed Rowan her coffee. "Let's ignore this for a moment until you're fully awake. Do you want to go for a walk or eat something first?"

Long walks on weekend mornings had been their routine for over a year, and during the warmer months, they often ended their journey with skinny-dipping in the lake.

"If you don't mind, I'd love to grab a protein bar or something and head out together. We can talk while we walk. We need to clear our heads before we can enjoy the weekend." Rowan drank almost half of her coffee at once and sighed contentedly.

"I have something even better." Maia pulled a plastic container over and opened the lid. "John gave us some homemade brownies when I picked up fresh eggs yesterday."

"Perfect." Rowan stretched her arms over her head, and her rumpled T-shirt pulled up to reveal toned abs. "I'll just get dressed."

"Mm-hmm. Perfect." Maia couldn't pull her gaze from Rowan's midriff. She'd rather they tumbled back into their warm bed. But Rowan was right; they needed to face their organizational problems.

"Okay, this seems like the best plan so far." Maia checked her phone where she'd been keeping notes during their walk. She scrunched her nose before quickly reading off her list. "Dad arrives on Christmas Eve, and we'll have dinner with him. On Christmas Day, we'll have brunch with my mom at Gabby and Ann's house and an early dinner at Martha's house with your mom. Later, we'll meet my dad again for his dinner and our after-dinner drinks at some restaurant we'll have to decide on. Then, the next day, we'll take him on a hike around here before he leaves again. Afterward, we'll meet up with both our moms and whoever wants to tag along."

Rowan sighed. "I'm already exhausted listening to you. I wish we could invite them all together and have one big party."

"Me too. I feel bad leaving my dad alone all day and also for setting time limits on the visits with our moms. But it's probably the only way." Maia closed the app and put her phone into her coat pocket. "Let's tell everyone about our plan later and get their input. For now, I want to enjoy the sunshine and quiet with you."

After hiking a two-hour loop through the woods behind their house, they reached the path down to the lakeshore.

Rowan pulled a pine branch to the side so Maia could pass without getting showered with the freshly fallen snow. From here, the lake looked like something from a fairy tale. It was frozen, and the sun glittered on the ice, coloring it in every shade from gray to blue. Most trees along the distant shoreline were dotted with white, and the tall, round rocks on the water's edge looked like they were resting under fluffy, white down blankets.

Jasper pushed between them, eager to get to his favorite playground. Maia stepped aside, and he dashed ahead, spraying them with fresh powder.

Laughing, Maia bent down and formed a snowball. She threw it past Jasper, and when he tried to retrieve it, it fell apart. "Oh no, look how confused he is."

Rowan laughed too. "Poor boy. Maybe I'll find a stick for him somewhere."

But before she could look, he had already forgotten about the vanishing ball and played with a piece of ice that had broken off.

As always, they walked along the lake until they came to their favorite place. Rowan leaned against the car-sized rock and opened her arms so Maia could snuggle close.

Immediately, Maia stepped into her embrace. "Sharing body heat is very important in this weather," she said.

"Absolutely." Rowan smiled and pulled her closer. Not that she needed the extra warmth—the memory of what they had done more than once at this rock during the summer left her hot and tingly.

For a few minutes, they just stood there and breathed each other in. This was perfect. Sunshine heated her face, the cold air was fresh and clean, and Jasper's happy barks echoed over the lake.

"What if we have kids?" Maia's voice was quiet but firm.

"What? Why? Do you want kids?" Rowan leaned back to study Maia's expression. She held her breath, and for a moment, the only sound was the slight crackling of the frozen lake.

Maia swallowed, and her beautiful dark eyes seemed to study Rowan intently. "Yeah, I always thought so. I haven't thought about it for a while. And you?"

"Honestly? It's not something I've seriously considered before." Rowan took a deep breath and tried to sort her jumble of feelings into words. Surprise, anxiety, excitement. And most of all, love. So much love. And it would be wonderful to share it with Maia and a kid. Or two? Whoa, the thought of two kids made her anxiety spike. Maybe start small. "But…yeah, I can see me…see us with a kid."

"Me too." Maia's smile was brighter than the sun reflecting on the ice. "I didn't want to spring this talk on you, but it just occurred to me that Christmases like this would be even worse if we had kids."

"True. Don't worry, I think this is one of the talks every couple should have before they get married. We covered where and how we want to live and finances early on and just skipped the rest." Rowan squeezed Maia tighter in her arms. "We got together so fast, but I wouldn't want it any other way."

"Me neither. But hold on, you mentioned something in passing that's almost as big as kids." Suddenly, Maia's gaze turned shy.

What had she said? Rowan replayed her last words. *Oh.* "Marriage."

"Yeah, marriage. We never talked about that either. I know you had a bad experience." Maia snuggled even closer. "Would you want to get married again?"

"Yes, of course." Rowan didn't need to sort out her feelings about that. They were crystal clear and had been for some time. She'd been thinking about the best way to propose more than once, but a frozen lake had never been the backdrop in her fantasies. "And you? Do you want to marry me?"

Maia inhaled sharply. "Are you…proposing?"

Rowan's heart raced faster than ever during a race, and rightly so, as this was more important than winning any swimming competition. Without losing eye contact, she stepped out of their embrace, took Maia's hands, and sank onto one knee. "I can't offer you diamonds or gold; I don't even have a wooden ring for you. All I can give you is my heart, my love, and my hands to build a future together. Will you marry me?"

Surprise, confusion, and happiness played over Maia's features, but there wasn't even a flicker of doubt. "Yes!" She slid down onto her knees too. "I love you and can't imagine a future without you. We don't need gold or diamonds to be happy—I only want to build our life together." Laughing, she threw her arms around Rowan and kissed her.

The softest lips met hers with passion and heat, tears of joy mingled on their cheeks, and, for a blissful moment, she got completely lost in the overwhelming feelings of love and happiness.

Loud and excited barks broke through her haze, and a wet and not-so-sexy snout suddenly pushed against their faces.

"Jasper!" Maia tried to simultaneously turn her head and nudge him away.

Rowan wanted to help, but the combined force of Maia and Jasper shoved her backward. One moment, they were entangled in the perfect embrace and the next, they had tumbled over onto the snowy beach.

After some more wriggling, laughter, and the promise of treats, they were finally upright again, with Jasper safely chasing another snowball.

Rowan took Maia's cold hand into hers. "So, we're doing this." She couldn't stop grinning. "When do you want to get married? In the summer?"

"A summer wedding has its perks. But I just had an idea." Maia brushed a bit of snow from Rowan's shoulder. "Why not this Christmas?"

"A Christmas wedding?" Nick jumped up, and his chair would have tumbled over if not for his husband's quick reflexes. "This Christmas? In two weeks? On Christmas Day?"

Daniel pulled him back down onto his chair. "So that's why you invited us over today. Congratulations. I'm happy for you."

"Yeah, I'm happy too. Ecstatic even." Nick grinned widely but shook his head. "But seriously, how can you organize a big-ass wedding in such a short time?"

"We don't need much. We just want to say our vows and have a Christmas dinner with everyone afterward." Rowan looked at Maia with a sheepish expression. "Right?"

"Right." Maia nodded. After they'd come home and warmed each other up—heat shot to her cheeks at the thought of how exactly they'd done that—they'd talked it over all evening. They had readily agreed on everything. "We just want our family and friends as witnesses and to spend a nice day with everyone. We don't need a big party, an extravagant cake, or special dresses."

"No dresses? Okay, I didn't expect Rowan to wear one, but don't you want to dress up a little?" Nick asked Maia.

"A little. We want to look nice—festive, not fancy." Maia put her notepad between them on the coffee table. "We brainstormed yesterday what we need, and the list isn't too long. The most important part is the paperwork—and we need to find an officiant."

"I'll do it." Nick leaned forward to look at the list.

"Our paperwork?" Rowan sounded doubtful. For her, the idea of paperwork was worse than pulling teeth.

"No." He grimaced. "I'll get an online certification or something. I'll read up on it, and then I'll officiate"—he looked from Rowan to Maia and back—"if you want me to?"

Maia only needed to exchange a quick glance with Rowan to know that they agreed. "We'd love you to."

"No singing," Rowan said at the same time as Daniel. They looked at each other and laughed.

"Hey! Why would you say that?" Nick pretended to be offended.

"Once a theater kid, always a theater kid." Daniel slung his arm around Nick's shoulder. "You'll do great without any songs."

"Fine. But I reserve the right to give a speech." He clapped his hands together. "I can't wait to get started. What else do you need from us?"

"We wanted to ask if we could rent the new event space in the brewery." Rowan sighed. "And maybe set us up with drinks and help us find a caterer."

This time, it was Nick and Daniel who exchanged a glance full of silent communication. Finally, Daniel nodded and looked back at Rowan. "You don't need to rent anything, and we'll decorate the space for you. And I have enough connections to find a caterer for any taste and budget. The drinks will be our wedding present."

"That's too much." Maia shook her head. She wasn't rich but had enough saved for a small wedding. She had a steady income and almost no living expenses as Rowan owned the house and Rowan's furniture-making business had done well last year too.

"Not up for discussion." Nick snatched the notepad from Maia's hand and ticked off the items. "We want to advertise the space for parties and weddings anyway, so you can be our guinea pigs—we'll call it PR."

Daniel leaned over his shoulder to look at the paper. "Let's go through the rest together."

Maia leaned back in her chair as they worked through the list, adding a few items and creating solid plans for almost everything.

She held out her hand, and Rowan immediately took it. Her grip was warm, firm, and gentle, all at the same time.

Maia had never thought it could be so easy to get married—and that it could feel so right.

"Why is it so difficult to get married? They always elope on a whim in movies and books." Maia shook the snow from her coat and stomped a few times to loosen it from her boots.

"What happened?" Rowan held out her hand for Maia's coat.

"Can I get a hug first?" Maia's cheeks were glowing red from the cold, and she looked as tired as Rowan had been feeling in recent days from working long hours to get the new event space in Daniel's brewery ready.

Without another word, Rowan pulled her into her arms. Despite the thick coat she was wearing, Maia felt cold, and melting snow dripped from her wool hat onto Rowan's shoulder. Shivering, Rowan pulled her closer.

After a few minutes, Maia stepped back with a long sigh. "Thank you, I needed that."

Hand in hand, they went into the living room, where a flickering fire waited.

Only after they sat on the sofa and snuggled beneath one of the old quilts that had come with the house did Maia seem ready to talk.

With a sigh, Maia held up her hand to tick off her points. "The weather is playing havoc with everyone's travel plans. Got a call from my mom, who said she'll come a day earlier, and my dad texted that he might run late. My former roommates in New York are unsure if they can make it. The marriage license isn't ready because the person responsible is on a spontaneous skiing trip, and the package with my dress is stuck somewhere in delivery limbo."

"I hate to add to your list, but I talked to the caterer today. She had some complicated questions about the kitchen equipment I couldn't answer. I hope Nick and Daniel can help her." Rowan didn't like being dependent on so many people and on such unreliable factors as the weather.

Maia rubbed her temple. "My headache is back."

"Let me." Rowan slid her hand along Maia's neck. It was the least she could do.

Maia's muscles were tight strings beneath her fingers as Rowan rubbed small circles up and down next to her spine. Sighing, Maia turned in her seat with her back to Rowan and relaxed into the massage.

"What were we thinking? Other people plan this for months, years even." Maia's tone was small and defeated.

"True. But this way, we only have a few weeks of this stress instead of a year? Sounds good to me." Rowan would have preferred no stress, but that wasn't realistic. "We can't control the weather, but we can be spontaneous about the date. Nick and Daniel don't need the venue for anything else, and they have commercial refrigerators to store most of the catering for a few days. And I'd marry you in scrubs. You looked hot in them last year."

Maia chuckled. "Only if you'll wear your tool belt."

"Deal." Rowan had planned on wearing the very nice suit she'd picked out with her swim training partner and new friend Kai last week, but she wasn't opposed to dressing down to lighten Maia's mood. "You know, we can always cancel the wedding and call it an engagement dinner if you want. That way, we can take more time to prepare and plan."

Maia shook her head. "Very tempting, but no. I want to be married to you more than I want a perfect wedding day, or even a stress-free party."

Rowan stopped her massage and gently pulled on one shoulder until Maia turned around. She needed to see her expression for this talk. "Do you think marriage will change anything between us?"

"Yes and no." Maia took Rowan's hand and slid her thumb over the callouses on her palm, returning the massage where Rowan needed it the most. "I don't think we can be more in love, and I don't doubt our dedication to this relationship. So that won't change. And I feel a rightness when I think of marrying you. I never had that before. The last time I had a fiancé, I said yes for a million practical reasons: because it was expected, because it was like another milestone to tick off on my list of life goals, because it would make my parents happy, because I needed the security of marriage to throw over my career. Now, I don't need to write a list of reasons. I know it's right, and I want to be your family. I want to put us first."

"I want to put us first too."

Rightness. The word echoed in Rowan's thoughts and gave a name to what she'd been feeling all along. She nodded slowly. "I know what you mean. I feel it too." And it was unlike anything she'd experienced before. "You know, I didn't feel it the last time I was married. I chalked it up to being stressed out because of my shoulder injury, my father's illness, and about giving up school." Rowan shuddered. That time in her life held a lot of painful memories, and her marriage wasn't even the worst of it. "I thought marriage would solve the problems between my ex and me and give her the security to stay with me in this small town. I didn't realize that marriage couldn't repair anything; it was like pasting a nice wallpaper over cracks in the wall. Everything looked fresh and new for a time, but then the structural damage just showed again."

"It would have been the same for Scott and me. I'm lucky that I got out of that situation so easily." Maia laughed without a hint of bitterness. A lot had changed in the last year. "Is it naive to believe that it'll be so different for us?"

"Maybe, but I wouldn't want it any other way." Long workdays with nothing but her trusted tools and reclaimed wooden boards as company had left Rowan ample time to think. She knew what she wanted and needed, and that was sharing her life with Maia. "We already are a family," she said, "but this marriage is a good way of showing everyone else what we mean to each other."

Christmas Day came more quickly than expected, and to Maia's surprise, every puzzle piece had fallen into place. With the help of Rowan's connections, they'd gotten their marriage license on time and found places for all their out-of-town friends and family to stay. The weather even cooperated. Not only did everyone travel on time and without incident, but also a beautiful, harmless dusting of fresh snow transformed the town into a movie-set-worthy winter wonderland. Even Maia's dark-green velvet dress had arrived unscathed after a few extra days in a random depot.

"Don't overdo it. I want to look natural." Maia scrunched her nose as her mom came closer with a makeup brush.

"Close your eyes." Her mom dusted some powder over her face. "You're practically glowing, I don't think anything I do will hide that."

It tickled, and Maia fought the urge to giggle. Her emotions had been on a roller coaster since she woke up this morning, and she was afraid she'd start crying any second.

"She's right. One look at your radiant smile and Rowan won't know or care if you have painted your face blue or pink." Ann chuckled as she continued to braid a silk ribbon and a strand of ivy leaves into Maia's hair. "Who'd have thought being a horse girlie would leave me with valuable skills?"

"Are you sure you don't want any eyelash extensions? They'd make your beautiful eyes pop." Her mom's voice was hopeful.

"I'm sure. I want to look today like I always do, not like a different person." Maia was about to bite her lip when she remembered she was wearing lipstick for once. At least it was in an almost natural rose color. "Or as close as possible. Too much makeup isn't me." It had taken her a while to accept that she'd never fit the beauty standards of her always meticulously made-up and well-dressed mom or her plastic surgeon dad. Mom had been disappointed that nerdy teenaged Maia had preferred textbooks to fashion magazines, but at least Dad had been happy that she'd chosen medicine—even if she didn't end up in a surgical specialty.

Nope, not today. Think of the future, not the past. "Rowan likes me exactly how I am." Maia squared her shoulders and opened her eyes. "And I do too."

"As you should. You're a wonderful person, beautiful inside and outside, with makeup or without." Her mom pulled her into a hug.

Maia squeezed her eyes shut to keep herself from crying.

"Aww. You two make me weep." Ann joined the hug.

"Um, I'm sorry, I'll come back later." Her dad's voice interrupted the moment. He sounded unsure—for the first time in as long as Maia could remember.

Both her mom and Ann stiffened and pulled back from the embrace.

"No, stay." Maia waved her father closer. She'd barely had time to talk to him since he arrived, and it would probably be harder to find time later, with even more friends vying for her attention.

"Maybe we should go and give you two some space." To Maia's surprise, her mom sounded neutral. It had been a long time since she'd used anything but an icy tone when talking about or to her father.

Maybe time truly did heal any wounds, or she was making an effort for Maia's sake. Both would be major improvements.

"Not on my account." Her held up his hands as if surrendering. "I'd just like a minute, and then I'll leave you for the rest of your preparations." He looked from Maia to her mom and back. "Is this okay with you?"

Wow. He was actually asking. Maia loved her dad, but sometimes he brought his surgical attitude home and expected everyone to follow his lead without question. "Yes, sure," she said.

He came closer and took both her hands. "I just wanted to tell you how proud I am of you. You went from a bad situation and not only thrived under pressure but actually ended up in a better place. Rowan is wonderful, and I'm so glad you found her. And this town isn't as bad as I thought either. You have a lot of wonderful people surrounding you here. John talked my ear off, and now I know more about chicken than I ever wanted." He chuckled. "But he also told me how you stepped up when he was injured, and later too, when his wife ended up in your hospital with pneumonia. Oh, and about your small hospital..." He shook his head with a wry smile.

Maia flinched. It would have been too nice if he'd left it at giving compliments, but it wasn't unexpected that he'd found something to criticize. He thought himself an expert on everything—except for chicken, apparently.

"I'd never have thought it possible, but I admire you for taking such a position at a local hospital. You're alone without other radiologists to support you, and that's a lot of responsibility. I talked to your colleague, Kai, earlier, and she had nothing but praise for how you've handled your workload and how much you've improved the work environment in the ED with your quick turnaround times. You make a real difference."

Blinking, Maia looked up to him. Did he really mean it?

His expression showed nothing but pride and love.

"Thank you for telling me, Dad." Maia swallowed. It had been a long time since he'd said something like this, and even though she'd gone her own way for quite some time now, it was still good to hear it.

He pulled her into a hug. "Love you, Maia."

After the double parental attack on her composure, she couldn't hold back her tears any longer.

Her dad said nothing about his fine suit or how she had to toughen up. Instead, he held her closer as she cried into him, not letting her go until her tears had run dry. When she finally pulled back, she smiled at him. "Thank you."

He nodded once and squeezed her arm. "I'll let you get ready now. See you out there."

After he'd left, Maia studied herself in the mirror. The carefully applied eyeliner had held, but wet streaks ran over her cheeks.

"Let me fix this." Her mom opened up her makeup kit again.

With a sigh, Maia closed her eyes. If she was honest with herself, she even enjoyed her mom's fussing today.

"Don't fuss." Rowan batted away Nick's hand.

"Just a teeny tiny bit more." Nick held up the hair gel. "Trust me."

Groaning, Rowan lowered her hands to her sides. "Just a little. Maia likes my hair the way it is, not stiff like dried-up glue."

"As if you'll have time to make out and get your hair mussed today." Kai snorted. "Let him do his job; he's good at it. I can vouch for him." She worked with Nick in the ED and had been a former colleague of Maia's in New York. Since they'd met last year, she'd become a good friend to Maia and Rowan, and her calm demeanor extended beyond the ED. It was the perfect foil for Nick's exuberance and just what Rowan needed today.

"This is not exactly in my job description as a PA, but I'll take a compliment from any quarter." Nick rolled his eyes and continued his styling. "You'll thank me once you see the pictures."

"Knock, knock." Rowan's mom tapped the doorframe twice. "Can I come in?"

"Sure," Nick answered before Rowan could say anything. "We're just about done, Debra. I have to go and get ready for the ceremony anyway." He nodded at Rowan. "Daniel will pick you up once it's time."

"If you don't need me anymore, I'll check in with Maia and escort her down." Kai squeezed Rowan's upper arm. "You'll do great."

"Thanks. I don't know what we'd have done without you." Rowan didn't know how to express her gratitude and relief that she had friends in her life she could trust and who always stepped up when needed. After the ceremony, she needed to tell Nick and Daniel what they meant to her.

"You'd have managed. You always land on your feet." Nick winked and left, closing the door behind him.

"Oh, Rowan, you look so..." Debra pressed a hand over her mouth and rapidly blinked, as if holding back tears.

Rowan frowned. Were those good tears? She had a hard time reading her mom's expression. She almost looked pained. "Is this okay?" She gestured at her suit.

"More than okay." Debra nodded and carefully ran a hand down Rowan's lapel. "You look so handsome." She swallowed. "Just like your dad when I met him."

Now, it was Rowan's turn to blink to keep her tears at bay—a losing battle. "Thank you, Mom."

"He'd be so proud to be here today. I'm sure he's still watching over us." Debra's voice was rough.

For a moment, they faced each other with silent tears running down their faces. Rowan wanted to hug her mom. Why was this so awkward? In the years after her dad's death, they'd drifted apart despite living and working together, and now that her mom lived in Florida, they didn't even see each other in passing anymore. She didn't know how to bridge that gap.

But today was her wedding day, and even if she didn't lean on the femme side, she was a bride too and could do whatever she wanted. If she wanted to hug her mom, she would.

Rowan opened her arms, and when her mom stepped closer, she pulled Debra against her shoulder. A familiar floral scent enveloped her. Her mom wore the same perfume she'd used for years for special occasions, like graduations, fancy dinners, or her wedding anniversary. It was soothing, and the choice made Rowan feel appreciated. She closed her eyes and let herself soak up the moment.

"Slow down." Kai's whisper was only audible to Maia as they entered the big event room arm in arm.

Maia didn't know if she meant her steps or her breathing, which admittedly bordered on hyperventilation. With a conscious effort, she slowed both. It wouldn't be fun to stumble or faint at her wedding, especially not in front of too many medical friends and family members.

Rowan was already waiting for her at the other end of the room. *Oh, wow.* She'd expected Rowan to fill out a suit nicely with those swimmer's shoulders, but this was next-level stunning. The dark-blue fabric hugged her closely in all the places that needed hugging. Her expression was even sexier, a mixture of anticipation, adoration, and traces of the same queasiness that plagued Maia's stomach.

When she got closer, Maia forgot all about Rowan's shoulders and could only look at her eyes. The navy fabric made her blue eyes pop, and it added depth. But the best part was the love shining in Rowan's gaze.

The ceremony passed in a blur, and only a few sensations penetrated the bubble of love Maia shared with the woman about to be her wife:

Rowan's warm and firm grip on her hand.

The surprisingly serious and soothing tone of Nick's voice. She barely understood the words, but he gently led them through the questions.

The cold metal of the ring Rowan slipped on her finger. When she returned the gesture in kind, her own hand shook as if she were back at her surgery rotation.

Rowan's soft, soft lips as they kissed. She could have kept kissing her forever, but finally, the applause pierced their bubble and let in her friends and family again.

"I love you." Maia mumbled the words against Rowan's lips, only for her.

"I love you too." Rowan had said it many times before, but today was different—special.

It wasn't only a declaration of feeling, it was a promise and a prediction of their future together.

Maybe marriage would change them—so far, it had only done so for the better.

If you want to read more about how Rowan and Maia met, their love story can be found in Chris Zett's *Flipping Hearts and Homes*.

To Madame du Barry, Who Deserved Better

by Jennifer Giacalone

Fleur lounged on the bed in her silk blouse and no pants, watching Renata slide into the sleeveless red velvet Chanel cocktail dress that they'd found at an estate sale a few weeks ago. They'd not imagined they'd have an opportunity to break it out this early, but Fleur was not complaining. She'd not have thought it possible to make Renata's lush curves look any more sumptuous, but she was happy to be surprised.

"Either fuck me or put your pants on," Renata needled, half-teasing, half-not. She preened in front of the mirror, adjusting the fit of the dress.

"No," Fleur said nonchalantly, "I'd like to enjoy you in that dress for a bit before I take you out of it." She stood and stole up behind her wife, laying a warm, moist kiss on the back of her neck, eliciting a soft little whine. Then she zipped Renata's dress up with a frustrating finality. Frustrating mostly for Renata, who had clearly been hoping for option A.

"Behave yourself tonight and we'll see what you get," she muttered into Renata's ear.

They'd moved out of Amsterdam proper not too long after they remarried and were now in a lovely little renovated farmhouse thirty minutes outside the city. It was spacious enough for Luca to have his own room when he came home from art school in Florence, and there was even a little barn that functioned as his studio in summer. It was modest, but compared to their old flat in Amsterdam West, it felt huge.

As luck would have it, their new home was a stone's throw from a three-star restaurant that they'd not yet found a justification to visit. And it needed one. Several hundred euros for a dinner would require one of them selling an organ, and probably one they would miss.

"Are you quite sure she said this was her treat?" Fleur asked again as they strolled through the mild spring evening in the restaurant's direction.

"Listen," Renata said, "I know it's too much. I wouldn't have accepted otherwise. She was very appreciative that we could get her and her young companion into the opening." She leaned on the words 'young companion' with a heavy dose of significance.

"So she's buying us a dinner that costs more than a houseboat. Seems reasonable."

"Listen. When your fabulously wealthy friend offers to treat you to dinner at a three-star restaurant, you say yes."

"So what has she been doing lately?" Fleur asked.

Renata waved a hand around vaguely. "Who knows? Enjoying life. And the *young companion,* I guess."

"A 'young companion,'" Fleur repeated, chuckling. "It would be just like her to go cougaring her way across Europe with some twenty-three-year-old lad in too-tight trousers."

"While her husband languishes in a Czech prison."

"Where he belongs."

Renata nodded her agreement and pulled her lacy shawl around her shoulders. The evening was damp and just this side of too cool for what Renata was wearing.

"I would think you'd know how to dress for Amsterdam by now, darling," Fleur said and threw an arm over Renata's shoulders.

Fleur herself was wearing a suit of pale-pink silk, which was perfect for the weather and looked especially fetching with the rope of freshwater pearls around her neck.

"Yes, but when I underdress, you're forced to always have your arm around me. Strategy, see?" Renata answered.

As they approached the restaurant, Renata gave a low whistle. "Would you look at that."

The restaurant was in a large glass structure off an old hotel that still received guests. It looked as if it might have been an orangerie or a greenhouse at one point, and with the massive hanging plant in the center of the room like a chandelier, it harkened back to that. It glowed warmly in the evening, inviting and sleek.

They entered a quiet, antique-looking reception area where a blonde thirtysomething hostess in a smart little vest greeted them.

They sauntered up to her. "Good evening, the two of us are meeting a friend here? The reservation is under—"

The hostess held up a hand. "Yes, of course, Ms. Cellini. She said you'd be along any moment."

Renata and Fleur exchanged mildly surprised looks.

"If you'll follow me."

The dining room, with its many standing plants and glass walls, almost gave the sense of eating outside. There was a soft hush to the background chatter, with each table backed by a curved, cushioned wall to absorb sound. Waiters glided back and forth with silver trays, carts laden with improbable, gravity-defying delicacies. The light was honey-colored and low enough to give atmosphere without being too dark to see one's meal. The space was accented with a lot of dark polished wood. This was as haute as cuisine ever got in Amsterdam.

They followed their host to a round table nestled against one of those curved sound barriers, where their friend and her "young companion" sat waiting for them.

"My girlfriends!" Oksana exclaimed, her face lighting up. She looked much as she did when they had last seen her: blonde hair coiffed expensively, neatly dressed—her silk suit was a bold blue, unlike Fleur's—and dripping in diamonds. She stood to greet them, first kissing Renata on both cheeks and then Fleur. She smelled of Tom Ford's "Lost Cherry," though she'd developed a lighter touch with her perfume than the last time they'd seen her. Her grip on Fleur's shoulders as she leaned in to kiss her cheeks was gentle enough but nevertheless gave an air of "strong enough to crush a few bones if she felt like it."

Fleur was glad that they'd ended up on this woman's good side.

Because Oksana's personality took up so much space, Fleur only now noticed her aforementioned "young companion": a brunette twentysomething woman in a black-spangled sleeveless dress, with wild, dark curls stuffed into an updo that was clearly plotting its rebellion from its hairpins. Elaborate script curled around one of her forearms in black ink, and one of her shoulders bore a lacy-looking pattern that Fleur couldn't quite make out.

"And this," Oksana announced, gesturing to the younger woman beside her, "is my young companion, Manon. Darling, say hello to my girlfriends, Renata and Fleur, lovers of art every bit as much as we are." Her Russian accent remained as thick as ever, almost cartoonishly so. Sometimes Fleur suspected her of playing it up to amuse herself.

Manon smiled, but there was something a bit distant about it. "*Avec plaisir,*" she said, nodding to them.

Fleur assessed the younger woman quickly. Her hands had the faded scars of lots of little nicks that they'd borne over the years, plus a few small, barely noticeable new ones. Short, well-kept nails. She worked with her hands, Fleur guessed. Her tattooed arms were not particularly muscular, so probably not a heavy trade. Probably working with small, sharp things: a seamstress, electronics repair, something like that. She was pale, with large, arresting blue eyes, and a little on the thin side, but not unpleasant to look at.

But what was perhaps the most stunning about her was the necklace she wore: a row of seventeen glorious diamonds, almost as large as filbert nuts, with a three-wreathed festoon and simple pear-shaped and star-shaped pendants dangling above her modest cleavage. All of this was to showcase a fabulous diamond that sat just above her heart.

"I see you're looking at Manon's necklace," Oksana commented.

"It's difficult not to. It's very impressive."

Oksana grinned like a cat and didn't say anything more.

The necklace was more than impressive. It was absurd. Even Oksana, who wore diamonds with her tracksuits, wouldn't be wearing such an incredible piece of jewelry. Who was this young woman, and what was she doing running around with Oksana and this necklace?

On their last encounter, about two years ago, Oksana had had a quiet but omnipresent assistant named Dasha. But there was no evidence of Dasha tonight, and something about the way Oksana briefly, almost unconsciously, touched Manon's shoulder as she sat down suggested that the young woman was almost certainly not a new Dasha.

Oksana flagged down a waiter, who appeared tableside as if by teleportation. Oksana had said she'd never been here before, but she'd clearly managed to fully ingratiate herself with the staff in the five minutes before Fleur and Renata had arrived.

"Jelte," she said, because of course she already knew his name, "let's have the eight-course tasting menu for the four of us, please?"

The tall, very blond waiter gave a little obsequious half-bow. "Of course, madame. And some wine?"

"Ah!" Oksana thought for a moment, then snapped her fingers. "No, I think you can bring two bottles of Moët for me and my girlfriends, yes?"

"Of course. Would you like to add the marigold egg caviar?"

Oksana gave him a dazzling smile. "Jelte, I'm Russian, what do you think?"

Jelte chuckled. "Of course, madame. For all of you, then?"

Oksana didn't even ask. "*Da, da,* yes, for everyone."

Fleur leaned over and whispered to Renata, "I don't even know what marigold caviar is."

Renata elbowed her and whispered back, "Expensive."

While Oksana chatted and flirted with Jelte, Fleur whispered to Renata, "Not half as expensive as that necklace on Manon. What do you make of it?"

"It looks fit for a queen," Renata responded quietly.

"Exactly."

The waiter disappeared, and Oksana returned her attention to her friends. "My girlfriends," she addressed them grandly, "you're looking so well! Much better than last time I saw you."

"Last time we saw each other was in an interrogation room in Monaco," Renata replied. "It was a hard night."

Manon raised an eyebrow at this. "These are the women who arrested your husband?"

"They have very good fashion sense for police, no?"

Polite laughter.

"We appreciated the cheese and caviar you sent, by the way," Fleur interjected.

They exchanged more pleasantries: Oksana asked about their new home, oohed and ahhed over the pictures and applauded their choices of art hanging on the walls, gushed over the painting of Luca's that they'd chosen to hang in the living room.

"I don't much care for abstract expressionism usually," Manon said in her French-accented English. "But his use of color is excellent." She turned to Oksana and, gesturing to it, murmured, "You should really buy one of his paintings, *cherie.*"

Renata puffed up with pride. She couldn't help it. "It is, isn't it? Are you an artist?"

"I would say so. I design and make jewelry."

Renata pounced. "Did you make that necklace?"

"I did."

"May I look a little closer?"

Manon gestured for her to go ahead.

Renata had some very strong feelings about diamonds, and Fleur could smell the blood in the water on this. She prayed that she wasn't about to make things weird in the middle of an absurdly expensive dinner.

Renata leaned in a little closer. It looked like she might be sneaking a look at her cleavage while she was there. But what could you do? The girl was wearing her art around her neck. "Very nice work."

"Thank you," Manon said, warming a little.

Oksana held up a manicured finger. "While the two of you have been getting married and moving to the country, I've taken on a little project." She gazed at Manon fondly for a moment, in a way that made Fleur wonder if she'd incorrectly assumed things about Oksana's sexuality.

"It's not little, *cherie*," Manon objected. She was quiet, almost aloof, but this was the second time she had addressed Oksana as "*cherie*," which didn't have to mean anything but could also mean everything.

"You're right, *zajka*, it's not little."

Jelte appeared with an ice bucket containing two bottles of Moët & Chandon. The conversation paused as he popped the first and poured. As he glided away, Oksana began speaking again.

"I'm learning a lot about the French Revolution," she began, which was definitely not what Fleur would have expected to come out of her mouth. "I started with the women painters, you know, because that's my great love, of course. But I met Manon, and she started to teach me about the jewelry. So much beautiful work!"

The subtler diamond collar around her own neck winked as she spoke.

"And, you know, the French crown was brought down by a necklace just like the one around my young companion's neck."

Renata knew more about jewelry than Fleur did, but even Fleur thought she recognized the design of it. "Is that a re-creation of a French necklace from the Revolution era?"

"Ah! It's better than that. It's *the* French necklace from the revolutionary era. Sort of." She sipped her Champagne and paused as the quiet atmosphere hung around them. "So, you know, Louis XV commissioned this necklace for his mistress, Madame du Barry, but he died before he could give it to her. Smallpox, I guess. So it was never paid for. The jewelers were stuck with this piece that they spent lots of money and years on. Can you imagine?"

"No," Fleur said sincerely. "I can't." The cost of that many diamonds alone would probably make her heart stop. She routinely dealt in tracking down paintings whose price tags soared into millions of dollars, but their worth was somewhat abstract, based upon what someone decided they were worth and was willing to pay for them. There was something more real about the cold, hard value of diamonds.

"So they tried to sell the necklace to Marie Antoinette. But she knew who it was originally for—her husband's mistress—so can you guess what she said?"

"*Allez frapper des pierres*?" Renata suggested.

Oksana chuckled. "That's go kick rocks, right? My French is not so good."

"It's getting much better," Manon assured her.

"What happened to Madame du Barry?" Renata asked.

"She was banished from the palace by her lover's successor," Manon said.

Fleur briefly remembered that she had merely asked Oksana what she was up to these days and was now in the middle of a history lecture, but it was interesting. "So how did the necklace bring down the French crown?"

"Don't be in such a hurry. They haven't even brought the first course."

As she said this, Jelte appeared with a cart and presented them with bubble plates made of red glass, in the center of which sat a little sculpture of pâté with an elegant, elaborate filigree of vegetables on top: curly slivers of red cabbage, carrot, and others, fashioned into a delicate crown. It was immaculate tweezer work for an amuse-bouche.

Oksana called for a toast. "To beautiful food, on a beautiful night, with my beautiful girlfriends."

Fleur raised her glass and added, "To the study of history."

Renata followed suit with, "To Madame du Barry, who deserved better."

Manon nodded with particular enthusiasm. They clinked their glasses against one another and settled into the spectacular vegetable pâté in front of them. Jelte had rattled off about a dozen ingredients, including avocado, stewed pear, macadamia nuts, and pinecones (pinecones!), but they all came together in a smooth, tangy, peppery, creamy marvel.

"Wonderful, no?" Oksana said after sampling her own.

"Delicious."

After finishing, Oksana lit once again into her story. "So. Dead king, banished mistress, and jewelers stuck with a necklace that could be about $17 million in today's money. Along comes a con artist—what was her name, *zajka*?"

"Jeanne de la Motte," Manon supplied, tipping her fork in Oksana's direction.

"Jeanne de la Motte. Con artist. Mistress to an influential cardinal who was on Marie Antoinette's shit list. Jeanne de la Motte told him she was close friends with Marie Antoinette. I'll patch things up for you, she says to him."

Jelte appeared with another cart, this one bearing a stainless steel "tree" with what looked like…rings, adorning its various branches?

"What have you got there, Jelte?" Oksana asked him.

"Ladies, these are ceramic rings, each with a gem, if you will, of veal tartare and caviar." One by one, he plucked a ring from the tree and slid it onto one of their fingers.

They sat there, looking at it with surprise, confusion, and amusement. "How are we supposed to eat it?" Fleur finally asked.

Jelte smiled. "Well, madame, any way you like."

Manon laughed, the first time so far that Fleur had seen her do so. "Like this, I think." She turned to Oksana and held the ring out to her. Oksana leaned down and ate the little gem of veal and caviar off with a good deal of eye contact. Then she offered her own ring to Manon for a similar treatment.

It was undeniably erotic. Fleur was definitely not imagining things. She wasn't sure before, but that was a flare across the bow.

Fleur gave a wicked little smirk and locked eyes with Renata as she put the ring up to her own mouth and closed her lips around the savory bonbon. She took a little more time than she really needed to with that. Renata squeezed her knee under the table.

"Fabulous," Renata exclaimed after she ate her own with a needless amount of eye contact and theatricality. "It's almost as fabulous as that ring on your finger, Oksana."

Oksana glanced at Manon, again with that measure of affection and pride that she'd shown earlier, and said, "Manon made it for me." She held it out to the table to show it off. They all admired the size of the rock and the precision of the curling pattern in the delicate gold band.

"*Bellissima*!" Renata exclaimed.

As they waited for the next course, Oksana continued with the story:

"So our con artist, de la Motte, she sets up a meeting between the cardinal and a Marie Antoinette lookalike, who happened to be a prostitute. Never underestimate a sex worker, right? She convinces the cardinal to buy the necklace so she can deliver it to Marie Antoinette on his behalf, to get him back in her good graces. He was on her shit list for some reason, I guess. De la Motte claimed that Marie Antoinette wanted the necklace, but certainly couldn't buy it for herself because it would look bad if she buys something so fancy when France couldn't even feed its people. She forges a royal IOU with Marie's name on it, and the cardinal brings this to the jewelers. They give him the necklace, he takes the necklace to de la Motte, and he waits for praise from the queen that will never come."

Fleur smirked. "How quickly was the necklace picked apart and sold?"

Oksana pointed a long, manicured finger at Fleur. "Instantly. Still warm from the cardinal's pocket. Boom. All over the black markets of Paris and London."

Jelte arrived with another cart. Another set of bubble dishes, this time orange glass. "Langoustines marinated in our house-made kombucha, topped with locally grown herbs and red onion."

Quiet fell as they sampled yet another beautifully arranged dish, eating slowly to savor each bite. Fleur knew she should probably slow down on the Champagne a bit, but it was excellent, the food was incredible, and her wife looked beautiful. And the mystery of Manon and Oksana had her curiosity thoroughly piqued. Oksana and Manon were chatting and joking quietly between themselves as they all ate, and Fleur's mind whirled. At one point, Manon leaned in to whisper something to Oksana, and Oksana's eyes closed for a moment at the brush of the younger woman's lips on her ear.

After finishing her langoustines in reverent silence, Fleur looked up at Oksana. "Poor Madame du Barry. She never got her necklace."

Renata snorted. "The monarchy was hoarding money, and the people were starving. Madame du Barry didn't need a seventeen-million-dollar necklace. And odds are they were blood diamonds anyway."

"You just said she deserved better," Fleur retorted.

"Yes, I meant it was cold-blooded of the new king to toss her out of the palace."

"Actually," Manon said, "to your comment, Renata, about the blood part of it, the odds are about fifty-fifty. Diamonds came from India then. They might just have been colonizer diamonds."

"Not a big improvement," Renata scoffed. "I don't blame the French for revolting at all."

"We're not revolting all the time," Manon said.

"You're never revolting, *zajka,*" Oksana said.

And there it was. Renata was not at all fond of diamonds because they mostly came with a history of suffering attached to them. The only one she would wear was the one in the ring Fleur bought her, and only because Fleur had gone to great pains to ensure that it was ethically sourced, presenting a certificate of provenance that it had come from Canada from a source that treated its workers humanely and practiced sustainable mining.

Oksana shrugged with a smile that could only be described as mysterious and changed the subject. "Thank you again, very much, my girlfriends, for getting us into the opening. It was beginning to feel very impossible for me, and I'm not used to that."

Fleur decided not to wait for Jelte to come around and poured herself a bit more Champagne. "Well, it is helpful to have good relations with all the local museum directors. They want us to come quickly when they need us."

"It was no trouble to get two more tickets." Renata glanced around, most likely wondering when the next cart of magnificent food was coming. "You know, Degas is the reason I met my son to begin with."

Renata launched into the story of when she was managing the gallery in Genoa and twelve-year-old Luca snuck in one night to sit and copy a Degas uninterrupted. It was the genesis of their relationship and led to Renata eventually adopting him.

The four of them were making quick work of the two Champagne bottles. Fleur gave herself license because it had been a stressful week and she was with good company. Oksana had ordered still another bottle of Moët. She was likely a much heavier drinker than either of them, but it still seemed excessive. That didn't mean Fleur was going to pass on just one more glass.

That was why it took well into the final dinner course—of dry-aged, hay-roasted duck with jus and celery stock—before she fully processed that as impressive as Manon's necklace was, it was missing a rather large diamond in the upper left festoon. There was a fitting there for one, but no gem. She wanted to ask about it, but she was having too good a time. She was hearing about fashion from Manon and Renata, and about caviar from Oksana, and the parade of fish dishes and elegant curries and delicacies served in beds of hay and topped with elaborate arrangements of vegetable filaments had entirely taken her attention.

She had even forgotten about the French Revolution.

Renata glanced at her watch. Fleur could tell she was slightly tipsy, but she still had her wits about her enough to announce, "After Jelte brings dessert, we really ought to go. Those newly discovered Degas masterpieces aren't going to come to us, after all."

"Bringing them to us!" Oksana exclaimed. "Why didn't I think of that?"

The table laughed.

Oksana had hired a sleek black Jaguar with a private driver and insisted on ferrying the four of them to the museum.

They settled into the sumptuous leather seats. It was a good thing they were comfortable, because it wasn't far to the city, but Amsterdam and cars did not get along particularly well. There was, in fact, a taxi stand at the Rijksmuseum, but getting to it would be another matter.

"You know," Oksana began as the car rolled off down the street, "I may have been exaggerating a bit when I said the necklace caused the French Revolution. But it didn't help. Even after everyone was arrested and the scandal broke, the French didn't want to hear about Marie Antoinette as the victim of a scam. They still believed she was spending big on jewelry and then stiffing the jewelers, on top of ignoring the suffering of the people."

"More of a last-straw situation," Fleur said.

"So really," Renata said, "nobody won, eh? The con artist ended up in jail. The jewelers never got their money. And Madame du Barry never got her necklace."

"I wonder what happened to all of those diamonds," Fleur mused. She knew that modern diamonds came with certificates of provenance like the one she'd gotten when she purchased Renata's, but she wasn't sure whether that practice stretched back to the era of the French Revolution.

"I can tell you," Oksana said, "but that's a story for later. *Much* later."

The journey through the streets of Amsterdam was excruciatingly slow, but the four of them occupied themselves with discussing the various exhibits in the major museums around Europe, Oksana effusively talking about her latest acquisitions and, as Manon had suggested, promising to buy some of Luca's art if she saw something she liked.

"How did the two of you meet?" Fleur finally asked as they sat motionless at a traffic crossing that seemed as if it would never free up.

"I was looking for a jeweler for a special project." She waggled her bedazzled fingers. "You don't think I wear off the rack, do you?"

"Oh, naturally," Renata said.

"She has a..." Oksana paused, screwing up her face in thought. "What is it?" She dropped her voice and tried to make it sound raspy, like Liam Neeson. "A particular set of skills."

Manon's pale-blue eyes twinkled in the dim of the car. "And I'm very good at what I do." Her hand rested over Oksana's in the space between them on the seat.

So, lovers; that much was clear.

After an interminable wait in the line of cars outside the Rijksmuseum, during which they discussed how interminable the wait was, they emerged into the cool evening to find a small swarm of equally well-dressed folk making their way inside. "I'm sure there will be more Champagne," Oksana announced as they walked hand in hand toward the entrance.

"I certainly don't need any more," Fleur replied. The night air was cool on her cheeks and felt good after the long, warm car ride.

"*Nyet*!" Oksana exclaimed. "There's always room for my two friends, Moët & Chandon!" She hooked her arm through Manon's tattooed one, and they marched toward the building.

Fleur could walk the Gallery of Honor in her sleep. She knew each Rembrandt, Vermeer, and van Ruisdael in it. They entered the softly lit hall, each panel of slate-blue wall gently illuminated to highlight the masterpiece that graced it. Bars on either side of the room beckoned with well-dressed waitstaff mixing sparkling concoctions. A podium was set up, which meant speeches at some point. Hopefully, they'd then be ushered into the gallery where the Degas were hung.

Oksana and Manon were still arm in arm.

Renata slipped an arm around Fleur's waist and asked quietly, "So, shall we separate them and see what the story is?"

Fleur raised an eyebrow. "Trading in gossip, Agent Cellini?"

"You're not curious?"

"Oh, you're damned right I am. You take Oksana; she likes you best. You know all the women painters in this gallery, yes?"

"There are only three, *mi amor*, don't insult me."

"Behave yourself," Fleur said, playfully stern.

"Or what?" Renata responded.

Fleur had come down a bit from the dizzy heights of her Champagne earlier but was still feeling loose and playful. She surreptitiously pinched Renata's behind as they walked. "Or I might have to march you out of here in cuffs."

"Promises, promises."

They caught up to Oksana and Manon. Fleur clocked someone already taking note of Oksana from across the room, so they would have to work quickly.

Renata tugged at Oksana's sleeve. "Oksana, I'm sure you've been here many times, but they only just added a few of the Dutch women masters to this gallery. Would you like to see them?"

These words would always work on Oksana. She seized Renata's arm and exclaimed, "Ah! Of course. You must show me immediately!"

As Renata guided her off, waxing poetic about Judith Leyster, Gesina ter Borch, and Rachel Ruysch, Fleur smiled over at Manon. "What do you say we go grab us all some drinks?"

Manon nodded in agreement.

"So how long has it been, you and Oksana?" Fleur asked casually as they strolled over to the nearest bar.

"Well, we know each other a year and a half, maybe?" As Fleur had predicted, one of Manon's dark curls had already begun to work itself free from her many hairpins.

"The particular set of skills, yes?"

Manon chuckled and rolled her eyes, and it was a little more warmth than Fleur had seen from her so far this evening. "Yes, she makes a lot of that joke, *fâcheusement*."

"Well, we enjoy being annoyed by the ones we love, no?"

Manon didn't say anything, but her amused look said a great deal. Fleur was very good at interrogation, but less so at being subtle about finding out what she wanted to know. "You've done lovely work on the necklace," she commented as they stood in line.

"Well," Manon said coyly, "I couldn't have done it without Oksana, you know. I mean, I *wouldn't* have. It was just a fantasy I had that I confessed to her one day, and she insisted I should do it." She offered a sly little smile. "You must know how impossible it is to say no once she gets an idea."

"I can only imagine."

They got to the bar. Fleur ordered herself and Renata a pair of white wine spritzers, something that would be light and sparkly but less lethal than yet another Champagne. Manon ordered a white wine and a vodka tonic.

As they waited, Fleur inquired, "So, forgive me, but I'm terribly curious. What is the *particular set of skills*?"

"Well, the jewelry, *bien sûr*, but also, my knowledge of history, and, of course..." A little mischief played around her lips. "I'm very good at magic."

"Magic?"

"*Oui*, like street magic, you know? Nimble fingers." She waggled her delicate fingers in the air, then held her hand out to Fleur. "I'll show you. Let me see your hand?"

Bemused, but intrigued, Fleur held out her hand.

"Ah, no no, the other one, please."

Fleur switched hands. "Now what?"

Manon took Fleur's hand in both of hers. "Now, I happened to notice, you and Renata have both got very lovely wedding rings, very nice." Her eye contact became incredibly probing and intense. "How long have you been married?"

"Well, we were married before, for five years, and then divorced for five, and now remarried for two."

Manon squeezed her hand. "It's so nice to see that love can conquer differences like that. What a beautiful story. I hope nobody ever steals your love away."

Manon released Fleur's hand.

"*Allors*, do you notice anything different?"

Fleur frowned, then looked down at her hand. Her own wedding ring was gone, replaced by one of Manon's, a braided gold band with small rubies. Her mouth dropped open. "How on earth?!" How had she done it? Fleur hadn't felt or noticed anything.

Manon laughed. She held up Fleur's ring between two fingers, grinning. "I told you, street magic." She held it out in her palm. "May I have my own ring back, please?"

Fleur dropped Manon's ring into her palm, took her wedding ring, and slid it back onto her finger. It was unnerving to have it off, even briefly.

Manon put her own ring back on. "I'm sorry. I hope I didn't alarm you."

"You did for a moment," Fleur admitted. "You must understand, that ring was rather hard-won the second time around."

Manon seemed genuinely apologetic as she took Fleur's drinks from the bartender and handed them to her. "I'm so sorry, I didn't know. I won't scare you like that again, I promise."

An announcement echoed discreetly through the gallery in English, then Dutch, then French. They would be opening the gallery to view the Degas exhibit shortly, it said. It was time to locate Renata and Oksana.

The museum was milking this opening for all it was worth, which might mean the pieces were nothing special and they had to get what they could from their novelty. It also might mean that they were about to see something extraordinary that, once it was released into the broader world, would lose the sense of magic one might have from seeing a master's work for the first time.

As they weaved through the milling crowd of well-dressed people, Fleur gave an occasional cursory nod or wave to museum higher-ups.

"They know you here," Manon observed.

An entirely new concern had sprouted in Fleur's mind: Manon clearly had skills that she was calling magic or sleight of hand but could easily be rebranded as a talent for pickpocketing. A rather impressive talent, actually. Oksana was surely someone who could take care of herself, as she'd demonstrated amply over the years, but Fleur couldn't keep herself from worrying that this young woman was taking her friend for a ride. While they weren't particularly close, Fleur liked Oksana and enjoyed hearing about her exploits. She didn't like the idea that she'd been honeypotted into an affair that might end in financial distress for her.

She wanted Manon to understand who she was dealing with.

"They do. I've been investigating art crimes for a long while now."

"You must be very good at it."

"I am. Renata and I together are a particularly good team too."

Manon smiled. "I like that."

They found Oksana and Renata lurking behind a pillar and presented their drinks. "I thought we should go a bit easy," Fleur said, handing Renata her spritzer.

"And I thought that you should not," Manon told Oksana with a wink. "Vodka tonic."

"So, why are you two hiding back here next to the Vermeers?" Fleur inquired.

"There's a man here I don't particularly want to see," Oksana said.

Fleur raised an eyebrow at this. It was hard to imagine Oksana avoiding someone. "Who?"

"Old business partner of my husband's," she said. "Dimitri Volkov and his *suka* wife, Ivana."

Renata discreetly pointed to a tall, dark-haired man of middle age in an expensive suit. He had a dark-haired woman on his arm in a silk dress that showed a lot of artificially enhanced decolletage. "That guy."

"It's not even really the guy. It's the wife," Oksana said. And then she muttered what Fleur assumed were probably some curses in Russian.

"Still, silly to be hiding," Renata said. "And not like you at all."

Manon began fussing over Oksana, gently rubbing her arm and speaking in soft, reassuring tones. Fleur couldn't quite make it out. She grabbed Renata's elbow and pulled her a few feet away. "So," she said quietly, "what has Oksana told you about the two of them?"

"Not a lot. But I don't get the impression this is her first woman."

"Well, listen, Manon just demonstrated her incredible pickpocketing skills while we were in the drink line."

The lights dimmed.

"What do you make of that?" Renata asked.

"I don't know," Fleur admitted, "but I don't like it. Do you?"

Renata looked over Fleur's shoulder. "I don't. But I also don't buy that Oksana would avoid anyone, much less some Russian gangster and his diamond-studded, fake-titted wife."

Fleur nodded. "I know."

As the evening's host was addressing the crowd in English, thanking them for being there and for their generosity to the museum, Renata squinted through the dim. "The Russians are moving a little closer… Do you know something? I could be wrong at this distance, but that wife has a ring that looks exactly like the one Manon made for Oksana."

Fleur tried not to gasp. "A ring? That was the trick she showed me. She took my hands, swapped her ring for mine without my notice and then immediately returned it, of course. But still."

Oksana's ring was beautiful. The work on the band, and the large diamond in it made for a real showpiece. Did Manon really make it? Or did she steal it?

Renata scoffed. "What do you think? Is she after that Russian's ring?"

"Maybe. And if so, does Oksana know it?"

"Shit," Renata hissed. "She's on the move."

While they'd been talking, Oksana had disappeared, and Manon was threading her way through the audience toward where the Russians were standing. It made sense. As the host went on, filling in the details of how the paintings were discovered, Renata and Fleur glanced around the room.

"Right," Fleur decided after a moment. "Let's interrupt this party, shall we?"

The two of them moved through the crowd as discreetly as possible, pursuing Manon's slender shape through the dim, trying not to lose her dark dress and dark hair in the sea of tuxedos and snappy suits. It still wasn't quite coming together, but Manon had no reason to be approaching those Russians, and with Oksana conveniently vanishing, it didn't feel as if they had much choice.

Renata managed to get hold of the younger woman's wrist when she was less than a foot from Ivana Volkov. "There you are," she said quietly into her ear. "Let's go for a walk."

"I was just going for an hors d'oeuvre," Manon objected. But she didn't seem as if she expected it to be believed.

"I'm sure. This way."

Fleur and Renata each took one of her slender arms and guided her off the floor. Fleur knew the interior of this museum like the back of her hand and led them to a small service area outside one of the hallways. Conveniently, a plastic chair sat pushed against a door, probably for a security guard or something.

"Have a seat," she said, gesturing to the chair.

Manon sat, looking up at them expectantly. She wasn't nervous. She didn't seem scared. "So?"

"What was it you were going to say to the Russians?"

"I wasn't going to say anything to the Russians."

"No?" Renata asked.

Fleur pulled up another plastic chair and sat down, directly facing Manon. Renata began prowling around behind her: their classic tag-team approach. It rarely failed them.

"So maybe you were just going after the ring, then?" Fleur pressed.

"What ring?" Manon asked, blinking innocently.

"What is your connection to that ring? It's exactly like the one Oksana says you made for her," Renata said. Her pointy heels tapped across the tile floor as she paced in circles behind Fleur.

"What would we find if we ran your ID in Paris?" Fleur asked. "Have you been arrested for pickpocketing?"

"Arrested?" Manon laughed. "No, never."

"I suppose that doesn't happen to good pickpockets, does it?" Fleur leaned forward and turned on her intense gaze, the one that made most suspects shrink.

Manon held up both her hands. "What are you two going to do? Arrest me? Detain me until the Amsterdam police can come pick me up? Why would you do this? I've done nothing."

"Oksana is our friend," Renata said, and her tone was laced with menace. "If you're involved in something that will bring her trouble…"

The heavy metal door squeaked and groaned open. They stopped. Manon looked up, and a small smile appeared on her lips. "Took you long enough, *cherie*."

Oksana stood there, her smile as dazzling as her jewelry. "Oh, my girlfriends, I knew you would be looking out for me."

Hands on hips, Renata looked ready to pounce on someone or something. "You knew we were going to be in here?"

Fleur stood. "Oksana, what the devil are you up to?"

Oksana grinned and sauntered in, letting the door close with a heavy, dramatic *thunk* behind her. "Why did you bring Manon in here?"

"Why do I get the feeling you know already?" Fleur's heart was thumping as it did whenever they found themselves embroiled in a chase.

"For trying to pickpocket, yes?"

"Yes, precisely."

"She didn't do nothing."

"We know," Renata said, her brow furrowed in irritation.

"But I did," Oksana announced. She held up her hand, showing off the ring. It looked exactly the same as it had when they'd admired it at the table in the restaurant.

"Stop playing around," Renata scolded.

"Let me explain."

"I for one, am dying to hear this," Fleur said.

Oksana leaned back against the wall and spread her hands apart in a grand gesture. "So, after de la Motte sold Madame du Barry's necklace for parts, they made their way through the black markets, as you know. But you would be surprised at how much evidence there was to track them. It turns out diamonds from the necklace that destroyed Marie Antoinette were prized by a lot of dealers. They weren't as hard to track down as you probably think. A few strands were sold whole, which made things simpler."

Fleur started to see the picture. "So Manon built this necklace…"

"Modeled after the original, using as many of the diamonds as we were able to track down. The project has been a year in progress already."

"But there's one missing," Renata said. "The one in that top festoon."

"You're so sharp," Oksana chuckled. "I wasn't lying about that Russian and his wife. I hate them. The diamond in her ring was the last one that we needed to complete the necklace."

"Why not simply buy it from her?"

"She wouldn't sell," Oksana said. "Believe me, I threw a lot of money at her. But out of spite, I think, she wouldn't sell. So Manon made a duplicate." She waggled her fingers, making the large diamond in the ring sparkle.

"And the plan was to have your little pickpocket swap them without her notice."

"Almost," Manon chimed in. "I taught Oksana how to do it, and she did it herself, because I have no reason to talk to those people."

Fleur almost barked out loud, gaping at Oksana. "You performed this little feat of close-up magic, did you?"

Renata shook her head. "I'm not even angry. I'm a little impressed."

"We made sure you would suspect her," Oksana went on, "so that you would entertain yourselves with chasing her and not be watching me."

They stood there under the buzzing fluorescent lights. What now?

"Now, you could arrest us, yes, but the ring I swapped is identical to hers, except for the provenance of the diamond," Oksana began. "It would be hard to explain what the crime was."

Renata glanced over at Fleur, who was feeling around in her purse for handcuffs. "And so this re-creation...with the original diamonds... First of all, why?"

Oksana looked at the younger woman with a softness that Fleur had caught glimpses of throughout the evening. "Because it was her dream, and I love her. Would you not make each other's dreams come true if it was within your power to do it?"

Fleur turned to Manon. "You mentioned that. But...*why* was it your dream?"

Manon crossed her legs and leaned back in her chair. "Because, my last name is Becú. I am the last living descendant of Jeanne Becú, better known to you as Madame du Barry."

She sat and waited with a triumphant little smirk, enjoying their faces as the denouement of the narrative became clear.

"If Madame du Barry couldn't have her necklace, at least it would go to her distant granddaughter," Oksana said.

"Christ, Oksana. Don't tell me all these diamonds are stolen." Fleur groaned. Because then she really would have to arrest them both, and she was not at all excited about this. The only person she'd begun the night thinking about cuffing was Renata.

"Of course not!" Oksana scoffed, offended. "I bought them all legitimately, except this one, because she wouldn't sell."

Fleur and Renata looked at each other. "So, it is a reconstruction of Madame du Barry's necklace, having tracked down and used the original diamonds," Fleur said slowly. "One could argue it belongs in a museum..."

Renata tilted her head, looking at the empty setting in Manon's necklace. "But no, the stones were all privately acquired. We would have a difficult time claiming it, and then authenticating it would be a bitch." She hunched down and looked closer at the empty setting, then straightened up.

"Tell me why you think Madame du Barry should have had this necklace," she demanded.

Manon's smile became a bit more bittersweet, her eyebrows pinching together. "You asked before what happened to her after Louis's death. Well, yes, she was banished, but that was not the end of her story. What people sometimes forget about the Revolution is that, yes, it was aimed at tearing down the aristocracy... at first. But then the zealots took over, and soon anyone—artists, craftsmen, bourgeoisie—could be swept up in it, labeled traitors, and next thing they knew, their heads would be rolling down the Place de la Révolution. Madame du Barry was using her fortunes from the royal purse to help get emigrés out of France. Not the wealthy ones—they could take care of themselves. Those of modest means who found themselves in the crosshairs of the fanatics for one reason or another. She was beheaded by the guillotine for her troubles."

"So you see," Oksana said, "together, we have re-created a lost piece of history and put it into the hands of the one person most entitled to have it. I make no promises what she will do with it, perhaps she can be persuaded to loan it to a museum. Perhaps *this* museum, if you can guarantee its safety."

Fleur understood what she was offering: the feather in her cap of placing a priceless piece like this in the Rijksmuseum. "Here? And not in the Louvre? Or at Versailles?"

"It would have to go to those places, of course," Oksana said. "But surely, if Manon decides she would like it to be seen, it could be arranged for a lengthy stay here in Amsterdam."

Oksana had once again managed to surprise them. And funnily enough, the bisexuality was by far the least of it. She had decided to put her significant resources into reconstructing the most infamous piece of jewelry in French history for the benefit of her young lover, simply because she loved her, and because she could.

"Do you have documentation for all the stones?" Renata asked.

Oksana nodded. "Except for the one on this ring."

Oksana had admitted to stealing the ring off Ivana Volkov's finger. Yes, she had replaced it with an identical one, and Volkov would likely never know the difference. Technically, it was still a theft.

But weighed against the importance of art and history that the finished necklace would represent, it felt trivial. Most diamonds came soaked in blood, but these were marked by the blood of rogues, revolutions, and a hundred stories of their travels through the markets of London and Paris to find their way back to the young woman who was arguably the rightful owner. In the proper hands, after centuries.

She looked at Renata. "The cop in me says we should arrest them. The art lover in me says we should go look at the Degas. What do you say, darling?"

Renata looked between Oksana and Manon, then back at her wife. "I think we should go look at the Degas."

Fleur pushed the front door open and stepped into the foyer of their home. She slipped out of her shoes and waited while Renata did the same.

"Why do you think she told us the truth?" Renata asked, flicking on the soft overhead.

"Clever people always want you to know how clever they are," Fleur said.

This was a truism as old as detective work itself. The mediocre thieves didn't play with taunting the police, but the clever ones? They were always tempting fate because they so badly needed someone to understand how difficult and daring their plans had been.

"I think it's more than that," Renata said. They strolled into the bedroom. "I think she wanted us to let us in on all of it. We may be the only people in her life who would appreciate it all, you know? The cleverness of it—I mean, for God's sake, we were the ones who got her into the opening in the first place—but also the importance of its history. And most of all…she wanted us to see how much in love she was. I don't know exactly what circles she moves in, but a Russian mob wife taking up with a younger woman? I don't think it would play so well, eh?"

There was sense to it, certainly. Still, it amused Fleur that Renata's sentimental self had chosen to see events in that way. "You softie," Fleur teased. She pulled Renata closer.

"Would you do that for me?" Renata murmured, gazing up into Fleur's eyes.

"What, track down a hoard of diamonds from centuries ago to help you reconstruct a necklace intended for one of your long-dead ancestors?"

"Yes."

"You don't even like diamonds."

Renata pressed herself to Fleur's chest, pouty lips inviting. "It's the principle of it."

Fleur unzipped the back of Renata's dress and trailed a finger down the exposed skin. "Then I would, without hesitation, track down masterpieces belonging to your ancestral line, thought lost to the centuries, no matter how long it took or how much it cost. Steal them, if necessary. Then," she went on, slipping the dress down Renata's shoulders, "I'd line the walls with them all and make love to you beneath them."

Renata shimmied out of the dress, which slid down her body and landed in a soft, rumpled pile around her ankles. "Now I want that."

Fleur thought of Oksana and Manon and how they fell in love and built something together. She thought of the diamonds on Manon's chest and how they would look on display in the Rijksmuseum. And she thought of a spread of paintings in heavy gold-leafed frames, lining the walls of their bedroom, perched on chairs and in corners, the tangible evidence of centuries of passion.

Fleur led Renata to the bed, and while she made love to her, she murmured in her ear the names of Italian baroque masterpieces that she'd chase down and buy and steal.

Curious about how their story started? Read *Art of the Chase*

Relationship Goals

by Liz Rain

Even when it was sunny in Seattle, the rain was never far away. I tucked my umbrella under my left arm so I could take Christine's hand as we walked. Her fingers, intertwined with mine, sent tingles all the way up my arm and into my brain. I nudged my shoulder against hers and lifted my face to the watery morning sun.

Going to our local café for a morning coffee was a strict part of our game-day routine. We were nearing the end of our first season playing together for the National Women's Soccer League team, Seattle Reign FC. I was a stalwart defender with the capacity for a quick rebound attack (yes, I've been described like that by other people, not just myself), and Christine was the star striker.

Over two years ago, she had given me a cold-shoulder snub when we played against each other at the World Cup – Christine for the USA and me for Australia. But despite many wrong turns, we had ended up together and now lived and played together for Seattle Reign in the middle of the year and in Melbourne in A-League soccer the rest of the time. We were both lucky enough to be in the squads for our countries too, so our life together oscillated between busy and downright exhausting.

As we entered the café, I breathed in the aroma of rich espresso and fresh-baked muffins. *Raspberry and white chocolate.* Our team nutritionist would flip if I ate one on game day, but I could get one to go and save it for tomorrow.

The barista, shrouded in a cloud of steam, looked up from behind the massive coffee machine.

"Hello, you two! Are you running late? I was starting to worry," he said.

"Emil, mate, you've gotta relax. We've got a night game, so the routine is –" I closed one eye, did the OK sign, and clicked my tongue.

"And you're going to get me the W, hey?"

"Oh, we'll win it alright," Christine said. "It's a must-win if we're going to make play-offs."

He wiped the steam nozzle off with a cloth. "That's what I like to hear. Now, you want your usual? No double-shots or wheatgrass or anything? I want that

W. You know this place has become an unofficial fan headquarters for the Reign since you two started coming here."

"No funny stuff, thanks. Just the usual," I said.

We wove our way through a cluster of people standing waiting for takeaways, and past couples and groups sitting and enjoying crepes and maple syrup, or plates stacked high with garlicky mushrooms and crispy bacon. Our favourite table, with the old chairs just like the ones at my nanna's house, was free, so we made a beeline. Just as we were about to sit down, a pair of girls about twenty years old jumped up.

"Hi, we're so sorry to bother you, but would you sign this for us?" one of them asked, her words tumbling out on top of each other.

"Sure thing," said Christine.

Emil motioned at me out of the corner of my eye, and I gave him a discreet thumbs up. He had offered to step in if ever fan adoration got a little too much, but we hadn't had to call upon his intervention so far.

"I'm Kiesha, and this is Sydney."

The fans each held out an official Seattle Reign fan program, one opened to a full-page picture of me, and one to Christine's page. Both programs quivered a little. *Awwwww.* My hands had shaken when I first got an autograph as a kid from my favourite soccer player Melissa Prinetti.

I scribbled a message and signed. "Hey, I've never read what this little blurb says about me. Do you mind?"

Sydney bounced on the balls of her feet and shook her head.

"Keeley McGee," I read aloud. *"Our thunder from down under spends her spare time eating Vegemite or trying to keep up with partner Christine Delacourt on hikes. But don't worry, she's no sleepy koala when it comes to shutting down the opposition."* I scrunched up my face. "Geez, they've laid it on a bit thick there. We get it, I'm Australian."

The fans gave delighted giggles.

"Here, what does yours say?" I flicked through the glossy magazine until I found Christine's page. *"Christine Delacourt is all class. Her silky skills make it rain goals, and her star power shines bright even when the weather is gray. Her number one hobby is finding the back of the net."* I narrowed my eyes even further. "Now that's way cooler than mine. How come yours is cooler?"

She arched an eyebrow. "They asked for input months ago. You need to start reading emails from Reign marketing. Or start checking your emails at all."

I shot the fans a look of wide-eyed incredulity.

They giggled again.

"It's hard to believe you two are even cuter together in real life," Sydney said.

"Social media didn't lie to us," Kiesha said. "We'll leave you to your coffee, I promise, but can I just say, Christine"—she turned so she was facing right towards Christine and looked her full in the face—"you provide such powerful queer, Black representation. It means everything. We live in Noxon on the Montana border, and it's not easy for me to see myself, or what I want to be, anywhere in town. But your strength inspires me."

"You don't know how much that means to me. Thank you. Can I give you a hug?"

"Yes!"

I stood back as she hugged them both. A lump rose in my throat. She inspired awe in so many fans with her work ethic and skill. Plus, it didn't hurt that she often looked like she'd stepped out of an expensive Reebok ad campaign. My insides swelled with gratitude that she had chosen me as her partner. It felt like a miracle. A part of me had expected the spine tingles to die down over as the months and years of us being together went by but, if anything, I felt them more now than ever.

I squeezed the fans tight when it was my turn to hug them. *So what if I'm Sleepy Koala sloppy seconds compared with my girlfriend?*

The fans waved to us as they left the café.

We sat down and Emil brought our coffees. "Do you ever regret that one Instagram post you put up of Mama's Romanian stuffed eggs?"

"Hah! We don't mind our spot being blown up when the fans are as sweet as those two. How about you?" I asked.

"Are you kidding? I love that I run a lesbian café! No mess, great tips, and lovely people!" He grinned as he jogged off to take the order of someone with bleached cropped hair, a dog collar, and a big ring through her nose.

Christine took a sip of her oat-milk iced latte. "I guess not all stereotypes are damaging?"

I chuckled. "I hope we don't have to switch coffee joints. We can if it all ever gets too much. But those two kids meeting their dead-set hero just now was wholesome as."

She closed her eyes and put her hand to her heart. "They're the generation that will save us. Can you believe the stuff they know? 'The power of representation of the marginalised'. When I was their age, I was more like"—she grimaced and put on a Frankenstein's Monster voice—"see ball. Get ball. Kick HARD."

I nearly did a spit take with my mocha. "Calm the farm, Granny May. We're probably, like, seven years older than they are. And you got way better grades than me in college. So if you were a dummy, I was a double dummy."

The light changed to green, and we turned onto Edmonds Way, a busy main road. We lived a thirty-minute drive from Lumen Field, where Seattle Reign trained and played.

I craned my neck to look ahead at a queue of tail-lights through the rain. "Traffic's pretty heavy." Coach was strict about being at Lumen two hours before match time.

Christine flexed her wrists as she kept hold of the wheel in a textbook ten-and-two position. I felt a flash of warmth for her precision. Her perfectionist traits had been a turn-off when we first met many years ago. I had seen them as a wall she put up to keep everyone out. But these days, I saw them for what they were—her love language. She looked after the both of us with diligence and care.

"I factored in about this level of delay. We should be right," she said.

"Hah! 'Ruhhght'. Your vowel slipped a bit there, Aussie. You've been hanging out with me too much."

She put her hand on my leg. "I could never spend too much time with you, baby. She'll be ruhhght, mate."

I chuckled as I watched raindrops course down the car window. *Geez, it really rains a lot here.* Melbourne weather could sometimes be crappy, but after months of living in Seattle, I was starting to hope for grey, drizzly days because at least they were better than driving rain for days on end. Now the weather was getting colder, it was even more of a bummer.

We started to move, along with the traffic ahead of us, but suddenly lost speed.

"What the?" Our car's dash went blank, and there was a faint whir like an old, boxy laptop computer powering down.

Christine flicked on the hazard lights and eased us off to the side of the road, getting us into a safe position just before our engine-less momentum ran out.

"What's going on?" I asked.

"I'm not sure. We charged overnight, so it's not out of juice." She leant forward and addressed the car. "Diagnose problem."

"I'm sorry. I don't understand this prompt. Please try asking in a different way," the smooth female voice replied.

"Shit." Christine muttered through clenched teeth.

"I'm sorry, I don't understand this prompt. Please try asking in a different way."

"Why aren't you working, you useless tin can?" She slapped the steering wheel.

The car didn't deign to reply, and the display screen went blank as well.

I put my hand on Christine's arm. "Hey, now, let's not piss off our ride. You know our future robot overlords all chat to each other once they clock off for the day. I'll have a look."

"Thanks, babe." She gave a tight-lipped smile. "I'll text the assistant coaches in the meantime and give them a heads-up we might be late."

"OK. Tell them not to tell Coach yet, though. I'm sure I can fix this." I jumped out of the car, and cold rain slapped me in the face. "Ergh!"

I ran around to the front. Cars sloshed by next to me. I ran my fingers along the hood's edge, hoping for a latch or release button. But the rim was smooth all the way around. I jogged back to the passenger side and knocked on the window. Nothing happened. I grunted in annoyance. Christine leaned over and opened the door from the inside.

"She's completely dead. No windows or windshield wipers or anything," she said.

"Oh, right." I leaned my head in, dripping water all over the shiny upholstery. It was a relief to give my head a break from the rain, at least. My arse was getting more and more soaked, though. "This tin can doesn't have a pull-tab. Hand me my phone. Ta. OK, Google!" I enunciated into the bottom of my phone. "How do you open the hood of a Dessaux D-series electric hatchback?"

"There is a lever under the driver's seat on the right-hand side. Is there anything else I can help you with?"

"Hey, that voice sounds a lot like the one of our car. Do you think they're sisters? At least cousins?"

Christine scoffed and shook her head as she fumbled around under her seat.

"Maybe we should start a trivia team with Car Lady and Phone Lady," I spread my hands and cocked my head. "Come on, we'd be pretty hard to beat."

The hood popped open. Christine grinned. "The trivia can wait. Get back out there, and get us going."

I saluted, wincing against the driving rain as I left the car. "Aye-aye."

I lifted the hood. Sleek plastic shapes, tubes, and wires sat there mocking me with their inscrutability. I put my hands to the sides of my face. *What were you expecting? Giant control-alt-delete buttons?* There was a smooth plastic tank in the middle of the high-tech riddle in front of me. I poked it gently. "Nope!" Nothing happened. I looked to the heavens and broke out in goosebumps as a rivulet of cold water trickled down my back. I ran back around to the passenger-side door.

"Well?" Christine asked as I sat back down and closed the door.

"Remember the original *Independence Day* movie?"

She narrowed her eyes. "Yeah..."

"Remember how the spaceship crashed and they prised it open and there was all the alien tech in there that they had no idea how to use?"

"Uh-huh."

"Let's just say our situation right now is a little like that. Actually, a lot like that." I gave two weak thumbs ups and an even weaker smile.

Christine threw her head back and laughed.

I laughed too, then I shivered and pulled my soaked tracksuit jacket across my chest.

"Poor baby! Here, let me get you my spare hoodie." She reached back and pulled not one but two neatly folded Reign hoodies out of her bag. "Here. One for your legs too. Take the wet sweater off."

"Oooo! I thought you'd never ask."

"For once, I'm not trying to get you out your clothes for the normal reasons."

"Awww, but I love the normal reasons." I dropped my bottom lip and gave her puppy-dog eyes.

She grinned and swatted her hand towards me. "Quit it, Keeley. Let me phone Dale and tell him we're going nowhere fast."

I waggled my head from side to side. "Maybe *you're* not. I'm one of the most promising first-season players, according to a poll on the NWSL's Instagram," I said in a stage whisper.

She fought down a laugh and swatted at me again. "Yes, hello. Our car's broken-down. Dead. Should we try and get a Lyft? No? OK. Yep. OK, I'll drop you a pin. Thanks. See you soon." She ended the call. "They're sending Melody to come get us."

"Oh, good. She's got great taste in music. She'll let us listen to Shania Twain on the way."

"Pffft. You and your country music."

"You'd think in the years we've been together, I would have moved the needle on your musical taste at least a little."

"Look, it's going to take more than Beyoncé putting on chaps and a cowboy hat to get me to listen to all that banjo nonsense."

"Wouldn't it be quicker to get a Lyft?"

"I thought so, but Dale checked with Chet, and he said it could end up taking longer, and he'd prefer it if Reign were in charge of getting his star players here, not some college dropout stoner riddled with viruses from too may airport pick-ups."

"Whoa, Chet. Way harsh."

I smiled and leaned my head against the seat. It was kind of cosy in our tin can, watching the cold rain pattering on the windshield. I looked over at Christine. My chest glowed warm, despite the chill of my wet clothes. It never ceased to amaze me how any situation, whether it was boring or shitty or even downright annoying, was bearable when I was with her. She was like hot sauce—she made everything better.

Christine caught my eye and schooched around so she was sitting sideways, her ear against the headrest. "What's up?"

"I was just thinking about how you're like hot sauce," I said, a little sleepily.

Her forehead creased. "OK..." She rested the back of her hand against my forehead. "Is there enough oxygen in here?"

"No. I mean, I hope so. I meant you make everything awesome."

"Awwww." She moved her hand so her palm lay gently against my cheek. "*You* do, you mean. Can you imagine how the old me would have handled this car trouble?"

"Uhhhhhh, a setback that threatened to cut into your game-prep routine? It would have been..." I winced, thinking of the Christine I had first met, wound up as tight as a ten-day clock.

"Exactly. But, hey, it will take Melody half an hour to get here, and at least half an hour to get us back to Lumen. I'll have to slash my pre-game physical *and* mental preparation." She brushed the corner of my mouth with her thumb.

Tiny fireworks went off in my brain.

Her eyes creased as she smiled. "But you've been up in here, tap dancing and cracking jokes to keep me relaxed. Thank you. You're my perspective, you know that? You ground me. When you're here, nothing bad can happen."

The glow in my chest got so big, it started to feel tight. "Aww, Chrissie." I leaned over and kissed her mouth. At a brush of her tongue against mine, my heart jumped, and I got a kick of desire. I reached under her shirt and dragged my hand her along her hip, wishing there wasn't a seatbelt and cup holders between us.

I felt her smile just before she pulled away slowly.

"We're going to steam up the windows if we're not careful," she said, pulling the hoodie I was using for a blanket back up around my shoulder where it had slipped.

"It wouldn't be the first time." I grinned, thinking back to a different vehicle in a city on the other side of the world.

Her lips curved. "No, it would not. We can't risk Melody catching us, though. She was raised very conservative in—"

"In rural Saskatchewan," I finished her sentence. "I know, I know. We can't make poor Melody blush, you're right. She's driving across town in this awful weather for us." I sat up. "Speaking of the weather—I just realised I didn't shut the hood. All the rain will be getting in."

"Oh, I don't think it will make any difference."

I hunched up my shoulders. "You *might* be right, but this is an electric car. Electricity and water don't mix. I saw a documentary once where someone murdered a lady by tossing her radio into her bath. While she was in it."

"Was this documentary an episode of *Murder She Wrote*?"

"No. Yes? Look, maybe. But I'm going to feel better if I shut the hood. We don't want to end up two fried lesbian sardines in a tin can by the side of the road."

She shrugged. "You're so right—I do not want that. You do you, boo."

I put the two dry-ish hoodies on the dash and took a deep breath, with my hand on the door to steel myself against the freezing rain. I pushed it open and jogged around again to the front of the car.

After I slammed the hood down, I tried to grasp the edge to make sure I'd done it right. My wet fingers scrabbled against the sheer surface. *OK. No bathtub electrocutions on my watch!*

A siren blared in my ear, and yellow lights blinded me. I shielded my eyes.

"Hey, are you Keeley McGee?" someone shouted.

I squinted up at a vast shape looming over me. "Yes," I shouted back. If this was the rapture, I figured there was no point trying to lie my way out of it.

"Oh, sweet! I'm a big fan. Are you having car trouble?"

When I shaded my eyes from the lights, I could make out a figure with a buzz cut.

A car horn blared, followed by a few more, blending into an angry chorus.

"Yes," I screamed over the hubbub.

"No problem! I've got you. Hop out of the way."

I jumped back into the car and watched as a tow truck pulled over in front of us.

"What did you do?" Christine asked.

"Nothing. The driver's a big fan and said she'd help us out."

She squinted out the blurry windshield. "I don't think Chet's going to like this."

"Chet needs to get the stick out of his arse. I've got a good feeling about this. Plus, we haven't even thought about sorting the car. Sure, Melody whisks us away to the game, but what, we have to get a towie at midnight tonight? And midnight towie has as much chance of being a crook as this towie we've got in front of us right now. You know the old saying—a towie in the hand is worth two in the bush."

Christine held up her hands in good-natured defeat. "I'll do anything to make you stop talking about 'towies' and their bushes up in here. Maybe at least she can drop us somewhere dry we can wait for Melody."

A figure in a black, hooded raincoat motioned at us to head towards the truck.

"Here goes nothing, I guess." Christine grabbed the bags from the back seat. "If we end up murdered on an episode of *Murder She Wrote,* I'm blaming your laissez-faire attitude."

"We'll be right," I yelled as we sloshed at a run to the truck cab. "They're not making the show anymore!"

I pulled the heavy door shut behind us. We sat close together on a thick towel covering a padded bench seat.

After some thudding and whirring, the other door opened and a drenched raincoat was slung past us behind our seat, followed by our driver plonking down next to us behind the wheel. "Holy shit! Christine Delacourt. You're my absolute favourite athlete! I'm Janet." She held out her hand, and Christine shook it.

I glanced skywards for a split second. If I didn't love her so much, it would have irked me that she got so much more adoration than I did. *It's not my fault my girlfriend is so easy to adore.*

"Now, you two have a must-win game at Lumen tonight. Let's get you there!" She started up the truck.

"Oh, Janet. Look, that's very kind of you, but we couldn't ask you to drive across town for us. If you drop us at the nearest mechanic, we've got someone from the Reign coming to get us," said Christine.

I might have imagined it, but her eyes seemed to rest on the tattoo of a topless mermaid, drawn in a thick blueish outline, adorning Janet's forearm.

"It's no trouble at all! You think I would have chosen this job if I didn't love driving? Plus, traffic heading this way is even worse. Your Reign FC person is going to be a long time coming."

Christine and I exchanged a look.

"Hey, we can do your plan, if you want. Totally. But my plan will get you there way faster. And I love Seattle Reign. It would make me happy to feel like I'm helping get the win tonight." Janet rested her hands on the steering wheel and waited for us to answer.

Christine glanced at me.

I grinned and gave a tiny nod.

Christine pointed forward with both hands. "Well, alright, then, Janet. Let's roll!"

Janet and I cheered.

"Let's get to the game!" Janet pulled the truck, still flashing its yellow lights, back out into the slowly flowing traffic. "My buddy Sanjay runs Tip Top Garage right near Lumen. I can drop your car off there afterwards."

I put my phone down on the bench seat between me and Christine and inclined my head towards it.

Christine's eyebrows shot up as she read that Tip Top Garage had a 4.9-star rating from 622 reviews. "Damn. I mean, yes please, Janet."

"Yeah, he's great with EVs. Tip Top. I guess it's all in the name!" She barked with laughter and slapped the wheel.

I laughed too. Not at the joke, which was objectively terrible, but with the joy of being on the road again thanks to our knight in shining armour. I even loved the tattoo.

"There's some more towels behind you if you're cold. You're supposed to stay warm before a game. Your muscles and stuff."

Christine grabbed a couple and layered them over us.

"You're smart to have these, Janet. Keeping your truck dry," I said.

"You kidding me? In this weather? You'd be crazy not to. I pick up a lot of stranded people. It's Seattle—everyone's wet."

I shouted with laughter. "You should put that on a T-shirt."

"Hah! Hell, yes. Make me a millionaire!" She slapped the wheel again. "Hey, I knew you'd be funny, Mac. I can call you that, right? You're always clowning around on Reign's socials."

"Yeah, Janet! You're a follower?" I asked.

"Heck, yeah. I got the Reign on, uh, whatever they're calling Twitter nowadays, Insta, TikTok, and I'm in all the Facebook groups. Love it. Love all the content."

"Nice!"

"Hey, I'm just going to text Melody and tell her to turn around," Christine said.

"Tell her Janet's gonna get us to the game!" I punched the air.

Janet pulled on a short chain above her head and gave some deafening blasts on the truck's horn, making Christine and me, and probably all the drivers in earshot, startle in our seats. "Get to the gaaaame! A-whoooooo!"

I rubbed my ribs, which were aching from laughter. "I'm so glad you picked us up, Janet! You're the greatest."

"Heck, yeah, I am. I'll often check in with people fiddling with their car hoods by the side of the road, so I slowed down, and I was like, 'Fuck, is that drowned rat out there Keeley McGee?' What did you think was under that hood, a big on/off switch?"

I chuckled and slumped back against the seat in defeat. "Look, maybe, alright?"

"Let's pump some tunes, people! Need some pump-up music. You girls like Melissa Etheridge?"

"Heck, yeah, Janet! To the gaaaaame!" I replied.

Christine braced for the volley of horn blares my war cry brought on. She entwined her fingers with mine under Janet's thick towel, which featured a beautiful illustration of a palm tree and beach ball bathed in yellow sunlight.

My heart soared as the truck picked up speed. The windshield wipers slapped in time with the bridge of the song as the three of us sung about coming home.

The clouds were heavy, but the rain finally stopped falling the moment we pulled into the players' carpark at Lumen Field. As we neared the entrance in the late-afternoon gloom, the truck's headlights picked up a group of people, some waving Reign flags. I wound down my window and could hear cheering and clapping.

"What the?" Janet asked.

"I told them how you rescued us, and they thought it would make great content for our social media," Christine said.

Janet's jaw dropped. "No way!" She opened her window and stuck her head out. "Woohooooo! Long may they Reign!!" She hit the horn again as we pulled up, causing Melody to drop her flag.

"This was your idea, huh?" I whispered to Christine.

Her lips curved. "Maybe."

We descended from the truck, and Janet ran around to meet us.

"Can you tell us what happened?" Reign's social media manager, Jordan, asked from behind the phone he held in front of him, recording.

"Well, now, you see, aww shucks, I can't talk. You tell them, Keeley," Janet said.

"Our car broke down on the side of the road, and Christine and I were completely stuck. Luckily, our hero, Janet, came to our rescue and got us to the game on time!"

Janet grinned.

One of our assistant coaches, Dale, stepped forward. "Well, you're actually still *a little* late." He glanced at Jordan. "Could I possibly nab these two so they can start their warm-ups? You know, for the game."

"In a minute, Dale," Jordan said, not taking his eyes off the video content his phone was creating.

Melody shoved something into my hands.

I shook it out. "Here, Janet. We would like to present you with this signed Reign jersey."

She gasped and beamed as I handed it to her.

"And this—pair of Reign socks, signed by…" I squinted at them. "Megan Rapinoe! Shit, I want these!" I clamped my mouth shut as Jordan shot a look at me that was clearly a language warning. "Are you a Rapinoe fan, Janet?"

"Am I ever," she said, clasping the socks to her chest. "She's my favourite athlete ever!"

I shot a look at Christine behind Janet's back. *Hah! You've been bumped down the pecking order too.*

She mimed a tiny *har-har*. "Janet, thank you so much! You saved the day." She gave her a big hug.

I did as well. "Deadset legend. Thank you so much."

Janet wiped a tear. "Thank *you.* Now go out there and win this thing for me, girls."

Dale swooped in and ushered us towards the players' entrance. Near the big double doors, he broke into a trot, dragging us along with him.

"...and I said to myself, is that drowned rat Keeley McGee?"

Just before we went inside, we turned to see Janet lit up by a bank of camera phones, regaling the group with a smile from ear to ear.

The rain stayed away. We were into additional time, 3-1 up and having fun. I had played well in defence, but Christine had really starred, getting two of the Reign's goals.

The opposition team, North Carolina Courage, had a goal kick, and it landed with me on the halfway line. Our goalie had moved up. I thought about doing the game-killing move of rolling it back to her. At that moment, two of the Courage's forwards moved towards the centre in anticipation of this move. A window opened in front of me. I sprang forward, dribbling up the sideline.

A figure in salmon pink appeared in my peripheral vision, but she was running heavy-footed. I burned her off for speed without even turning my head. I ran the ball right up to beside the penalty box. Two Courage players came to shut me down.

In the centre, Christine tried to make a move, but her opponent had her in a bear hug that would make a rugby coach proud. There was no way she could reach any pass I'd play. But our teammate, Kim, had a height advantage in a one-on-one at the left post. I faked to run towards the goal line but instead jumped backwards to give myself some space. Then I launched the ball with my right foot. My two opponents and I stood shoulder to shoulder as we watched it sail over the goalie's head.

The crowd rose.

Kim jumped, but too late. She made good contact with a header but mistimed so it bobbled up and over the net.

Gah! So close! I threw my head back in frustration.

The Reign fan army behind the net groaned, then applauded as the referee blew her whistle three times to signal the end of the match.

Christine caught my eye and gestured a chef's kiss in appreciation of my cross. Happiness surged through me like a tidal wave. We'd gotten the win, and the most stunning woman to ever play the game had me on her mind as much as I had her on mine. Life was good.

I shook the hands of the two Courage players closest to me and gave them both quick hugs and slaps on the back. We were all defenders, and I respected the hell out of them.

I jogged over to the referee and shook her hand. "Hey, number nine was all over Christine on that last play."

"Thanks for that note, Keeley. I have twenty-two players to keep an eye on. We can't all just watch Christine Delacourt." She gave me a wry smile as she turned to shake another player's hand.

After many more handshakes and a quick chat with North Carolina player, Ava, who also had played with me for Australia, our team congregated in front of the Reign fan army, our official cheer squad, who took up a large part of one end of the stadium.

Melody handed out markers, and the team made our slow way along the fence, taking selfies and signing autographs.

"Hi Keeley," a voice said as I moved along the line.

"Hi," I replied, followed by "oh, hey!" as I recognised the fans from the café that morning. "Kiesha and Sydney! Did you enjoy the game?"

"It was amazing! You played so well. Can we get another selfie with you and Christine? I'm making a photo collage on TikTok of our trip to Seattle, and it would be totally awesome to finish it with a photo with the both of you."

"Sure thing! Hey, Chrissie." I beckoned her, and she came jogging over. "Kiesha and Sydney asked for a selfie with both of us. Is that OK?"

"Of course! Hey, you two."

I took Kiesha's phone and leaned back for the selfie. "Say 'Reign!' Wait, no. Our mouths look weird. Say 'cheese!' That's better."

"I want a photo with Keeley and Christine!" said a voice.

"Me too!" said another.

We stayed put, together at the fence as a disorganised queue formed. Our teammates started to wander towards the change rooms.

"Don't look at Dale. He's going to tell us it's time to go," Christine whispered.

I shot a look back at the queue, which seemed to be getting longer rather than shorter.

We plastered on smiles for selfie after selfie.

One fan, her face painted white and navy blue, was in tears. "The two of you inspire me so much. You make me believe in true love."

Christine put a hand on her shoulder and smiled. "The most important love is the love you have for yourself. Tap into that, and good things will happen in your life. Take it from me."

I swear the woman visibly swooned, leaning back against the person behind her in the queue. I related hard—I was a little weak in the knees myself.

We snapped another selfie, just before Dale loomed right in our eyeline.

"Time to go, you two. Some of us want out of here before midnight."

"Aw. Booooo!" someone yelled from a couple of rows back.

"Sorry, everyone! Come and see us in the play-offs!" I shouted, waving both my arms.

We walked backwards as the remaining diehard fans gave us one last round of applause.

"Look. Is that...?" Christine pointed.

"Yeah, there's Janet. Hey, Janet!"

Janet jumped up and down from the fifth row, waving her hands.

Christine leaned in. "Is she..."

"Wearing her Rapinoe socks up to her elbows like Audrey Hepburn in *Breakfast at Tiffany's*? Yes, yes, she is."

She bit down a laugh. "I was going to say it looks like she's putting on a puppet show with two navy-blue Lamb Chops."

I covered my face to hide my cackle.

Christine slung her arm around my shoulders, and the crowd cheered.

She gave a delighted chuckle. "They like that, hey?"

"Sure do."

"Then they'll love this." She wound her arms around my waist and planted a kiss on my cheek.

I flushed with pure delight.

She looked at me with her face full of love.

My knees went weak all over again. Every cell in my body danced with joy that this woman, *this woman*, had chosen me.

The crowd of remaining fans was now roaring like we'd won the championship.

I walked down the race hand in hand with Christine, my insides thrumming like I'd won ten championships.

Further down, Dale turned around to check on us before he disappeared into the change rooms.

"He thinks we're going to run back out there for a curtain call," I said.

"The crowds love us, after all." Christine squeezed my hand. "Hey, I should have asked before I gave you that kiss. I figured a lot of people need a bit of good vibes injected into their lives right now. Sorry about that."

"Geez, don't be sorry in the slightest. I loved it!"

"I'm proud to be with you, you know," she said.

I opened and closed my mouth a few times, but no sound came out, as if trying to express how proud I was to be with her turned me into a goldfish. "You're, like, the GOAT. Of soccer and of life. I pinch myself every day that I'm with you," I was able to splutter.

"Can you imagine the me you first met doing something like that?" She shook her head and chuckled. "Uptight and terrified of happiness. I guess people can change."

My throat started to tighten up as I watched her walking there beside me, her hand in mine. We had both changed in the years we had known each other. Loving her had made me a better person in countless ways—kinder, more patient, more thoughtful. I understood Christine right down to her essence, and that we were linked by a strong bond that we strengthened every day. But change was the only constant thing in life. Things around us would always change, and we would continue to change and grow.

I grasped her around the shoulders in a tight hug. "I love you," I said.

"I love you too."

I kissed her mouth.

"Ah, jeez, not again!" Dale said, appearing at the change room door.

"You're quiet this morning," Christine said.

"You think so? Not jabbering away a mile a minute like usual?"

"Something like that." She took my hand.

We were walking through the little park outside of Lumen Field following our morning recovery session after the game, on our way to Tip Top Garage to pick up our car.

The owner, Sanjay, was letting us collect it on a Sunday as a special favour to his good friend, Janet.

It was a fine morning, although still a little wet underfoot, with a cool breeze rustling the leaves of the fir trees.

In truth, the night before had got me thinking, which was an exercise I tried to avoid for the most part. I had fallen even more in love with Christine, which was not a new feeling—it happened a lot. But all night, I hadn't been able to shake how she'd been talking about how much she had changed.

I usually took each day as it came and didn't worry about the future. Today, though, I had a restless excitement for how Christine and I would continue to change and grow together.

"I did want to talk to you about something, actually," I said.

"I'm listening, baby."

"You know how wonderful I think you are, and how happy you make me. I hope I get that across and you feel it."

"Wow, this is a serious talk. OK." She stopped walking and pulled on my hand so we were standing face to face. "I feel it, Keels. You make me so happy too."

A note of apprehension started to ding in my head. All my decisions since we had gotten together had been easy. Moving in together—easy. Accepting the offer to come to Seattle—easy. Even though starting a passionate fling with Christine in the middle of the World Cup had been risky, I was so drawn to her that, in hindsight, it had been the natural and easy choice.

The thing I was turning over in my mind would, in a lot of ways, rock the boat.

"We talk about the future kind of, but not really, hey?"

A little crease appeared between her eyebrows, and she was a little slow to answer. "Y-yes."

Right, just spit it out! I didn't want her to think I was breaking up with her. "I know it's hard to plan because any injury could completely turn our careers upside down. Here's the thing I know for sure, though. I want to be with you. Forever. Like, forever and ever."

The creased wiped itself away, and she broke into a smile. "Me too. One thousand per cent. Me too."

"Yesterday with Janet got me thinking."

"Oh, this is a conversation about Janet? That's an unexpected twist."

"Yes. I mean, we were broken-down on the side of the road, stranded, and the only people we had to call were people from our place of employment. Isn't that a bit cooked?"

She pressed her lips together and nodded. "You're right. We've been here for months, and we don't know anybody."

"In Melbourne, we've got Fletch and Viv. They're our found family. And you've got your tai chi ladies too. If we broke down on the side of the road, you would call any of them, right?"

"I would. Except Cynthia. They just took her licence because she's so incredibly old."

"See, you don't have your adopted nannas here."

"I never, ever thought about it. But it's true. I've been missing tai chi, but I like doing it in the park, and it's too rainy here." She nodded.

I raised my eyebrows and nodded along with her. "Exactly. I want to build a life with you, a whole life. In Melbourne, but also when we're away from it too. I'm not in this relationship on a month-by-month basis. I want the whole kit and caboodle. And I'm not sure this city is the place for our future."

The breeze picked up, and the other solitary person in the little park shoved their chin into their coat and walked past us in a hurry.

Christine's gaze lingered on them until they disappeared around a corner. She bit her bottom lip, then looked me in the face. "I'm in. I see it, I want the whole kit and the whole caboodle. We've been talking to Reign about extending our contract, but we haven't signed anything. Where do we go?"

"I have an idea about that. We've got our found family in Melbourne, but we've also got…"

"Lori! Lori in San Diego."

Her eyes shone, and my heart fluttered as I watched her think about living a life with her beloved sister in it. Lori was a flight attendant and lived close to the San Diego airport.

"Let's have our manager put in a call to the San Diego Wave. I hear they've got a good program down there. And I wouldn't be the only Aussie."

"And you know what else they've got in San Diego for *my* Aussie?"

I let out a long sigh. "Sunshine."

"Fucking, proper, melt-the-road, sunshine," she said, running one hand up to the back of my neck.

I got a jolt of anticipation, and sure enough, she did the thing she knew I loved—pulled my face towards hers and slid her tongue into my mouth.

I kissed her hard.

The future was going to be bloody awesome.

For the story of how Keeley and Christine met and got together (with a few bumps in the road in between) read *Onside Play*.

Vacation Vows

by Charley Clarke

It had begun with a simple question less than two months ago.

If you could go anywhere in the world, where would it be?

Taylor hadn't thought anything of it at the time, pillow talk before drifting off to sleep because her wife had a curious mind and liked to ask questions. Mack hadn't brought it up again until presenting her with plane tickets, a travel guide for Italy, and instructions to pick her top ten things to do and attractions to see.

Now Taylor found herself lounging on a pool floatie shaped like an alligator in the backyard of their rental villa outside Rome. Over the past two weeks, they'd done all the touristy things she'd requested, and today was a day to relax. She sipped a cocktail, something fruity that Mack had made for her, and in between pages of her book, she watched her wife do measured laps on the other side of the pool. Her *wife*. She still wasn't used to that. She didn't want to ever get used to it.

They had come such a long way in such a short time. This was the honeymoon they hadn't taken when they got married because last summer, their marriage had been nothing more than a business contract. Mack had needed a spouse in order to take over her family's company, and Taylor had needed help with her student loans and a bit of direction in life.

In the intervening year, they'd added love into the mix. It still made her giddy to think about sometimes. That woman over there *loved her,* and Taylor loved her right back, more than she'd ever thought it was possible to love someone. So, Mack's little sister, Sophie, had agreed to stay with Taylor's parents for a few weeks, allowing them this getaway.

"Babe?" Taylor called out when Mack paused at the edge of the water to catch her breath and check her heartrate.

"Hmm?"

Her curly hair was up in a ponytail, loose strands stuck to her cheeks and neck. A vision in the soft afternoon sunlight. It was enough to take Taylor's breath away.

Smirking, Mack turned to face her. "Earth to Tay?"

"Huh? Oh, yeah..." Taylor licked her lips to work moisture back into her mouth. "When you're finished, can you get me a snack?"

Mack looked pointedly at the small bag of pretzels in the floatie's cupholder.

"Something...not salty?" Taylor tried.

Mack only chuckled and swam over to the ladder. As she hoisted herself out of the pool, the practical rash guard she always wore clung to her body, showing off her sleek physique. But it was the mid-length swim trunks patterned with pink starfish that gave Taylor what she really wanted—a view of the curves of Mack's perfect backside. She bit her bottom lip to hide her grin as she watched her all the way into the villa. So she found her wife devastatingly attractive.

Sue me.

Mack returned a few moments later with fruit in one hand and a bottle of fresh water in the other. She sat at the edge of the pool, slipped her legs into the water, and held out the fruit. "Apple or orange?"

Taylor paddled the float closer. "Orange, please."

"Okay, let me peel it for you, then. You don't have anywhere to put the rind."

As always when Mack's thoughtfulness shone through, Taylor's heart grew three sizes.

"Thank you, babe," she said sweetly. "Will you happen to go back inside to throw the peels into a proper garbage can?"

Mack paused in her peeling to eye her suspiciously. "Why?"

"What can I say?" Taylor dragged her fingers through the crystalline water. "Hate to see you leave, but I *love* to watch you go."

The line pulled both an eye roll and a groan from Mack, which Taylor considered an excellent win. Mack set the half-peeled orange aside on a towel and slid gracefully into the pool. Desire heated Taylor's belly as her wife came closer.

Mack took the novel out of Taylor's hands and, rather uncharacteristically, tossed it onto the pavers where it wouldn't get wet.

Taylor couldn't lie. It sent a little thrill down her spine. Or maybe that was the hungry look in Mack's eyes.

"You...are...mischievous," Mack said, punctuating the words with pecks to Taylor's cheeks and nose.

"That's why you love me," Taylor teased, her voice soft and full of warmth.

"One reason of many," Mack murmured before capturing her lips in a deep kiss.

Taylor sank into it even though the angle was awkward. Mack's touch set her skin on fire, and she wasn't about to complain.

"Mm." She rested her forehead against Mack's. "That's nice to hear."

Mack wound her arms around Taylor's waist, the touch comforting. Taylor liked being held, and more than that, she liked being held by *this* woman.

Until Mack pulled her off the floatie and into the water. Taylor's embarrassingly high-pitched shriek didn't last long as she plunged under.

She came up sputtering and laughing and wiping the hair out of her eyes. "You asshole."

Mack pouted. Her arms were already encompassing Taylor's waist again. "How was I supposed to touch you when you were way up there?"

And, fuck, Taylor would forgive just about anything when those big, brown eyes were looking at her like *that*. Wrapping her arms around Mack's neck, she surged forward. Mack's hot and inviting mouth opened up beneath hers.

Without breaking the kiss, Mack grasped her thighs and lifted her. Taylor locked her ankles behind Mack's back and clung on tighter. When Mack's lips moved to her neck, she moaned. The fire in her belly became an inferno. Even the smell of chlorine in Mack's hair was turning her on.

"How long until we're supposed to call Sophie?" Taylor breathlessly scratched at the baby hairs on the back of Mack's neck.

"We have time."

Good, because if her wife didn't touch her in the next ten seconds, she was going to explode. She squirmed against Mack's belly, too hot and bothered to be embarrassed by the desperate noises she couldn't control.

Steadily, Mack's mouth traveled from the sensitive spot behind her ear down the column of her neck and continued. Taylor's breath hitched.

Mack trailed her fingers over the waistband of Taylor's swim shorts before dipping in the slightest bit. Smiling against Taylor's collarbone, she asked, "May I?"

"If you don't," Taylor panted, "I'll divorce you."

Mack only laughed, and then she dove in.

Taylor closed the dishwasher, dried her hands, and switched off the music playing on her phone. Since Mack had cooked dinner, a delicious eggplant rollatini, Taylor had cleaned up. Mack had wandered off into the backyard, and though they couldn't have been apart longer than twenty minutes, Taylor's heart fluttered at the prospect of spending the rest of the evening together—without time constraints, without true responsibilities. While the adventures Mack had taken them on were unforgettable, there was something special about relaxing in good company, especially since their real lives were hectic.

She slid open the French doors leading to the backyard. The sunlight was fading, but a golden glow still coated the scene. Mack had spread a picnic blanket on the lush grass and covered it with pillows. A bottle of wine, a corkscrew, and two stemless glasses sat on a tray beside the blanket. Beyond that setup, Mack walked back and forth in bare feet, her cell phone pressed to her ear as she talked to someone back home.

Taylor sighed fondly. She was about to sit down and open the wine when Mack ended the call.

Taylor made her way over. "That wasn't work, was it?"

Mack looked up sharply, and then her features relaxed. "Just Danny," she said as she met her halfway.

Taylor narrowed her eyes. She better have been talking to Danny the best friend and not Danny the CFO. "Talking about *work*?" she asked.

"No," Mack said, smiling. She tucked her phone away, reached for Taylor, and wrapped her up. "I promised, didn't I?"

"Yeah, but once a workaholic, always a recovering workaholic, right?" Taylor nuzzled into Mack's neck. "If you really need to, though…"

"I don't. I've been good!"

Taylor pulled back to fix her with a questioning eyebrow.

"I have!"

"Mm."

Mack's chuckle reverberated through her chest. "Come on."

She took Taylor by the hand and led her over to the blanket. They settled down, Taylor lying back on the pillows and Mack resting her head in Taylor's lap. Taylor tangled their hands together, taking comfort in the simple touch. The sky above was slowly darkening into a deep blue, and the crickets were starting to make themselves known. She couldn't think of a single thing that could make the moment more peaceful.

"It's so beautiful here," she murmured.

"Just wait until the stars come out," Mack said.

"If I could live here forever, I think I would."

"Do you want to?"

Taylor chuckled at the earnestness in Mack's voice. "Do *not* buy me an Italian villa, Mackenzie."

"Are you sure?"

Oh, this woman. Taylor threaded her fingers into Mack's hair and ran her thumb over her temple. "I love the life we already have."

"We could have a summer place."

That *would* be nice, but completely unnecessary. Taylor thought back to the trip they'd taken to the Poconos last November. A long weekend full of snow and smiles and each other. Maybe something like that—closer, and that their family could use throughout the year. And what about when they had kids? Traveling internationally with babies sounded like a nightmare.

Her hand in Mack's hair stopped of its own accord. It wasn't the first time she had thought about it. Far from. She hadn't mentioned it to Mack yet. Was this the right moment?

"Doesn't have to be here, though," Mack continued. "Could be anywhere."

Chickening out, she squeezed Mack's hand and said, "Hush for now."

"Okay."

They lapsed into comfortable silence, watching the stars pop out of the sky. Sophie seemed to be having fun at Taylor's parents', which was a relief. She hadn't been sure how that arrangement would go, but Sophie was an unusual twelve-year-old; she was getting a kick out of staying with a couple in their 50s.

"You know," she said, "I didn't expect to miss Sophie this much. I'm glad she's having fun, but..."

"Do you...want to go home early? We could if you really wanted to."

Taylor sighed. It was harder to go three weeks without seeing her friends and family than she'd anticipated. But she was abroad for the first time in her life! With the woman who loved her! She should be treasuring these moments. And she was. Of course she was.

"No, I don't. But maybe Sophie can come with us next time," she mused aloud.

Mack's lips tilted up. "To our *honeymoon*? How many of those are we going to have?"

"No, silly. On our next vacation. We can make it a family thing. Why? Do you *want* another honeymoon?"

"Can't have another honeymoon without another wedding."

There was something in Mack's brown eyes that took Taylor aback. Their wedding had been interesting, to say the least. At the time, she had found Mack odd and gorgeous and confusing. The whole affair had been overwhelming, and they definitely got married for the wrong reasons. Should they do it again, but right this time? Would Mack even want that? She preferred private displays of affection over showy occasions. That was part of why their ceremony had been small in the first place.

And even though Taylor *knew* she loved Mack, and knew Mack loved *her*, this was unfamiliar and scary territory again. The past nine months had been lovely, but they hadn't prioritized talking about the future. They were content to simply be together.

Taylor decided to skirt the issue. "You're not planning on exchanging me for a better model, are you, Mrs. Watson?"

"A better model doesn't exist."

"Smooth talker."

"Only with you," Mack admitted.

"What are you really asking, Mack?" Taylor said softly. Their brains worked differently, so sometimes directness was the best route.

Mack shifted a little to better look at her. "We weren't in love when we got married. And not everyone knew what was going on."

Taylor took a deep, calming breath. On their wedding day, only a handful of people had known the reason behind their marriage was to help Mack secure her family's company and to help Taylor pay off her mountain of student debt. And after they fell in love, they'd had to come clean with the most important people in their lives. *That* had been a fun conversation with her mom. Even the memory of it made her wince. At least they'd had the sense to tell her parents when Sophie wasn't around. Spare her the drama.

Mack pulled her attention back with a squeeze of her hand. "Lots of little girls have an idea of their dream wedding. You didn't get a chance to live out those dreams. Is that...Is that something you'd want? A do-over?"

Taylor had never even thought about it. In a way, their ceremony had been right on brand for their unconventional relationship. "I don't think there's anything to do over," she said. "A wedding's just a day. I think marriage is more about what we build together, and we're doing a pretty solid job."

Mack hummed lightly. Taylor studied her face even as Mack avoided her gaze. They were still learning about each other, but she knew what that noise meant.

She cupped Mack's cheek and ran her thumb over her skin, a gentle plea to look at her. "Babe, whatever it is, you can tell me."

Mack finally turned her head to meet Taylor's gaze. "Our anniversary is in two days, you know?"

"Are you worried I forgot?" Taylor teased, thinking of the first-edition Agatha Christie that Shane had helped her track down and that was currently tucked away into a closet upstairs. The first anniversary was paper, and Mack loved a good mystery novel.

"No! I know you didn't forget."

Taylor was starting to put the pieces together, but she stayed quiet, waiting for her wife to say it in her own time. She just kept brushing her thumb over Mack's perfect cheekbone.

"I never dreamed of a big wedding. I never really dreamed of a wedding at all." Mack played with Taylor's fingers, twisting her wedding ring to and fro. "But ever since things changed between us, I can't help but feel like how we got married doesn't really reflect us."

"Well," Taylor said wryly, "our timing's always been a little off."

Mack frowned at the reminder of their first interactions, of how long it had taken to get their shit together.

Taylor smoothed the crease in her forehead and said, "I'm just saying. It fit us at the time, I think."

"Right. So, shouldn't we have something that fits us now?"

"You want to have another wedding?"

"Not necessarily. I don't think either of us needs something huge." Mack, animated now, sat up. "But I would like to renew our vows. I want you to know that I mean them now and that I always will. And I think…I think our anniversary would be a good day to do that."

Taylor's heart melted, and she couldn't keep the grin off her face. She pressed her lips to her wife's, a quick but reassuring kiss. "I know you mean them, Mack, and you know I mean them too." Another kiss, this one longer. Butterflies fluttered in Taylor's stomach. "But yes. Yes, that sounds perfect."

"Yeah?" Mack said through a laugh. "You'll marry me again?"

"I'd marry you every day if that's what you wanted."

Mack kissed her again, deep and insistent. Before Taylor realized it, she was on her back again, Mack's comforting weight atop her.

"I don't think we should do it on our anniversary, though," she said through a blissed-out giggle.

Mack pulled her lips from Taylor's neck. "Why not?"

Breathing hard, Taylor sank her fingers into Mack's luscious hair. "Because that's two days from now, and we should have our family there."

Mack studied her. Taylor could tell she really wanted to renew their vows on their anniversary, for the symmetry, but they'd built a life together over the past year, and their loved ones should bear witness to that progress. That was more important than anything.

"When we get the family together, then?" Mack finally asked.

"Yeah. When we get the family together." It could wait a few weeks.

Taylor kissed her again, and for a while, there was no more talking at all.

"Mm, where you going?" Taylor groaned.

Even without opening her eyes, she could tell it wasn't fully morning yet. And if it was still this early, why on Earth was Mack awake and rustling around?

"Going for a run," Mack said quietly.

Taylor shifted the pillow beneath her head. "'S' too early."

Mack chuckled, the bed dipping as she sat beside Taylor. She tucked some hair behind her ear and kissed her temple. "I'll be back before you know it. Go back to sleep, love."

Taylor groaned again and leaned into the touch. "Try to remember it's vacation, babe, okay? Wake me up when you get back, and I'll make you breakfast."

"Sounds fantastic," Mack said with a quick kiss to her lips.

Taylor snuggled back into her pillow and was almost asleep again when Mack closed the door softly behind her.

The next time she woke up, the sun streamed brightly through the cracked curtains. She stretched, enjoying the pleasant soreness in her muscles. As much as she missed home and their family, she could certainly get used to long nights and lazy mornings. But where was Mack? A glance at the time on her phone told Taylor she should be back from her run by now.

Pushing her hair out of her face, she stumbled into the en suite bathroom for her morning routine. When she was done, she threw on a short satin robe embroidered with *Mrs. Watson* and left it untied. A gift from Mack. Well, if Mack had already made breakfast, Taylor would have to find another way to take care of her. Maybe a nice shower together. Besides the fun to be had, Mack had a weakness for Taylor washing her hair.

She crossed the room, but as soon as she opened the bedroom door, she froze. Voices wafted up from downstairs, and it definitely wasn't just the TV or a podcast. They had *company*. A whole group! On their *honeymoon*.

Why? And *who* had tracked them down in Italy?

Oh, if it was anyone from work, Taylor was going to have words with her wife.

She sighed. No wonder Mack had insisted she put on pajamas before falling asleep last night. Which meant Mack had expected the company. That rascal.

Hands on the banister, she listened closer.

Wait. She recognized that voice. And that one. All of them, actually.

Grinning in disbelief, she hurried back into the bedroom, threw on actual clothes, including a bra, and rushed downstairs to meet her family. She was barely into the living room when Sophie sprang up from the couch and launched herself into Taylor's arms, squealing all the while.

Taylor squeezed her twelve-year-old sister-in-law back. "Hey, kiddo! I missed you!"

"You better have," Sophie said as she hopped down. "I missed you too."

"Hopefully she didn't miss us *too* much," Emily said, getting up from the couch where she was sitting with Shane and Jade. "I think she and Mack had some better things to do."

Taylor's face heated, and she swatted Emily's shoulder before pulling her friend into a hug.

"What?" Emily asked innocently. "I'm talking about all the historical sites you've gone to."

"Right," Taylor said. "But seriously! What are you doing here? What are all of you doing here? This is crazy!"

The living room was full. Her stepsister, Poppy; Poppy's husband, Jeff; and their three-year-old, Leo. Danny was here too, looking fondly amused at the ruckus. Taylor hugged everyone, even Danny, and some of them twice.

"Guess you like the surprise," Danny said wryly.

"Mack flew us all out," Shane said.

"What, and she set this all up last night?" Taylor asked, bewildered.

"Nope!" Sophie beamed. "This was the plan from the start. Two weeks alone and then a week with us!"

Jade squeezed Taylor's hand. "Mack thought you'd enjoy a true family vacation."

Taylor shook her head in disbelief. No wonder Mack had wanted to rent such a huge property. She looked at Poppy. "Mom and Dad?"

"Kitchen!" Poppy answered brightly. "Mack's making everyone pancakes!"

She found Mack standing over the stove, doing just as Poppy had said and chatting with Taylor's mom and stepdad, who sat at the counter on high stools, drinking coffee and munching on fresh fruit.

"Darling!" Abby said when she walked in. "Come here, come here!"

Taylor hugged both of them. Over her mom's shoulder, she saw Mack looking at her with a loving smile. Tears burned her eyes. She really was so lucky. So *happy*. "I can't believe you're all here," she said as she pulled away and wiped her eyes.

"Neither can we!" Abby said.

"I'll admit—it was a little hard to keep it a secret this long," Henry said.

"How long?"

"Oh, I don't think Mack booked anything until she knew we could all make this week work." He turned to her. "Isn't that right?"

Mack nodded.

Weeks, then. Likely months.

Taylor was still marveling at her wife's thoughtfulness and at how well this had worked out when Abby squeezed her bicep and said, "We'll give you two a minute."

She and Henry took their coffee into the living room, leaving them alone.

Mack turned back to the stove, scooped four pancakes off the griddle, set them on top of the stack, and poured batter for the next. Taylor sidled up behind her, resting her hands on her hips, gripping firmly, trying to control herself from sliding them up her abs to her breasts; their entire family was twenty feet away.

"Do you have something to say?" she murmured into Mack's ear.

Mack smirked. "I told you I wasn't talking to Danny about work last night."

"You're sneaky."

"Henry was right, though. It *was* really hard to keep it a secret. I don't like lying."

"I know you don't." Chuckling, Taylor kissed her cheek and nuzzled into her. "Wasn't really lying, though. Just keeping a surprise under wraps. A surprise that's made your wife very happy."

"Yeah?" Mack asked quietly.

"Yeah," Taylor murmured back, happy to give however much reassurance Mack needed. She slipped her palm under Mack's shirt and pressed it against her stomach, basking in the warmth of the touch. "How did you know?"

Mack hummed.

"How did you know I'd actually *want* my mom and everyone to join us on our honeymoon, hmm?"

Mack flipped the pancakes before twisting in Taylor's embrace.

Mack hummed. "You mentioned once or twice that you had good memories of your family vacations, so I thought, why not try it out with our big, crazy one?"

Once or twice. Because Mack listened and loved her, and it made Taylor feel incredible. She wanted to give all that positive energy right back to her.

"And I thought they'd like spending a week at an Italian villa," Mack continued.

Taylor swallowed the lump in her throat and brushed a stray curl behind Mack's ear. "I'm sure they will. You will too, right? It's a lot of people under one roof for a whole week."

Mack shrugged. "It's a big house, though. I'll manage."

She turned back to the pancakes, and Taylor reluctantly loosened her embrace.

"I guess I should go and make sure everyone's settled. Unless you need help with breakfast?"

"No, I've got it. Tell them it'll be ready in about ten minutes."

"Great. Thanks, babe."

Breakfast was a chaotic affair. Afterward, Mack wiped her hands with a napkin, pulled something from her pocket, and dropped to one knee.

The conversation around the table came to a halt.

Grinning, she popped the little clear capsule open, dumped the contents into her palm, and held it out for Taylor. The object in her hand was a silly plastic ring from a gumball machine, what she'd joked about proposing with the first time.

Taylor's laugh abruptly turned into a sob as her heart skipped a beat. Oh God, she was so far gone for this woman, and they were already married.

Mack took her hand and rubbed her thumb along the back of it. "Don't cry," she said quietly.

"I don't know why I'm crying," Taylor said from behind her palm, "but it's a good cry. Promise."

"Okay."

Mack's expression was soft. She looked up at Taylor as though she could drink in the sight forever and never be satisfied, which only made Taylor cry more. She was being so *silly*.

When Mack asked a silent question, furrowing her brow and twisting her lips, Taylor nodded for her to continue.

"Taylor," Mack said after a deep breath, "when we got married last year, I believe we had good intentions but the wrong ones."

Taylor let out a wet chuckle, and someone—probably Danny—snorted at that.

"But over the last fifteen months, we've gone from almost strangers to allies to friends, and now we're here. You're the love of my life, Taylor, and I want to make sure you know it and everyone else who loves you knows it, and that's why I'm asking you to renew our vows in front of our whole family. Will you do that with me?"

Nodding, Taylor wiped the tears from her eyes. "Yes, of course. I love you so much. Of course I will."

Amid the claps and whoops, Mack slid the plastic ring onto Taylor's finger. When she got to her feet, Taylor wrapped her in a tight hug and tucked her head against her shoulder.

"I have to say," she said quietly, "as sweet as the last one was, I prefer this proposal."

Amid the cheering, Mack just pressed a soft kiss to her lips.

Even though it was summer, the night was cool and they had a fire going in the living room hearth—"for atmosphere," Jade insisted—as they relaxed with coffee or wine after a full day of running around the countryside.

"So," Taylor said, interrupting the low chattering, "since you were all in on this little secret, should I assume there's a plan for tomorrow?"

Glass of whiskey in hand, Danny chortled. "Taylor, it's *Mackenzie*. She always has a plan."

Unable to argue with that, Taylor snuggled closer into her wife's side.

"We've taken care of everything," Emily said. "Shane will act as officiant."

"Except it's not official—didn't need to get ordained or anything—so I'll be more of an emcee to guide the ceremony," Shane interjected from beside his fiancée.

"Right," Emily continued. "We brought clothes for you and Mack, and your mom offered to cook chicken with mac and cheese as our celebration meal."

Taylor gasped. "My favorite!"

Abby rolled her eyes fondly. "As though my daughter-in-law would ask for anything but your favorite. And Jade's making devil's chocolate cake."

Taylor pressed a quick kiss to Mack's flushed cheek.

"You don't have to worry about a thing," Jade assured her.

Mack tipped her head from side to side. "Well..."

"What?" Taylor asked. "What does that mean?"

Mack cleared her throat and said, "Everything's taken care of but the vows."

Oh. Taylor let out a breath. That didn't seem too hard. Their first go-round had involved only the standard marriage agreement—until death do them part and all that, and of course, it had all been lip service. The intention to get divorced in a year's time had put a bit of a stain on their promises to one another.

"I want to write mine," Mack continued, "but you shouldn't feel obligated to."

Taylor looked into Mack's deep-brown eyes. Her wife would never force her to do anything she didn't want to. Taylor wasn't the best at saying how she felt. She preferred to show affection physically, through touches and kisses and hugs. But this ceremony was going to be special, and they would be in front of the people who mattered. So, yes, Taylor wanted to give that to her.

"I want to," she said.

Smiling brightly, Mack squeezed her hand and pressed a kiss to her temple.

Taylor melted into the touch and wondered how she could ever put words to the warmth that bloomed within her chest when Mack looked at her.

It turned out that writing vows, even for the person you loved with your whole heart, was actually difficult. While Sophie, Jade, and Danny swam in the pool and everyone else watched a movie or lounged inside, she had settled on a chaise lounge on the patio with a notebook and pen. Not that she had anything to show for it after twenty minutes. Her love was so big, and extra sweet for having been so unexpected, that she didn't know where to start when trying to put it into words.

She looked over the lines she had written, corny and trite, and scratched them out. Sighing, she ran a hand through her loose hair. Mack wanted this to be special, and no matter how inelegant she was with words, Taylor wasn't going to screw that up with lackluster vows.

"Hi, sweetheart."

She looked up to find her mom approaching with two glasses of wine.

Abby held one out as she settled into the adjacent chaise. "Thought you might need some help."

"You can say that again," Taylor said with a snort. She downed half the glass of wine in two swallows.

Abby raised her eyebrows. "Taylor?"

Sheepish, Taylor set the glass down on a side table. She wiggled in her chair to find a more comfortable position and avoid her mom's knowing gaze.

"Wanna tell me what's going on up here?" Abby asked, tapping Taylor's forehead.

"Nothing. Writing vows is stupid hard. It's like there's actually nothing in my brain right now."

Abby regarded her closely for a few seconds. "I know you're not getting cold feet, so what is it? What's stopping you?"

Taylor let out a long breath, closed her eyes, and rested the back of her head against the chaise. "It's just... She's probably going to have amazing vows, and I... I just love her so much, and I'm going to sound so stupid trying to tell her."

"Your vows don't have to be perfect, sweetheart. In fact, I guarantee they won't be."

"But I want them to be. She deserves perfect."

"You're putting a lot of pressure on yourself for something that's supposed to be celebratory."

Biting her lip, Taylor didn't answer. She didn't need her mom to tell her that, but she also didn't know how to *stop* pressuring herself.

"You know, when you first told us you had faked your relationship..."

Taylor sucked in a sharp breath and tried to hide her wince.

"I couldn't really wrap my head around it because it was so obvious you loved each other," Abby continued. "And after you explained it, I expected to be angry that you'd lied—"

"I'm sorry," Taylor said for what had to be the millionth time.

Abby waved her concern away. "I know why you did it. But what I'm saying, Taylor, is we had watched your love grow for months by that point. You don't have to prove it to anyone—not to your wife and especially not to yourself."

"Mom..."

"The words don't matter so much," Abby said, squeezing Taylor's knee, "it's what's underneath that she cares about. And no matter what words come out of your mouth tomorrow afternoon, she's going to be happy because you're *showing* her how much you love her." She stood up, kissed her on the temple, and said, "You've got this. I believe in you." And then she was gone with a wave, taking her wineglass with her.

Taylor tapped her pen against the empty page. Now her chest felt loose enough to breathe more freely. Maybe her mom was right—that the words didn't matter as much as the underlying intention. Falling in love with her fake wife hadn't been part of the plan last year. She hadn't needed to follow a script for that, so why would she need one now?

She was making this so much harder than it needed to be. She closed the notebook, drank the rest of her wine, and walked back inside, leaving the empty notebook on the chaise. She was going to do things her way because Mack loved her exactly the way she was.

Taylor closed her eyes to soak up the afternoon sunlight that came through the window. Today was shaping up to be much less stressful than their original wedding day. Emily and Shane had cooked everyone breakfast, a group had gone to the store to fetch groceries for dinner, and now her friends were helping her put on the jewelry to go with her simple, lightweight dress. They had brought her two options, one floral and one solid white. She opted for white this time.

Jade clasped a gold necklace around Taylor's neck and squeezed her shoulders as they looked into the mirror. "You're stunning."

Putting the last bobby pins into Taylor's hair, Emily let out a whistle. "Do we think Mack's going to cry? I think she's going to cry."

Taylor blushed. "She's seen me dressed up before."

"And she gets emotional every time because that woman is head over heels for you," Emily said with a fond smile.

Taylor looked down at her sandals, suddenly shy. "It's good I'm head over heels right back, then."

Jade clapped excitedly. "Ooh, this is the best day! It's all of the excitement of love but none of the stress of the wedding!"

Beaming, Taylor pulled them both into a tight hug. "We couldn't have made it this far without you two. I love you."

Emily squeezed back. "Yeah, without us, it would've taken you ages to get your heads out of your asses and confess your love."

"Gee, thanks."

"You got it together much faster than we expected you to, though," Jade added.

A knock at the bedroom door cut off their embrace—and Taylor's exasperated laughter.

"Come in," she called.

Instead of Mack, Sophie opened the door. At twelve years old and still sprouting, she was eye level with Taylor now. The beige linen shorts and vest over a white shirt emphasized her gangly frame. Jade took Emily's hand and led her out into the hall, closing the door behind them to give Taylor and her adorable sister-in-law privacy.

"Sophie," Taylor said cheerfully, holding her arms out.

Sophie immediately stepped into them. "You look beautiful," she said.

"Thank you." Taylor tugged at Sophie's vest. "You look very smart."

Sophie preened. "Thanks! I've been told I clean up well."

"Yes, because your life as a middle-schooler is so hard," Taylor teased, "especially during summer vacation."

Sophie rolled her eyes. "So funny. I have something for you."

"Soph... That's sweet, but—"

"No arguing." She retrieved something from her pocket and held it out in both hands. A watch. A lovely one.

Gingerly, Taylor accepted it. Mostly silver with some gold in the middle, it was more elegant and expensive than any watch she had ever owned. It matched the one Mack wore that once belonged to her father.

"It's beautiful," she breathed.

"Look at the back."

Taylor turned it over. Etched into the metal were the words: *Every day, every second, I choose us.*

Tears burned her eyes, and she had to swallow the sudden lump in her throat. She didn't know for sure, but she had an inkling of the watch's provenance.

"My dad gave it to my mom on one of their anniversaries," Sophie said, wistful. "I asked Mack, and she agreed that you should have it."

Taylor's heart was so unbelievably full; she couldn't push the words out. She put a hand over her heart and the other on Sophie's shoulder. Finally, she sniffled and cleared her throat. "Sophie, are you sure?"

"Yeah," Sophie said with a soft smile. "She would have wanted you to have it, I think. She would have loved you. They both would have."

"You think?"

"Yeah." Sophie nodded vigorously. "You gave my sister a safe place to be herself."

Taylor couldn't hold back the tears any longer.

"Oh, no, don't mess up your mascara," Sophie said.

"It's fine, it's fine." Taylor took the tissue Sophie offered and dabbed at her eyes.

Mack didn't talk about her parents all that often, but Taylor was grateful for the details she did get, usually when it was late at night and quiet, when Mack was sleepy or had had an extra glass of scotch. She'd gathered that Mack took more after their dad and Sophie more after their mom. As much as she would have liked to have met them, to have been able to tell them they raised wonderful daughters, she was at least glad to hear memories of them.

She pulled Sophie into a tight hug. "I'm sure I would have loved them, too."

Mack was waiting for her when Taylor, accompanied by Sophie, came down the steps.

Sophie grinned at her sister before skirting around and joining everyone else in the backyard.

Taylor dropped down the last stair and took in her wife. Similar to Sophie, Mack wore a white button-down with the sleeves rolled up under a beige linen vest and matching pants. No tie or jacket, which made her looked relaxed. What made her look even more relaxed was the easy smile on her face.

"You look radiant," Taylor said, resting her hands on her wife's shoulders and pressing their foreheads together.

"Radiant?" Mack murmured. "That's a new one."

"It's true."

"I like it." She nuzzled Taylor's nose. "You take my breath away."

Taylor shuddered. Mack's hands were warm on her waist, her lips so tantalizingly close. She breathed in her spicy, comforting scent.

Mack pressed soft lips to her forehead. "Ready when you are, darling."

This time around, Taylor carried no flowers. Instead, she took her wife's arm, and they floated down the makeshift aisle together as an instrumental version of "A Thousand Years" wafted out of a portable speaker. Patio chairs flanked the aisle, and even though the walk was short and the guests were few compared to last summer, she was grateful for each person here. Her family was all she needed. At the end of the aisle, just in front of the small gazebo, Shane waited for them with a wide grin.

As they reached him, they turned to each other and clasped their hands.

"All right?" Mack whispered. She was glowing in the afternoon sunshine.

Nodding, Taylor murmured back, "Perfect."

Mack gave Shane a little nod to begin.

"Welcome!" Shane said to their small gathering. "We're here because Mack is one of the most generous people on the planet and let us all crash her and Taylor's honeymoon."

Taylor squeezed Mack's hand as everyone chuckled.

"But we're here mostly because Mack and Taylor wanted to acknowledge the love that has blossomed between them over the past year, and they wanted to do so in front of their beloved family. First, though, I'd like to ask anyone who would like to share a few words with the couple to come up here now and do so."

Jade was first, reciting a poem by Rumi, and it went on like that. To Taylor's surprise, every single person had something to say, whether it was a poem, a quote, song lyrics, or a bit of advice. Even three-year-old Leo giggled happily from his dad's shoulders as Jeff and Poppy read a passage from *Captain Corelli's Mandolin*. It warmed her heart, and by the time Sophie had sung "I Choose You," Taylor was holding back tears, but the way Mack rubbed her thumbs over the back of her hands soothed her.

"Thank you, everyone," Shane said. "And now, the reason we're here. Mack and Taylor will reaffirm their union with the vows they wrote. Mack?"

Mack took a deep breath and let go of Taylor's hands so she could pull a folded piece of paper from her pocket. She looked into Taylor's eyes and smiled.

"Taylor," Mack said, "before you came into my life, I was walking around in the dark without even realizing it. I put everything in my life into boxes because it was easier that way. I kept my heart locked up and pretended that was okay, pretended that was how I wanted to live, pretended it didn't hurt. Then you came into my world. Everyone here knows we got off on the wrong foot—twice, somehow."

Taylor shook her head while everyone chuckled.

Mack squeezed her hand and continued, "You brought light into my life without even trying to, and all of a sudden, the only thing I knew was that I didn't ever want to go back to what it was like before you. For a long time, I didn't think I deserved a love like this."

Taylor bit her lip to keep the tears from spilling. Mack deserved the world and all the goodness it could possibly offer.

"But you helped me realize that I do," Mack said. "I fell in love with your spirit, your goodness, your intelligence, your humor, your joy. I can only hope I've enriched your world as much as you have mine. I am honored to be the person who gets to witness you bloom and grow with each passing day, the person you come home to every night, the person you can lean on for support and love. I want to spend the rest of our lives helping you shine as brightly as you help me. I love you, and I will keep loving you until the end of time."

She marked the end of her speech by kissing the backs of Taylor's hands.

Taylor couldn't hold back the tears anymore, letting them slip down as she stroked Mack's cheek.

Shane raised a hand toward her. "And Taylor?"

She took a deep breath. Everyone was looking at her expectantly, but the only gaze she cared about was the brown one right in front of her.

"Mackenzie," she said through a calming exhalation. "I didn't write anything down, and somehow I think that doesn't surprise you."

Mack's chuckle was affectionate.

"I tried, but it's almost impossible for me to put into words how much you mean to me, how much our family means. Part of nurturing this relationship was learning how to communicate with each other, and since I've learned how much you value directness, here are my promises to you."

As Taylor sniffled, Mack dug a tissue from her pocket and helped dry the tears.

"Thank you, baby," Taylor whispered.

Mack pressed a gentle kiss to her forehead, warm and calming.

Taylor took another breath, squeezed Mack's hand, and continued, "I promise to take the foundation we built over the last fifteen months and continue to create something wonderful. I promise to listen to you, to be a shoulder for you to lean on, to be your partner in life and in love. I promise to be patient when we disagree, to give you warmth when you're cold, to be your peace when you're tired. But, most of all, I promise to wake up every morning and love you more than the day before. I love you so much, Mack."

Mack's grin widened, if that was even possible.

Taylor matched it because her heart felt so full, and the joy needed to spill out somehow. Yes, they were legally married already, but Mack had been right. The simple act of standing in front of their loved ones and proclaiming their devotion to each other was nothing short of magical.

"Ladies," Shane said, "you've reaffirmed your love before the most important people in your life. You may now seal those promises with a kiss."

Taylor threw her arms around Mack's neck and pulled her down for a searing kiss.

Mack enthusiastically obliged.

For a small party, it was a lively one. Music and laughter drifted up into the sky as they all danced on the soft grass after dinner. Taylor—warm on happiness and, she would admit, comfortably wine drunk—twirled Sophie as the others danced around them. Then Mack tapped on her sister's shoulder and politely asked to cut in. Sophie grabbed Danny as her next partner, and Taylor was all too happy to sidle into her wife's arms.

As it neared dark, Henry lit up the fire pit. At first, only he and Abby sat there, fondly watching their children and their friends. Jade's playlist got mellower, and the rest wandered off the grassy dance floor to join them.

When Taylor got close to the love seat Mack had chosen, Mack stretched out an arm to beckon her over. Taylor curled into her side and pressed a kiss on her cheek, enjoying the flush that rose to Mack's face. Mack ran her thumb over the wristband of Taylor's new watch, her mom's watch.

"As lovely as your first wedding was," Henry said, "I have to say, this was very special. Thank you for letting us be a part of it."

"And for bringing us on vacation!" Shane chimed in.

Poppy clapped brightly. "Yes, I'm *so* excited! This is a dream!"

"I'm glad you're enjoying yourselves," Mack said. "And you're welcome, of course. Thank you—thank you all—for being here. Experiences don't mean much without people to share them with."

Taylor squeezed Mack's thigh. "I don't think we'd be here without you. It's because of this family that Mack and I have come so far, so thank you, and thank you for helping us celebrate."

"I'll cheer to that." Emily raised her glass of wine. Once everyone had followed suit, even Sophie with her sparkling juice, she said, "To family!"

"To family!"

"And to love," Taylor added, feeling warm and content.

"To love!"

"You're still out here," Mack said as she walked into the quiet yard.

"Mm, it's a gorgeous night." Taylor was lounging on a chaise, gazing up at the curtain of stars. "Come here."

Mack slid onto the chaise beside her, and Taylor resettled onto her wife's chest, shivering as Mack scratched lightly at the back of her neck.

"Good day?" Mack asked.

Chuckling, Taylor pressed a kiss to her jaw. "The best, babe."

"It was okay I invited our family to crash our honeymoon?"

"It was a nice surprise! And I did say I wanted the family there if we renewed our vows."

"You did."

"Today was perfect."

"It was, wasn't it?"

Taylor answered with a soft, reassuring kiss, grateful for Mack's thoughtfulness. They lay there in comfortable silence watching the stars. Even with the night air cooling, Mack's arms warmed her. She could stay like this forever.

After a few minutes, though, she couldn't hold it in any longer. She'd been thinking about it almost constantly for the past two days. She had to at least start the conversation. "Mack?"

"Hmm?"

Taylor sat up to look into her wife's eyes. "I'm going to say something that you're going to need some time to think about, okay?"

Mack licked her lips, uncertain.

"It's nothing bad. It's just a big decision, and we're going to need a lot of time to think about and discuss it, okay?"

Mack nodded hesitantly.

Taylor pushed a stray curl behind her ear and cupped her face. "I know we did a lot of things in the wrong order, and we probably should have talked about this a while ago, but..." She let herself breathe, let herself find calm in the moment. "What do you think about...expanding our family?"

Mack blinked slowly.

The cogs were turning, but Taylor could tell she didn't want to say the wrong thing. Not that she could say anything wrong. Whatever they decided, they were in it together.

"What are you saying?" Mack asked.

Taylor slid her hand to the back of Mack's neck, playing with the baby hairs there. "I'm saying...I want to have a baby, *your* baby."

Mack raised her eyebrows and gaped like a fish.

Taylor put a solid hand on her chest. "Not tomorrow, you know."

"Well, no, that's biologically impossible," Mack said, almost to herself. "Babies need nine months to gestate."

Taylor could only hum with amusement. She loved watching Mack think both quietly and aloud. "You don't need to say anything now, and we don't even have to decide for a few years."

"Okay."

"Okay."

Mack's brow furrowed. "But I think there are factors we should consider."

"Of course. Anything in particular on your mind?"

"Sophie's still young. I think she should have more time to be a kid on her own, not a twelve-year-old aunt with a baby in the house."

"Agreed."

Mack's brow furrowed. "Just like that?"

"It's a good point," Taylor said with a shrug, "and this isn't something to rush. We're making the decision as a team. Any other thoughts for tonight? Or we can table it for a while."

"I..." Mack licked her lips again, then fell quiet. Her gaze lost focus, and she rubbed her thumbs idly over Taylor's hips.

"Just you and me, babe," Taylor said in a voice as soft and as soothing as the starry sky. "You can tell me anything."

When Mack looked back up, her eyes were glassy. Her grip tightened a fraction. "You'll be wonderful, I know, but do you really think I'll be an okay mom? That's a lot of faith to put in me."

"I have all the faith in you. You're already an incredible sister, and I know you're going to be an incredible mom. And we have lots of time to prepare." When Taylor kissed her, it was a tender promise, and she knew Mack felt all the emotions she couldn't put words to.

Mack's arms squeezed her waist, and she smiled beneath Taylor's lips. "Thank you," she whispered.

And Taylor understood. It was a thank-you for believing in her, for helping her believe in herself, and for the life they were building together.

"You're so welcome, my love." She got to her feet and pulled Mack up, too. "Now come on. I have a present for you."

This is what happened after the epilogue. Read *The Business of Love* to discover how their love story began.

Buckaroo

by Cheyenne Blue

The sun had just risen when Hayley pulled the week's dinner suggestion sheet from the kitchen door at Ghost Gum Station. She scanned it. As usual, Jools's mum's lasagne was there—did the station hands never get fed up with that?—but the suggestion with the most votes came from one of the backpackers who'd requested a Sicilian pasta dish.

Easy as! But wait until the hands found out—after they'd devoured it—that the dish contained anchovies!

Hayley grinned in not-so-fond memory of when she'd first arrived at Ghost Gum, nearly two years ago. Then, the diet of meat, potatoes, and frozen vegetables had been filling, if a little dull. But now that she was the station cook, things had changed up, and the weekly suggestion sheet was one of the most popular changes.

She continued into the kitchen to start breakfast. She was mixing pancake batter when the thud of feet made her turn around. "Hi, Gill. Coffee's on."

"Thanks, Hayley." The station owner ambled over and peered at the batter. "Are you going to add blueberries? Pretty please?"

"Sure, seeing as you begged so sweetly."

"I didn't just come to grab coffee and influence breakfast." Gill settled on a stool at the counter. "I've got a favour to ask you. Well, you and Jenna, but it's mainly about you."

"Oh?" Hayley raised an eyebrow. "Am I going to like this?"

"I hope so. Although it would mean some flexibility. You and Jenna are on holiday in a couple of weeks."

"Yeah!" Hayley grinned. "A week in a tropical paradise. Blue ocean, white sand, palm trees, and a cabin by the water."

"Your first holiday since you returned to us from New York." Gill nodded. "Hayley, you can say no to this. My sister Wendy and her partner Glen have a station over in the Northern Territory: Bilby Downs. It's about one hundred and ten kilometres east of Alice Springs."

Hayley nodded. "Yeah, you've mentioned it."

"Every year, they hold the Bilby Cup, a cross-country horse race on the station. It's hugely competitive and has a first prize of five thousand dollars."

"Didn't Wes compete last year?"

"He came fourth, which was pretty impressive, given the competition." Gill drained her coffee. "Thing is, Wendy's cook has broken her leg, and they don't have anyone capable of serving great food over the duration of the Cup. We're talking sixty hands, plus thirty or forty of Wendy and Glen's friends, and investors in the station who fly in especially. Fine dining is part of their experience. There's an assistant cook who's good but inexperienced and is struggling to cope. Wendy's heard about you. She begged to borrow you for Cup Week."

Hayley's stomach sank. Going by Gill's face, she could guess when that was. "It's the week of our holiday, isn't it?"

"It is, yeah." Gill patted the stool next to her, and Hayley slid onto it. "Which is why you can say no. You could refuse even if it wasn't."

"Gill, we've got flights and accommodation booked."

"Wendy pays well. I won't lie; it's a totally full-on job for a week, but she'll pay you the senior cook rate and double-time once you get over forty hours for the week." She grimaced. "Which will probably be sometime on the third day. She'll also pay your travelling time and fuel costs."

"If this is instead of a holiday, I won't do it. Jenna and I have been looking forward to a break—"

"You won't miss out! Wendy suggested you drive over, towing the horse float. We've got one of her mares here, and she needs to go back. You can have three weeks for the trip—it's a three-day drive each way with the float, and you'll need a few days before the Cup to settle into the kitchen and do some preparation. We'll pay for your flights and accommodation to be changed—and give you and Jenna an extra paid week of holiday when you've finished."

Hayley sucked her lower lip. "Who's going to cook here while I'm gone?"

"Don't worry—it won't be me. When I covered your weekend away, Red offered to cook instead. He's never cooked more than a toasted sandwich in his life but swore he couldn't do any worse than me! But the last time I talked with Slugger, he was muttering about being too young to retire. I think I could probably tempt him back for the weeks you're away." She side-eyed Hayley. "No longer than that, though. We'd miss you and your cooking too much."

Hayley's fingers twitched. A chance to stretch her cooking skills—fine dining for thirty people. Was she up for that challenge? *Hell yeah.* Maybe, too, she'd earn enough to pay for that second week's beach cabin with Jenna.

"Think on it, and talk with Jenna. But there's a sweetener for her, too. As you'd be taking the horse float, she could take Bucky and enter the Bilby Cup. Bucky's such a fast horse, she'd be in with a chance." Gill slid from the stool. "Now, I've distracted you from the brekkie prep. Want me to do anything to help?"

"No!" Hayley swatted at Gill's hand with the whisk. "Get out of my kitchen before you touch something and wreck brekkie!"

Laughing, Gill left.

Hayley went back to the pancakes. Her hands mixed and flipped on autopilot while her mind was far away. About eight hundred kilometres away on an unfamiliar station in the Northern Territory. Somewhere she'd never been, despite it being close to Ghost Gum—as close as anywhere was in the Australian outback. The Territory, where the dirt was redder, the ghost gums whiter, the landscape more dramatic in the East MacDonnell Ranges.

And a road trip with Jenna, her love. Three days' slow drive. They'd camp along the way. A frisson of excitement tickled her skin. Why, that would be a holiday in itself. Until they arrived and she had to cook for one hundred people. Well, she already cooked for thirty at Ghost Gum. And her years in a New York diner had given her the skills to cook for more.

By the time she banged the old saucepan with the ladle to summon the hands for breakfast, Hayley had reached a decision: If Jenna would come, she'd do it.

Jenna looked up as Hayley slid onto the bench next to her with a plate loaded with scrambled eggs, toast, and, because this was Hayley and she ate a lot of plants, a couple of grilled tomatoes and some mushrooms.

"Hey." She took in Hayley: compact muscled body, her vivacious face with the floppy brown hair that hung over her eyes—longer now than when she'd first arrived from New York. Even wearing an old T-shirt with a cooking-oil stain on the front, she was gorgeous.

And she loves me. The thought still had the power to make Jenna melt.

"Great brekkie, Switch." Red looked up from where he was stuffing his face with pancakes. "Did Jools's mum's lasagne win the dinner poll again this week?"

"Not this week. It'll be a surprise." Hayley wiggled her eyebrows.

Red's girlfriend Jools pushed her plate away. "We'll keep voting for the lasagne. It'll win again."

"It wins every other week. Aren't you sick of it yet?" Jenna asked.

"Not in this lifetime. Or the next. And my honey loves it too." She made goo-goo eyes at Red, who squirmed.

"Young love," Hayley teased. "You two are so sweet."

Red beat his chest. "I am man; hear me roar."

"He roared all right last night, when I—"

"Argh, no!" Jenna covered her ears. "I don't want to hear about your sex life."

"When I accidentally dropped a workboot on his toe." Jools stood. "We're off to Last Chance Bore. The pump's broken." She dragged Red up. "Come on, lover boy. Shift your arse."

"She's so romantic." Red followed Jools out.

Hayley swivelled to face Jenna. "Gill came to me with a proposition this morning."

Jenna listened as Hayley related what Gill had said. "Do you want to do it? Because that's a great deal—I'm in, if you are. Imagine if I won the Bilby Cup!" Excitement pooled in her stomach. The Cup needed an agile horse with stamina and speed. Bucky was perfect.

"You and Bucky leave me and Turtle in your dust when we gallop. Yeah, I'm up for it." Hayley's eyes shone. "You and me, long outback nights and unknown roads—"

"The Plenty Highway has road trains. Not so unknown."

"Unknown to me. New and exciting scenery—"

"It's just like here, except more sand dunes."

"Camping by ourselves, just you and me and a million stars."

"Now you're talking!"

Two weeks later, Slugger pottered around the kitchen, opening doors and drawers and inspecting the contents of the walk-in fridge and freezer. "It's good to be back, Hays. Seems you've made a few changes."

Hayley lifted a shoulder. "Every cook makes the kitchen their own. You know that."

Slugger harrumphed. "Don't expect it to look like this when you get back, then." He hauled a fifteen-kilogram bag of lamb chops from the freezer. "Reckon this'll do for dinner."

Hayley smothered a smile. Slugger's food was plain and wholesome. But she doubted there'd be any complaints. "I've made two large pans of Jools's mum's lasagne. It's at the back of the freezer. That'll do for your first day off."

"I remember that lasagne. It's tasty as."

"Recipe's in the file on the bench if you want to give it a go."

"I might at that. This old dog is up for new tricks. I ain't dead yet, Hays."

She wrapped her arms around him in a giant hug. "No! With your heart pumping good as new, you've a long way to go."

When she released him, even the tips of his ears were pink. "Now git from my kitchen and go pack. Your woman is already loading the ute."

With a laugh, she fled. The hands and her kitchen would survive under Slugger's control. Indeed, there was no one she'd rather leave in charge.

Hayley sat in the passenger seat, her leg bouncing as Jenna drove south from Ghost Gum Station toward Boulia. The horse float with Bucky and Kitty, Wendy's mare, rumbled behind them. Their bags, a portable fridge, and the swags were roped on the tray, already covered with a fine layer of red dust.

She pulled the bag from her feet onto her lap. "I have snacks. Want a muffin?"

Jenna reached over and grabbed one. The ute wobbled then straightened. "When have I not wanted anything of yours?" She flicked a glance over. "Your food, your company, your kisses. Your body."

Hayley leaned across the gap between the seats and ran a hand down Jenna's thigh. "Keep talking, silver-tongued one."

"You're the one with the silver tongue. And I can't wait to be on the end of it tonight."

Warmth pooled in Hayley's belly at the thought. "Yes, tonight. Us together, under the stars. Do you know where we'll camp?"

Jenna shrugged. "Not a clue. We'll pull over somewhere away from the road."

"That sounds perfect." Hayley leaned back and stretched her legs. "I love how we can just camp somewhere quiet and no one bothers us."

Three hours later, after a stop in the tiny town of Boulia for coffee and to check the horses, they drove along the two-lane highway toward the Northern Territory.

Hayley scanned the pancake-flat landscape of red dirt and scrubby trees and watched a willy-willy as it lifted the dust in a lazy spiral before dropping back to earth. Kangaroos resting in the shade didn't stir as they passed.

Around four, Jenna slowed and turned onto an unmarked set of two-wheel tracks that wound through the mulga. "This looks promising. If it keeps going, we might get a good camp."

Branches scraped the sides of the float, and behind them the horses shifted restlessly. After a few minutes, the track passed a bore and continued to a rise at the base of some jumbled red rocks. Jenna halted and got out. "This looks good. There's a bit of feed for the horses over there, and a clear area for our camp here."

Together, they unloaded the horses. Bucky sprang backward down the ramp, nearly pulling the rope from Jenna's hand in his eagerness to escape the confines of the float. Kitty was more decorous, and in a few minutes, Jenna had erected the temporary pen and given them water and feed. The sun still scorched the sky, promising a hot night.

Hayley soon had a campfire going and their chairs out. She held up an icy beer from the fridge. "I'm sure you're not interested..."

Jenna bounded up and grabbed the beer from Hayley's hand. "This is the best part of the day."

Hayley waved away the flies. "I thought I was the best part of the day! Especially later. Silver tongue, remember?"

Jenna popped the top of the beer. "I haven't forgotten." She took a long draught, then set the can down. "You're the best part of my life, Hayley." She hooked her fingers in the *V* of Hayley's shirt and tugged her closer, until their lips met.

The long, drugging kiss had Hayley's head spinning, and she gripped Jenna's waist. Her lips pulsed hot when they broke apart. "Later. That's a promise."

The brilliant daylight dropped into evening, darkness falling like a blanket. They ate a dinner of chops and corn cooked on the fire, and potatoes done in the ashes, washed down by another beer. Bucky and Kitty grazed. Somewhere close by was the hop-hop of a kangaroo; even closer, the whine of a mosquito. The moon rose, huge on the horizon.

Jenna released the swags from the back of the ute, pulling out the mattresses to set them together on the tray to make a double bed. They each had a quick wash, then relaxed on their bed to watch the stars. Soon, though, Hayley couldn't wait and slid slow, seeking hands over Jenna's skin, around her small brown-tipped breasts, along her ribs and into the indent of her waist.

Jenna arched her back, raising her breasts, silver in the moonlight, to the sky.

Hayley caressed each nipple before sliding lower, over Jenna's flat belly, down the valley between her thighs.

Their world narrowed to the touches and tastes of love. The inarticulate noises of pleasure, and the softness of skin on skin.

Jenna came under Hayley's tongue; Hayley by the stroking of Jenna's fingers.

They lay together, pulling the thin sheet over them, Hayley rested her head on Jenna's shoulder as together, they watched the moon rise higher and the stars appear in their blaze of glory.

"The Northern Territory! Stop! I want a photo at the border." Hayley leaned forward.

The sign was underwhelming, just green metal with bullet holes, graffiti, and a pile of beer cans at its base. Hayley posed, swinging on the pole.

"Idiot," Jenna said as she snapped pics on her phone. "It's just a straight line on the map."

"This is the first time I've been to another Aussie state. Or territory. One day, I'd like to do a Big Lap, like the grey nomads do. Maybe when I'm old. Maybe we'll do it together."

Jenna's breath caught. While she and Hayley were an established couple, their plans had yet to go beyond a holiday, Christmas, the day-to-day life at Ghost Gum Station. "Are you saying you want us to grow old together?"

Hayley stopped swinging. She came across and wrapped her arms around Jenna, pressing a kiss to one cheek, then the other, then her lips. "That's exactly what I'm saying." She drew back. "Do you want that?"

Jenna blinked fast to clear her misty eyes. "That's exactly what I want. We've just never looked that far ahead before."

Hayley licked her lips. "We haven't. But when I look ahead, I see a future with you in it. Hopefully, at Ghost Gum. Maybe somewhere else. But always together."

"And here, in Australia? Maybe you'll get homesick for New York someday."

"I already do. Sometimes I miss that city so bad, it hurts. And I miss my friends, particularly Mad. I'll go back to visit at some point, but I'll return. I'll come back to you, and to my friends, and to my life here."

Jenna's heart swelled so there didn't seem room for it in her chest. "Maybe I'll come with you for that visit."

"I'd love that. Show you how my life was before I met you. You'll be horrified!"

"Not as horrified as you were when you first came to Australia."

Hayley laughed. "If you come to New York, you'll never think Mount Isa is a city again." She went over to Jenna, wrapped her arms around her, and pressed a kiss to her mouth. "But before we go to New York, we have to get to Bilby Downs."

Once into the Northern Territory, the Plenty Highway turned into a wide, corrugated dirt road and stretched straight and empty as far as Hayley could see. Mindful of the horses, Jenna slowed to around fifty kilometres per hour.

A road train thundered past in the opposite direction, and Jenna slowed even more as they were enveloped in a choking cloud of dust that seeped in and hung about the cabin in a haze.

Jenna pulled in for fuel at a tiny community, and they sat under the shade of a spreading tree to eat sausage rolls bought from the shop and watch the kids and dogs playing in the dust. Then she stood and hauled Hayley to her feet.

"If we get going now, we might be able to camp near enough to the next roadhouse to get brekkie there tomorrow."

Hayley's eyes shot open at sunrise as Jenna slid from the mattress. "You going without me?"

"Never." Jenna leaned over to kiss her. "Was going to check on the horses. If we get an early start, we'll be at Bilby Downs by mid arvo."

Hayley sat up and stretched. "As long as the roadhouse coffee is browner than dam water, that sounds good to me."

An hour later, fortified by bacon-and-egg rolls and coffee that was indeed thick and dark, they rejoined the Plenty Highway. It was still early, and there were no other vehicles. Jenna slowed to let a mob of cattle cross, then sped up again.

Hayley propped her elbow on the sill and watched as the smudge on the horizon that was the MacDonnell Ranges drew closer. Spinifex circles and red termite mounds dotted the baked landscape. She sighed. To think when she'd first arrived in Australia, she'd found the landscape monotonous. Flat as a blueberry pancake and not nearly as interesting. There was always something for her to see, now that she knew how to look: a solitary dingo watching them from the shade of an acacia, the abrupt U-turn of a glossy black-coloured snake as it retreated to the side of the road away from the vibrations of the ute, a mob of emus, feathery skirts bouncing as they ran.

It was gone three when they pulled onto the track leading to Bilby Downs. Whereas Ghost Gum was marked only by a battered sign at the start of the entrance track, Bilby Downs had an actual entrance with security cameras and a smooth, graded road that led past the barn and yards to a modern homestead surrounded by an oasis of green.

"They have better bores," Jenna said, apparently reading Hayley's mind. "Wendy married into this. Bilby Downs is nearly twice the size of Ghost Gum Station—over a million hectares. They breed stock horses as well as run cattle—hence the Bilby Cup. You can close your mouth—the flies will get in." She grinned. "I was the same the first time I saw this. It's a different world, that's for sure."

Jenna swung the ute around and stopped near the homestead, and they both got out and walked up to the door. The bell was a klaxon, and its blare made the horses in the float stamp their hooves.

A white woman answered the door. It had to be Wendy. She had Gill's rangy build and wide, welcoming smile—the one that had welcomed Hayley to Ghost Gum nearly two years ago when she'd arrived fresh from New York City, having won the life-swap competition.

"Hi, Jenna, it's good to see you again." Wendy hugged Jenna, then switched her gaze to Hayley. "And you must be Hayley. I'm so happy to meet you. Thank you so much for agreeing to step in."

"No worries," Hayley said. "Happy to help."

"I hope you're still happy next week! Let me show you where you're staying and where to put the horses. Follow me." She jumped into a modern Toyota and led the way toward the barn.

Kitty came down the ramp first, with a little prance and a toss of her head, then stared all around her.

"She knows she's home," Jenna said.

"She does." Wendy stroked Kitty's neck, dusty after the day's drive. "She's looking well. Thank you for looking after her." She waited while Jenna backed Bucky down. "Your horse has a stall in the main barn, and there's a paddock if you prefer to turn him out with other horses."

"Stall's good," Jenna said. "Keep him nice and fresh to outrun the rest of you in the Cup."

"Good luck with that." Wendy lifted an eyebrow. "Competition is fierce this year. There's even a cowboy from Arizona competing. He's been working at a station the far side of the Alice—going to be tough to beat."

"He doesn't have Bucky." Jenna ran a hand down her horse's hard neck.

"I love your confidence." Wendy put Kitty in the adjoining stall to Bucky's. When the horses were settled, Wendy led them over to the accommodation buildings. "Our cook, Sal, has gone to her parents' place while she's in plaster. She's happy for you to use her quarters."

"Quarters" was too basic a word for the modern building. A wide veranda ran around all four sides, with a doorway on each side.

"Our manager and assistant managers have the other three units," Wendy said. "But our cook is just as important, so Sal has the fourth." She flung open a door and gestured for them to enter.

Fans turned on the high ceiling, and the open space was larger than Hayley and Jenna's old cottage at Ghost Gum. A new-looking couch faced wide windows and looked over the veranda to where the MacDonnell Ranges rose in craggy red majesty.

"Stocked kitchenette over there," Wendy said with a wave of her hand. "Bedroom and bathroom through here. Air conditioning controls by the door."

"Very different from home," Hayley said with a grin. "Thank you, Wendy. You're spoiling us. I assumed we'd be camping."

"Sal works hard and long, so she needs to be comfortable—and so do you. I hope Gill told you how full on it is when the Cup's on?"

"She did," Hayley assured her. "All good."

"You'll have an assistant most of the time. Zach's good but not experienced enough to run things this week. He covers on Sal's days off, though, so he knows his way around the kitchen. He's stepped up since Sal broke her leg." Wendy hesitated. "I'd love to give him a few days off...Would you be okay to—"

"I can start with tomorrow's brekkie," Hayley said. "Zach can show me the kitchen, then I'm fine if he wants time off."

Wendy's shoulders relaxed. "That would be great. Thank you, Hayley. You and Zach can sort it out." She swung on her heels. "I'll leave you both to it."

Once Wendy had left, Hayley turned to Jenna. "This is amazing!" She pressed the bed. "I bet this is really comfortable."

"Air conditioning, too!" Jenna said with a grin. "We might never leave. Although we'll have it at Ghost Gum soon."

"Awesome." Ceiling fans could only do so much. "No more sweaty nights. Well, not from the heat." She waggled her eyebrows.

"There'll always be our favourite sort of sweaty nights." Jenna came over and looped her arms around Hayley's neck. "But in the meantime, I hope we're not going to be too tired to take full advantage of these gorgeous quarters and big bed!"

A bubble of excitement expanded in Hayley's stomach. The kitchen at Bilby Downs was *amazing*: spacious, functional, modern, and laden with gadgetry that Hayley could only dream of. And air conditioned.

A young First Nations man swung around from the bench as she entered. "Hi, if you're looking for a snack, you'll find sandwiches in the fridge in the rec room."

"I'm not right now." Hayley advanced into the kitchen. "I'm Hayley Reed, the cook from Ghost Gum Station. You must be Zach."

Zach's teeth flashed. "Welcome, Hayley. I'm so happy to see you." He fanned himself. "I've been trying my best, and no one's starved—not yet, anyway—but it's intense."

"I hear you've done good. Wendy spoke well of you."

Zach blew a breath. "Thanks. Looking forward to a few days off, though. I'm going to see my mob on the other side of Alice. I'll be back a couple of days before the Cup. Wouldn't miss that." He washed and dried his hands. "Want the tour?"

"Can't wait. This set-up is amazing!"

"It is. I learned to cook working the outstations and musters. I thought I was the greatest, and then I came here. Sal soon set me right." He led her to a board by the door. "These are Sal's suggested menus for the next week. You don't have to stick with it, though. You can do whatever you want."

Hayley followed along, head reeling. This was massive. This was intense. She hoped she could manage it.

Jenna lounged on the supremely comfortable couch with the view to forever. One hand held a cold beer as she waited for Hayley to finish in the shower.

Hayley had rushed in, eyes alight, praising the amazing kitchen. Her chatter had continued until Jenna pushed her toward the bathroom.

Jenna had tagged along with Megan, one of the hands, and had a tour of the barns and yards and the horse-breeding side. Bilby Downs was incredible. But it had grown from the original family-run station and now had part foreign ownership. Megan worked purely with the youngsters. Jenna had shaken her head in bemusement. It sounded wonderful to be so focused, but it wouldn't—couldn't—happen at Ghost Gum, where one day she'd be repairing fences, another checking stock, and a third building nesting boxes for a school project with Rory—Gill and Malc's youngest.

A curl of worry twinged in Jenna's belly. Hayley was the best cook Ghost Gum had ever had. What if she wanted to work somewhere with the comforts of Bilby Downs? Hell, what if she wanted to move here? Station cooks were hard to get, even harder to keep. If Hayley wanted to move, she'd be snapped up.

And if Hayley moved, what would that do to them and their relationship?

Jenna took a mouthful of beer and shook her head to clear the intrusive thoughts. There was no sense in worrying about something that may not happen. She and Hayley were solid enough that they would talk about such plans—if they ever came about.

Hayley was her love, her partner, her best friend. Maybe one day, she'd be her wife. If Hayley left Ghost Gum, Jenna would go too.

But she hoped she wouldn't have to.

"We only learn the course for the Bilby Cup the evening before," Megan said. "All entrants get a mud map showing the four checkpoints. It's up to you which route you take. You can drive around to reccy your route, but you can't ride it beforehand. It's usually around four kilometres."

Jenna nodded. She hoped Hayley would be free to go with her. Although Hayley wasn't the most experienced rider—indeed, she'd learned at Ghost Gum and was initially so bad that Gill had affectionately called her Ghost Gum's worst jillaroo—she had keen eyes.

"Last year, there was a storm the night before the Cup. The creek came up and went down again overnight, but the bed was still boggy. Many riders had chosen to cross it at one particular point, but I knew it would be bad, so I went a longer way around. My horse wasn't fast, but I still placed quite high." Megan grinned. "Insider knowledge."

"Don't suppose you want to drive around with me once we have the map?" Jenna asked.

"Nah, sorry. I've got a great horse this year. I might be in with a chance, so I'll keep my knowledge to myself." She tapped the side of her nose. "Bucky's fast. You could do well."

"Be nice. But mainly, I'm doing it for the fun of it."

"Aren't we all?" Megan led Jenna to where a grey mare gazed out of her stall. "This is Pinky, short for Bilby Downs Pink Lady. She's my ride."

Jenna appraised the mare's deep chest, clean legs, and strong hindquarters. The perfect stock horse. She'd be agile and fast. Megan and Pinky would be serious competition.

"The bloke from Arizona is the one to watch," Megan said. "He's riding a horse we bred and sold on. He's apparently a crack rider, utterly fearless."

"Fearless isn't necessarily a good thing," Jenna said. "I prefer bold with healthy respect myself."

Megan laughed. "You got it, sister." She nudged Jenna companionably. "Your partner did a great job in the kitchen last night. Those beef-and-Guinness pies were fantastic. Hope she keeps doing different stuff this week."

"She probably will." Jenna stored up the compliment to pass on to Hayley.

"I'm riding out this morning. Gotta keep fitness up on some of the Cup entrants. Want to come on Bucky?"

"Sure." Jenna grinned at her new friend. "Gotta learn the land while I can."

Hayley blew her damp bangs up from her forehead. She'd been at Bilby Downs for four days, and so far, so good. Food for station hands was all about good quality and excessive quantity. But today, the station investors and guests were starting to arrive, and they expected fine dining. Beef-and-Guinness pies wouldn't cut it.

She pulled down her menu sheets. Tonight, there were only thirty guests. Easy-peasy, lemon squeezy. Blue-cheese-crusted filet mignon with port wine sauce was tonight's offering. A mixed mushroom risotto did double duty as a side dish and a vegetarian main meal if that was sprung on her. Zach had returned from his days off and would handle grilling the steaks. Staggered dining meant the hands would be fed before the VIPs—something good, but plainer than filet mignon. That left Hayley to prepare the sauce and side dishes and to plate up. A coconut panna cotta was already chilling in the walk-in fridge.

"Hey." Jenna entered. "Do you get a break soon?"

Hayley nodded. "Now works." She took a couple of cold drinks from the fridge, and she and Jenna went across to the rec room veranda and bagged one of the couches.

Hayley stared east, over the rough, red range. "This is amazingly beautiful. I wish I had Turtle here so we could go for a ride."

"We could probably borrow a horse for you. Something quiet."

"Maybe after the Cup. How's Bucky?"

"Fighting fit and raring to go. Despite what she said about not sharing insider knowledge, I've learned a lot from Megan."

"You gonna win the Cup?" Hayley nudged Jenna's ribs. "You gonna win that sweet five grand so our holiday to the beach is a *really* good one?"

Jenna laughed. "I wish. Word from Megan is the hotshot from Arizona is the one to beat."

"Maybe. Maybe not. My money's on an assistant manager from western Queensland."

Jenna kissed her. "I love your confidence."

"Seriously, though, this dude from the States—he may be some star rider over there, but does he know the outback like you do? Does he know his horse as well as you know Bucky?"

"He's been here a few months. He's not totally raw."

"My money's on you when the betting opens."

"Put a few bucks on Megan too."

"I will. But not as many as I put on you." Hayley drained her drink and stood. "I gotta get back or you won't eat tonight."

"Course for the Cup is out." Jenna crashed into the kitchen the next day where Hayley was stirring a pot of chilli. "Got time to come with me to check it out?"

Hayley tasted the chilli she was cooking. A bit of sugar to offset the tang of the canned tomatoes and it was pretty much perfect. She dragged her thoughts away from meal prep. Could she get away?

"Go," Zach said from the bench where he was unmoulding desserts. "We've only got the pudding for the hands to do. I can handle that."

"Thanks." She shot him a grateful grin and removed her apron. "Back in an hour."

Jenna bounced along, the keys to the ute jingling in her hand. "Can you drive so I can look?"

"Sure." Hayley took the keys. For a moment, the memory of the first time she'd driven one of the station utes flashed into her head. She'd never driven a stick shift before, and she'd hit the barn door and nearly run over Jenna. Now it was second nature.

Once in the ute, Jenna spread out a large piece of paper. "The race starts and finishes here." She pointed to the large paddock near the homestead. "And these are the four checkpoints, numbered one to four." She tapped each one on the map. "Riders pick up a token from each one as proof they were there. The map shows the fence lines, the creek, the checkpoints, and nothing else."

"The obvious way would be a big circle." Hayley studied the mud map.

Jenna pulled a pen from the glovebox. "You'd think. But this fence line"—she tapped the map between the second and third checkpoint—"doesn't have a gate, and we can't jump wire fences. Then there's a claypan that stretches between the third and fourth checkpoints. It's pretty mucky at the moment, so the choice is to go around or risk going across the middle. I'd like to check if there's anywhere on the fence line between the second and third points where it's possible to get across without having to retrace nearly back to the start, and look at the claypan, and, well, just look generally."

"Gotcha. How about we check out the claypan first?"

Hayley drove slowly in a direct line toward it. Ahead, the flat area glistened as the salt crystals caught the sun. She stopped on the edge and shaded her eyes as she peered out over the flats.

"No cattle tracks heading across," Jenna said. "That implies it's too soft. Let's head around anticlockwise. That's potentially the shortest route."

Hayley followed a rough vehicle track around. A herd of feral goats leaped away from them, bounding down to the edge of the salt, where they stopped. Even they didn't cross.

The line of a dry creek beckoned. Hayley weaved in and out of gum trees and across the sandy bed before accelerating up the far bank.

"I'd have to slow through the trees," Jenna said, "but Bucky's so agile, he might gain ground on some of the pure speedsters."

"I thought all stock horses would be able to weave," Hayley said. "Mustering cattle and all that."

Jenna grinned. "You're right. But Megan told me that every year, some people enter horses that are unbeatable in a straight line but not as good at anything else. They never win. That's why the course is as it is—to encourage the true stock horse."

"Facts." Hayley nodded.

They completed the claypan loop. Only one cattle track led out toward the centre.

Jenna studied it. "It weaves a lot. I don't think it's worth taking."

Large, blue circles on the ground marked each checkpoint, which were difficult to see from a distance. Jenna stopped at each one, turning a slow three-sixty.

Hayley watched in silence. Jenna was a very visual person—she was no doubt fixing the landmarks in her mind.

Hayley headed toward the next checkpoint.

"There's a gate to the south," Jenna said. "Gates will be open. But I want to see if there's anywhere to the north I could cross."

A line of dust rose where other vehicles headed south toward the gate. "That'll be other riders checking the course," Jenna said. "Try to look like you work here so they don't follow us."

"I do work here. Right now I do, anyway."

Jenna gripped her hand. "Ghost Gum loves you, Hayley. Don't forget."

"I won't." She squeezed Jenna's fingers. "And I love you. I'll never forget that either."

The ute meandered along the fence line in second gear.

"Look." Jenna pointed. "What's that?"

Hayley stopped. A five-metre stretch of wire fence had been rolled back, and downed timber replaced the wire.

"That's been done deliberately." Jenna kicked the bottom log, which didn't shift a centimetre. "It's pretty solid. No wire, so it's jumpable."

Hayley swallowed her apprehension. "It must be nearly four feet high."

"A bit over a metre, I think," Jenna said. "Too high for some. Not Bucky."

They retraced to the gate to cross the fence line, then went north back to the timber jump, and then on to the next checkpoint.

A dense stand of mulga stretched in both directions between the last two checkpoints.

Hayley stopped the ute. "Go around, or go through?" Cattle tracks wound their way in, and dust wallows showed where the cattle had rested in the shade.

Jenna sucked her lower lip. "Let's walk." She led the way along the widest track. Ten minutes later, they were on the other side.

"Maybe through. It'll be slow, but it'll give Bucky a chance to recover after the long gallop. I think most people will go around, which is a lot longer." She nodded. "I've got my route."

It was still dark when Hayley crept from bed on Cup Day. Jenna slept on, lying on her stomach, one arm reaching toward where Hayley had lain. It was tempting to kiss her awake and see where that led them, but she resisted. This would be a busy day for the both of them.

The coffee was brewing, and the breakfast muffins were out of the oven when Zach appeared. Not a morning person, he poured a coffee, grabbed a muffin, and finished both before he said. "I'm here, I'm alive. Let's get to it!"

Jenna saddled Bucky, nerves twanging like a wire fence in a storm. Hayley had insisted she eat something, and the roll sat heavily in her stomach,

Bucky pranced as she led him out of the barn. Megan was already there with Pinky. They mounted and rode over to the starting corral.

"The betting favourite is Rick, the Arizonan." Megan nodded toward a man on a rangy chestnut.

Jenna searched the crowd for Hayley as they rode toward the start. She was nowhere in sight, but then she burst out of the crowd alongside her.

"Thought I'd missed you," Hayley rested her hand on Bucky's shoulder. "Lunch took longer than expected, and then I had to get my bets in. Crowd is heaving at the bookies' ring. I got fifteen to one on you, and eight to one on Megan."

Jenna reached down, and Hayley went up on tiptoes. Her lips brushed Jenna's—soft, warm, loving. "Good luck. Ride like hell, and come safely back to me."

"Always." Jenna's lips tingled from Hayley's kiss.

The loudspeakers crackled, then the race caller told all riders to assemble at the start. Jenna's stomach turned over, and she ran over her plan in her mind. The other horses and riders—maybe forty of them—seemed so much fitter and faster than her and Bucky. Maybe she should go around the mulga rather than through it. And—

No. She slammed a wall down in her mind. She had her plan; she and Hayley had talked it through. It was the right one for her and Bucky.

She reached the start line, where horses and riders were already jostling for position. Where was the Arizonan? She couldn't see him in the melee at the start line. She nodded at Megan. "Good luck."

"You too."

Jenna stroked Bucky's neck, and his skin shivered under her palm. "You and me, Bucky. Let's see what we can do."

"One minute." The loudspeaker ended in a squeal, and one horse whipped around and bolted.

When the ten-second countdown started, Jenna moved Bucky toward the corral's west side. A ute horn blared the start, and the horses streamed across the line. Jenna leaned forward, letting Bucky stretch into a gallop. Most of the riders were heading northeast, to the gate, led by Rick the Arizonan, while only a dozen or so headed toward the claypan. *Interesting*. She pushed them out of her mind, concentrating on picking the best line to the checkpoint.

Bucky was the fourth horse there. Jenna flung herself off Bucky and grabbed a token from the bucket—a miniature blue rubber duck. She remounted and galloped toward the point she'd fixed in her mind, where a large ghost gum shaded the creek. Bucky was galloping easily. The horses in front of her slowed as they reached the trees lining the creek and, with great bounds, plunged through.

She steadied Bucky for the soft sand, not wanting him to strain something, but in a minute, they were through the dry creek and racing around the claypan toward the next checkpoint.

Jenna overtook one horse and let Bucky stretch on the flat run. She didn't look back. This was about her and Bucky, not the other riders. As she propped to a halt at the bucket, the leading riders were already remounting and turning south toward the gate. She slid off Bucky and snatched the token—a pink duck this time—then remounted.

A rider galloped up as she turned toward the fence. Megan. Jenna dithered. The leading riders had gone south to the gate. If she went north, would Megan follow? She shook herself. Megan almost certainly knew about the alternative route. She urged Bucky into a gallop and headed north without looking back.

A couple of minutes later, she turned Bucky and steadied him for the jump. He hesitated, and she ran a hand down his shoulder. "You can do it, boy."

With an enormous leap, Bucky was over and stretching back into a gallop. The third checkpoint came up fast. Horses and riders approached from the other direction, and the area was a cloud of dust. Jenna ducked her head and located the bucket through watering eyes.

She picked out a yellow duck from the bucket, squashing it into her pocket with the other two.

As she galloped away, Megan came up on her left. They shared a quick grin, then Megan pushed Pinky past. The mare was barely blowing.

Jenna aimed for the slight gap in the mulga she'd earmarked before. The shortcut would let Bucky catch his breath and maybe give her an edge over Megan, who even now was on a course that would take her around the trees.

The thicket loomed, and she let Bucky slow to a canter, then a trot. He ducked and weaved and jinked through the scrub, jumping low branches. Jenna guided him in the right direction but let him pick his speed.

Her shirt snagged on a branch, jerking her sideways. The material tore in a loud rip. *Damn, my lucky shirt.*

They burst out of the scrub, and she pushed Bucky back into a gallop toward the last checkpoint. There were no other horses around. Where were the two horses who had been in front of her? Where was Megan? Maybe they'd all thundered past while she was weaving through the mulga.

Then she saw a dust trail coming from the north. Horses. She switched her gaze back to her route. Bucky was blowing hard, and sweat streaked down his shoulders. "Good boy. Not much further."

She grabbed a green duck from the last bucket, remounted Bucky, and turned him toward the finish.

One long gallop, most of a kilometre. Who was ahead? Who was closing in fast from behind? And the riders who'd gone the other way—including the hotshot from Arizona. Had he already crossed the line and was celebrating his win?

Bucky's hooves pounded the red dirt, and he streaked on. The yards came into sight, but at that distance, Jenna couldn't tell if someone had already won.

Bucky stumbled slightly as he crossed a gully where the dirt was soft. Jenna gave him his head and let him right himself, and he recovered. But he was flagging, his pace slower. Sweat darkened his neck and shoulders.

The finish loomed, maybe a couple of hundred metres away. Jenna's heart pounded in time with Bucky's hoofbeats. She raced through the open gate in the fence line without slowing.

Noise filled her ears: Bucky's laboured breathing, the creak of her saddle, and, somewhere to the side, another horse's hoofbeats. She flashed a glance. Megan. Pinky's nostrils were blown wide, but she was gaining slowly on Bucky.

One hundred metres to go. And coming from the other direction, three riders, one ahead of the others: the Arizonan in front, looking as relaxed as if he'd just set out on a picnic ride.

Jenna looked to the finish. People lined the yard fence, and the cheering and whooping grew louder as they approached. She crouched lower and urged Bucky on. He flicked an ear back and increased his speed. Pinky dropped back, her nose now level with Bucky's hindquarters.

Jenna glanced at the Arizonan. He was coming fast—impossible to tell which of them was in front.

"It's anyone's race coming up to the finish," the loudspeaker blared. "It's Rick Schmitt on Generous Joe, Jenna Dwyer riding Buckaroo, and Megan Dellacqua on Pink Lady."

Bucky's ears flattened. The dust cloud from the horses' hooves nearly obscured the finish line. Was she in front? Jenna couldn't tell. Megan was close, but the American was closer.

The three horses pounded across the finish, and the timing chips attached to their bridles beeped almost simultaneously.

Bucky's ears pricked, and his head disappeared between his forelegs as he lived up to his name, letting rip with three enormous bucks. Jenna laughed but managed to keep her seat. Bucky slowed, dropping into a loose walk, his head down, blowing hard. Who had won?

"It's a photo finish, folks," the loudspeaker announced. "We need to check the chips to know the winner."

A hand came around to collect their tokens and chips and ticked their names off on a sheet.

Jenna rode over to Megan. "Great race."

Megan nodded. "You too. I think it's between you and Rick. I hope you've got it."

Rick swept off his hat with a gallant bow. "Good ride, ladies."

Jenna slid to the ground. Where was Hayley?

Then she was there, her compact figure in dusty jeans and a green shirt, pressing close to Jenna, her arms around her neck, tugging her head down to kiss her.

"You were amazing. My heart nearly stopped when I saw you come racing up. And then Bucky lived up to his name—I have no idea how you stick on him when he bucks like that." She paused. "You're in the money—at least third."

The money. Jenna had forgotten, but, yeah, she'd win something. "Money for our holiday."

Hayley patted Bucky, who nuzzled her shoulder. "Bucky was incredible."

"He was." Jenna led him over to the water trough, and he drank.

Other riders were finishing, and the corral filled with dust and with sweating, blowing horses.

Hayley gripped her hand. "That was more exciting than Broadway after dark. Wait until Gill and the others hear!"

Jenna looped Bucky's reins over her arm and turned to Hayley. Her love. "I was racing back to you."

"Oh?" Hayley arched an eyebrow. "I thought you were doing it for the excitement, to prove you're the best rider, that Bucky is the best stock horse. And for the five grand you might win."

"Them too. But knowing you were here cheering me on was the biggest incentive." She brushed her lips over Hayley's. "I love you."

"And I love you too. Even though you taste of dust." Hayley deepened the kiss.

The loudspeaker crackled. "We have the results, folks. Can the first five riders mount and return to the stand?"

"Good luck." Hayley worried her lower lip. "I'm daring to dream here."

Jenna mounted Bucky and edged up to Megan. "Good luck."

Megan's teeth glinted in her dust-covered face. "You too."

The loudspeaker crackled again. "The results."

The fifth and fourth places went to riders from local stations.

"Third place," the announcer said, "with a prize of fifteen hundred dollars..." A pause. "Megan Dellacqua from our own Bilby Downs, riding Bilby Downs Pink Lady."

"Congratulations!" Jenna shouted as Megan rode up to collect her prize—a white ribbon and a cheque.

Megan waved and gave a thumbs up, patting Pinky.

"In second place, and only a nose behind the winner, for a prize of three thousand dollars..."

Butterflies leaped and turned in Jenna's stomach. Second was amazing. Second would give her bragging rights and a decent cheque. She'd be happy with that. But still the butterflies circled, and the refrain beat in her mind: *What if I've won? What if it's me?*

"All the way from Arizona in the United States, it's Rick Schmitt, riding Carlton Station's Generous Joe."

Jenna froze for a second, then she grinned, and it became a laugh of sheer delight. She'd won! Over the crowd cheering, she swore she heard Hayley's whoop. She turned to congratulate Rick. He offered her a rueful smile. "Thought I'd just pipped you. Congratulations, Jenna. That was a darn fine race."

The static in her head, the cheers, and hollers of the crowd increased. She'd won! She leaned forward on Bucky's neck, hugging him hard. What a horse he was!

"And first place for the five thousand smackeroos goes to Jenna Dwyer of Ghost Gum Station in western Queensland, riding Buckaroo."

She urged Bucky forward and leaned down to accept the blue ribbon and an envelope with the cheque. She cantered back to the others, laughing as Bucky let loose another huge, triumphant buck.

Turning, she scanned the crowd, looking for Hayley.

Then she was there, running up, arms outstretched to hug Bucky around his neck. Jenna slid from the saddle so they could celebrate properly. With a kiss. A long kiss that had the people nearest them cheering them on.

"My girlfriend, the Bilby Downs Cup winner," Hayley said when they broke apart.

Jenna's head spun. Five grand was a fantastic windfall. Why, they could have a better holiday, she could add to her savings…or she could buy an engagement ring.

Maybe.

Maybe that's what she'd do.

Hayley jogged back to the kitchen. Her face ached from grinning, and the few hundred she'd won from the bookies put a bounce in her step. To make the day even better, there was only the three-course dinner to prepare tonight for thirty-eight people. Well, for forty. While Jenna and the other winners would also eat with the investors and guests, Hayley would make sure she and Zach also ate well; Hayley was adamant about that. The station hands and visitors would eat from the many foodtrucks.

She pushed open the door to the kitchen and gasped. Black smoke coiled out to meet her. Zach stood in front of the open ovens, flapping a tea towel.

"What's happened?" Hayley hurried over. *What's gone wrong? What's burned?*

Zach's eyes shone white in his dark face. "It's the osso buco. I put it in the oven and went to watch the Cup. But when I came back, the kitchen was full of smoke. The food's ruined. I'm sorry Hayley, I set the ovens way too high." He blinked fast and his mouth worked looking as if he was about to cry.

Shit, fucking shit, and double fuck. There weren't enough cuss words invented for this. The osso buco agrodolce with kale pesto was a spectacular dish, redolent with herbs, sweet with orange vincotto and balsamic vinegar that she'd had delivered especially from Alice. And to think she'd chosen that dish because it would slow-cook during the afternoon when she and Zach were enjoying the festivities.

Zach sniffed and dashed a hand across his eyes.

She laid a hand on his arm. "Hey, it's a mistake that could have happened to anyone. We can fix this."

"How?" Zach sniffed again. "We've got less than two hours."

"We have the tagliatelle we were going to cook. We just need something to replace the beef."

"There's chicken breasts."

Hayley went over to the pantry. "Pecans, Worcestershire sauce." She turned to Zach. "Ever made pecan bourbon chicken?"

He shook his head.

"Do you know anyone who'd have a bottle of bourbon we can use?" At his nod, she continued, "Tell them we'll replace it with two bottles if we can have it now."

Zach disappeared down the steps.

Hayley removed the burned casseroles from the oven and scraped them into the bin, then set about preparing the chicken and other ingredients.

Zach returned a few minutes later, clutching a litre bottle of Jim Beam. "Hope this is okay."

"Perfect." Hayley set the bottle down on the bench. "We don't need the classy stuff. Okay, this is what we do..."

One and a half hours later, Hayley flipped back her bangs and grinned at Zach. "We did it!"

The chicken was ready; breasts rolled in crushed seasoned pecans and pan-fried. The bourbon sauce was ready to be heated, the vegetables and tagliatelle prepared for last-minute cooking.

The hired waitstaff attended to last-minute presentation in the dining room.

Hayley and Zach had finally sat down for a few minutes with a cup of tea when one of the waitstaff burst into the kitchen.

"Hayley, I thought you said the main was chicken? The menu cards mention osso buco."

"Shit!" Hayley leaped to her feet. "Thanks, Manda. I totally forgot." She worried her lower lip between her teeth. "How are we going to redo forty handwritten menu cards in the next twenty minutes?"

"Could we just tell people about the change?" Manda said.

"It would take too long. Jenna has good handwriting; can you spare anyone on your staff? If we all write a few, we'll get it done. Just."

"I can spare a couple. I'll ask for volunteers." Manda disappeared back to the dining room.

"My girlfriend's got great writing," Zach said. "I'll ask her. Unless she's been celebrating too hard, she'll do it."

"Let's go." Hayley ripped off her apron and headed for the barn, Zach behind her.

Jenna, dressed in her best jeans and shirt for dinner and with a beer in her hand, was talking with Megan and Rick.

Hayley panted up. "Sorry, sorry. I need to borrow Jenna for a short while."

Jenna let herself be towed away. Swiftly, Hayley explained what she needed.

"Of course." Jenna set down her beer. "Do you need more people? I think Megan might be willing."

"Sure. Please ask her, and I'll see you at the kitchen."

Hayley was sorting the blank, stiff cards they used for menu cards and finding pens when Zach appeared, out of breath, with his girlfriend.

Hayley flashed her a smile. "Thank you so much." She directed Amie to the bench where she'd propped the menu for people to copy.

Where was Jenna? Hayley's stomach turned over. This dinner was the culmination of her cooking stint at Bilby Downs. She'd wanted to go out on a high. Could anything else go wrong? But then Jenna bounded up the steps to the kitchen. She kissed Hayley, her lips soft and tasting of beer. "I've brought a few people to help."

Behind her was Megan, and behind Megan, a line of maybe a dozen people. Some were dressed in floaty dresses or jeans and dress shirts, others were in the dusty clothes of working hands.

Hayley gaped, and then a grin spread. Outback people helping outback people. Of course they were willing to help, even with something as small as this. She directed them over to the bench where Zach was scrambling around finding more pens.

People clapped her on the back or shook her hand as they filed in.

"Gotta help you," said one woman dressed in dusty jeans. "The tucker's been great this week. Thanks, mate."

Jenna sat at the bench copying the first card in her neat handwriting.

Hayley went up behind her and wrapped her arms around Jenna's neck and pressed a kiss to her cheek.

"You're the best girlfriend."

"I know."

She felt Jenna's smile under her lips. "All these people taking time away from their fun to write a stupid menu card."

"It's no biggie. It's what we do out here."

"It is."

"You get that. You understand life out here, Hayley. The good and the bad."

"You're the best of the good. As well as the winner of the Bilby Cup."

"There is that." Jenna turned her head so that Hayley's lips met hers. "And those winnings are going to give us one fantastic holiday. I'll contact the accommodation tonight. See if we can upgrade to one of their luxury units. After all, we'll need comfort to plan the rest of our life together."

Did Jenna mean what she thought she meant? Hayley's heart melted like butter on a hot pan. "Whatever you're planning, whatever we decide, whatever we do, as long as we do it together, I'm happy."

"Me too." Jenna set down her pen and turned into her arms. "Me too."

They took their leave from Bilby Downs a couple of days later. Zach hugged Hayley. "Thanks, mate. Wendy's given me the cook's job until Sal returns. Said you told her I was able for it."

"You totally are." Hayley hugged him back. "Hope I get to sample your food again. And if you're ever in western Queensland, come see us at Ghost Gum."

Zach grinned. "Maybe."

Jenna and Megan were laughing together, bumping fists. Bucky waited in the float.

Wendy came over. "Thank you both, so very much. Hayley, we couldn't have found anyone better to stand in for Sal." She handed Hayley a sealed envelope. "This is on top of your wages. Our guests were impressed and had a whip around for you."

Hayley took it. "Thanks, Wendy. I didn't expect this. It's been a pleasure."

"I won't offer you a job as Gill would kill me, but if you ever decide to move on from Ghost Gum Station, there's a place for you and Jenna here."

Hayley reached for Jenna's hand. "I'll remember that. But my life and heart are bound to Ghost Gum."

"I thought you'd say that." Wendy hugged Hayley, then Jenna. "Gill and Malc are lucky to have you."

"We're lucky to have them," Jenna said. "But mainly, Hayley and I are lucky to have each other."

Enjoyed this glimpse into their life after the happy ending? Discover how their story began in *Switcheroo*.

A Presidential Declaration

by Lola Keeley

Connie leaned back in the heavy leather chair that had been her constant companion over seven years in the Oval Office. The faces around her had changed, the meetings ranged from the banal to the stuff of anxiety dreams, but through it all she had at least been seated comfortably.

She almost laughed aloud at that ridiculous way of measuring her time as president. Now that it was in the final stretch of her second term, all anyone wanted to talk about was legacy, and building a library, and the upcoming election that had no incumbent, leaving Connie feeling a little like yesterday's news. After being relentlessly in the spotlight for so long, first as Governor of California and then President, it was pleasant to be a little forgotten.

Well, at least until the Democratic Convention in a few weeks' time. With no nominee leading the pack, and Connie unable to serve a third term thanks to the Constitution, all focus would be on her once more. While she wanted more than anything to leave the country in safe hands, the polling numbers spoke to a shift in the national conversation, and the Republican nominee was making great strides while her own party was in disarray. She did not envy whomever had to run against them.

Before that though, she had a special event of her own to attend. One she had never imagined when she became a widow, or when running for office. It had been a staggeringly big deal to admit to her bisexuality while contesting a bitter election battle, but Connie had done so. It hadn't remotely been on her radar that she would meet a brilliant, hard-headed heart surgeon during her first term as President, but Emily had come crashing into her life all the same.

Connie reached for the candid snap of them both atop the Eiffel Tower, where they had both ended up proposing at the same time. It was one of her absolute favorite images, up there with the first photo of her cradling her newborn son, Zach, and the moment in both her Inauguration ceremonies when she had taken the oath of office.

It was all such a long way from law school and starting out as a Los Angeles District Attorney. Sometimes, Connie wondered if that might have been enough for her, a satisfying life without constant daily scrutiny. She set the photograph in its heavy silver frame back down on the sturdy desk where she signed bills into law and issued vetoes of legislation she would never support.

There had been plenty of occasions when it would have been easier and less frustrating for all concerned if Connie had simply stayed single for the duration of her presidency, but even in the toughest times the thought of being without Emily had been the only truly unbearable thing. So the extra security and the additional threats had been weathered, and somewhere along the line the press and the majority of the country seemed to just accept their relationship with a shrug.

She had been asked, once, in an interview that was recorded and never aired after she was shot, whether she would give up her job if it was the only way to be with Emily. It had startled Connie to feel the 'yes' forming on her tongue, and the interviewer had sensed it coming. Luckily, no tape existed of that moment any more, but Connie still wondered at times if she should tell Emily that it had happened. They both loved their careers, and their families, but it seemed as though they had survived and even thrived this long by not forcing each other to choose.

Connie swirled the last of the bourbon in her glass, the half-melted ice clinking against the crystal. Tomorrow would be her wedding day, her second, and the eyes of the world would be on the White House. Perhaps it would have been prudent to wait until she had left office, but in terms of a symbolic gesture, they didn't get much bigger than the White House's first same-sex marriage for a sitting president. She squeezed her eyes closed at the weight of those words, even inside her own head.

Other people could run off, to Vegas or any state with a short waiting time for a marriage license. Other countries, secretive places that only a handful of people could enter. Connie had offered just that to Emily, but they'd settled on the public spectacle.

And that spectacle was now less than a day away.

Emily Lawrence had spent large stretches of her life being awake at 4am. As a child she had woken far too early every day, dragging the rest of the house out of bed as soon as they would let her. After the trauma of losing her parents in her teens, the nightmares had put paid to a solid night's sleep for years. As for medical residency? Sleep had been a myth, a grabbed hour whenever she could steal it.

While being a successful surgeon and Head of Department had afforded her the chance to mostly pick her hours, there was always an on-call emergency waiting to rear its head and disturb that peace of the wee small hours. Was it any wonder she slept so lightly?

"I can hear your wheels turning," said a sleepy voice next to her, partly muffled by a huge pillow. "Something on your mind?"

"Nope. Just awake," Emily said, turning on her side to witness the half-awake and beautiful face of her fiancée. Even in the half light of the earliest morning, it knocked Emily a little giddy to see the woman she loved in such a peaceful state. "Why? Is something happening today?"

"Just a breakfast meeting with the Joint Chiefs." Connie's eyes finally opened, the reality of her schedule as the most powerful woman in the world sinking in once more. "Then after that I thought I might blow off work, go shopping or something. Any plans?"

Emily reached across and tapped Connie on the tip of her perfect nose. "Well, I heard some woman is going to try and marry me in this old building. Apparently it's some kind of a big deal."

"Wouldn't you rather be in surgery?"

"You have to know that I'm going to do both. In fact, I scrub in at seven."

Connie propped herself up on one elbow, the strap of her silk chemise sliding down as she did. "We should have spent this night apart, you know. It's tradition."

"There's a lot of tradition around two women getting married at the White House, is there? And we've had to spend too many nights apart so far as it is. Once your term is over, I don't plan on us being away from each other that often."

"Is that so?" Connie leaned in to kiss Emily, soft and fleeting. "I might hold you to that."

"Did you want to go back to sleep?" Emily was aware that she probably wouldn't do much more than doze if she tried.

"Not really. This might be our last chance for some privacy today. Before long the staff will arrive, and the stylists, and the press, and our families..."

Emily grimaced just a little. Thankfully she was used to performing under pressure, but even her steady confidence wavered a little at the thought of the attention that would beam into every moment of their special day. "That's not counting the dignitaries, celebrities and party donors who would have been offended not to receive an invitation."

"I'm sorry about that," Connie said, brushing a strand of dark hair from Emily's face with her usual care. "I know this should just be about us, really, but we did agree—"

"That it's important to show the world how wonderful this is, that we're making a commitment and making it part of the country's institutions. I haven't changed my mind on any of that, don't worry."

Emily confirmed her agreement with a kiss to Connie's collarbone, right where the slipped strap used to sit.

"But still?" Connie pressed, looking for something in Emily's eyes once she pulled back again.

"Just a little stage fright. Nothing I can't handle."

"Nothing we can't handle." Connie made her correction while taking Emily in her arms and pulling her close. "Now what can we do instead of sleeping?"

"I'm sure we'll think of something," Emily said, and despite the way her mind had been whirring, all the chatter quietened with Connie's first kiss.

For a long time, Emily hadn't imagined she would have a wedding day. Commitment to one person had never been the focus, not with a career that took all of her time and energy. Since meeting Connie though, the prospect had seemed less optional and downright necessary.

Just like starting her wedding day with some light surgery.

Sure, other women might want a light breakfast with mimosas, or book out the first hours of the day to spa treatments and professional makeup artists, but neither of those had ever been Emily's style. Instead, one of the most important days of her life was beginning in the secure and sterile walls of Operating Room 1, and amongst the nurses and doctors in their surgical gowns, stood one of her usual Secret Service agents, Joseph, his military bearing giving him away even though his black suit was well covered. At least he had agreed to taking off his omnipresent sunglasses indoors.

Satisfied with the blood flow to the exposed heart in her patient's chest cavity, Emily allowed herself a moment of pride over a job well done. Only her resident clearing her throat from behind her surgical mask spoiled the moment, and with a wince of reluctance, Emily nodded. She set her scalpel down on the tray of used instruments, and smiled at the glint in the resident's eyes at the prospect of getting to close up. It seemed like a long time since Emily had been so keen to operate that she would gladly take any task in the process.

"Thank you, everyone," Emily said, stepping back from the operating table with her hands held up, still clad in bloody latex gloves. "I know I'll be seeing you later, but I don't want anyone rushing the cleanup here, okay?"

Her favorite surgical team comprised most of Emily's few additions to the wedding guest list. Even some of her oldest friends had been wary of the glare and security hoops of a White House wedding, and it was hard to blame them. Dropping by a friend's house for coffee really had become a thing of the past, so it was a lot to ask of anyone to come and spend an insane day in the Washington fishbowl.

Still, Sutton and Rebecca would be there. Emily had faced almost everything with her sister at her side, and Rebecca was a good boss if occasionally a difficult sister-in-law. At least the arrival of baby Toby had softened her a little, and it had made Sutton happier than Emily had seen her in a long time. That he resembled their much-missed father had just been the icing on the familial cake.

They would form the core of Emily's side on this day of expanding their family officially, but Connie and her son Zach had already felt like Emily's family, and her future, for quite some time. Riding out an assassination attempt, and Zach's college application process had left them in this pleasant position of celebrating the last year of Connie's second term with a vow that they would both take more seriously than just about anything.

Joseph followed her into the scrub room as she cleaned up.

"Joseph, you don't have to hover."

"Yes, ma'am." He pulled off his mask and gown with evident relief, pausing only to throw them in the waiting trolley before resuming his alert stance, shoulders back.

"You're going to 'ma'am' me even on my wedding day, aren't you?"

"I would expect so, ma'am." Joseph flashed a rare but genuine smile in her direction. "But don't worry, we'll stay out of the official photos."

Emily snorted as she disposed of her surgical wear, and when she had washed up and was down to her unblemished scrubs, she led the way to the locker room. Where she had previously shared with the other attendings, a private space had been set up for her, another security demand from the Department of Treasury. Emily could hardly complain when their Secret Service agents had already put themselves on the line to keep her and everyone important to Connie safe. It was a little lonely, sure, but it let more people sleep better at night.

After a brief blast of a shower, she opened the closet that had been provided instead of the standard locker. Where Emily was sure she had folded up some running gear for the trip back to the White House, whisked from building to car to building, instead she was greeted with a beautiful cream-colored pantsuit.

"Uh, Joseph? Is this your way of critiquing my wardrobe choices? Because the main event is hours away and I have a pretty white dress for that."

"Don't ask me, ma'am. One of the other agents was handling the bags."

"Well, I could just put my scrubs back on. If this is coming from Francesca in the Protocol Office, I don't care how scary she is, I will be having words."

Joseph shrugged, before retreating to the doorway once more. "Someone seems to want you to have those nice clothes today. It wouldn't be so bad, right?"

Maybe Rebecca was to blame. As hospital administrator and a family member, she would have access to switch things around. Since nobody but White House staff had been involved in the wedding planning, perhaps this had been her contribution into keeping Emily presentable at all times. The PR of having the president's fiancée on staff, even with a limited schedule, had been quite the coup for the hospital.

Grumbling, Emily pulled the suit from its hangers and noted the camisole and underwear that came with it, perfectly complementary in champagne silk. She was used to changing in record time, but these days every change came with the necessity of restyling her hair and applying at least the basics of makeup. The paparazzi never got close enough thanks to the agents, but with super-powered zoom lenses that didn't always matter.

With a final glance in the mirror, she deemed herself acceptable for the sake of the car journey back to the White House. She would have preferred to run it, chase out some of the nervous energy fizzing in her muscles, but often that kind of open-air exercise was more trouble than it was worth.

To her surprise, Joseph didn't lead her to her usual exit. Assuming something had been changed because of the wedding, Emily fell in brisk step with her small protection detail as they made their way to a loading bay that she hadn't even noticed the entrance to before.

Instead of the usual hulking armored cars she had become used to traveling in, Emily stopped in her tracks at the sight of two far more discreet SUVs. The cars were downright sporty compared to the tank-like things that living with Connie had introduced Emily to.

"Joseph?"

"Ma'am?"

"You're not about to kidnap me because you think this wedding is a mistake, are you? Because that really doesn't sound like you."

Joseph let a rare smile show for just a second, fixing the cuff of his crisp white shirt where it peeked out the sleeve of his jacket. "You know we have to keep things fluid, this is just changing it up to not draw extra attention today."

Emily nodded. "Attention is the one thing I don't think we'll be short of for the next few hours."

She slid into the backseat of the waiting car, barely noticing as everyone else took their spots with a synchronized slamming of doors. The engines had already been purring, so they sped off smoothly into the still-quiet streets of the nation's capital.

The route from the hospital to the White House had become a familiar blur to Emily. She checked her phone, the one only a handful of people would ever have the number for, and was surprised to see no message from Connie. No matter how busy the day, they would usually check in quickly after a surgery or a big meeting. It hadn't been difficult to keep track of both schedules, not with Emily's reduced caseload and all the staff supporting them both.

Just when they should have made a turn, Emily was surprised to feel the car go straight on. She glanced out but saw no road closures, no traffic or anything that would prevent their regular route.

"Something up?" She asked, checking each agent to see how they reacted.

As cool as ever, Joseph turned back from the passenger seat. "Just a slight change in plans, ma'am. Security protocols tightened up for today."

Which Emily completely understood. In fact, she should have expected it. She would have believed it too, if her inner compass wasn't already aware that they were heading away from the White House, and showing no signs of turning back in the right direction.

Connie paced the mahogany-paneled office like a tiger in a cage. Only a few determined strides and she was out of space, forced to turn around and retrace her steps. She was aware of everything crowding her in this space that was most certainly not her own. The leather-bound books that had probably never left the shelves, since it was quicker to search most of their content online anyway. The heavy velvet curtains that seemed to date back to the Revolutionary War, at least judging by the faded stripes of sun damage.

She heard one of the agents at the door shifting their weight, someone coughed gently and tried to muffle the sound. All that was missing from her agonizing time alone was a huge ticking clock, but thankfully the room didn't contain one of those.

"Mom?" The door opened to reveal Zach, too tall and too handsome to be the same baby she had raised, immaculate in his gray suit and champagne-colored tie. "Have you heard anything yet?"

"No," she marched up to pull him into a hug, not caring if her own dress might crumple a little in the process. "But it can't take much longer, don't worry."

"How are you so cool about this?" Zach pulled away, that little bit more embarrassed these days by displays of motherly love. No matter how close the bond, teenagers were always a little awkward for a while. Connie managed not to take it personally, even though sometimes it felt like her heart might break.

"Because I have a little something called faith, oh son of mine. Do I look okay?"

"Yeah? I mean, I guess? You look happy for sure."

The compliments were a little backhanded, but Connie still treasured each one. "Thank you for guessing. Can you keep everyone else updated for me? I want to do the first part myself, that's all."

Zach grinned at her. "I bet you do. And trust me, it's better for all of us if this bit happens behind closed doors.

A commotion in the hallway, then. A flurry of solid footsteps and an unmistakable voice demanding answers from seemingly everyone she could think of.

"I'll be right outside, Mom. I'll tell Sutton and Rebecca, and we'll all be waiting for you."

Connie nodded, watching him slip out of the door. She braced herself, spine straightened and fingers laced together at her waist. Cool, calm, utterly in control. Well, except for the small hurricane of butterflies that seemed to be fluttering in her stomach. How could a person sail through addressing the United Nations but be nervous about talking to one person?

"What the hell is going on?" Emily arrived in the doorway as her protective detail melted away from her with evident relief. With her cheeks flushed and her long, dark hair slightly mussed, she was a sight for sore eyes. And that was before Connie took in the silk camisole and light-colored pantsuit that matched her own.

"Well… surprise?" Connie decided to keep it short. As a politician, she knew when it was no time for a big speech.

Emily hadn't recognised the underground parking lot they eventually stopped in, and she sure as hell had no idea which marble hallways she had been led through. The strange old dean-style office she ended up in was not one that she had ever seen before either.

But at least at the end of her journey, there was Connie.

"Is there some kind of threat? Do we have to call it off?" As the daughter of assassinated parents and the fiancée of a president who had also had her own brush with threats and actual death, Emily could do nothing but jump to the worst case scenario. Her own heartbeat thundered in her ears, the beats too rapid to keep track of.

"What?" Connie seemed startled at the question. "Oh no, no, nothing like that. Oh Emily, I'm so sorry. I wasn't thinking when I changed up the plan, I just wanted to give you what you really wanted from today." She stepped in close, taking Emily's hands in her own.

"You did? What does that mean?" Emily felt her pulse start to slow, the rhythm of her breathing starting to follow the rise and fall of Connie's chest, right in front of her.

"Today, all the pomp. Also the circumstance. We'll still do that, it's still important."

"Okay…"

"But I wanted something just for us. Nearest and dearest only, something the rest of the world doesn't get to be a part of."

Emily looked around the room, and spotted the black robes hanging in a half-open closet, the gavel resting on the paper-strewn desk. "Something private?" Emily had almost forgotten what the word meant. Even in their most unannounced and remote retreats at Camp David or private country estates, the presence of staff and security always hummed along somewhere in the near distance. It had been the price to pay for falling in love with Connie, and Emily had paid it willingly, but accepting something and liking it were two very different things.

Connie kissed her then, not the lazy, gentle meeting of their lips that started the day, but a sudden heat of pressure and excitement that made Emily's breath catch in her throat just a little. This was the woman she wanted to marry, and she was damn well going to do it.

"Won't this mess up everything planned for later?" Emily asked when they finally parted. She was glad Zach had left the room so promptly. No teenager wanted to see his mom and almost-stepmom looking at each other this way.

"No, we just do it twice. It's only bigamy if it's not the same person both times. Trust me, of the two of us I'm the one that's been married before. Plus, the lawyer thing."

"Practice a lot of marital law from the Oval Office, huh? Must have missed the sign."

Connie rolled her eyes with her usual fondness. "Oh yes, I've been meaning to speak to you about all those billable hours we've been spending together. Could get expensive, doctor."

"I'll raid the change jar at the Residence. So obviously Zach is here, but won't we need more than one witness?"

"Even if we didn't," Connie said, leaning against the stranger's desk. "Sutton and Rebecca are here. With Toby, of course. Can't have him growing up and finding out he missed one of his aunties' weddings."

"Toddlers worry about that a lot, good call." Emily couldn't bite back her grin, though. Of course Connie knew that family meant everything to both of them. She would never have considered doing something this important without the essential people there. Almost all the people Emily truly needed would all be in one room.

Waving her hand vaguely in Emily's direction, Connie clearly had something else to add. "And Dima, too. You can't get married without a maid of honor, at least one of the times."

Emily went over to hug Connie at the news her best friend would also be there. Of course she had asked Dima to be in the official wedding, but that invitation had been bluntly declined, with plenty of love. Dima didn't know whether people would pay more attention to her Russian nationality or her status as a trans woman, but either way she was in no hurry to become a walking target for podcasting morons and conspiracy theorists.

"You're amazing, did I mention that before?" Emily murmured her question against the side of Connie's neck. "Don't even tell me how you arranged the clothes switch, I want to preserve the mystery."

Connie hugged her back tightly. "I'll brag about it later, after a glass of champagne or two. But I think we should maybe get around to the whole secret ceremony before the very very public one starts. And before we crumple these outfits completely."

"That sounds like you want me to let you go," Emily said. "That can't be right."

"Only temporarily," Connie replied. "And don't worry, I already know you're never really letting me go."

"Why not?" Emily had to ask.

"Well, look at me… I'm a real catch," Connie said, and they both dissolved into giggles for a moment. Then Emily did release her embrace, but only so they could go and become legally even closer.

The tiny courtroom didn't seem to be one that was in use very much. It had that distant-shelves-in-a-library feel of air not often disturbed. Connie had loved spaces like that during law school, and it felt right to be doing this here, in some obscure corner of the district court system.

Right now, live news feeds around the world would be speculating on her hair choices and the politics of her dress designer, or maybe whether the canapes would give an indication of who was under consideration for presidential pardon. Whatever the speculation, it was where it belonged - outside and far away for the moment.

She took Emily's hand in her own, and they stood in silence side-by-side for a moment, watching the welcome and wanted hubbub created just for them. Familiar faces only, the agents hanging back in the hallway, although a few of them had become family of sorts too.

Sutton bounced little Toby on her hip, his curls bouncing along with the motion. Rebecca never really took her eyes off their son, even as she stood off to the side a little, in conversation with Ramira.

Connie beamed at the sight of her best friend dressed more casually, not in one of her razor sharp business suits she used to reign over the entire West Wing. The light summery dress looked perfect on her, and as she caught Connie looking at the gathering, she waved them over.

"Emily, Connie, you both made it! I have to say, I won't miss these last minute schemes of yours, ma'am."

"No ma'am-ing at private events. You promised," Connie said, only slightly scolding.

Ramira shrugged, unable to drop the habit fully. The woman was nothing if not a professional.

"I can't say I was expecting this when I sent an orderly to sneak an outfit into your locker," Rebecca said next, greeting both of them with a firm handshake. Despite being their sister-in-law, or at least Emily's officially, that formal manner never completely dropped. Connie understood it, and it had to be at least partly rooted in the fact that she was Emily's boss, but there was no hiding that it pained Emily ever so slightly to be held at arm's length.

Which thankfully was not the case between the sisters themselves, with Sutton pulling Emily into a group hug with her nephew almost immediately. Connie was not exempt after all, being tugged into the melee as well a moment later. She received their welcome gratefully, with a quick kiss on the top of Toby's adorable head. He'd be well provided for with a teacher and the head of a hospital for parents, but having a doctor and a president for aunties certainly wasn't going to hurt. Connie already spoiled him rotten with most of her assets tied up in a blind trust until she left office, so there would be no stopping her once she and her credit cards were released in a matter of months.

"I knew you'd be in on it." Emily teased Rebecca once the hug had come to an end. "How come I'm not allowed to break rules at work, but you can engage in government conspiracies about my outfit choices?"

"Just be grateful Connie already picked the suit," Sutton said. "Otherwise this one would have sent you in scrubs. Not exactly the pages of Vogue over at Blackwell Hospital, is it?"

"I have some very fashionable sneakers, thank you," Emily replied, not seeming remotely offended. Siblings got to make a little dig that others just didn't. Connie was going to enjoy making this rabble of people her family officially; she'd missed so much of this when it had become just her, Zach, and her former mother-in-law. Too many only children in their own family, and too many people already gone too soon.

"Are we ready?" Said a voice from the door to chambers.

Connie looked to Emily one last time, checking she could speak for them both. "I do believe we are."

The voice that sounded across the room was familiar to Emily, an itch of memory that she couldn't quite place. When she looked to the door, she saw the judge in her robes, a petite elderly woman with dark skin and graying hair, brown-black eyes sharp and flitting over every face in the room. Definitely someone who didn't miss a single thing from the bench, that was for sure.

"Sutton, Emily, I fear you won't remember me. But I remember you both very well." The judge's voice sounded like a memory even as she admitted to having crossed their path some time before.

"I'm sorry, I feel like I know you from somewhere, but I can't place it…" Emily said, trailing off as her cheeks flushed a little.

"I'm Mamie Keaton, and your mother clerked for me right out of law school. We kept in touch, she brought you girls to visit when you were so little. And I wrote an article in support of her nomination. That's the only thing I ever regretted in my life. I'm so sorry."

"Don't be," Sutton said, and Emily echoed her in the sentiment. "She was proud to be nominated to the Supreme Court, and I don't think she'd ever have taken it back. Nobody could have known what would happen."

It was only to be expected that they would think of their parents on such a special day, but Emily put the pieces together quickly.

"You did this?" She turned to Connie, who gave a humble nod in response. "You found a judge to marry us who was someone so important to my family?"

"Well, obviously I had some help, and Judge Keaton does work right here in Washington. I didn't move any mountains." Connie tucked a golden strand of hair behind her ear. "I thought it would be another way to include them in the day. I know how proud they'd be of you."

Witnesses be damned, Emily launched herself across the mere foot of space that separated them and hugged Connie close enough to crumple both of their outfits completely, and she didn't give a single damn.

"Thank you," Emily said, leaning back just far enough to look Connie in the eye. In gratitude, in love, and in disbelief that she got to marry this woman, Emily kissed her soundly on the lips.

Judge Keaton broke the spell of the moment. "Now ladies, let's save that for after the vows please. I assume we're all ready?"

Emily answered with just about much certainty as she'd ever had in her life. "Hell yeah we are."

Connie felt her heart skip as they shuffled into place before the judge. Had she been this nervous at her first wedding? It seemed so long ago, almost like it happened to another person. But her husband Robert, Zach's father, couldn't have asked for anyone better than Emily to be her second act. Everyone in the room knew that too, and Connie most of all. Whatever lay ahead after the toughest mission of her life, she would face it with the most wonderful woman she'd ever known, and that was saying something.

Did it really all come down to saying some simple words in front of a handful of their favorite people? Every other major decision in Connie's life had usually been accompanied by a screaming crowd, or a table surrounded by stern-faced generals waiting for a critical answer. In comparison, taking this step felt as easy as stepping off the diving board at her favorite pool, and every bit as thrilling.

Only when Judge Keaton got to the first really important bit did Connie realize she hadn't been listening to the ceremony at all.

"Now I'm guessing everyone here is on your side, but I still have to ask that if anyone here knows of any reason or impediment why these two should not be married now, speak now or forever hold your peace."

And despite herself, Connie held her breath for a moment. She allowed herself one glance at her loved ones, and saw only encouraging smiles in return. "Good," she muttered, and a ripple of muted laughter went around the room.

"I'll take that as a no," the judge said. The rest was a blur until the really important question, and that one Constance Calvin was very certain of her answer to.

"I do," she said. It seemed like an eternity until it was Emily's turn to repeat those words back to her, but when she did it seemed like no wait at all.

"You may now kiss a bride," Judge Keaton said, and as applause broke out from their family, Connie wrapped an arm around Emily's waist and did exactly that.

No consideration of angles or optics, and all the things that would be jostled over at the ceremony later. No need to cut the beautiful sensation short, or worry what people would say afterwards. When they finally broke the kiss, Connie felt a small tear escape.

"I promised myself I wouldn't cry!"

"Me too," Sutton said, the first to come and hug them both, Toby handed off to Rebecca this time. "But who doesn't cry at a wedding? It's the one time it's basically a free pass."

"True," Emily said, but made of sterner stuff, her eyes were barely glistening.

Connie knew though, that private tears would come later, when it really was just the two of them. Emily didn't give into overwhelming emotion that often, but when a patient loss really hit or a past trauma raised its head, she knew she was safe to cry in front of Connie. Or now, to cry in front of her wife.

They accepted the flurry of hugs, and as Connie waved to Jill and Joseph, the brother and sister Secret Service agents closest to them all, she got to hug Zach one more time without him squirming away.

"It's going to be good, mom. And you'll have someone to hang out with when I'm at college."

"Bold of you to assume that means I won't be visiting you every weekend."

"Moooo-om."

"I kid, I kid. You're my only son, I have to mess with you at least a little." Connie patted his cheek as she said it. She turned around to look for Emily, catching her in conversation with the judge.

"Hey," Emily said as she slipped back to Connie's side. "We're really married, huh?"

"We are," Connie said. "What did the judge give you?"

"Oh, just some papers my mom wrote when they worked together. Drafts, things that nobody needs to keep somewhere. I'm going to share them with Sutton."

"That's lovely," Connie said. "Like getting a new piece of her even after all this time."

"Apparently there are some postcards between her and my dad that she left behind as well. I hope I'm not too scandalized. I don't know if I can ever thank you for finding Mamie, but that can wait for now. Today is about us."

Connie bumped her hip gently against Emily's as everyone chattered around them, passing out tissues and keeping Toby entertained. "You really don't mind a surprise extra wedding?"

"Mind?" Emily looked at her, incredulous. "Honey, I loved marrying you so much I think I'm going to do it again in a couple of hours. What do you say?"

"Just what I said before, Emily: I do."

Want to know how their love story began? Read *Presidential*, where these two first meet.

Weekend Getaway

by Thea Belmont

Selene/Vivienne

Vivienne stowed her bag in the car's trunk before she stepped back to close it. The air was chilled, despite the bright blue skies.

She turned to say goodbye, her sister hurried off the veranda, a picnic basket in hand. "I know it's only a short trip, but there's some coffee and sandwiches for you and Selene both," she said, handing the basket over with a warm smile. "Hope you have a lovely birthday celebration, Viv."

Vivienne rolled her eyes, but took the basket from her to place it on the backseat of the car. "Thank you, Hattie, but it will only be a few hours' drive. We don't need to stop along the way."

"Never know," Hattie said. "There may be some delays or a flat wheel, and you'll be thankful for that warm bit of coffee."

She meant well, and as much as Vivienne wanted to argue, she bit her tongue and gave a short nod. Her sister was supportive, in her own way, and it was enough for her to soften and smile. "It's appreciated."

Wrapped warmly in gloves, a jacket, and a scarf, Vivienne's niece, Claudia, watched from the veranda. A familiar knowing smile sat bright on her face.

It was Claudia who'd first brought it up, weeks before Vivienne's birthday, casually asking when Selene might finally make her move into the Carter household official. "Her cooking is better than yours," Claudia had informed her, cheekily. "So it would be better if you could ask her before I go off to college."

This weekend…if all things went well, Vivienne would broach the topic.

"Right," Hattie said, stepping back. "I trust you've got everything, but were there any errands here you needed me to run while you were gone?"

"No, Hattie. But thank you."

"Don't rush your trip, enjoy it. Lord knows that once classes start up again, you'll both be busy little bees."

That was undoubtedly true. Vivienne smiled and gave a short nod and then she was climbing into the car.

As she drove off, she checked her rearview mirror. Smiling, Claudia and Hattie waved as Vivienne pulled away before heading back inside. Hattie had already moved out to her own place, and was only staying the weekend to look after Claudia.

The house felt different without her sister residing there in the last year. But as of late, most days Selene would stay until dinner. Usually sleeping over on the weekends. They still had a family Sunday dinner together with the four of them.

Something that Vivienne had worried would be awkward, given Selene was Claudia's high school principal. But her niece had taken to her in the last year.

The weather was cold. Freezing really. To prep for picking up Selene, she placed the heaters on high and the seat warmer on for both herself and the passenger side.

Selene stepped out of the house, dressed in a dark coat and black woollen stockings, her thick hair spilling over her shoulders as she stepped off the stairs, her eyes catching Vivienne's before she headed around to the back of the car.

Even now, Vivienne felt as enamoured with her, as the first time she'd stood before her.

After stowing her own bag in the trunk, Selene slid into the passenger seat, her eyebrows arching in question as she turned to Vivienne. "Seat warmers, my, my what other gifts do you have for this weekend?" And then she was leaning forward, pressing a kiss to Vivienne's lips before a protest could be argued.

Vivienne sighed into Selene's soft lips, that familiar flutter igniting in her chest.

She leaned back, captivated as a soft smile graced Selene's features. "You look so lovely."

"In a woollen sweater and slacks?" Vivienne asked, her eyebrow raised. "I think you're lovesick."

A soft laugh escaped Selene, but her gaze lingering on Vivienne's face. "More than likely," she said. "But I'm all the richer for it."

There was a pause, and then Vivienne hesitated, wondering if she should bring up what they agreed to. "We don't have to play this weekend. I'm not your client any more, I don't want you—"

She was shushed as Selene pressed a single finger to her lips, a bright smile on her lips. "Ms Carter, I am delighted to accompany you this weekend. I believe we discussed arrival at the hotel in the city, and then tomorrow we would go to the art museum, before some recreational shopping until at last, dinner. Is that correct?"

"It is."

Selene had a way of easily bringing them into role play. Taking the reins without ever making Vivienne feel that she was out of control. If anything, she felt utterly and completely at ease, knowing that at any time they could break the scene and it would be just them again.

"I have a feeling this weekend is going to be a lot of fun." Selene's fingers found Vivienne's, their hands entwining, before Vivienne squeezed.

And just like that they fell out of the scene. A quiet tell to ease each other back into the selves.

Vivienne pulled onto the road, flicking her car's stereo to play a radio show for their first hour. It was mostly a conversation starter, and they both took to it quickly, discussing the hosts' opinions and then going off on their own tangents, getting into a disagreement over the semantics of morality versus ethics, a topic that few found enjoyable in Vivienne's circle, and yet Selene was eager to battle against her.

Selene's mind was as sharp as hers, she'd read as much as Vivienne had, but having had a very different life, filled with foster homes and struggling finances, came at different viewpoints—whereas Vivienne had never once known what it was like to not have a safety net. Instead she'd attended private school and boarded, expecting to grow up, financially succeed, and look after her sister.

"Did we pass the roadhouse?" Selene asked suddenly, twisting in her seat to look at a passing road sign.

"A few miles back. Why?"

"It was a landmark that I used to measure how far away we were from the city."

"The GPS is right there," she said, pointing to the screen in the centre console.

Selene looked at it and then to her. "I prefer landmarks. There's something more *real* about going, 'ah, yes, the dog statue, we must only be an hour out, now'."

Vivienne rolled her eyes and shook her head. She used GPS for any of her lengthy trips, even when they were for something as simple as a direct highway to the city. "We're only two hours out. You can sleep if you want to."

"Hmm. There's definitely something that I want to do." Selene turned her head to look at Vivienne mischievously. "Two hours is a very long time, and I didn't see you at all yesterday."

No, Vivienne had been busy preparing for the trip. "And what, exactly, would that be?"

"Coffee."

Vivienne blinked. That was unexpected. "Coffee?"

"Why? What were you thinking about?"

Ah, that was the game, Vivienne realised. She was going to be teased this weekend to continue to build suspense. "As it is, Hattie packed us a light morning tea. Would you like to pull over somewhere?"

"There's a place up here, on the right," Selene said. "I used to stop here all the time when I travelled back and forth for conferences."

A little further along, there was a road that peeled off to a rest stop. There was a public restroom, but also picnic tables. Parking had allocated places for caravans, but Vivienne drove into the car parking, before climbing out of the car, into the brisk air, and taking the picnic basket aside. It was an old wicker basket that opened up with red lining. On the lining were individual spots for cutlery, plates and cups to set into.

Just as promised, Hattie had packed coffee, chocolate chip cookies, that her and Claudia had baked, and tomato and cheese sandwiches nestled with an ice pack to keep them chilled.

A cool breeze swept around them, prompting Selene to snuggle close to Vivienne. She had the coffee in grip and smiled. "This is nice," she said, sipping at the hot coffee.

Vivienne eased, leaning against Selene. It was nice, despite the chill. Before them was an open area of trees and grassland, the early morning frost dripping from the greenery.

She didn't usually take time to stop, outside of filling up the car. The faster they arrived at a destination, the better. But Vivienne wouldn't deny that sitting here, and taking a moment to enjoy the travel with Selene was far more enjoyable.

"I was thinking…" Selene said, moving to sit up.

Vivienne's chest tightened, hoping that Selene wasn't going to ask her to move in. She had a carefully laid out plan to ask.

"Maybe…we could go away for the summer. For two weeks?" Selene finished.

Vivienne softened and smiled. "Where were you thinking?"

"Anywhere. By the beach, on top of a mountain, I don't care. Somewhere you speak the language and can impress me with your dialect."

Vivienne laughed. "South France is lovely in summer. How does wine and cheese in a chateau sound?"

"Perfect."

The remainder of their drive moved to soft discussions, dipping into light-hearted stories of their travels. Vivienne talked about her time in the south of France, and how she made her way from place to place, until she ended up in Paris. Selene then cheekily discussed art thefts and conspiracy theories on the Mona Lisa, but when Vivienne tried to pry into discussions of artists or their bodies of work, Selene remained vague—advising that she couldn't wait to show her around the museum.

It left Vivienne hungry and eager for their upcoming tour through the galleries.

The open road turned into the suburbs and then quickly, they were on the motorway, taking them into the city and navigating hellish city drivers.

Once they arrived, Vivienne parked in the hotel lot before she pulled out their bags.

Selene had a mischievous smile on her face as she quickly took back her bag, tutting that she didn't want her to know any secrets.

"And what secrets do *you* have?" Vivienne asked.

Selene grinned at her. "Almost there. Soon we'll have an entire hotel room to ourselves where we don't have to worry about who else may be around to hear."

Vivienne scoffed, looked away and walked towards the entrance. The concierge desk stood to the immediate left, and after confirming her name and credit card, they were provided with their room keys.

It was past midday but not quite evening and Vivienne planned to enjoy the next few hours with Selene, uncaring as to whether they missed dinner. They stepped into the elevator, Selene moving to stand close beside her.

As the doors slid shut and Vivienne pressed their floor number, her hand instinctively brushed against Selene's.

A comforting warmth radiated from Selene's hand as her fingers curled around Vivienne's. With a soft sigh, she rested her head against Vivienne's shoulder, a silent expression of contentment.

"There's no expectations," she told Selene. "Tonight we can just rest. Enjoy our own company in a hotel far away from work."

"We'll see how we feel," Selene teased with a glance.

Their room was spacious, there was a bed, a kitchenette, a bathroom with a sizeable shower and separate bath large enough for the both of them. There was a television mounted to the wall, before a lounge, separating the bed from the kitchenette in a small sitting space with tasteful city photography on the wall.

They set their bags down, and then Selene put her hands around Vivienne's waist and kissed down her throat.

"How about we order in for dinner and I show my appreciation for this lovely weekend you've booked for us?" Selene asked. "I want to take my time to ensure you understand my gratitude."

Vivienne warmed at the comment, turning to press her lips to Selene's. Her girlfriend's fingertips undid her slacks, tugging the zipper down. "And what about my gratitude?"

"Tomorrow," Selene promised, her breath soft against her lips. "I want to taste you."

There'd been a time where Vivienne had wondered what domestic bliss would feel like with Selene. She'd thought that, like in sex, Selene would vie for control, tugging and teasing only to occasionally permit it to be the other way around. But Vivienne was wrong on both parts.

She was no longer Selene's client, which meant that the last year she had explored a new dynamic with her, filled with love and respect and patience.

She knew that Selene was content to have her head on Vivienne's chest, an arm around her waist and saw no reason to deviate from it, preferring to fall asleep listening to her heart. Whereas in sex, Selene was as excited to be led as she was to lead—or in some cases, mutually work with Vivienne to bring them both to new heights of ecstasy.

The powerful side of the dominatrix could be brought present at any moment, but the respect between them never wavered. They were never unequal, no matter the power-play. And the last year, Selene had taught Vivienne more about that than before.

It made the scenes they did more fun. Vivienne was able to relax, even when a riding crop was dragging around her hips in warning. The excitement pulling at every breath. She wanted to be pushed to the edge, because she knew, underneath it all, she was loved and respected. That nothing either of them did would ever be a cause of embarrassment or shame. Their moments in sex were fun, cathartic, and sometimes soothing.

There was also the occasional laugh when things went wrong or became silly—but never at the other's expense.

Selene had spent the early months of their first meetings to ensure she knew this and Vivienne had spent every moment since, ensuring she treated her with the same respect.

Reaching out, she dragged her fingers through Selene's hair and felt as her girlfriend's hands tightened on her waist, a moment before she relaxed back into a deep sleep, her breaths becoming long and slow.

Peeking down at her, warmth hummed through Vivienne, anticipation still prickling on her skin for tomorrow.

Her home had always been at the Carter Manor. She'd travelled the world, lived in other houses and apartments, but a sense of home had always been where she'd grown up in Oakwood. And yet…each moment she spent away from Selene, she was realising that she was homesick. Somehow, she felt as much at home as being with Hattie and Claudia.

Vivienne reached over to the bedside table, and flicked the lamp off, holding Selene close as she kissed the top of her head and pondered one question she'd asked herself before making any lifelong decision.

If this was for the rest of their life, would she be content?

In the depths of her heart, she knew she would be more than that.

She wanted to spend the rest of her life waking up with Selene in her arms.

Vivienne awoke to lips on her neck, kissing down her throat and shoulder, before she inhaled the scent of coffee.

Selene stood before her, wearing only a bathrobe and holding a mug of French press coffee. "Good morning, darling. I had a peek at your itinerary and noticed that you were hoping to leave in the next hour, so I thought that you might want to wake up, despite how cute your snores are."

"I don't snore," Vivienne muttered.

Despite the end of her comment, her chest fluttered at the thought that, although Selene didn't feel the same way about a need for itinerary on a weekend getaway, she understood that it was important to Vivienne they follow it. Vivienne had spent a fair amount of time perfecting it to maximise the weekend and ensure every moment led up to where she needed it to.

"Thank you," Vivienne took the mug of coffee and brought it to her lips, feeling her shoulders relax. "Did you have any thoughts about the itinerary?"

"Breakfast at the hotel, then a walk around the park, before arriving at the art gallery where it was noted that you expect me to provide you with a grand tour." Selene paused to pose dramatically, which only further served to reveal her naked body beneath the robe.

Vivienne's eyes dropped, shamelessly admiring the view as she nodded. "You did promise, after all."

"I'm not sure an open-ended comment about my time of hopping between galleries for free food consists of…promising. But for you? I'll make the exception." At that, Selene reached forward with one hand, tilting Vivienne's eyes to face hers. "Thought you might be worn out from last night."

"Hardly."

Selene's hand shifted to cup her cheek before she leaned forward and kissed her again. "I should get ready," Selene advised, "before I distract you any further."

Vivienne smiled, sipping her coffee.

By the time she'd finished waking up, Selene had dressed and began to do her hair and makeup.

Vivienne got up and started to dress. As she watched Selene comb her fingers through her hair, fixing wayward strands into place, she couldn't help but remember what she'd looked like caught in ecstasy, her hair unravelling around her.

"Mm?" Selene's gaze met hers in the mirror.

"Thinking about what I plan to do to you tonight."

There was a soft laugh. "I never would have expected the shivering woman on my doorstep to become so cocky."

"Cocky?" Vivienne scoffed, pulling the jacket tighter around her. "You haven't seen me at my worst. Now, shall we finish getting ready? I don't enjoy being off schedule."

Selene smiled at Vivienne, before returning to the mirror. "I can be persuasive," she teased.

Vivienne reached into her bag and tucked a small present away into her coat pocket.

As they made their way downstairs, to the hotel restaurant, Vivienne continued to tap at the box, as if it might suddenly jump out of the coat.

Not that it would matter. It wasn't an engagement ring. It wasn't something pricey. But when she'd imagined the moment, it had been with the key.

In the hotel restaurant, Vivienne felt Selene's eyes gaze to her over and over again, as if she knew each time Vivienne was tapping at the box.

As they sat at a table, Selene placed her hand over Vivienne's. "You seem anxious. Is there anything I can do?"

"Hardly anxious."

Selene gave her a knowing look. "I thought we promised to be honest with each other and our feelings?"

Vivienne relented. "I haven't done a romantic weekend away in quite some time. I want it to be perfect."

"The best stories come from mistakes, too," Selene said. "Whatever happens, I am happy to be here with you."

"What do you think of the local art museums?" Vivienne asked.

Selene, taking the hint, allowed the conversation to drift about her own history with the arts and its patrons, coloring a strange picture of a young, starving Selene using exhibition openings as a way to drink free alcohol and talk to artists by chance whilst dining on platters of dried fruit, cheese, and cold meats.

"I became a server at a catering company for a short time. We got to take the leftovers home. Including the wine. All very exciting—but eventually I tired of the pay, and was offered a tidy sum to model for artists. I enjoyed that more."

Vivienne smiled. "I've done it for a partner, but I preferred photography."

"Oh, I recall," Selene teased. "I do love your candids. Especially when I'm busy in meetings. Makes them go faster."

Vivienne hummed softly, before her gaze drifted to the clock on the wall, noting the advancing hour. "I think we should traverse through the park if the weather holds."

They exited the hotel, the cold air washing over them. Vivienne reached into her pockets, pulling her gloves on, and Selene did the same.

Taking a deep breath, cool air filled her lungs as she tilted her head to look up at the sky. It was likely to snow later, but for now, it was just a cold winter's day, with a thick cloud cover. Stepping closer to Selene, she slid her hand around her waist, feeling an eased comfort from her presence.

They walked through the streets together, stopping to get takeaway coffees to keep their hands warm, and then both of them spent the next ten minutes complaining about how horrible the coffees were before discarding them when they no longer supplied warmth.

It was easy to laugh with Selene, to pause as they waited for street lights to change, and see her expression warm as she caught Vivienne staring.

More than a year had passed, and with each day, she found herself falling deeper in love with Selene.

Vivienne was at ease, not worrying about work, or family, or life. It was as if every worry was a tangled mess that Selene helped to spool into something tidy. Something easier to address. And when that was too large to tackle, Selene had a way about her that could make Vivienne forget her worries.

She couldn't recall the last time laughter had bubbled up so freely that her head tilted back. But with Selene recounting her disastrous first babysitting job from her mid-twenties, such unrestrained joy came effortlessly.

Detailing the horror of a child who had been so good at hide and seek, Selene feared he'd run away. Only to later find him having fallen asleep in a laundry hamper.

"Did you ever want children?" Selene asked. "Before Claudia?"

"I did," Vivienne said. "But Claudia came before I found any partner I wanted that with."

"Do you still want children?"

"No," Vivienne said. "For a while, I considered it. And…then," she paused, swallowing. She wanted to push the feelings away and snuff them down. But Selene had been so open and so candid with her.

"We can talk about something else," Selene said softly, pausing on the path to look at her. "There are ducks over there."

Vivienne glanced over to where her girlfriend pointed and looked at what, decidedly, were not ducks. If anything, they looked to be a collection of sculptures. "You need to get your eyes checked," she said before smiling.

Selene blinked back at her, frowning. "You can't see them?"

A soft laugh escaped Vivienne as she reached out, her fingers gently adjusting the lapels of Selene's jacket, smoothing them with care. "When we return home, I kindly request you have your eyes checked, because those, my love, are stone statues."

Selene frowned and then looked away. "Fine. But you'll have to come with me to hold my hand."

At that, Vivienne tried to swallow back a laugh. "Are you telling me that you're afraid of the optometrist?"

"Deathly," Selene said before giving a small giggle, as if unable to contain the ridiculousness of her statement.

Vivienne warmed at the sound, lacing her arm around Selene's waist again. Their steps were slow and steady as they tried to find sync with one another. The conversation had moved on, but Vivienne could still feel the question pressing between them. "I worried that it would affect Claudia," she said. "That's why I never pursued it. I didn't want Claudia to ever doubt that I loved her as my own. I've seen what it does to children and she's suffered too much."

"You've sacrificed a lot for her."

"I don't regret it," Vivienne said. "When I see the young woman that Claudia is becoming, I am so proud of her. I wouldn't change a thing." She paused then, reflecting on the last year. "Perhaps I would ask she not get into so much trouble with her school's principal, but it seemed to work out well for us."

"Mm. We wouldn't be here if I hadn't considered suspension. I could have done without the proceeding headache of school fights—but I'm pleased to see that she hasn't had so much as a detention since last year." Selene drew her closer. "You're a good mother, Vivienne. God knows Claudia has turned into the woman she is because of you."

"Oh, headstrong and argumentative?"

"Well, I would have said authoritative, but yes, you can be headstrong too," she teased, kissing her temple. "But it's an admirable trait."

"And the argumentative side?"

"Mm. It makes you a good academic," Selene teased, "Where are we on the itinerary, by the way?"

Vivienne softened and reached into her pocket to pull out her phone. She tensed for a moment, uncertain if the box was still in her pocket. Relief washed over her as her fingers found it nestled securely on the opposite side of her jacket. "We have time to stroll."

"Oh, to stroll do we?"

Vivienne hummed, taking Selene's arm in hers once more and pressing her head to Selene's shoulder. "Stroll," she confirmed. "And you can tell me about why you became a teacher."

"Oh, now that is a story," Selene said. "I was in the peak of my career and no longer a starving ragamuffin on the street, so—"

"You lived on the street?" Vivienne asked.

Selene flushed. "For a time," she admitted, "But it was a very long time ago, and only for a few months. Now—"

"Why were you on the street?"

"Vivienne," Selene said, "Do you want that story or the story about how I was inspired to teach?"

Vivienne contemplated the question, relenting to listen to Selene. "Teach," she said, "But you can tell me the other story later."

Selene nodded and then began detailing what the peak of her career looked like and how she'd begun attending exclusive art openings with clients. One such client was a private school principal who had specific fantasies about being a teacher in need of punishment from her principal.

"She wanted me to be exact in the role. Each session I would get notes about what a principal would say or do, what I needed to do, and I ended up reaching out to a friend who was catering a conference. I helped out, listened to a lot of the speeches, thinking that I was getting some research and some free food to take home...and instead found myself entirely enamoured by the idea of becoming a teacher. I thought I could make a difference, even if it was only with one child." Selene paused then, biting her lip as she looked to Vivienne.

"So...why high school?"

"In part, I wish someone at the schools had known the signs of a neglected foster child and could help out. The work I do with the school isn't perfect, but I won't allow any of the children to be disadvantaged. I look out for the signs of a struggling student. Listening to the PTA discuss things like divorce, or financial struggles, to see what I can do for the students. If I've only made a difference for one child, then it was all worth it."

Vivienne softened, her arm tightening around Selene. "You've made more than one child safer. Claudia has assured me of that."

When they arrived at the art museum, Vivienne purchased the tickets to the modernist collection and pressed her hands in her pocket, feeling the lump.

Though a few patrons wandered through the other galleries of the art collection, the current room was blessedly empty, offering Vivienne the perfect chance to stand close beside Selene and quietly appreciate the artwork.

"This one appears to be more impressionist than modern," Vivienne said, baiting Selene.

"Ah, that's because modern art overlaps impressionists; it's when artists began to become experimental," Selene advised, "both with form and style, but also the mediums they used. This is an oil painting, but that one there is a lithograph, which allowed the middle-class to buy prints instead of commissioning new artwork. Essentially reforming how we view and obtain art." She continued on, detailing how Manet came into modern art, wishing that the *Luncheon on the*

Grass was here to share with Vivienne–whilst teasing her in the next breath that she should pose nude for her by the river in summer.

"Seems risky," Vivienne pointed out.

But Selene smiled. "If we go to the South of France, it won't be. It'll just be french."

Perhaps, then, Vivienne decided.

Most of the art was studies on the female form, and as Selene talked about the mixed media component, detailing art history with German and Dutch art schools, Vivienne listened attentively, following Selene's gestures to the way the strokes of the pencil or paint, the use of the colour. And as Selene became truly, utterly distracted, Vivienne found herself utterly enamoured.

"See this shade of yellow? It's chrome-yellow, the same shade is used in Van Gogh's Sunflower series. It's made with lead and some well-known carcinogenic, so these days there's a 'safer' paint to use, but a lot of artists choose to use this one because they prefer the pigment."

Vivienne smiled. "What would you prefer if you were painting sunflowers?"

There was a soft, focused look and then a smile. "Depends on the lighting and what surrounds it. If you were wearing a crown of sunflowers, I would use purple amongst the yellow. Because the light would bounce the red tones of your hair against the flowers."

There was an undeniable charm in someone being so intelligent and gazing at you with such adoration, their fingers gently tracing paths through your hair.

"It's lunchtime," Vivienne said when Selene's hand dropped away. "Did you want to sit at the Museum's restaurant, or did you want to go out somewhere else?"

Selene tilted her head, a silent question in her eyes at the shift in topic, before a slow, warm smile spread across her face. "Here's fine."

They dined at the Museum's restaurant, sharing the tasting plate while drinking before returning to the galleries.

A contemporary collection had Selene continue to talk about each piece they stepped before, studying the didactic panel, before her voice, warm and confident, began to ponder about the choices.

Vivienne couldn't help but drink in her words as if she were a student again, attending an art history conference.

There was something beautiful about watching passion—in such a way that Vivienne found herself thinking about their future. What art would they collect? What new up-and-coming artist would they discover?

"I feel as though I've taken up all the conversation," Selene ducked her head. "I'm sure you didn't intend for such a prolonged lecture about why we have to view the lens of class when we look at art."

Vivienne shook her head. "It was exactly what I hoped for."

"Anyone else, and I would think they were flattering me," Selene said, before she leaned forward, pressing a kiss to her lips. "What's next on the list, darling?"

"Nothing until this evening. I thought we could…" she trailed off.

Selene's eyes met hers.

"Go wandering, maybe I could buy a new dress. I've been meaning to buy some new lingerie if you'd like to come help me choose something?"

"Is that so?" Selene asked. She pulled back, smiling as her eyes ran over Vivienne's clothes. "I think I can be of assistance."

They made their way into the heart of the city, drifting through shops.

"Was there anywhere that you wanted to go, as well?" Vivienne asked.

"Oh, no, I›m quite happy to follow," Selene said, her head tilting. "Lead the way."

Vivienne followed along as they browsed the clothing shops. Selene's demeanour was thoughtful as her fingers skimmed across the racks of dresses, considering the styles with the focused air of selecting attire for a job interview.

Even as Vivienne teasingly walked through a lingerie store, Selene merely nodded approvingly, her expression soft.

Vivienne didn't know how, but there was a power shift. Suddenly, she felt as if Selene was leading, though she still deferred to Vivienne, inquiring about what the plans were for the rest of the day, and made no effort to direct her otherwise.

It was maddening, distracting. But more than anything, it was strangely having an effect on her. There was a challenge set.

Vivienne tried on a new bra, asking Selene's opinion.

Selene slid into the dressing room and glanced her over, drinking in the red, shibari-inspired bra. The matching underwear hung on a hook beside her, the absence of fabric obvious.

"Is it too much?" Vivienne asked, knowing it wasn't. "Not for tonight, but next weekend. I thought that while Claudia was away with her friends, you and I could…"

Her words faded as Selene's fingers found her bare waist, pulling Vivienne close until they were pressed together.

The material of Selene's black woollen cloak rubbed against her bare skin as her girlfriend's fingertips trailed up her waist, to her ribs and thumbed at the twisted rope that made up the band around her ribs.

"I could do this for you," Selene whispered. "After dinner. I brought some silk rope. If you'd like me to tie you up, all you had to do was ask."

"So not this one?"

Selene smiled, her lips brushed at her throat, a blunt nail ran along Vivienne's ribs. "If you want rope, I want to be the one doing it. Not this manufactured design."

There was something there in her voice. Strong, commanding and yet as she met Selene's eyes, she knew why.

Turning around, facing the woman, she smiled. "Do you really think that some corporate design would ever match your skill?"

"No. But it gives me ideas," Selene said, before her eyes flicked to where the bottom half of the lingerie hung. "Will you let me tie you up tonight?"

"Depends," Vivienne said.

"On what?"

"On how dinner goes." She stepped away, removed the red bra and picked her own up. She was pleased that her plan had the desired effect as Selene stepped back, watching her redress. There was a flush to her lover's cheeks. Her blue eyes appeared darker with the dilated pupil. She only hoped that it added to her evening plans instead of hindering them.

"Before dinner, we could—"

"No," Vivienne said, biting on her tongue to stop her pleased laugh. "I want you to wait. And then you may have me however you want…so long as I get to taste you."

As they made their way back to the hotel to prepare for dinner, Vivienne noted that Selene had returned to carefully placed touches. One hand on the middle of her back, a gentle touch against her arm. A strange, chaste choice in touch following the change room.

No kisses, no longing looks, no fingertips that tugged at her coat, or arms that slid around her waist.

There wasn't even a flirtatious remark.

Good. It meant that she was entirely flustered.

At dinner, everything changed. It was a luxurious restaurant, and Vivienne had booked a private seating with a set menu and wine pairing. Which meant that they were seated on a private balcony, separate from any prying eyes.

They were in the chill winter air, two heaters standing tall behind them, warm enough that Vivienne was able to comfortably remove her jacket as Selene did the same.

Selene looked good, in a dark, tight-fitting dress that went off the shoulders. Enough so that Vivienne wanted to forgo the meal and get directly into that evening's plans, but she held strong.

She also knew she looked good, and would run her fingertips over the wine glass, drawing Vivienne's gaze to the fingertips, before bringing the glass to her lips, licking at the wine droplets.

Swallowing, Vivienne looked aside, and ignored the toe of the shoe, dragging against her calf.

"What are you thinking about, Vivienne?" Selene purred, setting the glass back down.

"You."

"Do tell?"

Vivienne slowly shook her head no. "Not until dessert."

They were on their second course, and therefore their second wine pairing, when she reached behind her, checking the jacket pocket and felt a spike of anxiety. "I…" she began, and flicked her eyes up to Selene.

The mischief slid away from Selene and the woman sat up, setting her glass aside. "Yes?"

"I hope you don't mind me being sentimental here. It's been over a year since I've had the pleasure of meeting you. I got to know you in your private life, your professional and now your personal. I've come to realise—"

The waitress interrupted and cleared their finished plates, offering a polite inquiry about their satisfaction with the meal before refilling their water glasses. But Vivienne felt all the more parched as Selene's shoe accidentally brushed against hers before she made an apology and shifted in her seat.

How was it that she could look so utterly seductive doing nothing? Was it the way she lifted a hand to brush her hair from her eyes, or how she glanced at Vivienne and smiled with such a knowing look?

Once the waiter had departed, assuring them their next course would arrive shortly, Selene's gaze drifted towards the balcony. The sprawling cityscape seemed to capture her attention.

Cars passed, lights changed on the tall buildings, and Vivienne thought about how she wanted this moment to imprint in her mind forever.

"You were saying?" Selene prompted.

Vivienne flushed, looked away, and finished her wine, focusing back into the moment. "I suppose, what I'm trying to get at is..."

Movement caught her eyes. The waiter arrived with a fresh bottle of wine, next in the tasting presented by the sommelier who began a detailed explanation of the next dish as he presented the accompanying wine, discussing the color and palate, before he poured it into fresh glasses as the previous ones were discreetly removed.

Vivienne felt sorry for whoever the dish-hand was. From three courses already, she'd felt there'd been over nine plates of food and three sets of wine glasses between them. She couldn't imagine what the rest of the tables were like on top of that.

A small wagyu pastry with a wasabi-soy sauce blend was set out. To be enjoyed in its entirety, the waiter said before leaving.

Selene picked it up and then leaned forward, presenting it to her. "In its entirety," Selene echoed. "Open wide."

Vivienne leaned forward, her gaze dropping momentarily as her lips parted. Then, she felt the delicate touch of Selene's fingers placing the pastry on her tongue. Her mouth closed around it, her tongue and lips sucking over the fingertips, drawing them in as she looked into her eyes. She watched desire bloom across Selene's face before releasing her fingers from her lips.

Selene took a deep breath, then her mouth parted with a soft exhale as she gave a soft laugh. "I'm going to tie you up, just like that first time, Vivienne. But this time, I will fuck you."

"Is that so? And what about what I want?"

"We could step into the bathroom for a moment," Selene said.

"Mm. Not until dessert," Vivienne said, sipping her wine.

The box in her lap felt sturdy. She flicked it around once, twice and then smiled at Selene before she set the box on the table. It was large enough for a bracelet.

Selene's eyes went wide, curious. "I thought I was the one who was meant to be giving you a gift."

"Open it," Vivienne said.

Selene's eyes flicked to hers and a familiar, knowing look crossed her face. "This wouldn't happen to have anything to do with some hints that Claudia was dropping recently...about how her Aunt Hattie had moved out, and she was left with your awful cooking except for the evenings I visited, and wouldn't it be easier if I lived closer to the school rather than so far outside of town?"

Vivienne closed her eyes for a moment, trying to hold back something between a laugh and an annoyed sigh. "I thought she'd stop meddling with us."

"I suspect she was trying to angle if I was as interested as you," Selene said. "But she's seventeen, now. And hasn't yet worked out how to be subtle…much like her mother." Selene's gaze held a directness that was impossible to ignore.

Vivienne felt as though an old knot in her chest had unraveled. "I can be subtle."

"Yes, the constant checking of your pocket all day was certainly subtle," Selene teased. But her eyes were bright. "There's nothing more that I would love than to move in with you and Claudia both. So as long as you promise to come to the South of France with me."

"I promise."

Only then did Selene open the box, and her eyes lit up as she picked up the set of keys on a black keyring. Hanging from it was a keychain with a star map engraved with the constellation from their first meeting.

"I may not physically be able to give you the stars, but I hope you know that there's little I wouldn't try to do for you."

"Vivienne Carter…" Selene blinked as she looked up at the sky. "I am wearing very expensive foundation and you are going to make me cry!"

Reaching out, Vivienne took Selene's hand and squeezed. "I love you."

"I love you too," Selene said.

When dinner had finished, Selene led her down the street, fingers brushing against her hand.

It was busy, the city filled with people enjoying their evening, heading out in the cold to their next destination. But Vivienne felt as though every noise drained away as she leaned against Selene.

"Did you ever think this would happen?" Selene asked, as they waited at the lights to cross the street back to their hotel. "When you called my number?"

"When I booked a dominatrix, did I think I'd fall in love with her?" Vivienne laughed. "No. But my life has been all the richer for it."

If you enjoyed this story, you can read how their love story began in *Principle Decisions*.

Almost Perfect

by Tiana Warner

This was supposed to be the moment. Barefoot in the sand, romantic speech rehearsed, the tropical sun shining down on us as I ask Cate whether she's ready to talk about marriage—whether she'd be open to me proposing soon. See, you can't just *pop the question* on someone like her—an A-list celebrity, Hollywood's hottest, a woman whose entire life is put under a microscope every time her relationship status changes. You've got to plan it carefully, to ask her permission and let her know it's coming while keeping the details a secret.

It has to be just right. It has to be perfect.

Instead, sand kicks up behind us as we race along the beach, our sweaty hands clasped, while a trio of paparazzi snap pictures of us in swimsuits like we're endangered wildlife.

My lungs burn. My thighs scream. We weave through sunbathers, dodging inflatable unicorns and children wielding plastic shovels. A gaggle of teenagers on a blanket gasp and scrabble for their phones, holding them up like medieval villagers brandishing torches.

"Oh my God, that was Cate Whitney!"

Their voices fade behind us as we push faster.

This is *not* how the morning was supposed to go. This isn't how *any* part of our romantic Hawaiian getaway was supposed to go.

"This way," Cate whispers, barely audible over the hissing waves and the shouts.

"Cate! Just one picture!"

We veer onto the boardwalk, and I let out a high-pitched "eep!" as we narrowly avoid a surfer lugging his board. He glares at us, his annoyance melting into shock as he realizes who nearly mowed him down.

"I *knew* Mandy shouldn't have made you post a picture," I hiss. My words jolt as my toes catch on the rope barrier separating the boardwalk from the pool deck of whatever hotel this is. Cate's fingers tighten over mine, saving me from a face-plant. Now, *that* would be a photo.

"I know. You were right," she says, her voice strained. "People must have recognized the background."

The paparazzi are still shouting.

"Give us that gorgeous smile!"

"Have you two talked about marriage?"

I groan. The romantic atmosphere we've cultivated over the past two days has shattered like a dropped champagne flute. Our quiet beach strolls, kisses, sex in our luxurious suite…all reduced to tabloid fodder. Not to mention the important subject I was about to broach, stolen by a random man shouting it at us. Fantastic. How am I supposed to ask her about marriage now? She'll think I'm only asking because of public pressure.

We navigate a maze of lounge chairs and huts surrounding a multi-tiered pool, trying not to fall into one of the many hot tubs. The faint scent of chlorine replaces the salty sea air. A lazy river winds through it all, flowing through a garden and beneath an artificial waterfall. As our bare feet slap the wet stone, my chest is so tight, I can't breathe. Two years of therapy techniques desert me as sweat breaks out across my skin. I've been working on my crippling camera fear, but being ambushed by paparazzi while my pale ass is hanging out of a tiny bikini is a new level of unfair.

"Try to ignore them," Cate pants beside me. She yanks me behind a cabana and cups my face with her other hand. Her chest heaves, her eyes wide as she holds my gaze. "Are you okay?"

"Living my best life," I say. Now is not the moment to dive into my deepest thoughts and feelings about having bikini photos taken without my consent.

My hair pokes into my eyes, the short, sandy-colored locks damp with sweat, and I push it back irritably.

Cate squeezes my hand, seeming to read me. The concern in her eyes is heart-melting. "Come on. In the lazy river."

She makes a break for it and jumps in, her shorts still on over her yellow one-piece. The splash obscures her beneath the turquoise water.

There's no time to consider. Leaving my own shorts on—my phone is back at the hotel, thank God—I take a flying leap, tucking my knees up and doing a cannonball.

The cool water swallows me, chlorine burning my nose. My ears ring. I force my eyes open and find Cate swimming under the waterfall. Staying beneath the surface, I frog kick after her.

The thunderous roar of the falls fills my head—and, with it, a surge of hope. This leads into a tunnel. The cameras won't be able to follow.

On the other side of the falls, I emerge with a gasp, wiping water from my eyes. Before I can get my bearings, Cate's fingers close around my arm, pulling me away from the tunnel's entrance. We slosh through the waist-deep water, our legs moving slowly, and duck into an alcove.

Our heavy breaths fill the space.

The arched ceiling is high and designed to look like a cave. There's a swim-up bar across from us, but it's not even 10 a.m., so it's not open yet. It's just us. Us, and a couple of giggling kids paddling by on inflatable flamingos, oblivious to our presence.

"That was, um, resourceful of you." I sink down to my shoulders and lean back against the cold wall, fighting to catch my breath. This was not how I envisioned spending our morning, but at least we've found a refuge.

"The hotel staff should shoo them away," Cate says, sinking down next to me. "I'll have them call Ken, and he can escort us back."

I nod, suddenly wishing we'd asked her bodyguard to shadow us on our walk. *Yeah. Great way to kick up the romance.*

My heart is pounding against my ribs. I close my eyes, breathing meditatively, but all I achieve is a flashback to that time in Vancouver when we had to hide out from the paparazzi in the back room of a witchy shop. Some things never change.

Cate's warm hand brushes my cheek, soft and reassuring. "You okay?"

I meet her gaze. Her ice-blue eyes, usually sparkling with mischief, are filled with concern.

"Sure." My voice is shaky.

Cate doesn't buy it, frowning as she pushes a soaking lock of blonde hair away from her face. "I'm sorry, Rachel."

"Don't. It's not your fault."

She shakes her head, her brow furrowed. "I should've told Mandy no. But with the film coming up, she wanted to make sure my social media—"

"You don't have to explain yourself to me." I drift closer until our legs tangle beneath the surface, our skin slippery from sunscreen. I slide my hands around her waist. Being here with her—feeling the heat of her body through the thin, wet material of our swimsuits—helps ease the tightness in my chest. The panic recedes, replaced by a different kind of breathlessness. With Cate, I always feel safe. Loved. Accepted. She's my comfort, my adventure, and my home.

A drop of water glides down her cheek. I catch it with my thumb, letting my hand linger. Even after three years together, touching her feels surreal—like I'm still that starstruck fan who couldn't believe Cate Whitney knew my name, let alone loved me back.

I stay still, drinking in how perfect she is. The tropical sun has given her skin a golden glow, and even with her hair plastered to her face and her usual effortless style disrupted, she's breathtaking. More droplets glide down her face, neck, and chest, where her low-cut swimsuit plunges between her breasts.

She pulls me closer, the water swirling around us. "I was going to take you to this amazing secluded cove I found a few years ago," she murmurs, her voice taking on that low, husky tone that drives me wild. "It's just down the beach from here."

"Another time, then," I whisper back, a pang of regret in my stomach. This morning should have been special. I've spent weeks planning this conversation, imagining different ways I could propose, even imagining what our wedding would be like. This morning was going to be a step toward our future.

But her celebrity status always has other plans.

Cate's eyebrows furrow, mirroring my disappointment. Beneath the water, her hand brushes against her shorts, as if she's realizing she's still wearing them. Personally, I'm uncomfortably aware of my wet shorts flapping around my thighs. Ew.

With a sigh, Cate returns her hand to my neck, her elegant fingers tracing my jawline.

As always, her touch sends a shiver through me, making me forget about everything but her. I lean forward and melt into her. The world outside the tunnel—people's shouts and laughter, scraping chairs, the rhythmic slap of flip-flops on concrete—fades beneath the rush of the waterfall.

"Well, as long as we're trapped in here..." Cate murmurs, her lips brushing mine.

Chlorine mingles with her familiar taste as I close the distance. Her lips part for me, her playful tongue sending a surge of heat through my middle. The tension in my shoulders eases, and as her hands slide lower and pull me flush against her, I exhale into her mouth. Kissing her like this over the last couple of days—in the ocean, in the pool of our own hotel, on our private patio—has revved up my desire for her more than ever. I can barely handle the feel of her warm, irresistibly soft skin against mine beneath the water, not to mention the way her swimsuit leaves little to the imagination.

I let my hand wander between her thighs, and she hisses into my mouth. "Rachel, there are people around."

Her lips curve into a mischievous smile, and I smile back, letting out a breath of laughter. Maybe being forced into this hiding spot isn't so bad.

Click-click-click.

We freeze. Pull apart. Turn.

Behind the slush machine on the closed swim-up bar, a camera lens points through a small opening like the barrel of a gun. The paparazzo grins as he captures us in mid make out, and my stomach plummets. I meet Cate's eyes and see my own horror reflected there.

This is about to be everywhere.

So much for our private getaway.

Four days earlier

"You should pack a couple more formal pieces," Abby says, her arms overflowing with a mountain of clothing plucked from my walk-in closet. She dumps the whole thing onto the bed and shakes her dark hair back, out of breath.

"But I want to travel light!" I protest, reaching past the avalanche of suits and dress pants for a pair of sensible khaki shorts.

The usually pristine king-size bed and hardwood floor are a disaster zone of clothes, shoes, toiletries, and even the stack of medical journals I need to review for my next research presentation. It makes the room…well, a lot like my old apartment when I lived with Abby. I mean, it smells nicer here, with Cate's perfume lingering, but the chaos Abby and I have created in the last hour is weirdly comforting. Like, no matter how fancy my life with Cate becomes, Abby still treats me as the same humbly awkward grad student.

Abby puts her hands on her hips. "Fine. But don't come crying to me when Cate proposes in front of a tropical sunset and you're dressed like you're about to mow the lawn."

Heat floods my cheeks, and I glance at the open door, even though we're alone. Cate is out running errands, but the idea of her overhearing Abby's assumption is mortifying. "She likes me this way. And this isn't a proposal trip." I forcefully shove the khaki shorts into my carry-on suitcase as if to squash the nervous butterflies in my gut.

Proposal? No. Important conversation about our future? First on the agenda.

"Uh-huh. Just pack *one* more. This one." Abby plucks a lavender suit from the clothing mountain.

It's the one Cate bought me a few months ago for our third anniversary, which I wore to the award ceremony for my team's work in radiation therapy modeling. I can still picture Cate beaming at me from the audience while I stumbled through the speech she helped me write.

The suit's delicate fabric shimmers in the daylight streaming through the bay windows. I chew my lip, my stomach twisting into a knot. "It's not too formal for Hawaii?"

"You can leave the jacket off. Picture it: Romantic dinner overlooking the water at sunset, barefoot stroll along the moonlit beach, Cate gets down on one knee..." She frames my face with her fingers, sighing dreamily.

"Stop it," I groan, sinking down onto the bed. A stray hanger clatters to the floor. "You're going to make me act all weird and nervous the whole trip."

Abby perches next to me, bouncing on the mattress. "You still *want* to get engaged, don't you?"

"Of course! But we have to talk about—"

Abby kicks her feet and gives an excited squeak.

"—it before we do any asking!" I persist. "And I *know* there'll be a huge media frenzy when it happens, and the *world* will be watching and judging and... I don't know, it's scary looking at the failure rate of celebrity marriages. I love her too much to have our relationship reduced to something for the tabloids."

"Hun, your relationship has been all over the tabloids since you met."

I shoot her a glare. "Not helpful."

"Look, whatever happens with the media, you've faced worse, and you came through stronger."

"I guess..." I grab a pillow and hug it to my chest, breathing in Cate's familiar scent. There's also this nagging fear that I can't handle being married to someone so famous. Every time I think I've gotten used to the spotlight, something throws me off balance.

But then I remember how Cate looks at me when we're alone, and I want that forever.

Abby tilts her head, an understanding smile on her lips. "She loves you, Rachel, and this trip is special. She's planned this romantic getaway in paradise for just the two of you—"

"The two of us plus her bodyguard," I mumble. Nothing is ever *just the two of us* when Cate is this famous.

"Well, yeah, but it's not like Ken is going to be spooning with you at night."

I smile.

"I just think you should be prepared with a couple of nice dinner outfits in case she's got something in mind for this trip." Abby tosses the lavender suit at me. "The choice is yours. But you look super hot in this."

I look between the suit in my arms and the shorts in my open luggage. Everything I've packed so far represents safety, comfort, the familiar. The suit represents... Well, considering Cate gave it to me on our three-year anniversary and Abby is now telling me to wear it in case I get proposed to, it represents a hell of a lot. It's a future I'm both terrified of and desperate to run toward.

I let the lavender fabric glide between my fingers, remembering the way Cate's eyes lit up when I tried it on. It's the sort of outfit I never would've bought for myself in my old life, the sort I can continue to wear to red carpets, dinners, award shows—all as Cate's wife.

Wife. The word in connection to Cate has my heart doing a jig.

I gently fold the suit and pack it. It wouldn't hurt to be prepared—just in case we're about to start the next phase of our life together.

After a six-hour flight, we're finally here. The scent of plumeria and coconut wraps around me like a hug as we step into the lobby of our five-star Hawaiian hideaway. I let out a contented sigh, transported back to our first hotel stay together when we practically threw ourselves at each other after a night of shameless flirting. I'm as overwhelmed today as I was back then by how luxurious some hotels can be.

The lobby is open to the outdoors, letting the tropical air drift in. Beside the front desk, a waterfall cascades down a moss-covered wall, and overhead, crystal chandeliers catch the light. Colorful birds strut around a koi pond. Best of all is this impossibly beautiful woman holding my hand, casting a dazzling smile at the hotel staff.

I am in actual paradise.

"Welcome!" the receptionist says, her professional demeanor cracking slightly as she recognizes Cate. Her eyes dart between us, and I brace myself for the usual fawning, but she manages to hold it together as she checks us into their Ocean Suite.

I let out a breath and squeeze Cate's hand. I've come to appreciate small moments of normalcy.

After we get our room keys, Cate looks at her phone and sighs. "Mandy needs me to post a pic." She glances around, maybe searching for a suitable backdrop.

"Now?" I ask. The last thing we need is to broadcast our location to the world.

She must read the panic in my tone because she pulls me in and kisses my cheek. "I need to promote *Hidden Agendas*. I won't tag where we are."

Maybe one day I'll feel like we aren't inviting the whole planet into our private lives with every shared photo. But for now, with rabid fans stopping her whenever we're out in public, I think I have the right to feel like our privacy is on thin ice. Hell, last time we went out for dinner, someone took a photo of me with my shirt billowing out in the wind, and I had to endure a week of people speculating whether I was pregnant—including Mom, who called to ask me outright. As if it's possible for Cate and me to have an "oopsie."

Trying to hide my trepidation, I take Cate's phone. This is what loving her entails—balancing our private moments with her public life. So, I snap a photo of her in front of the mossy waterfall, carefully angling it so the hotel name isn't visible. The first try is stunning, of course, with her radiant smile and her golden hair fluttering in the breeze. God, those cheekbones.

Before I hand the phone back, I exercise my girlfriend rights and pull her in to plant a kiss right on one of those perfect cheekbones. She laughs, an adorable flush creeping up, and types a caption.

Getting in some much-needed R&R before diving back into work. Excited for you all to see #HiddenAgendas, in theaters on March 26!

"That's fine, right?" Cate asks.

I shrug. I'm not the person to ask for social media advice. "Sure."

She posts it. "Shall we?"

We step through the lobby's back doors and onto a golf cart, where a bellhop drives us along a paved path winding through the garden. By the time we walk into our suite to find a bucket of champagne, pineapple, fragrant tropical flowers, and chocolates, I'm back to forgetting the outside world exists. Could this be any more incredible?

The door closes behind the bellhop, and Cate crosses the living room to roll open the wall-to-wall sliding glass door. The air conditioning shuts off, and warm, humid air drifts in. Our second-floor balcony offers a breathtaking ocean view, the setting sun glinting off the water. In the silence, palm fronds rustle, and crashing waves are faintly audible in the distance.

I step out onto the patio with her, which feels like a sanctuary floating above the resort grounds. Two plush chaise lounges, a small table and chairs, and a round daybed with white cushions fill the space. Solid privacy walls on either side ensure we're sheltered from prying eyes. The isolation has me letting out a big breath. Nothing but the endless ocean and palm trees are in my line of sight. "Cate, this is perfect."

She spins, her glowing smile making my heart miss a beat.

I step closer, and she tucks my hair behind my ears, cradling my face between her palms. She holds me like that for a moment, her gaze darting over my face, before leaning in and pressing her lips to mine.

The kiss is tender at first, and then her lips open, and a familiar passion seeps in. Her hands flutter down my neck, arms, and waist, leaving trails of heat like I'm lying in the sun. I move with her, letting her guide the kiss, responding to her with soft moans. I tangle my fingers in her hair, the scent of her shampoo and perfume intoxicating. We stay suspended in the moment for a long time before we break apart, breathless and tousled.

"I could get used to this," I say, glancing out at the setting sun. Standing on this private patio, looking out at the empty ocean, it feels like the world is just us. No media noise, nobody else clambering for Cate's attention.

"I'm just happy to wake up with you every morning," she murmurs, not taking her eyes off me. "No matter where we are."

My heart skips at this reminder of the subject I want to broach. *Every morning.* We're already living together, so it's easy to imagine how it would feel to wake up as her wife. A thrill shoots through me like I'm standing at the edge of a cliff.

"I love you, Cate."

"I love you too," she says before locking her lips over mine again.

Well, we've got time. As she pulls me over to the round daybed on the patio and pushes me onto the plush cushions, I don't want to stop where this is going. I grin, and before I can catch my breath, her tongue is in my mouth and her fingers are fumbling for my zipper.

"Here? Outside?" I ask between kisses, my hands automatically moving to tug her dress upward.

"Nobody can see us but the birds," she responds, climbing on top of me. "I need you."

I can't argue with that.

As pleasure ripples through me and the prospects for this vacation stretch out ahead of us, giddy excitement washes over me. This is going to be a hell of a good trip.

Two days later

What a horrible fucking way to start the trip.

Emerging from the waterfall tunnel, I swipe water out of my eyes, coughing. The paparazzi are gone, but our moods are sour as we stomp back to our hotel with Ken.

"Didn't think we'd need him to escort us on a morning stroll," Cate mumbles as we traipse back through the sand with him lurking a few steps behind. Her shoulders are tense beneath the cover-up he brought her, the back of it soaked as her hair drips down.

"Yeah…" I cross my arms, soaked and shivering, chlorine still burning in my nose. My shorts rub my thighs, and my own clinging cover-up is damp and cold.

Paparazzi are part of the deal, I remind myself, fighting with a surge of resentment over the whole situation. *We met because she's a celebrity, and this is what being famous entails. She wouldn't be the Cate I know without this.*

Still, I'm allowed to wish, aren't I?

The awkward silence as we arrive back at our suite kills any possibility of broaching the marriage topic. Ugh. I'll have to find another opportunity.

I turn on the shower and peel off my wet shorts and bikini, needing to wash the chlorine out of my hair and the sticky sand off my legs. The bathroom is open concept, the shower easily big enough for two. "Want to join me?" I ask, hopeful that we can still salvage the morning.

"You go ahead," Cate says from the other room. "I want to make some calls."

"Oh." I try to mask my disappointment. "Okay."

I step under the rainfall showerhead, letting the hot water cascade down my scalp and shoulders. Steam billows out, but as blissful as this is, the tension doesn't really melt away.

I refuse to let the media ruin this trip. I *have* to find a moment to talk to her about our future. Maybe tonight during dinner? She made a reservation at a nice restaurant…

No, there will be people around. Staring. Listening. I want somewhere private where nobody's going to interrupt us or take surreptitious photos of us.

When I get out and wrap myself in an ankle-length white bathrobe, I find Cate on the patio. She's on the daybed in her own bathrobe, her bare feet curled under her. My heart flips just looking at her. I can't let today's chaos bother me. I've learned that we can't control it, but we can choose how to respond to it. We can keep holding each other tightly through it all.

An idea strikes. "Hey, let's go snorkeling later. We can take a boat to the middle of the open water where there are no crowds… Even if there are people around, our snorkel masks will be a good disguise."

She turns her bright smile onto me and waves her phone. "You're kidding. I've just booked us a snorkeling excursion after lunch. We're taking a private catamaran to a crater an hour away, and the spot is reserved for us alone."

I smile back, picturing the two of us floating in the turquoise water, surrounded by colorful fish and sea turtles. And here is one of the perks of her fame: In the time it took me to shower, she secured us a private snorkeling trip in the middle of paradise. "Sounds perfect."

Her eyes light up, and the look on her face reminds me that this is what matters—the way she makes my heart skip every time she smiles. The way we read each other's minds and always prioritize each other over everything else. The way I feel, deep in my core, that she is the person I want to spend the rest of my life with.

Sitting across from me on the catamaran, Cate's hair is pulled back into a braid, loose strands whipping around her face, her eyes hidden behind oversized sunglasses. Her relaxed smile tells me she's enjoying the rocking motion.

I, on the other hand, have never sailed on a catamaran, and each crest and dip makes my stomach toss around the truffle pasta I had for lunch. Ugh, the open water. The bliss of the first five minutes has evaporated as I focus on our destination: a half-moon of volcanic rock jutting out of the sea ahead. I just need to make it there, and everything will be fine.

Cate smiles at me, and I smile back, hoping it doesn't look strained. I try to concentrate on how beautiful she looks with the sun catching the gold in her hair, and her effortless grace as she shifts with the boat's movement. But another wave hits, and my intestines tie themselves in a knot. Of all the ways I pictured the marriage conversation going, projectile vomiting wasn't involved in any of them.

At last, the captain cuts the engine, plunging us into silence.

I take a deep breath of salt air and diesel fumes, which does nothing for my queasiness. Ahead, waves froth against the mound of exposed volcanic rock, seabirds squawking as they perch on top. Below, waves slap the hull, making it rock some more, and shadows move beneath the surface.

Ah, first seasickness, now sharks. Great start.

They're just fish and harmless reef sharks, Rach. They wouldn't send us in otherwise.

I hope, anyway.

We put on life jackets, flippers, and snorkel masks, which are all cold and damp. It's not the most attractive look for the romance I'd like to cultivate, but whatever. It's possible I'm not going to find the perfect situation for this conversation.

"Cute getup," I tell Cate.

She does a little model walk in her flippers, which looks so ridiculous that I burst out laughing.

"See you in there." She jumps backward into the water with the confidence of someone who's done this before.

"See…see you in there…" I say valiantly, though she can't hear me.

I opt for a more careful approach and use the ladder to climb in, the toes of my flippers catching on everything.

Yeah, this is *so* not sexy.

The water is a lot colder than the hotel pool, and I gasp as the waves attack my rib cage and shoulders. The life jacket rides up under my arms, and my flippers feel like lead weights as I try to kick. I'm a decent swimmer, but the ocean is vast and wild and full of mysteries I'd rather not think about—like whatever just brushed my leg.

Please be seaweed.

My insides twist as we swim away from the boat. Waves froth, looking a lot bigger from this angle. Okay, being out on the open water near a ring of volcanic rock is a little more unnerving than I anticipated. My hands shake as I adjust my mask.

Clinging to my motivation for coming out here in the first place, I suck in a breath. "C-Cate, I've been wanting to talk—"

"A turtle!" she exclaims, spinning on the spot and dunking her face back into the water.

"Already?" I swim closer and plunge my face in. It's hard to breathe through the tube, and my mask isn't tight enough, so cold water seeps in at the edges. I cough, surfacing to catch my breath. Salt coats my lips, and I wipe them, but, of course, salt also covers my arm. I push the mask tighter over my eyes, put the tube back into my mouth, and try again.

As the bubbles clear, a dark shape moves beneath my toes.

It's a turtle all right—and below it? The ocean floor is *way* down, and there is a fucking shipwreck lying there, sea life teeming around it. Coral and slime cover the ghostly structure, which is hazy through the murk.

The heebie-jeebies seize my legs, and I'm overcome with the sensation that every one of my organs is trying to escape through my mouth. I pull my face out of the water with a gasp. "Nope, nope, nope…"

Ahh, the carefully constructed speech I was about to make, reduced to a long string of "nope" as I swim frantically back to the catamaran.

"Rachel!" Cate calls after me, but I can't stop. I need to get back on the boat.

I thought snorkeling was supposed to be less creepy than scuba diving. Hovering safely at the surface should theoretically stop this sort of panic from happening.

The captain extends a hand to help pull me back on board, and I seize it like it's my only hope of survival. He's a local in his forties with a muscular build, and he pulls me out of the water easily, calling out reassurances that I can't register.

I sit on a bench, gasping for air.

Cate catches up and grips the ladder, floating beside the boat. She pulls the snorkel mask up to her forehead. It's left marks around her eyes, which might be funny if I wasn't busy trying to breathe.

"Sorry." I whip off my own mask and rub my face. "Never done this before. I didn't expect to be right over a shipwreck."

"That's okay." Cate offers a little smile. "It freaks me out a little too. We can move the boat if you want. Somewhere shallower?"

My stomach churns. That...might help. At the very least, there might be fewer waves to toss us around and make me sick. "Maybe."

Frustration twists in my gut, mixing with the rising nausea. Why couldn't we have a normal snorkeling trip? One where we didn't have to sail an hour away from civilization to have a speck of privacy? This is ridiculous. We're floating all over the ocean to try and have some peace.

Cate studies me closely, a deep crease between her eyebrows. "Before I saw the turtle, you said you wanted to talk?"

"Oh. No, it's nothing." The moment is gone, and the captain is steps away, able to hear every word.

The catamaran crests a wave, and my stomach heaves.

"Rachel?" Cate takes a step up the ladder, searching my face, her eyes widening. "You okay?"

"I'm—" My stomach lurches again.

Oh no.

"It's just the—the waves—" My mouth goes very, very dry.

Then, a rush of saliva.

No, please don't...

But there's no stopping it. I lean over the side of the boat and empty my lunch into the Pacific Ocean.

We skip our dinner reservation, ordering room service so I can recover. Cate gets the macadamia-crusted mahi-mahi topped with a mango-papaya salsa. I order saltine crackers and ginger tea. We're both determinedly not checking our phones, sure we'll find that bikini make out picture plastered all over the internet by now.

"I should've warned you about the catamaran," Cate says after we've both showered and wrapped ourselves in fluffy robes. "They're horrible for seasickness."

"It's not your fault," I mumble, though a part of me blames her status for our constant need to escape—for the fact that we always have to go to great lengths just for privacy. It's a shameful thought, and I can't meet her eye as I accept the tea from her.

She sets up her meal on the little round table on the patio and sits down, looking elegant with her plate of mahi-mahi and glass of white wine. I stay on the daybed with my legs crossed and a pile of individually wrapped saltine crackers beside me. The setting sun casts golden light over everything, and a warm breeze carries the sound of distant waves and the scent of tropical flowers.

It would be perfect if not for the ruined mood.

We eat in silence for several long minutes, me taking little bird bites in the hopes that the crackers stay down. It's been three hours since I puked in the ocean, and after taking my second shower of the day and brushing my teeth extremely thoroughly, the garbage feeling in my gut is finally receding.

As I crumple up the final saltine wrapper, I say, "I just wish we didn't have to worry about *where* we go snorkeling. We could've waded into the ocean right down there with everyone else." I motion toward the distant shore.

Cate looks at me sharply. Pauses. "We can, if you want," she says finally, an edge in her voice.

"But you know what'll happen." My words come out harsher than I intended. It's hard to stay calm when every second in public becomes a performance for strangers' cameras. We can't even kiss without someone capturing it.

She pushes the last bite of food around her plate, her shoulders slumped.

Guilt punches me in the chest. What am I doing? Am I seriously blaming Cate for other people's disregard for her privacy? "I'm sorry." I scoot forward on the seat and reach over to put my hand on her thigh. "It's just frustrating sometimes."

"I know," she says softly. "I'll have the concierge arrange activities for us that don't involve snorkeling, seasickness, or crowds."

I try to smile. And as she clasps her fingers over mine, the smile comes easier. Out of all the places we've gone so far on this trip—beaches, restaurants, pools, the catamaran—my favorite is right here. This hotel. This patio.

She puts down her fork and moves to the daybed with me. "I can think of an activity that will cheer us both up."

My heart skips at the closeness. After all this time, she still makes me feel like I have a giddy crush. Maybe that's partly why the marriage question is such a big deal—because sometimes I still can't believe this is real. What did I do to deserve someone this amazing?

"Hm, like a board game?" I ask, the joke dying on my tongue as she leans over and kisses my neck.

Her lips curve into an irresistible cheeky smile. "I was thinking I could eat you for dessert. Keep going until you forget about today—until you forget your own name, maybe."

A fire lights inside me. "That sounds way more fun than snorkeling."

She tugs at my robe to expose my shoulder, and her damp hair tickles my skin as she leaves a trail of kisses. She smells like the hotel's shampoo—honey and citrus. My eyes flutter closed as she peels my robe open further, exposing my breasts. Her lips keep tracing a line back and forth across my clavicle.

What *is it* about this patio? I think we've had sex out here more than in the bed. Is it the tropical air?

In the next breath, all thoughts leave my head, and my body takes over. I push her onto her back and climb on top, kissing her hard.

She lets out a surprised gasp into my mouth and brings her knee up to hold me to her. "Mm, Rachel..."

I graze my lips against hers. Her tongue darts out to tease me. Our breaths quicken. I fumble with her robe, untying it. After that brief excursion today, she already has tan lines.

As I run my palms up her waist and over her breasts, I let out a moan. I'll never get tired of the sight of her sprawled naked under me.

I trace my lips and tongue along her neck, then down the center of her chest, savoring her taste.

She squirms, her fingers working clumsily at the knot of my robe.

"Take your time," I tease.

"You're making me—lose all coordination," she murmurs breathlessly.

She gets it untied at last, and I slide my body along hers, relishing the feel of our bare skin against each other. I part her legs with my knees, enjoying the soft moan she makes in my ear.

"Rachel," she breathes into my neck, "you're supposed to be the one on your back right now."

I smile, teasing her for a little longer before rolling us onto our sides. "How about this?"

"Good compromise," she whispers.

Our knees bump as we slide our hands between each other's legs. The familiarity in the way we touch each other, the way we know exactly what the other needs, makes my heart swell. We kiss deeply, each of us knowing what to do with our fingers to make the other gasp, finding that rhythm we've perfected over our three years together.

She lets out breathless noises into my mouth, and I comb my fingers through her damp hair, knotting it in my fist.

"I'm so lucky I have you," I murmur.

"S-same," Cate whispers, her breath hitching.

She's losing herself, a hungry look in her eyes that never fails to unravel me. Everything around us fades as she brings me closer to the edge, her fingers moving expertly between my legs.

"Cate, I'm—oh—you're too good," I whimper, opening my eyes and struggling not to come too fast.

"You're close?" she asks, breathless.

I nod, biting my lip.

"Good. Me too."

Knowing she's ready to finish tips me over the edge. I arch into her, kissing her hard. She hits just the right tempo, and I stifle a cry into her mouth.

A moment later, she shivers, and her moan is loud enough that someone could hear. I try to smother the noises she's making with my mouth, but as pleasure courses through me in waves, all I care about is how good her fingers feel and how sexy she is as she comes on my hand. Her hips rock uncontrollably against my fingers until, at last, we both fall limp.

We melt into the daybed and let out slow breaths. My brain is a haze, my eyes distantly registering the sky turning yellow with the sunset and the swaying palm fronds overhead. My skin dances, the warm tropical breeze adding to the pleasure tingling through me. What were we even talking about before this?

"Still seasick?" Cate props herself up on an elbow.

A surprised laugh escapes me. "Oh yeah. I forgot we were on a catamaran today."

She grins. "Well, I'm glad to have found a cure for motion sickness."

"What, orgasms?"

"Yep. Want to submit the research paper for me?"

I laugh and squeeze her cheeks between my thumb and forefinger, planting a firm kiss on her lips. "I love you."

"I love you too."

"And for the record, this *was* better than snorkeling," I say, leaning my head back.

"What, sex on a hotel patio?"

"Yep."

She laughs. "Such a romantic."

After we clean up, we return to the daybed to cuddle, gazing out at the stunning orange sunset.

There's not a lot of daylight left, but the whites of Cate's eyes are bright in the setting sun. She's looking at me hard, like she's deep in thought.

"What?" I ask, my voice coming out sleepy.

"I've been trying to create a perfect moment since we got here," she says. "The morning beach walk, the snorkeling excursion, tonight's dinner reservation... But it's occurred to me that the perfect moment is right here."

I smile. "I love it when you get all mushy."

She chuckles, propping herself up on an elbow again. "Since arriving on this trip, this suite—this *patio*—has been a more intimate and private place than anywhere else. I'm happy here."

I'm so glad she feels the same. "Fully agree. So are you saying we should stay on this patio for the rest of the trip? Because I'm game."

I'm only half joking. Yeah, it's nice to do other stuff, but damn if this isn't perfect.

"Not quite. But what I *am* saying..." She sits up and looks around. "One sec."

Before I can piece together what she's on about, she shrugs into her robe and disappears into the suite.

A minute later, she comes out with her hands behind her back. "Okay, listen. This vacation hasn't gone to plan. There's not much about our relationship that has, and the fact we're here shows how—how strong we are." Her voice trembles. "I think if we can get through all this media nonsense, we can get through anything."

I sit up, pulling my robe over my shoulders. Why is she nervous? Wait, what's going on?

My gaze drops to her arms, her hands still behind her back.

My face goes numb. *Wait.*

"I want to spend my life with you, Rachel," she says, sinking down onto her knees and edging closer to the daybed so we're at eye level.

"Me—me too," I stammer. My heart is beating out of my chest. I can feel how wide my eyes are, and I hope she sees that this isn't panic—it's pure, barely contained excitement. "Cate—are you—is this—"

From behind her back, she produces a black velvet box.

My breath catches, a wave of dizziness hitting me. *OhmyGodohmyGod... This is really happening.*

Cate opens the box, revealing a ring. The trio of diamonds sparkle in the fading sunlight, catching the last rays. It's breathtaking.

I cover my mouth to hold in a flood of tears. Or a scream. Or both.

As my eyes prickle, I can only stare at Cate, the woman who has changed my life in a more wonderful way than I ever could have imagined. She looks more vulnerable than I've ever seen her—nervous, open, just a normal girl doing something very scary.

"Rachel, I can't imagine my life without you. You're my best friend, my anchor, my everything. From the day we met, you've been so special to me. You've always seen me—the real me." She takes a deep breath. Swallows hard. "Will you marry me?"

I throw my arms around her shoulders before she finishes asking. "Yes! Of course!"

She gives a shaky, wet laugh, her eyes glistening.

My hands are shaking so much that I have to help her slide the ring on. We laugh, both of us wiping our eyes.

"Wait, so—" I huff out a breath to try and get my voice back. "So the beach stroll, and snorkeling, and the dinner reservation—"

"All attempts to propose," Cate says, a little bashful.

My eyes sting, and I blink back more tears. "You had a ring on you all that time?"

"I did."

I cover my mouth again, trying not to sob. "Oh my God, Cate. I've been trying to broach the subject of marriage with you all this time, and you—you—" I take a deep breath and shake my head in disbelief. "So that's why you checked the pocket of your shorts when we were in the tunnel? The ring was in there?"

"Didn't fall out, thank God."

"And if I hadn't thrown up on the catamaran..."

She lifts a shoulder. "It was a risky plan, anyway, bringing a ring into the ocean."

I chuckle and rake my fingers through my hair, feeling like I'm floating. "I love you."

"I love you too."

I pull her onto the daybed with me. "You're right, you know. We're strong. Like, I know this announcement is going to come with a lot of buzz and cameras and stuff, but... Maybe that doesn't scare me as much, as long as we're together. It's all part of us."

She leans her head on my shoulder. "I'm so happy to hear you say that."

The ring on my finger is practically glowing. I can't believe this is happening.

"We won't announce it until you're ready," Cate whispers.

"Thanks," I whisper back, though I'm admittedly bursting to tell Abby.

We cuddle into each other as the world plunges into darkness, both of us growing sleepy. Stars come out, bright and sparkling in the inky sky, and the temperature stays comfortable.

"Cate?" I murmur.

She lifts her head. "Yeah?"

"That was the most amazing proposal a girl could ever ask for." I cup her face, feeling her cheeks lift into a smile.

"It wasn't anticlimactic? I wanted to make a grand gesture, but—"

"No. After all we've been through, the comfort we have right here is perfect. It's everything I could have dreamed of. And anyway…" I wave my hand at the gorgeous view. "You can't tell me this isn't grand."

She catches my hand and looks at the ring, brushing her thumb over the sparkling diamonds. We look out at the sky together, the night peaceful and quiet—as if the whole world is just the two of us.

Enjoyed this glimpse into their life after the happy ending? Discover how their story began in *From Fan To Forever*.

The Apostate's Creed

by Carrie Byrd

The return address wasn't necessary. Just one quick glance at the shiny brown envelope covered in turkey stickers and orange glitter and Jillian Reed knew exactly who'd sent it.

She dropped their junk mail on the dining room table, then tore open the seal.

You are cordially invited to attend
A Friendsgiving Celebration
and St. Rita High School Survivors' Reunion
at the lovely home of Ms. Jessica Marie Bruno
hosted by her only daughter, Ms. Emily Margaret Bruno

Friday, November 26, 6:00pm
1402 Hazel Drive, Gladbeck

Bring a dish of your choosing (leftovers encouraged) and your favorite dinner party question!!
Text Emily with any questions or if you saw a cute dog recently

Jillian grinned. Sure, Emily Bruno was technically an adult now, but in some respects, their former student was still the same enthusiasm factory she'd been at fourteen. If reincarnation was real—it wasn't, obviously—then Emily had probably lived a former life as a Roman candle.

Some show's theme song blared from the living room TV, interrupting Jillian's focus. *Tiny Houseboat Hunters*? The hell kind of name was that? Was the houseboat tiny, or were the hunters tiny? Were there guns? Did the hunters shoot the houseboats?

Didn't matter. Jillian wasn't interested. Much.

"Hey, Freckles." She waved Emily's invitation in the air. "Just got something in the mail you'll like."

From her prone position on the nearby couch, Mattie Belman lifted her head in obvious interest. She rarely left the living room on her afternoons off, exhausted from a near-constant schedule of teaching theater classes, working the odd Starbucks shift, and play rehearsals. In between her commitments, reality TV was about all she could manage.

The couch pillow's corduroy pattern decorated Mattie's round cheek. If the word *adorable* was in Jillian's vocabulary, she could apply it here. Theoretically.

I could kiss those indents until they disappeared. The thought flared inside Jillian. *I can kiss her whenever she wants, whenever I want. No one's gonna stop me. I get to have this.*

More than three years since she'd come out for the first time, her voice ringing to the rafters from St. Rita's auditorium stage, and those realizations still felt like the promise of Christmas morning.

She'd get to have her girl for the rest of their lives, in fact. That gleaming sapphire on Mattie's ring finger, put there by Jillian just a few weeks ago, told the happiest story Jillian could ever imagine.

Reflexively, Jillian rubbed her thumb against her own engagement ring, a slim gold band she'd had studded with three tiny rubies: Mattie's birthstone. She never took it off. Ever. Not even to shower or lift weights. In fact, she'd made sure to show it off to the Queens College women's soccer team, who'd all made appropriately exuberant noises over their assistant coach's news.

"Did we get the Williams Sonoma holiday catalog?" Even at a distance of fifteen feet or so, it was easy to tell that Mattie's big brown eyes were sparkling. "It's gonna be hard to outdo last year's thousand-dollar countertop Neapolitan pizza oven, but I have faith. Hoping for a fondue pot made from diamonds this season."

"Emily Bruno's throwing some kind of party the day after Thanksgiving. In Gladbeck."

"Emily? A party?" With a delighted smile, Mattie sat up straight, her dark curls bouncing. "Oh, cool beans."

Unadulterated affection surged through Jillian. A ridiculous phrase shouldn't sound that appealing. "Freckles, 'cool beans' is incredibly dated, and, worse, it's a horrible insult to the joy I get from a piping hot burrito."

Mattie appeared unfazed. "You'll live. So we're going, right? Will all our kids be there?"

Our kids. Admittedly, that phrasing was odd, given that Mattie and Jillian planned on being happily child-free for the rest of their lives. But after that last year at St. Rita's—the year they'd put on an absurd musical that changed all their lives, the year Mattie had trebucheted her smile and stubbornness against the stone castle of Jillian's heart—their former St. Rita students were, and always would be, theirs. To protect, to cheer for, to—

Yes, Jillian would admit it: To love. While there was breath in her body and brain in her skull, Jillian Reed would love their kids.

"No clue who'll be there," she said and tossed the invitation onto the table. "But of course we'll go. We'll be down at Mom's, anyway. And we haven't seen any of the kids in months, besides Izzy."

Mattie rose from the couch and crossed over to Jillian. She wore a fitted green sweater that nicely advertised the eighth wonder of the world: her glorious breasts. "Speaking of, I wanted to check in—how are you feeling about seeing your mom?"

Jillian stiffened. "Fine."

The word sounded perfectly normal, but Mattie's eyes still narrowed. "I don't buy that you're 'fine,' honey. You haven't seen her for more than three years. The last time you were in that house, among other things, she said God didn't call her to judge you *or* your cousin who got arrested for domestic assault. Like it was the same thing."

"I was *there*." Jillian set her jaw. "And she hasn't said anything like that since we started talking again. Look, she's trying. Imperfectly. So am I." In fact, her mother had been the first one to reach out after Jillian had cut contact, sending a letter that felt like a tentative hand. She'd extended the Thanksgiving invitation this year, too.

Mattie, now close to Jillian, reached up and cupped her cheek.

As always, Jillian leaned into the curve of that gentle palm, the softness of Mattie's skin. Her eyes fluttered shut. Forget the beach or the mountains—this was her vacation spot. This was paradise.

"I know you're doing your best," Mattie murmured. "I just worry."

The last time Jillian had spoken to her mother, two weeks ago, she'd relayed the brand-new engagement news. *I want you to know that I'm very happy,* she'd told Mary, trying not to grit her teeth. *Happier than I've ever been. I would like it if you could be happy for me, too.*

A long, long pause, the kind you could live in if you let yourself. Then her mother had said, *I've always placed my happiness in God's hands.*

Jillian straightened up. No. Her mother didn't get to be here. Not in their cramped little Queens apartment with the upstairs neighbor who played EDM before dawn, their leaky bathroom faucet, their kitchen the size of a drink coaster. Not in their perfect home that held the only person who had ever truly known Jillian Reed and said *yes, yes, give me more.* This place was sacred.

It had taken her forty-four years to understand the real meaning of that word.

"I've got something better for you to do than worry about me," Jillian informed her fiancée with a smile she knew would guarantee Mattie's distraction. "Wanna tear yourself away from houseboat murder and head to the bedroom with me for a bit?"

Sure enough, Mattie brightened immediately. "The bedroom? Why not right here?"

She hopped up on their tiny kitchen table and spread her legs just a bit, her gaze never leaving Jillian's. That gorgeous gleam in her eyes blazed like a promise, a challenge, a beacon.

Desire rolled open inside Jillian, pushing away any lingering unpleasantness. She placed her hands on Mattie's thighs and leaned in. "You think I can't wait, don't you? You think I can't control myself when it comes to you?"

Mattie grinned, catlike. God, that smile. You could power the M train with it.

"I can do anything I want," Jillian told her. She didn't say *as long as I have you.* She didn't have to. "I'm Jillian Reed."

"You're better at it than anyone else," Mattie said and kissed her.

"So how are you feeling about seeing your mom?"

Jillian glowered. Was her therapist in cahoots with Mattie? Had the two of them secretly texted each other to strategize a two-pronged emotional assault? Unsportsmanlike conduct. She'd already talked about this subject last week for two entire minutes. "Isn't there something more pleasant we could discuss? I hear toenail fungus is making a regional comeback."

"It's your fifty minutes." No matter how crabby she got during sessions, that gentle tone never left Robert's voice. "If you're not ready to talk about Thanksgiving, you don't have to."

Goddamn it. When he put it like *that.* "I'm not scared to talk about her."

"I didn't say you were."

"I just—don't feel like it. Okay? There's nothing wrong with that."

"I didn't say there was."

Jillian crossed her arms over her chest and settled back into the couch. Too bad physical intimidation was unacceptable in a therapeutic environment. At six feet tall, she towered over Robert. "We've talked Mom up and down and back and sideways for the last three years. She's a Catholic grandmother. She makes great scrapple. The Pope's too liberal for her. She hates that I'm butch and bisexual, and she's under the illusion that I'm still a believer who's at least got a chance at Purgatory. That's Mary Reed. Done."

"All right," Robert said calmly. "I hear you. That's fine."

Good. She'd won this one.

Jillian waited.

Silently, Robert looked at her.

She looked back, not breaking eye contact. Standoff at the O.K. Corral, only the turf was an eighty-one-year-old woman, and Robert kept patience in his holster.

Finally, she announced, "I don't like the way that house assaults my nostrils. It smells like Febreze, floral perfume, and the polyester couch cover. Everywhere else, I've got an iron stomach, but that combination puts me on a direct flight to Queasy City."

"Sounds very unpleasant," Robert agreed.

"Any sane person would agree that's plenty of reason not to want to be there."

"Sure. Absolutely. Any other reason coming up for you?"

Jillian pressed her lips together.

Honestly, she didn't have it that bad, comparatively. Most people had strained relationships with their parents, didn't they? Matter of fact, Jillian was luckier than most; for a long time, she'd had her dad, who always made sure she knew that he was on her side.

She'd been his little girl. Now she was no one's little girl. Just her mother's discarded doll.

No. That was a lie. She was Jillian Reed, retired professional soccer player, former coach to the thirteen-time-winning St. Rita Peacemakers, and the greatest assistant coach in the history of the Queens College women's soccer team. She was a goddamn hurricane wrapped in human skin. She was Matilda Belman's fiancée.

"I don't want Mom to hurt Mattie," Jillian burst out and had to clench her right hand to keep it from clapping over her mouth.

If Robert was surprised by this declaration seemingly from out of nowhere, his placid face didn't show it. "How do you think she'd hurt Mattie?"

Jillian didn't have to think. "Verbal paper cuts. Her specialty. She thinks she's *helping*." She really did. That was worse, somehow.

"So what would you do if she made a cutting comment to Mattie?"

"I'd tell Mom to knock it the hell off."

Robert made a quick note on his pad. "That sounds like an extremely reasonable reaction. Let me ask you something. What would you do—what *will* you do—if your mother makes a cutting comment to *you*?"

"Beg pardon?" A curl of unease in Jillian's stomach.

"You'd stand up for Mattie, you said. Would you stand up for yourself?"

Of course I would, Jillian wanted to say. *I'm Jillian Reed. Nobody takes a swipe at me without losing all their claws.* But her mother was in a category of her own. "I'd—I don't know. I've stood up for myself to her before."

"When you came out to her?"

"And when I told her she didn't know what was right for me." More than three years ago. "After I'd let Mattie go because I couldn't own up to who I was. What I wanted."

Robert nodded. "So why aren't you sure you can stand up to your mother again?"

Because I haven't seen her in a long time. Because she's trying to accept me. Because she'll get angry. Because, no matter how old I get, when I'm around her I'm still a little girl.

"Because," Jillian said softly, "I want Mom to love me."

The serene expression on Robert's face slipped into something that looked like pain. Slowly, he put down his pen.

"Do you want your mother to love you more than you want to love yourself?" he asked her.

And for the first time in years, Jillian Reed had no idea—no idea at all—what to say.

In some ways, Mattie was even more nervous about this visit than Jillian.

Honestly, Jillian couldn't blame her. After all, Mattie hadn't met anyone in the Reed family yet—other than her brother, Brian—and a Thanksgiving visit, spread out over the yawning stretch of three days, was a hell of a way to get introduced. Then there was the fact that Mattie was Jewish. As far as Jillian knew, her mother and her brothers weren't antisemitic, but Catholics didn't exactly have a long-standing reputation for religious tolerance.

"Paul's the one who fishes, right?" Mattie asked as she got out of their rental car. "And his wife runs that organization, what's it called, Nice Irish Kids?"

Jillian was already pulling their suitcases out of the trunk. "You're mixing up Paul and Jimmy. Paul fishes, but it's Jimmy's wife you're thinking about—she's on some committee for the Friendly Sons and Daughters of St. Patrick."

"I still can't believe that name is real. Speaking of names, she's—Michelle?"

"Melissa."

"Shit." Mattie slumped a little. "I'm going to mess this up, aren't I?"

"Hey." Jillian left the suitcases and put a comforting arm around her fiancée. "The hell kind of talk is that? You can't mess up any of this. So what if you call someone by the wrong name? Every single Reed in this house should be getting on their knees in gratitude because you decided to grace them with your exceptional presence."

Mattie gave her a small smile. "Yeah?"

"You're the best damn actress in all of New York. You're sunshine personified. You've got more brains than a zombie apocalypse. Your heart's big enough that it just might be medically concerning. And besides all that, you're going to be my wife." Just saying it made happiness ray from Jillian's chest, so strong, it must've been visible. "Nothing else matters, Freckles. You got me?"

Mattie slid her arm across Jillian's waist and squeezed briefly. "I should be reassuring you, not the other way around."

"Why? I'm perfectly fine." And she was. She definitely was.

Somehow, Jillian's childhood home looked far less imposing than the house in her memories. Come to think of it, the house's paint seemed more faded, too. And had the mailbox always been that crooked? She couldn't remember. Three years away did a number on you, apparently.

The concrete pathway leading up to 3205 Malabar Street was threaded with cracks, some of them new. Jillian could feel her heart pulsing inside her neck.

"Honey," Mattie murmured as they stepped up to the front door. "Just remember, okay?" She held up her pointer finger in the air.

You're my priority. They'd made that promise to each other in the first days of their relationship. The finger was their shorthand reminder. *You come first. No one else. I've got your back.*

In response, Jillian lifted her own pointer finger and pressed it gently against Mattie's. It was the closest she'd get to kissing her fiancée on her mother's porch.

A sound inside the house, very near, made them both jump apart.

Jillian froze in place as the front door swung open, the creak of it like the last clicks of a roller coaster before the drop.

"Hello," her mother said. "I heard you on the porch. Thought I'd save you the trouble of ringing the doorbell."

She's an old woman.

The shock of it nearly made Jillian take a step back. It wasn't like she'd been in denial—at eighty-one, Mary Reed was old by anyone's standards—but over the last three years, there'd been a noticeable change. The lines mapped across her mother's face had deepened. Her paper-pale cheeks were sunken. And her posture was slightly stooped now, wasn't it? She'd used to be nearly as tall as her only daughter.

Who was this old woman who lived in her mother's house?

"Hi, Mom," Jillian said.

Her mother took in Jillian, gaze traveling from feet to crown. "Well." She didn't seem to know what to say. They had that in common. "Well. You look—different."

Jillian resisted the impulse to touch her short, light-brown hair, cropped about an inch from her scalp. She'd shorn it off just a couple of weeks after the last time she'd seen her mother, more than ready to lose the weight of expectations it carried. "Yeah. I do. Mom, this is Mattie."

With a wide smile that concealed any nerves, Mattie reached through the doorway for a handshake. "It's a pleasure to meet you, Mrs. Reed. Thank you so much for hosting us."

After the briefest hesitation, so small that it could be measured in milliseconds, her mother shook Mattie's offered hand. "Well," she said again. "My goodness. Aren't you a pretty girl?"

Yes, Jillian wanted to say. *Yes, as a matter of fact, I happen to be engaged to the most beautiful woman who's ever existed; you're correct for noticing it.*

Mattie didn't seem to know how to answer.

"Why don't you come inside?" Mary continued. "You can get settled and say hi to the boys."

Jillian lifted her carry-on suitcase over the threshold, Mattie following behind. The eldest of "the boys" was almost sixty; regardless, they'd all still be "the boys" for as long as her mother lived.

If the house exterior seemed different, the inside looked just the same: a mausoleum of oversized 1970s furniture and shag pile carpet. In the entry hallway, decades of family photos lined the walls, arranged around a large portrait of her parents just after their wedding. Jillian knew that picture like she knew how to execute a perfect sliding tackle on the field; every millimeter of it was acquainted with every millimeter of her.

"Who's here?" she asked as her mother led them up the stairs. "Is everyone coming?"

"Not everyone." Mary gripped the stair banister tightly as she climbed, not turning around. "Sean and Julie are in Philly this year—you know Kayla had her baby last month."

No, Jillian did not know that her nephew's wife had given birth. That made her a great aunt, technically, although considering her nearly nonexistent relationship with her nieces and nephews, the more accurate term was probably "aggressively mediocre aunt." She followed her mother down the upstairs hallway.

"And Frankie's with Christine's family in Wilkes-Barre. Though why he'd choose to spend the holiday with those obnoxious people over his own flesh and blood is anyone's guess."

Jillian's stomach roiled unpleasantly. She had a pretty good guess, and it was a safe bet her mother did, too. Of her five brothers, Sean and Frankie had withdrawn the most after she'd come out, choosing radio silence and a yearly Christmas card. "Paul and Jimmy?"

"Throwing a football in the backyard with Noah. Savannah's somewhere with her nose buried in that phone of hers, as always. And Brian said he'll be by tomorrow morning. I know he's champing at the bit to see you." Mary pushed open the door to the bedroom Sean and Frankie had shared decades earlier. "You'll be staying in here."

You was a tricky pronoun. It could mean *you two*, or it could mean *you, my daughter*, or it could mean *I'm hiding behind my words because it's too painful for me to openly acknowledge that you're sharing your life with a woman.* Jillian peered into a room she hadn't seen in years.

The bedroom had been long since stripped of her brothers' personalities, but one familiar detail remained: two parallel twin beds jutting out from the far wall.

Behind her, Mattie made a soft noise.

"We're filled to the brim this weekend." Her mother didn't look at Jillian. "Paul and Jimmy beat you to the two big beds, and the spare room's the only one big enough to hold the kids. This is what's left."

It was a very reasonable excuse. It was also undeniably true. And yet.

"Oh, don't you worry, Mrs. Reed," Mattie said cheerfully. "We'll make do just fine. I don't think it'll be too hard to push the beds together."

The jolt of sudden anxiety that sliced through Jillian jockeyed for attention with her sharp pride. *That's my girl.*

Mary blanched. "Well, then. I'll just be down in the kitchen. Lots to do."

"I'll come help you." Jillian's offer came instantly. "After I unpack."

Her mother nodded, then placed a tentative hand on her daughter's arm. Held it there, the warmth of her touch seeping through Jillian's jacket.

"Welcome home, Teeny," she said softly, and in those three words Jillian heard the reflection of her own grief, her own fear, her own deep longing. "Welcome home, my girl."

Thanksgiving Day was incorrectly named. More like Thanksgiving Year, given how slowly each minute was passing. Was it really only ten in the morning? Maybe Jillian's watch was off. Maybe she'd entered an alternate dimension. Maybe her mother's house somehow defied the march of time.

At least they weren't sitting around, twiddling their thumbs and snatching at awkward conversation. *Idle hands are the devil's workshop,* Jillian's grandmother had always said, and if you defined the devil as your own discomfort, that was more or less right on the money.

The yellow-and-green tiled kitchen was packed with people and heat. Her mother flitted between oven and sink while her sisters-in-law prepped a green bean casserole. In the background, a radio played Frank Sinatra, a crooning voice that yanked Jillian back in time.

Mattie hovered over a nearly filled pan, shredding egg bread for stovetop stuffing. She'd volunteered the night before, and Mary had given her a task so simple that Jillian had done it as a little kid.

"Oven's ready," her mother announced, brushing her hands across the front of her wine-red apron.

That was Jillian's cue. For years, Mom had lifted an eighteen-pounder without breaking a sweat, but aging had stolen her strength. She'd never had much weight on her; now, though, she looked as if a good sneeze would launch her backward so fast, she'd break Usain Bolt's record in reverse.

Carefully, Jillian carried the dressed turkey across the kitchen and deposited it in the oven cavity. At least she'd have some decent food as a reward for getting through the day.

Her mother seemed satisfied. "We're right on schedule," she declared. "Assuming Tracy hasn't been put out of commission by those onions."

Paul's wife wiped the wet upper half of her cheek with the back of her hand. "Oh, I'm good, Mary. Promise. Melissa's finishing them up."

Had Tracy ever called Mary Reed Mrs. Reed? Had any of her sisters-in-law? They must have. And at some point, her mother had told them, "Call me Mary," a statement Jillian tried to imagine her repeating to Mattie. Couldn't.

Then, with a quick glance in Mattie's direction, Jillian's mother added, "I meant to say earlier."

A long pause followed while Mattie continued to shred.

"Mattie," Jillian said, because apparently her mother couldn't. "Mom wants to tell you something."

Mattie spun around, apprehension obvious in those big eyes. "Oh! Yes?"

"We have Kosher salt." Her mother's tone was pleasant, but she didn't seem to know exactly where to look. "Picked some up from the market on Tuesday. For your religious dietary needs."

Luckily, Jillian had perfect control over her facial muscles. Good God. Well, whatever else that statement was, her mother was clearly making an effort. Mattie was almost certainly the first Jewish person her mother had ever been around for more than two minutes.

"That's very thoughtful, Mrs. Reed." To her immense credit, Mattie, who loved a hot dog as much as any Gentile, didn't burst into helpless laughter. "Thank you. I really appreciate it."

Before Mary could respond, the kitchen door next to Jillian swung open.

She had just enough time to gasp in delight before two strong arms went around her, and then her brother, Brian, was lifting Jillian off the floor, squeezing her so hard, the breath went out of her lungs.

"Teeny!" he cried out and spun her in a full circle before dropping her again.

Brian was five years older than Jillian, her closest brother both in age and bond. In childhood, she'd followed him around like a puppy, and although she'd long since stopped chasing Brian, the adoration hadn't faded one bit. He was kind, loyal, and one of two living people who'd always accepted her without condition.

She squeezed him back, hard. Oh God, were those tears lodging in her throat? Humiliating.

"It's been ages." Brian pulled back, a wide grin blooming. "When was the last time—spring, right?"

Jillian could feel the heat of their mother watching them. Yes, the last time she'd been to Gladbeck had been in April, on a visit to Mattie's parents. Of course, they'd avoided Malabar Street like it was a dark basement in a horror movie. But here Brian was, unintentionally reminding Mary that her daughter had spent three years doing everything she could to stay away.

She wouldn't think about it. Wouldn't let herself focus on the old sting of alarm that popped up every time she stepped out of her mother's ruler-straight line. "Too long, buddy. Hey, how's the shop doing?"

Brian's expression darkened slightly. "Not great. Let's save that for another time, though. I want to hear how my baby sister is. And—" He looked around the kitchen, and the bright delight on his face wiped away any shadows. "Mattie! You're here! It's so good to see you, pal! Oh. Hey, Melissa. Hey, Tracy."

Jillian beamed, her first honest smile since yesterday's drive. It felt great to see Mattie getting preferential treatment from at least one other Reed. Jillian wasn't the only one in the family with taste.

Exclaiming happily, Mattie rushed over to hug Brian.

"I, uh, didn't know"—Brian released Mattie, then glanced at Jillian—"if you'd make it, Mattie."

Meaning, of course, that Brian wasn't sure if Jillian would bring Mattie home with her. That had been a necessary condition of the visit. *Either both of us are coming or neither of us will,* she'd told Mary, and her mother had said slowly, *Well, if you insist on an ultimatum —*

Mary cleared her throat. "No greeting for your old mother?"

"I see you all the time, Mom." But Brian gave her a quick kiss anyway. "Teeny's special."

For a moment, Jillian thought her mother might disagree.

"She is," Mary said quietly.

There it was again, that undercurrent of longing in her mother's voice. It tugged somewhere deep inside Jillian's stomach. Did her mother really see her as special? And, if so, who was she imagining? The dutiful daughter who, despite her failure to be the feminine girl Mary wanted, had always tried so hard to please her mother? Or did she mean the real Jillian Reed?

Three years ago, Jillian had told Mattie, *I always thought Mom didn't see me. But I realized I was wrong. She does see me. She just doesn't like what she sees.*

Maybe things could finally change.

"I'm gonna steal these two away for a bit, Mom," Brian announced, wrapping one arm around Jillian's shoulders and the other arm around Mattie's. "We've got some catching up to do." He turned to Mattie. "That play you're in, when's it opening?"

"In three weeks," Mattie replied, just as Mary said, "Play? You're an actress?"

Incredulous, Jillian stared at her. She'd told her mother that Mattie was in theater. Right? Something that foundational to who Mattie was? There'd been half a dozen phone calls over the past couple of years, plenty of time to share.

But she'd left Mattie out of those conversations more often than not. Easier to avoid the subject. Safer.

This time, Mattie didn't hide her incredulity, although she recovered quickly. "Uh, yeah. Yes. I'm an actor. Off-Broadway."

Mary made a small noise of neutral acknowledgement and didn't comment further.

The ensuing silence was pregnant with everyone's discomfort. Almost in unison, Melissa and Tracy turned back to their casserole prep.

"She's also a teacher," Jillian added, way too late. "That's how—"

We met, she meant to say, but her mother was already looking over at the onions. "Not so thin, Melissa. If you slice them too thin, it ruins the flavor."

"Let's go," Brian said, low, near Jillian's ear. "While she's distracted."

Jillian didn't have to be told twice.

On their way out of the room, Mattie in front of her, she let herself stare at the back of her fiancée's head, those dark curls just as hypnotic as the first time she'd seen them, touched them. Never mind her past. This, right in front of her, was Jillian's future.

She wanted so badly to take Mattie's hand in hers, squeeze it hard in reassurance. *I'm sorry I didn't tell her. You're not my secret anymore. I don't want you to think I'm ashamed of you. It's not you. I'm not ashamed of* you.

This year, the Reed Thanksgiving dinner gathering was small enough that everyone could fit around the oversized dining room table. Without Sean, Frankie, and their families, they were down by half; Paul and Jimmy's older kids, currently in college, had apparently elected to go home with their significant others.

Jillian tried not to stare at her youngest nephew, Jimmy's nine-year-old son Noah, who'd grown about two feet since the last time she'd seen him. What did he know about his aunt? What had Jimmy and Paul told their kids in the past three years about her absence?

"So, Teeny," Paul began.

Startled, she swiveled her head to look at him.

Paul speared another slice of turkey off the chipped Corning cornflower-blue plate, ready for seconds even though they'd been at the table for just fifteen minutes. "When are you gonna give up on this whole idea of being a New Yorker and come back home?"

His voice was light, but Jillian wasn't in the mood. "Great question. When are you gonna give up on this whole idea of being someone with a full head of hair?" She stared pointedly at the top of his head, where a few dozen strands struggled in vain to hide a bald spot the size of a handmade doily.

Next to him, Paul's teenage daughter, Savannah, let out a bark-laugh that earned her a sharp glare from Tracy.

Paul flushed. "You never could take a joke," he muttered.

"I love jokes." Jillian shoveled a scoop of mashed potatoes onto her fork. "I'm related to one."

Before Paul could jab back, Brian interjected. "Paulie, who you got for the game? Dallas or New York?"

It worked. Paul lit up with the kind of glow that only sports hatred could kindle. "You think I'd ever bet on Dallas? Me? I used to ask Our Lady if she'd get her son to drop a 300-pound linebacker on top of Troy Aikman's right hand."

Brian, across the dining room table from Jillian, met her gaze for just a second and gave her a tiny wink.

"Oh, Paul!" Mary's shocked gasp had more than a little delight in it. "You *didn't*."

"Swear to G—swear on my heart." Paul raised his eyebrows at Mattie. "You better not be a Cowboys fan, Mattie. Now *that's* an unforgivable sin. I mean, not that you've done anything—well, you know. I'm just saying, if you root for those guys, we're gonna have some words."

Jillian didn't have to look over at her mother to know that Mary's lips were pursed.

"I'm actually not much of a football girl," Mattie offered brightly. "But I do watch the Steelers with Jillian sometimes. Sorry about your O-line, by the way. I don't really know what that is, but I know it's not doing something. Or it's doing something badly. Right, h—Jillian?"

Honey, she'd almost said, and no wonder. For a long time now, they'd used pet names almost exclusively, to the point that hearing her real name come out of Mattie's mouth felt surreal.

"Bang on," Jillian agreed. "Defensive tackles get through that O-line faster than greasy children go down a water park flume."

"Dad used to love game days," Jimmy said suddenly. He'd been quiet most of the dinner, not unusual. "Remember? He'd park himself in that ratty old recliner, and anyone who'd join him would get a lecture on why Ernie Stautner was the greatest defensive player in Steelers history."

Brian grinned. "One time I told him Joe Greene was better. Pretty sure that almost got me kicked out of the family."

He clearly didn't mean anything by it, but Jillian couldn't help the wince that briefly hunched her shoulders. Their dad hadn't known the truth about her sexuality—or had he? Sometimes she wondered—and while she was nearly positive he would've come around, that wasn't the same thing as being *sure*. Which would've been the bigger sin to him: preferring Joe Greene, or his only daughter choosing agnostic bisexuality over a straight, Catholic life?

A decade after her father's death and she could still conjure up the faint, jagged scent of motor oil that always clung to his cotton shirts.

Sudden pressure around her left hand. Mattie had grabbed it under the table. Jillian squeezed back, hoping it was enough to communicate her appreciation.

"Man, I really miss the guy." Paul stabbed a glazed carrot piece. "Sometimes I forget and think he's still here, even after all this time. And then I remember. Weird."

"I miss him, too," Brian said quietly, then looked up at the ceiling. "Miss you, Dad. All of us do."

"Father Mike says that only God and those with him know for sure who's in heaven," her mother observed. "And I know it's blasphemous to go against Church teachings—but I'm positive he's living forever with Christ. We might miss him, but he's better off where he is."

"Amen," Melissa said ardently.

Envy, unexpected and furious, tugged at Jillian. She'd had that same certainty once, and although she wasn't a believer anymore—hadn't been for many years—agnosticism was a hell of a lot less comfortable than religious conviction.

"Dad always says Grandpa Jack's in heaven." Noah twirled his fork through his cranberry sauce, stopping only when his mother laid a warning hand on his arm. "When I say my prayers, I say one especially for Grandpa just to really make sure God's paying attention to him. But it's gonna be a long time until I can get up there and see if it's working right."

"That's my sweet boy," Mary crooned.

Jimmy smiled fondly at his son.

For some reason, Savannah scowled, staring down at her half-finished plate, and the expression on her face was surprising enough to lock Jillian's gaze onto her.

Savannah was, what, fifteen? Sixteen? More than old enough to call bullshit.

She'd never noticed before, probably hadn't ever examined Savannah closely, but the kid looked uncannily familiar, especially with that scowl. Like looking into a mirror, but thirty years ago: sharp cheekbones, a pointed chin, brown eyebrows that slashed across pale skin, near-black eyes. Her outfit even resembled the kind of clothes Jillian had worn in high school. Baggy jeans, an oversized men's T-shirt. The only real difference was their hair: in high school, Jillian hadn't been allowed to cut hers as short as Savannah's was now.

Jillian's heart felt a little tight.

"I miss Dad a lot," she said truthfully. Couldn't be the only child of Jack Reed at this table who didn't join in on this conversation. "It's nice to think he might still be around somewhere."

No one said anything. Quiet sat in the room.

Oh, shit. She'd used the conditional tense.

Shit. *Shit*. This was what happened when you weren't on constant guard. Why the hell had she thought she could partially relax, even for a second?

"What does that mean, Teeny?" The soft lilt of her mother's voice promised familiar thorns. "'He might still be around somewhere'?"

"I think Jillian just wanted to—"

"Mattie." Jillian cut her off. Mattie didn't understand the nuances here, no matter how much she wanted to help. "I'm fine."

Mattie glanced at her with worry in her eyes and seemed to search for something in Jillian's face. Didn't appear to find whatever it was.

In the few seconds of reflection Jillian could snatch before hesitation got dangerous, she weighed her next words. It was obvious: she should reassure Mary that, like any good Catholic, she was sure her father's soul still existed in some form. Easier. Safer.

Robert, in her ear: *Do you want your mother to love you more than you want to love yourself?*

She knew what the right answer was supposed to be. But Jillian's answer was yes. Her answer would always, always be yes.

Jillian inhaled, about to speak.

"She means none of us actually know for sure if Grandpa Jack's soul is still out there," Savannah said abruptly. "I think that's pretty obvious."

Jillian closed her mouth. Shock licked up the hairs on her arms.

"Savannah," Tracy gasped. "Your father and I didn't raise you to say things like that. You apologize to Grandma Mary right this second."

"Apologize for what?" A light in Savannah's dark eyes sparked. "All I did was explain what Aunt Jillian meant. I didn't say I agree with her. Although—" She sat back in her chair. "I do agree with her, actually. I know that's not allowed in this family, or whatever, but she isn't the only skeptic here."

She caught Jillian's gaze, and a current of understanding snapped between them.

"You're too rebellious for your own good, missy." Slowly, Mary lay down her fork next to her plate, then delicately dabbed the corner of her mouth with her napkin. "Not to mention rude. If I was in charge of you, there would've been consequences to your behavior long ago."

"Glad you're not in charge of me," Savannah muttered.

To Jillian's shame, her burning satisfaction at hearing this couldn't survive the flood of her relief. Someone else was under her mother's microscope, even temporarily.

If the Queens College women's soccer team could see the great Coach Reed now—this flinching, hesitant woman who'd choked on her own silence—they'd think she'd been body snatched.

"I'm so sorry, Mom." Jimmy seemed truly mortified. "Van, what's gotten into you? Why would you speak to your grandmother like that? You know better."

"Does she, James?" Spots of color dotted Mary's pale cheeks. "When she's been raised with such a free hand? When she gets to act just the way she wants without anyone bringing her back in line?"

Next to Jillian, Mattie shifted in her seat.

Jillian felt numb. She'd been brought "back in line" plenty over the years by her mother's sharp tongue.

"You never controlled her properly," Mary continued. "And now you can see the results."

"What's wrong with me, Grandma?" Defiance scorched Savannah's expression, the sudden blaze of someone who'd been waiting a long time to speak up. "I want to know."

Like looking into a mirror—

"You're a beautiful girl," Mary told her. "You've been given every opportunity to walk the right path. And yet you sit there with that sullen, defiant attitude, determined to offend me."

—except that mirror didn't show Jillian; it showed someone who loved herself enough to say—

"And what if I don't think your path is the right path?"

—that the order of nature loved her, too, just the way she was—

"Please," Tracy said despairingly. "Not here."

Mary pressed her lips together in a thin line. "Then I'll pray you change your mind."

"Stop!"

It burst out of Jillian's lungs like a detonation.

Paul actually recoiled, as though the blast of her cry had pushed him backwards. Melissa and Tracy looked stunned. Jimmy's gaze went to his lap. Noah braced his palms against his ears. Savannah watched her, wide-eyed.

Mattie's breath was audible, short and heavy.

Fear, sudden and overwhelming, threatened to smother Jillian, a plastic bag that wrapped tightly around her head. Somehow she managed to stand up and force herself to look at Mary.

This was for Savannah, wasn't it? She could do it for Savannah.

"I beg your pardon?" Her mother's pale eyebrows crawled up her forehead.

"She's just a child!" Jillian cried out.

"I'm very aware she's a child, Jillian Louise. That's the entire—"

"You can't *talk* to her like that! You can't tell her she's on the wrong path just because she isn't doing what you think God wants her to do! Do you know what it does to a person when they hear that?" She pushed a trembling fist against her chest, as though she could somehow touch the words rushing out of her. "Do you know how it feels when someone tells you that who you are is *wrong*? It shreds something inside of you. And you can't tape that part of yourself back together.

No matter how hard you try. Even if you're lucky enough to have someone who tells you a thousand times over that you're right and good and wonderful."

"You're putting words into my mouth. I never said—*that*. It's her behavior I don't like. And for heaven's sake, I won't have you dictating how I can speak to my own—"

"She's just a child, Mom." Jillian's voice broke. "*I* was just a child."

Her mother blinked once, then twice, then a third time. "I think," she said finally, "that you and I should go somewhere else. Somewhere private. You appear to have a lot to say to me."

On the verge of protesting, Jillian thought better of it, and then, with all the effort of a weight lifter, nodded her agreement.

Silently, she watched her mother rise from the table, placing her napkin over her plate.

Tentative fingers pressed lightly against the small of her back. Jillian looked down at Mattie.

Want me to go with you? Mattie mouthed. Her eyes were bright and gleaming, her forehead pinched with concern.

Jillian shook her head and gave Mattie a small smile she hoped was reassuring. *I've got this,* she meant. *I need to do this. It's time.* Finally, after more than three years—after forty-four years—it was time.

The only downstairs room with any real privacy was her father's old domain, the den. Dark, with wood paneling, and small enough that a real-estate agent would label it "cozy," the room's centerpiece was the ratty old recliner in front of the 15-year-old TV.

Jillian couldn't help it; her eyes went immediately to the headrest cushion, where the back of her dad's head had rubbed the fabric smooth over decades of use. Any remaining signs of her dad's physical presence were more comforting than photos or most memories.

Her mother sat down on the small couch against the wall, then gestured to the recliner, indicating that Jillian should take a seat.

"I can't," Jillian said automatically.

"Yes, you can." Mary sniffed. "He wouldn't want you kids making a mausoleum out of that recliner. Furniture's for sitting. Sit."

Fair point. Jillian sat down and swiveled the chair to face her mother on the couch just a few feet away.

"So. You were implying that I've damaged you irreparably," Mary said evenly. "Continue."

Jillian couldn't read her mother's still face. Strange, considering how thoroughly she'd memorized every microexpression over the last four decades.

Remember who you are. It was her own voice, not her therapist's.

Jillian thought about the Queen's College soccer field, the sweat and dirt that crusted her players after a long and ferocious practice, the power that surged through her when she took a wide stance on the sidelines, the way the breath burst from her lungs when she shouted her commands.

And somewhere behind her eyes, there was Mattie, always Mattie, her arms open.

"I know we don't ever talk," Jillian managed. "That's not how this family operates. But"—she took a deep breath—"you were right. I do have some things to say to you. So I propose that we pretend, just for a few minutes, that we're the type of people who share their feelings openly."

Mary's expression was still illegible. "I'm listening."

Jillian's tongue felt thick in her mouth. She could begin by sharing her first clear memory of her mother, the time she'd been sent to her room for attempting to cut her long hair with a pair of kids' safety scissors. Or the first time she'd been called a dyke, by another fifth-grader. Or how she'd spent half of her adult life burying herself in a world that had no room for someone like her. That only over the last three years had she been able to pull out the dirt clotting her throat, wipe away the darkness over her eyes, dig through the ground with short nails and all her desperation.

She could try to begin with an introduction to the real Jillian Reed.

"I want things to be in black-and-white," she said slowly. "Always have. I get it from you. Good and bad. Right and wrong. Winners and losers. The world's easier to navigate that way. Simpler. Shades of gray are for elephants and English majors."

The corner of her mother's mouth tugged up just a little.

"You know why I want things to be like that?" Jillian splayed her hands against her thighs, pressing into the wool fabric. "I figured it out maybe a year ago. Obvious, looking back. It's because *I'm* not black-and-white. And it's made my life—difficult. I've never been able to fit myself into a box. I wasn't good at being a girl. I didn't act or think like the other girls did. And you—I know I disappointed you. I wasn't the daughter you'd prayed for. You made that very clear."

"Teeny—"

"Don't you know how much I always wanted to be what *you* wanted? I spent forty years oscillating like a sped-up table fan between what you thought I should be and what felt right to me. Always somewhere in between the two. Gray, gray, gray. But then"—another deep breath—"then I met Mattie. And I know you don't want to hear it, I know it offends you, but, Mom, she brought me back to life. No, not back to life. She gave it to me in the first place."

"*I* gave you life," Mary said quietly.

"You gave me existence. She gave me life."

Mary sucked in quick air, then dropped her gaze to the floor. Finally, she said, "I see."

"Do you?" It was clearly impossible for her mother to understand, but Jillian had to try anyway. The urge was a rope tied to her ribs, tugging her forward. "Before Mattie, I had my students. My Peacemakers. All that mattered was teaching them how to win. Everything went outward. Nothing went in here." She jabbed a thumb into her chest. "I couldn't keep anything in here without losing everything. But after Mattie came along, I figured out that even if I lost everything—if I lost the daughter I tried so damn hard to be—with her by my side, I'd gain the person I've always been."

A strange, incomprehensible look shadowed Mary's face.

"I want you to know," Jillian continued, "that I'm done oscillating. This is it, Mom. This is who I am." She gestured at her short hair. "One setting. And I hope—I hope you want to get to know that person. I hope you still want to love me." Only the barest hint of a tremor in her voice. "I love *you*. I'll never stop loving you. But I'm trying to love myself, too."

There. It was out. Her worst fear and her biggest hope.

She leaned back against the chair and waited, sick with anticipation.

"Let me make something perfectly clear," her mother said.

"What?"

"You are my child, Jillian Louise." Her sharp jaw set in a rigid line. "God gave you to me. And his design is perfect."

Jillian wouldn't let despair in, not where her mother could see it. "Can't you allow for the possibility that God might've designed me differently than you think he should have?"

"You're not listening. You are my *child.*" That sharp jaw trembled. "I'd prayed for a daughter for so long. You were God's answer. If I was disappointed, it was my sin. Never yours."

Was the room tilting somehow? That would explain why Jillian suddenly felt so dizzy.

"I didn't understand you," Mary continued. "Your father did. You were a good girl, he said. The way you dressed, your fixation on sports, your obsession with getting attention—none of that was a problem to him. He'd tell me to quit criticizing you. But I didn't see it as criticism. I saw it as helping you be the person you were called to be." She pressed her hands against the couch seat. "And now you, too, are telling me that I was wrong."

"I'm trying to—"

"I should have listened to him."

Jillian fought to remember how to breathe.

"I've had a lot of time to reflect and pray on it. More than three years. But when we started talking again, I"—she twisted her hands together—"didn't know how to bring up the subject. Maybe I didn't want to say it out loud. But you're right. Your father was right. This is who you've always been, since you were a small child. The problem was that I wanted to make you in my image, not God's. That was wrong of me."

Jillian wanted to exhale, let out her fear. Couldn't, not yet. "Just a few minutes ago, you were telling Savannah that she was following the wrong path. How's that any different?"

"That girl gets pleasure out of shocking and offending me." Mary lifted her chin. "It's not who she is that I take issue with. It's her bad behavior. Rude and intentionally provoking."

It wasn't the time to observe that Savannah's rudeness was almost certainly a response to her grandmother's expectations. "All right, fine. But it's not just about how I look or who I am. The Church says it's the action that's sinful. And I'm marrying a woman."

Mary exhaled, her discomfort apparent. "Yes, you are."

"Then how do you reconcile those two things?" She tried to keep the distress out of her voice and couldn't. "That's part of who I am. Mattie's partner, Mattie's future wife. How can you accept me and not turn your back on something that defines you?"

Again, her mother paused. Her forehead wrinkled, skin drawing together in what looked like pain. "You want the truth, Teeny?" she said finally. "I don't know."

Why had Jillian asked when she already knew the inevitable answer? She turned her head away, momentarily unable to speak.

"But I'll find a way."

Jillian's head whipped back to look at her mother again. Mary's shoulders were back, her posture rigid with conviction. Her eyes were burning.

Hope, baby-new and starved, began to crawl through Jillian.

"The Church," her mother continued, "has been my bedrock for my entire life. It gives me the Sacraments so that every week I can be in the presence of God Almighty. It provides me with rules for how to live according to God's word. It shows me that God has always known and loved me, even before I was formed. It's stitched through every part of my soul."

"I know," Jillian said quietly.

"However," said Mary, "you, my girl, *are* my soul. You and your brothers." She leaned forward and gently placed a hand over Jillian's knee, as though touching something precious. Maybe she was.

Jillian's eyes stung. Her heart shuddered in her chest. Her cheeks were wet.

"I love you." Mary's voice was so soft, Jillian almost couldn't hear it. "God knows I do."

They sat there in silence, her mother's blue-veined, wrinkled hand still on Jillian's knee.

After a while, Jillian covered that hand with her own and held it. Came home.

"You're sure you're okay?" Mattie asked for the third time in five minutes.

Lying on the now-conjoined twin beds, her cheek resting against her fiancée's sternum, Jillian said for the third time in five minutes, "Yes. This isn't some delay tactic, Freckles. I'll tell you all the details when we get home. Not before. These walls are thinner than an Amish phone book."

"But—" Mattie hesitated. Jillian couldn't see her face, but she knew Mattie was biting her lower lip. "It sounds like it went well? I'm just looking for the headline, promise. No details."

Jillian felt like a wrung-out washcloth, her limbs limp and heavy. After a lifetime of denial, her mother had finally seen her for who she really was. Seen, and turned toward her, not away. You couldn't sum up the weight of that in just a few words. "About as well as it could've gone."

"That's incredible." Mattie pressed a kiss into the top of Jillian's head. "I'm so happy for you, sweetheart."

Yes, happiness was merited. But somehow, Jillian couldn't marshal any feeling other than thick exhaustion. "You be happy for me. I'll just lie right here and stare at the magnificent Ashkenazi Highlands." Her face was right in front of Mattie's breasts, after all.

Mattie giggled. Even the smallest trickle of her laughter sounded more beautiful than the roar of a stadium crowd. "I like your brothers, by the way," she said. "I mean, you already know how much I love Brian, but Jimmy's nice, too. And, yeah, Paul's loud and a little obnoxious, but he means well. Anyway, I'm loud, too."

"That isn't new information," Jillian said dryly, remembering the time a neighbor had knocked on their front door, asked them to keep it down, then sheepishly congratulated them on their sex life. "You're doing great with everyone. Mom even wanted to know if you were allowed to celebrate Christmas. I think she was asking me if there was some Jewish law forbidding you from crossing her threshold when she's got the tree up."

"Your mother's mind is fascinating." A smile curled in Mattie's voice. "So I take it she doesn't completely hate me?"

"No one could hate you. It's against the laws of nature and probably physics."

"You did," Mattie reminded her. "Once upon a time."

Jillian closed her eyes. She could feel the warm, buzzing place where the line of her body met the curve of Mattie's. Beneath her ear, the muffled thump of Mattie's remarkable heart beat in reassuring time. "I never hated you, Freckles. Not for one second. I hated how being around you made me feel."

"When I first came to St. Rita's, you mean."

"Yes." For the first few weeks of that school year, Jillian had been eaten up with resentment, paranoia, and—worst of all—humiliation. "Then you nonconsensually bulldozed me with that relentless charm of yours, and I was powerless to resist."

"And after *that*, you realized I was the person you were fated to be with," Mattie said dreamily. "Well, following a few tiny roadblocks we don't need to rehash."

Jillian didn't comment. Instead, she snuggled in closer and wrapped her left arm around Mattie's waist, hoping an embrace would be enough of a reply. Once before, Mattie had alluded to fate bringing them together, and, thanks to a well-timed kiss, Jillian had gotten away without responding.

"You *did* realize that, right? That I was destined to be yours? Your cosmically intended person?"

Clearly Jillian wouldn't be getting away this time. "I realized that I was ridiculously, horribly, transformatively in love with you," she said honestly. "Around the time I spent an entire hour combing the internet in search of the perfect wrapping paper for your suitably casual Hanukkah present."

Mattie pushed herself up into a sitting position, which meant Jillian had to follow suit. "That's not the same thing, though."

Her gorgeous eyes were wide with what looked like worry. Jillian swallowed. "You're right. It isn't."

"I see you as my destiny." Mattie's expression tightened. "You're telling me you don't see me like that?"

She was hurt. That much was obvious. And every molecule in Jillian's body strained toward the sudden and desperate need for clarification. She couldn't let Mattie misunderstand something so important.

An old, hard voice, familiar as bone, murmured to her. *How could anyone ever understand you?*

Jillian pushed it away.

"It's not what you think," she said quietly. "I don't see you as my destiny because that would mean I thought some higher power—God, the universe, whatever—brought you to me. And I don't believe that, Freckles." She took a deep breath. "I don't know if there's something greater than ourselves, but I'm certain about this. Some unseen cosmic force didn't create my love. *I* made us happen. And so did you. Not God. Not the universe. I took a hammer to my existence and shattered it because I wanted, more than anything, to build a better one with you. Loving you is the greatest decision I've ever made."

Mattie's mouth parted softly. "Oh," she managed.

"I spent forty years turning away from myself, and without you, I might've spent another forty doing the exact same thing. I'm not powerless against the way I feel. I'm powerful because I choose to feel it."

God hadn't created Jillian Reed in his image. Jillian Reed had created herself.

Now there were tears shimmering in Mattie's big eyes. Understanding sparkled there, too. She nodded shakily, then reached out to grab Jillian's hands.

"I like that even better," she said and smiled through her tears. "I really, really do. You're pretty spectacular, you know that?"

Jillian lifted Mattie's hands to hers. Kissed them, making little marks of tenderness. "Are you seriously phrasing that in the form of a question? Have you met me before?"

Mattie laughed, her face luminous.

The exhaustion Jillian had felt just a few minutes ago was gone, replaced by a deep, aching gratitude. To be seen, to be fully known, and to still be loved, not despite that knowledge but because of it—it was the greatest gift she'd ever received.

"Oh, my light," she whispered, full to bursting. "If I ripped down the sun with my bare hands, there'd be no difference with you in the world."

Mattie's cheeks flushed, and it was her turn now to kiss Jillian's hands, her lips warm and satin soft.

"There's one thing," she said softly after she lifted her head again, "that is definitely destined, and I won't hear any arguments against it. Not that I think you'll try."

"Oh, yeah?" Whatever this was, it was going to be good. "Let's hear it."

"That talented mouth of yours," Mattie murmured, "between my legs. Right this second, if you're willing."

Now *that* was the kind of fate Jillian could wholeheartedly believe in.

Without hesitation, she eagerly scooted down the bed and got herself into position as Mattie bent her legs, feet pressed down on the faded quilt, ready to receive. Oh God, Jillian was lucky. More fortunate than any woman alive.

Blessed are you. She pushed up Mattie's skirt. *Blessed are you forever.*

Friday, their last full day in Gladbeck, made Jillian feel a little like she was in a pickleball game, playing the role of the ball. Between looking at twenty thousand photos of Savannah's new girlfriend—"Grandma doesn't know yet, but I'm thinking of dropping the bomb right as we're leaving, like literally halfway out the door"—destroying Brian in a two-person backyard soccer game, getting the rundown of extended family updates from her mother, and a late-afternoon visit with Mattie's parents, there wasn't much time to relax.

Not that Jillian knew the definition of the word anyway.

Before she had time to take a breath, her finger was on the doorbell of Emily Bruno's mother's house. It was the second time in three days she'd stood on the front porch of a modest Gladbeck home, waiting to be let in. This time, though, apprehension didn't cramp in her veins.

Jillian and Mattie were holding hands.

"What's the over-under on how long it'll take Emily to pounce on us?" No note of the last few days' strain in Mattie's voice, just amusement. "I'm thinking eight, nine seconds."

Jillian was about to take the under when the door opened on a short, beaming woman maybe a few years older than Jillian, with a face that seemed more unguarded than a spring flower. Jillian knew, with the kind of instinct she never doubted, that she would get along with Jessica Bruno just fine.

"Hello!" Emily's mother beamed at them. "I'm Jess. Welcome, welcome. Come on in! The kids are all hanging out in the family room."

They entered, exchanging greetings and the sort of basic social lubrication that was Jillian's shaky third language, after English and soccer.

Mattie handed Jess the Tupperware containing leftover stuffing. "My future mother-in-law's specialty," she said brightly. "Hope you don't already have four of these."

"Thank you! We don't, but even if we did, there's absolutely no such thing as too much—"

Out of her visual periphery, Jillian had just enough time to register a blur of movement before the impact.

She staggered a little, looked down, then laughed. Emily had her arms wrapped around Jillian's middle and was hugging her tightly from her right side.

"Okay, Red, okay," she said, not bothering to keep the delight from her voice. "I had no idea you were training to become a nose tackle. Not half bad."

"I've been looking forward to this for weeks!" Emily let go, then stepped back. Her carrot-red hair was a staticky halo around that bright, animated face. She wore the exhilarated look of someone who, even at eighteen, couldn't quite believe her former high school teachers were actually inside her house. "We even decorated sugar cookies to make them look like soccer balls so you'd feel more at home. Because our home's your home tonight."

That generosity was textbook Emily. For absolutely no reason at all, sudden tears pricked at the corners of Jillian's eyes.

Emily then tackled Mattie, delivering a repeat performance that was just as good as the first, and Mattie spun around, turning the tackle into a bear hug. She'd always had a particular fondness for Emily, almost from the start. Jillian had a suspicion that Emily reminded Mattie of her younger, less filtered self, even if she'd never said so out loud.

"Let Coach Reed and Ms. Belman catch their breath," Jess told her daughter, smiling. Then, to Mattie and Jillian, "Can I take your coats?"

It wasn't possible to pause Emily; the only setting she had was fast-forward. "Oh! Everyone's in the den!" She counted off on her fingers. "Kylie, Aubrey, Sophia, Olivia, Kiara, and Izzy. Kiara and Kylie weren't going to come home for Thanksgiving, but when I told them you were going to be here, they changed their minds. You haven't seen them for a while, right? Or Olivia? I mean, you haven't seen *me* for a long time, either. I know Izzy comes over a lot because they're in New York, too, but—oh, guess what? Olivia cut her hair and it looks so—"

"Hey, Red," Jillian interrupted, shrugging off her jacket. "I'm going to stop you right there before your larynx collapses. Why don't you show us where the den is?"

It was nothing like the den in her childhood home.

This room had a wall of windows on one side that let in the sharp autumn light, a plush cream carpet, several couches and chairs that looked soft enough to disappear into, and a large braided rug in rainbow colors. This room was filled with sound and laughter and the sprawling bodies of six college students, six adults who, once upon a time, had been under her care and protection.

They still were.

Izzy was the first to look up and see Jillian and Mattie, their eyes widening. A grin split across their face, and Jillian couldn't help but mirror that smile with one just as wide. Izzy—brave, determined Izzy, who'd told their father that he could accept them for who they were or lose their child—was the best of a truly outstanding bunch.

"Jillian!" Izzy cried out just as the others all whirled toward the doorway, surprise and delight on their faces. "You made it!"

"You can't call her that!" Emily objected while the others stood up, chattering excitedly. "She's Coach Reed, Izzy. She's always Coach Reed."

"I am," Jillian agreed, and slid her arm through Mattie's, clasping it tight. "But I'm Jillian, too. I've told you before, Red. You can use our first names. All of you can."

"Only if you want to," Mattie amended.

"That's so weird, though." Olivia's new haircut looked like she'd handed the stylist a picture of Leonardo DiCaprio circa 1997. She looked at Mattie, her round cheeks stained pink. "Just—what? Call you Mattie? Just like that? I don't know."

Apparently, time and space hadn't diminished Olivia's obvious crush on her former theater teacher one bit. Mattie was still oblivious, somehow, and Jillian wouldn't tell her. More fun to see if she'd ever figure it out on her own.

"Say less," Kylie declared. "You're Jillian. And you're Mattie. See, Liv? Super easy."

Kiara laughed and elbowed Kylie. "Yeah, you sound like you feel extremely normal about this and not at all like you're cosplaying being an adult."

"It's gonna take me some time," Aubrey added. "Like, ten years."

Sophia blinked, clearly fascinated by the new pathway opening before her. "I would actually like to call Ms. Belman Ernestine. It's my favorite name."

"Not one of the options, Sophia," Mattie said gently.

All right. Enough chit-chat. "Kids!" Jillian barked, not letting go of Mattie.

Instantly, the room quieted.

"We're not kids anymore," Izzy pointed out. "The whole first name thing kinda supports that. All of us are at least eighteen now."

"You're *my* kids." Jillian glared at her, the sort of stare that meant, *Tough shit, I've claimed you for life*. "Mattie's, too. And you've all forgotten something. Except Emily here."

Emily, who loved getting things right, beamed.

"What'd we forget?" Kiara asked.

Jillian looked at Mattie and grinned. Without moving away, she flung her free arm wide.

Half a second later, Mattie did the same.

Ours. They stood there together, open and laughing, as their kids all ran toward them.

Curious about how their story started? Read *Loser of the Year*.

Tent for Two

by Jae

"So…" Steph sat cross-legged beneath their parents' poolside pergola and swirled the ice cubes in her fruity cocktail. "Big anniversary coming up for the two of you next month. Any plans?"

Claire couldn't believe nearly a year had passed since she and Lana had said, "I do." The old saying *time flies when you're having fun* was definitely true for marriages too.

She smiled at Lana, who was sprawled on the lounge chair next to hers in her beloved capris, flip-flops kicked off, tanned legs stretched out as if she didn't have a care in the world, enjoying the gorgeous fall weather in LA. *Life's too short for boring T-shirts* was printed in bold letters across her ample chest.

"Or are you just going to keep working?" Steph added when neither of them answered right away.

In the past, Claire admittedly would have made that mistake—always putting work first. But since she had met Lana, her priorities had shifted. She sat up in her lounge chair and straightened her spine. "Of course we have plans. Well, ideas."

Her sister waved her stainless-steel straw. "Let's hear 'em."

"I was thinking maybe a wine-tasting tour in Napa. Or a spa day, followed by dinner at The Ambrosia Palace."

Steph rolled her eyes. "Seriously? You want to celebrate your anniversary at a restaurant where you spend half the night trying to figure out what fork to use? Doesn't sound like something Lana would enjoy."

Before Claire could push her sunglasses down her nose to shoot her sister a withering glare, Lana shrugged. "I can handle forks. It's knives I have a problem with." She laughed and turned to Claire. "Remember that steak house in Philly?"

As always, Claire marveled at her ability to poke fun at herself and not let Steph provoke her—two skills she, herself, was still working on.

But Steph was right about one thing: The Ambrosia Palace wasn't Lana's style. While she didn't mind dressing up every once in a while, Lana preferred a more laid-back atmosphere.

Luckily, Steph was distracted by staring at their parents' pool, where her girlfriend, Rae, sliced through the water with powerful strokes, giving Claire a moment to discuss it with Lana.

She reached over and took Lana's hand. "Your little knife mishap was hilarious. Even the waiter thought so...once he recovered. Seriously, though, if you could pick anything for our anniversary—any place or activity at all—where would you go?"

They had been traveling a lot since getting married, but with the exception of their honeymoon, it had all been for work—Claire's work. Whenever Lana hadn't been on set or in her recording booth, she had joined Claire on her book tour, making sacrifices without complaint. Now Claire wanted to spend their anniversary doing whatever Lana would enjoy most.

"Hmm..." Lana sipped her iced tea while she seemed to consider the options.

"Don't think about it for too long," Claire added. "Just say the first thing that comes to mind."

Lana grinned. "We both know I'm good at that." She put her iced tea down on a small glass table and said, "Camping."

Claire had been about to nod, ready to agree to whatever Lana wanted. Now she froze. "Camping?"

"Camping," Lana repeated, her hazel eyes twinkling with excitement. "No email or Wi-Fi, just the two of us, snuggling next to a campfire, stargazing, rebelliously ignoring your no-carbs-after-six rule and roasting marshmallows."

The mental images darting through Claire's mind weren't quite so romantic: spending the night shivering in a leaky tent, peeing in the bushes, eating cold beans out of a can, being devoured alive by bugs or, worse, a bear.

Steph nearly spilled her cocktail as she bent over, howling with laughter. "Oh my God! Can you imagine Claire at a campground? Her idea of *roughing it* is a hotel without room service!"

Claire smoothed her free hand over her linen pants. Admittedly, she and the great outdoors were not the best of friends. Her only experience with camping was oohing and aahing over photos from their friends' camping trip as she sipped a glass of pinot noir in her air-conditioned home, but that didn't mean she was going to back down now. "I'll have you know I'm perfectly capable of roughing it if I want to. I'm not some delicate flower. I just wonder if November will be the best time for a camping trip."

"We're in Southern California, honey. It's not like we'll freeze to death."

"Yes, but nights can get chilly, and I'm a thin-blooded Californian, not a cold-resistant Easter Coaster like you," Claire replied.

Lana grinned at her. "That's what campfires, sleeping bags, and warm wives are for."

Claire didn't want to sound as if she was making excuses, especially not in front of her sister. Lana had picked camping, so that's what they would do. "All right. We'll go camping."

"We're talking *real* camping, right?" Steph asked. "Not glamping in a deluxe cabin with gourmet meals and a hot tub."

Claire nodded stiffly. "Of course we're talking real camping. Besides, who says I can't cook a gourmet meal over a campfire?"

Lana leaned toward her. "Are you sure?" she whispered, her deep voice resonating through Claire in a way that sent goose bumps down her body, despite the warm October temperatures in LA.

"Absolutely," Claire said even as her stomach did a backflip. If this wasn't proof that marriage didn't kill romance, then she didn't know what was. She lightly bumped Lana's shoulder with her own, attempting to mask her nerves with a teasing smile. "I've gone outside a time or two before, you know? If you want to go camping, I'm all in."

Lana studied her for a few seconds longer, and Claire knew her wife saw through her bravado. But Lana didn't call her bluff. "Great! It'll be fun; you'll see!"

Obviously, they had different definitions of fun, at least when it came to outdoor activities.

Claire squared her shoulders. She would say yes to even more ridiculous things than camping for Lana. One night in the woods wouldn't kill her... hopefully.

Who knew that a camping trip could be so much fun?

Well, at least the planning part of it.

Over the past week, Claire had pored over campground review sites, product tests of tents and air mattresses, and recipes for healthy campfire cooking.

A steady stream of packages had arrived all week, and now the living room of their West Los Angeles home was starting to look like a camping gear store.

Color-coded plastic bins filled with metal plates and mugs, flashlight batteries, and other camping essentials lined one wall. Meal plans, checklists, and maps of the area were spread across the coffee table, and a sleeping bag was draped over the couch after Claire had tried it out earlier.

On Friday evening, Lana left the recording booth they had set up in the former guest room and paused in the doorway. Her eyes widened as she took in the gear that had arrived while she had been working on the latest audiobook she was narrating.

Admittedly, Claire had spent too much money on things she would probably never use again. But she couldn't help herself. She wanted to make it an unforgettable weekend for Lana.

"Oh wow." Lana crossed the room and picked up the clipboard that held Claire's checklist. "This list would make NASA jealous! You do know we're just going camping for one night, not gearing up for a ten-year mission to Mars, right?"

Claire shrugged. "You can never be too prepared. We only celebrate our one-year anniversary once. I want things to be perfect, so I'm not just going to wing it. No surprises."

"But surprises are the best thing about camping."

"Only if it's good surprises," Claire replied. "Not if it's raccoons raiding our supplies or the campfire getting out of control."

Lana chuckled. "Okay, I'll give you that. But…" She peered at the checklist. "Bear spray?"

"You can't charm a bear with your enchanting personality."

"Why not?" Lana playfully batted her lashes. "I managed to charm you, didn't I?"

"Not right away. I remember calling my agent, demanding she find another actress to play the role of my fiancée because you were driving me up a wall." Claire laughed at the memory, glad her agent hadn't listened. "You only started to grow on me once I dipped you back against that palm tree and fake-kissed you."

"Fake-kissed?" Lana fanned herself with the clipboard. "That kiss didn't feel fake at all."

Heat shot up Claire's body. She would never forget their first kiss at the office party either. "It didn't feel fake to me either. I thought you had to be the best actress in the world." They both chuckled. "But a bear won't give you the chance to win it over with your kissing skills."

Lana shuddered. "Not that I'd want to. The only one I'll be kissing for the rest of my life is you. So it's a good thing there are no bears in the Santa Monica Mountains."

Claire lifted her finger. "I found an article online that said they sighted one in 2023."

"Okay, okay, the bear spray can stay on the list, just in case that one lone bear wanders into our campsite," Lana said with an indulgent smile. "The emergency flares have to go, though. It's a campground right off PCH, honey, not the Alaskan wilderness. Plus we don't want to start a wildfire."

"But what if—?"

Lana put down the checklist, cupped Claire's face in her hands, and kissed her. "What if we just have fun? You're adorable when you're in hyperorganized planning mode, but you worry too much."

Claire wrapped her arms around Lana, pulled her even closer, and kissed her again, this time a little longer. Lana tasted of the herbal tea with honey and lemon that she always drank while narrating. "Have fun," she murmured against Lana's lips. "I think I can manage that as long as I'm with you."

"Good." Lana kissed her a third time, then let go. "Now come on. Take a break from your checklist, and keep me company in the kitchen. I'll make grilled cheese sandwiches for dinner."

"Grilled cheese sandwiches?" Claire raised her eyebrows. "Whatever happened to my no-carbs-after-six rule?"

"Hey, you are the one who keeps insisting we shouldn't wing it when it comes to our camping trip. Grilled cheese sandwiches are great camping practice."

"That's your excuse now?" Claire muttered but still followed her to the kitchen with a smile.

Two weeks later, the weekend of their big adventure had finally arrived.

It was early Saturday afternoon when they pulled up to their assigned campsite, following the directions the camp host had given them.

They had taken their time, enjoying the drive up the Pacific Coast Highway, and had even stopped for an early lunch at a seafood restaurant just a few miles from the campground. Truth be told, Claire hadn't been in a hurry to leave civilization behind.

Lana had pointed out that the area wasn't exactly remote. There were plenty of ranches and wineries, not to mention a visitor center and even a luxury retreat.

But Claire couldn't get over the fact that there was no Wi-Fi or cell reception. She had drawn the line at peeing in the bushes, though, and had insisted on a place with restrooms and shower facilities. There was no way she would crawl into her sleeping bag grimy, covered in bug spray, and reeking of wood smoke.

At least the sign posted near the entrance showed that the day's fire danger level allowed campfires in the designated fire rings, so they wouldn't have to use the camp stove or be stuck eating granola bars for dinner.

Lana threw open the passenger door and bounded out of the car as soon as Claire had parked it. "We're here!" She waved her arm as if presenting a luxury resort. "Doesn't it look picturesque?"

That wasn't the word Claire would have used to describe it. *Rustic* was more like it.

Their campsite was tucked between two massive, old sycamore trees. A sturdy wooden picnic table stood nearby, flanked by two worn benches. Other than that and a fire ring, there wasn't much to see. Their campsite consisted of just a patch of dirt and bits of grass.

Twigs crunched beneath Claire's brand-new hiking boots as she followed Lana.

"Mmm, can you smell that?" Lana stuck her nose in the air like a Golden Retriever.

"Yeah. Wood smoke." The smell had hit Claire's nostrils as soon as she had gotten out of the car. She managed not to wrinkle her nose.

"No, I meant the ocean air! You can even hear the waves from here."

Claire strained her ears. Lana was right! The distant roar of the ocean drifted over from the other side of the highway. Okay, that was a nice perk.

"Let's go for a walk on the beach once we've set up the tent." Lana got the nylon bag that held the folded tent and pole segments from the car as if she couldn't wait to get started.

Claire put their air mattress for two and their rolled-up sleeping bags down on top of the picnic table and unfolded the instructions that had come with the tent. "Step one says to find level ground and clear it of rocks and branches."

Lana strode to a spot between the two sycamores and tossed aside a couple of twigs. "Check."

"Step two—"

"No need to read all of that," Lana said. "I've set up a tent a million times. Just sit down and relax. I've got this."

Claire gave her a disbelieving look, but who was she to interfere with the more experienced camper? She perched on the edge of a wooden bench, careful not to get a splinter, and watched as Lana got to work.

Lana spread a tarp over the spot she had picked, then unfolded the tent and placed it on top of the ground cover. Once she had turned the zippered door the way she wanted it, she assembled the two long tent poles, snapping them into full size.

The sight of her was so captivating that Claire forgot to double-check every step of the instructions. There was something incredibly sexy about a competent woman—and Lana certainly looked as if she knew what she was doing.

Her tan skin gleamed in the mid-November sun, and the muscles in her arms flexed as she connected two pole segments. Her short-sleeved T-shirt said, *Camping hair—don't care,* and her ponytail was indeed coming loose, with several of the wavy, light-brown strands escaping from her pink scrunchie.

God, she looked good out here. Okay, she looked good *everywhere,* as far as Claire was concerned.

"You're staring," Lana called over without glancing up from where she was pushing the poles through the sheaths crisscrossing the top of the tent.

"I'm supervising," Claire called back.

"Right." Lana inserted one end of a pole into a metal circle in one corner of the tent, then went to the opposite corner to secure the other end.

The lightweight pole bent into a bow shape, lifting up the roof of the tent.

But just as the structure was starting to look like an actual tent, the end of the pole Lana wasn't holding on to popped out.

The half-assembled tent collapsed into a heap of orange polyester, the poles clattering down on top of it.

Lana sent a sheepish look at Claire. "Oops."

"I thought you've done this a million times before?"

"Um, maybe I was generously rounding up. Plus mine was a one-person tent, while this is a tent for two. Maybe setting this one up is a two-person job."

"That's what the instructions say." Claire got up, went over, and held one end of the pole in place while Lana secured the other.

This time, they balanced glances at the instructions with Lana's more intuitive approach, and within minutes, they had placed the rain fly—an outer tarp—on top of the tent and hammered the stakes into the ground, anchoring the structure in place.

It might have been silly, but pride filled Claire as she stood side by side with Lana and glanced at the dome of the tent.

"Not too shabby for a couple of city girls." Lana slung an arm across Claire's shoulders, while Claire wrapped hers around Lana's soft middle. "We make a good team."

Claire hummed her agreement. Maybe camping wasn't so bad after all… even though she didn't look forward to sleeping in that thing, with just the thin polyester walls separating them from the woods and whatever creatures might be lurking there.

But the way Lana's face lit up made it all worth it.

Lana squeezed her shoulder. "I saw a sign for firewood at the visitor center. How about I grab some, and you can blow up our air mattress?"

"Deal."

"If you get lightheaded from all that blowing, I promise to give you a piggyback ride to the beach later."

"Your leg would start to act up if you tried that. Besides, what do you take me for—a spontaneous person who sets out on a camping adventure without doing any research?" Claire shot her a superior smirk. "Of course I brought an air pump."

Lana chuckled and pressed a kiss to Claire's cheek. "Of course you did. Be right back." She headed toward the car.

It was only once Lana had driven off that Claire remembered they hadn't yet unpacked the tub that held the air pump—it was still in the back of the car.

Claire groaned. Maybe she'd have to take Lana up on that offer of a piggyback ride.

After setting up the rest of their camp, Claire and Lana had spent the afternoon at the beach, which was only a ten-minute walk away.

They'd had the secluded cove almost to themselves.

The rhythmic crash of the waves and watching the antics of the seagulls had been the perfect antidote to the chaos of their arrival.

When the wind had turned sharper and it had gotten later, they had returned to their campsite to make dinner.

Lana knelt next to the fire ring. She had pushed up the sleeves of her fleece jacket, clearly unbothered by the crisp air. Her brow furrowed in concentration as she stacked the wood in the shape of a log cabin—crumpled newspaper and dry kindling in the center, then bigger pieces of hardwood around it.

The scrape of a match broke the quiet.

"What, no rubbing two sticks together?" Claire teased as she hovered nearby.

Lana chuckled. "No, thanks. I'm hungry and want to eat sometime this century." She leaned back on her heels and watched with a satisfied smile as the fire crackled to life.

"I'm impressed. Where did you learn how to do that?"

Lana brushed her hands together and stood. "My stepfather."

"Which one?"

"Stepdad number one. He took Avery and me camping every summer when we were kids, even after he and Mom got divorced."

Claire wrapped one arm around her. "I'm glad you had him in your life."

"Me too."

They stood close to the fire, warming up after the chill of the windy beach as they waited for the flames to burn down a little, giving them a nice bed of coals to cook on.

But when Lana moved to get their cooking gear, Claire held her back. "You've done your part. Now it's my turn to impress you."

"You don't have to cook," Lana said. "I know it's not your favorite thing to do. I could toss something on the—"

"No. You cook at home nearly every day. It's time for me to repay the favor. Besides, I don't want you to think I'm completely useless out here."

"Hey." Lana gently tapped Claire's nose. "You're never useless. I know I would have forgotten half of the equipment we need without you. Last time I went camping, I forgot to bring something really essential."

"The tent poles?" Claire asked.

"Worse." Lana dramatically widened her eyes. "The s'mores."

Claire gasped and clutched her chest. "Oh no! However did you survive?"

"It was a close call," Lana replied with a very serious expression. When Claire laughed, Lana's lips curled up into an affectionate smile. "I love making you laugh."

Which happened constantly. Never in her life had Claire laughed more than in the two and a half years since they had first met, and now she had a chance to show Lana her appreciation. She gestured toward the camping chairs they had brought. "Sit, relax, and prepare to be amazed."

"By all means, Chef Renshaw. The kitchen is all yours." Lana swept her hand toward the fire and plopped down in one of the folding chairs.

Claire set to work. Her meticulous preparation now came in handy. Every cooking utensil was neatly lined up in a plastic tub, in the order in which she'd need it. She drizzled oil into the large cast-iron skillet that sat on the grill over the fire.

As the oil heated, she opened the large cooler and pulled out the Tupperware containers with the cubed chicken and the veggies she'd chopped at home.

In no time, the mouth-watering aroma of sizzling meat, garlic, onions, and apples filled the air.

She glanced over at Lana, who had her legs stretched out toward the fire, her arms folded behind her head, and was watching her with an impressed expression. "That smells amazing! Leave it to you to find a camping meal that is both healthy and yummy!"

Claire had scrolled through hundreds of recipes until she had found the perfect one. She knew Lana loved hearty dishes with an unexpected ingredient, so the apple chicken stir-fry should be right up her alley.

She turned back toward the fire and reached out to slide the skillet a little to the left, so it wasn't directly above the flames.

Pain flared through her fingers.

With a yelp, she jerked back and dropped the skillet.

It bounced off the edge of the grill, tumbled down as if in slow motion, and landed upside-down in the dirt.

The smell of burnt onions stung Claire's nose.

The YouTube video she had watched on campfire cooking had failed to mention one thing: how hot the handle of the skillet would get over the fire.

"Claire! Are you hurt?" Lana jumped up and rushed over. She gently cradled Claire's hand and inspected it.

"I'm fine." But their dinner wasn't. It definitely couldn't be salvaged. Tears stung Claire's eyes—not from pain but from frustration.

The campground didn't have a store, at least not during the off-season, and the nearest place to get groceries was fifteen miles away.

So much for making this perfect.

But throwing a fit would make it worse, so Claire knelt and started to clean up the mess. "I'm so sorry. We might have to eat tomorrow's oatmeal for dinner." She peeked up at Lana, who grinned, completely unfazed.

"I wouldn't mind at all. But how about we have this instead?" Lana strode to the cooler, rummaged around for a few seconds, and then triumphantly held up a package.

Claire stared at her. "You brought hot dogs?"

"You can't go camping without hot dogs, so I brought some, just in case. But don't worry. They're the least junky hot dogs you'll ever eat. They're turkey, the buns are whole-grain, and the condiments organic. I know it's after six and—"

Claire got up and kissed her. "Doesn't matter. I'll gladly have a hot dog… and even eat a couple of s'mores for dessert."

This time, they worked together, skewering the hot dogs and roasting them over the crackling fire.

They ate with their camping chairs set next to each other, the fire warming them as the night air grew cooler.

Afterward, Claire licked a bit of mustard off her bottom lip and leaned back with a contented sigh. "That was surprisingly delicious. I guess it's true what all the YouTube videos said: Everything really tastes better outdoors."

"Just wait until you try the s'mores."

"Contrary to popular belief, I've had s'mores," Claire said.

"Not mine." Lana opened a package of marshmallows, speared two onto roasting sticks, and held them over the fire until they were golden brown. Then she leaned one stick against the grate so it could toast a moment longer while she assembled the first mini sandwich with graham crackers. But instead of a square of chocolate, she used a peanut butter cup.

"Oh my God," Claire muttered as she watched, her mouth already watering. "I didn't take into consideration how dangerous it would be to let the woman who knows all my secret vices make my s'mores."

Lana leaned forward and held the treat just inches from Claire's lips. "And the not-so-secret ones," she added, her voice even huskier than usual.

Their gazes locked as Claire cupped Lana's hand and with deliberate slowness brought the s'more even closer. Carefully, she took a small bite, letting her teeth graze Lana's skin.

The moment the gooey sweetness hit her tongue, a soft moan escaped her.

"Good?" Lana asked, sounding breathless. Her cheeks were flushed, and Claire had a feeling it wasn't just from the soft orange glow the fire cast across her features. Lana brought her thumb to the corner of Claire's mouth and wiped away a bit of melted chocolate.

"Perfect," Claire replied without breaking eye contact.

And despite their string of camping mishaps, this moment really was.

Claire bridged the space between them again, this time to kiss Lana. "Thank you for being my knight in shining armor and saving dinner." She glanced at Lana's chest. "Well, knight in a ketchup-stained fleece jacket."

Lana smiled against Claire's mouth. "Anytime. Happy anniversary."

"Happy anniversary."

Their lips met in a longer kiss, but before Claire could deepen it, the smell of burnt sugar hit her nostrils. "Uh, your marshmallow is on fire."

Lana quickly wrenched her mouth away and grabbed the stick she had leaned against the fire ring, but it was too late. Her marshmallow had burned to a crisp. Groaning, she slumped against the back of her folding chair. "God, this trip will make you hate camping!"

Claire smiled. "I don't hate it."

"No?"

"No." She stole another kiss—and the stick Lana held on to. "Come on. I'll make you a special s'more, and this time, no distractions."

Claire insisted on doing the dishes while Lana finished her beer next to the nearly burned-down fire.

When Claire was done, Lana took her hand and tugged her toward the tent. "Come on. I'll show you the constellations."

Claire arched her brows at her. "That's not a euphemism, is it?"

Lana laughed. "I wish. No. The tent walls are a little too thin and the other campsites too close for that. But there's one more camping tradition I'd like to introduce you to: stargazing."

She pulled one of their sleeping bags from the tent, unzipped it, and spread it over a patch of grass a few steps from the fire.

Was this really a good idea? The sleeping bag would reek of smoke all night, and the chill in the air made Claire shiver. Now that the sun had gone down, the temperatures had dropped to the forties. She pulled the blanket she had wrapped around her shoulders more tightly around herself, but it wasn't enough to fully ward off the cool breeze from the ocean now that they weren't as close to the fire.

Lana seemed to notice and quickly grabbed another blanket from the tent. She stretched out on the sleeping bag, invitingly lifted the blanket, and patted the space next to her. "C'mere."

Claire shoved her hesitation aside and crawled onto the sleeping bag.

As soon as Claire settled beside her, Lana covered them both with the blanket, while Claire put her own on top. They lay on their backs, shoulders touching, and Lana's body heat kept her warm as much as the blankets and the lingering heat of the embers did.

The night sky was stunning. With no moon and no city lights, the stars appeared brighter, standing out against the darkness like diamonds on a black velvet pillow.

The distant sound of waves blended with the occasional pop from the embers. Every now and then, laughter from a neighboring campsite drifted over, but it felt as if it was in another world that couldn't touch theirs.

Beneath the blankets, Lana took her hand and pulled it onto her chest. With her free hand, she gestured upward. "This is Ursa Major—the only bear you'll encounter tonight." She moved her fingers to the right. "And that one's Hippocampus Stellaris."

Claire squinted. "Where?"

"See those five stars? They form the seahorse's tail."

With a lot of imagination, the stars might indeed form the shape of a seahorse. Or it could have been a fish hook or a question mark.

Lana moved on to another patch of the night sky. "And that's my favorite—the Great Squirrel. There's one ear, and over there is the other. See?"

Claire had just opened her mouth to tell her how impressed she was by Lana's astronomy knowledge, but now she snapped it shut and turned onto her side to study Lana. "The Great Squirrel?"

"Mm-hmm." Lana kept a perfectly straight face, but Claire didn't fall for it.

"You're making all of this up, aren't you?"

"Not all of it. I think that one"—Lana gestured toward the first constellation she had pointed out—"really is Ursa Major. But I forgot the other constellations. It's more fun like this anyway."

Claire gave her a fond smile. Making up constellations was such a Lana thing to do.

Lana squeezed the hand she still held. "Try it. Make one up."

Claire hesitated. "I'm not the most creative person."

"Hello? You wrote a book!"

"A self-help book on relationships," Claire said.

"A self-help book with some very *creative* ideas and exercises." Lana tapped her hiking boot against Claire's. "Come on."

"All right." Claire searched the night sky. "Ooh, I've got one. Look over there." She stuck her hand out from beneath the blankets and gestured to the left.

Lana leaned her head closer until they were cheek to cheek so she could make out where Claire was pointing.

"That's the Celestial Alpaca."

For a second, Lana stared at her. Then she burst out laughing, loud and carefree, unconcerned with the other campers who could hear her.

Claire couldn't help laughing along. She loved Lana's booming, unrestrained laughter and her infectious joy in the simple things.

"And if you focus really hard, you can make out Coffee Spill Rising over there." Claire pointed at a random group of stars, making Lana laugh harder.

They cuddled closer and took turns pointing out fictitious constellations, each name more outlandish than the one before.

When Lana finally came up with "Nebula Nap Time," Claire stood, folded the blankets, and pulled her up from the sleeping bag.

"Come on. I think it's nap time for us too."

They doused the remaining embers of their fire and locked the cooler and all remaining food in their car, where it couldn't attract animals.

Then, using Claire's newly acquired headlamp, they made their way to the campground facilities for something Claire had looked forward to all day: a hot shower.

Claire had rarely felt this miserable. She had been lying awake for an hour, staring up at the ceiling of their tent.

If there was a patron saint of first-time campers, he or she clearly hated her.

All showers at the campground facilities had been filled to the brim with tokens, so there had been no hot water.

Instead of a long, relaxing shower, they had rushed through a quick wash with cold water to rinse off the sand from the beach and get rid of the wood smoke.

Freezing and with her hair still smelling of hot dogs, Claire tossed and turned in her sleeping bag. As predicted, it reeked of smoke because they had used it for stargazing.

She wrinkled her nose, yearning for her lavender-scented shampoo, soft silk sheets, and a proper bed.

The air mattress she had picked easily accommodated two people, but it dipped toward Lana's side and had deflated just enough to make her hips ache whenever she turned. Each time she moved was also accompanied by a squeak of the material, forcing her to lay as still as possible so she wouldn't wake Lana. The inflatable pillow beneath her head was too hard and just as noisy as the air mattress, making it impossible to find a comfortable position.

Every now and then, the croak of a frog at a nearby creek cut through the still night air, drowning out the soothing sounds of the ocean and keeping her wide-awake.

How could Lana sleep amidst that ruckus?

Or was she awake too?

Lana's sleeping bag rustled as she sat up.

A moment later, the battery-powered lamp on the tent wall flared to life.

Claire squinted against the sudden brightness.

Lana's head brushed the polyester roof, making her already messy hair stand on end with static.

Despite herself, Claire couldn't help smiling.

"Can't sleep?" Lana asked. "You look…miserable."

"And you look adorable." Claire smoothed down Lana's hair and sent her a smile that probably didn't look very convincing. "I'm fine."

"I'm so sorry about the showers. About everything." Lana hung her head. "I never should have let Steph badger you into going camping. I had a feeling you would hate it, and I don't know why I—"

"Hey, I told you I don't hate it," Claire said.

Lana gave her a doubtful look, but Claire continued.

"And I didn't agree to go camping because of my sister. This past year, you sat through most of my promo events, suffering jet lag and hearing me read the same passages from my book again and again, without complaining even once."

"Why would I complain?" Lana seemed honestly confused. "It was fun!"

"See? That's the attitude I love and admire. You make the best of any situation and manage to have fun, no matter what. This weekend, I decided to take a page from your book. For once, I wanted us to do something you would enjoy instead of letting my schedule determine how we spend our time. But I don't think I managed too well, so if anyone should apologize, it's me."

Lana blinked and ran a hand through her chaotic hair. "It doesn't work like that, Claire. Just because I went to your readings doesn't mean you have to go camping. A healthy balance in a relationship doesn't have to be a mathematically equal tally."

A hint of a grin tugged on Claire's lips. "Did you just quote my own book at me?" God, that might be the cutest thing ever. Possibly also the hottest.

Lana nodded. "Chapter four is my favorite. Well, other than the sex-on-the-kitchen-table chapter, of course."

Claire gave her a playfully stern look. "You know there's no such chapter in my relationship book."

"I'll have to deduct a star, then."

They grinned at each other, then sobered.

Claire pulled one arm from her sleeping bag, sat up, and took Lana's hand. "Look. I'll admit that I felt a little sorry for myself a minute ago. You know I get grumpy when I'm cold and have PMS. But that doesn't mean I'm not enjoying our adventure."

"All of it?" Lana asked with the tiniest smile.

"All of it," Claire confirmed. "Except for the shower and the ruined dinner—although that did turn out more than okay." Another shiver went through her. "And the subzero temperatures at night."

Lana chuckled. "Subzero? It's like, what—fifty degrees?"

"Forty-five," Claire said. "Practically freezing by Californian standards."

"I can help with that—or rather, you can."

"Me?"

Lana nodded. "I'm married to an amazing woman who did three hours of research before deciding on the best sleeping bags, and I vividly remember the feature that was the deciding factor."

"They zip together!"

They looked at each other, then couldn't move fast enough, unzipping their individual sleeping bags and zipping them together, creating one large cocoon.

Snuggled against the warm shelter of Lana's body, Claire relaxed for the first time in an hour. Instead of the hot dog and wood smoke smell, Lana's familiar scent filled her nose. "Oh my God." She let out a moan. "I'm a genius."

Lana chuckled and kissed her forehead. "Yes, you are. Now that you are no longer a freezing genius, do you think you'll be able to sleep?"

Claire nodded, her eyes already drifting shut. "Lana?" she mumbled sleepily.

"Hmm?"

"I really don't hate it."

"Good."

That was the last thing Claire heard before she fell asleep.

Claire woke with a start.

For a few moments, she lay still, not knowing what had wrenched her from deep sleep. She was warm and reasonably comfortable, still cuddled up to Lana, who was sound asleep.

Then a noise drifted through the fabric wall—a faint but deliberate scratching just outside the tent.

Claire stiffened. Her heart started to race. With trembling fingers, she searched for the flashlight in the dark—more to have a club-like weapon than for the light it would provide.

The noise came again.

It didn't sound like a squirrel or another tiny critter just passing by. Claire's mind showed her something much bigger—something with huge teeth and sharp claws that could easily slash through the flimsy layer of polyester separating them.

"Claire?" Lana mumbled sleepily.

"Shh," Claire whispered. "There's a bear right outside the tent!"

Lana sat up and rubbed her eyes. "Like I told you, there are basically no bears in this area, just mountain lions."

That wasn't exactly a soothing thought either.

A more insistent scratching came from the tent door.

Lana clutched her own flashlight. "It's probably just a deer or a raccoon," she whispered, but her usually deep, sensual voice came out high-pitched. "Or maybe a skunk."

Claire used every meditation technique she knew to calm herself. She would not be a camping wuss again! This time, she would be Lana's knight in shining armor instead of waiting for Lana to rescue her.

As silently as possible, she unzipped their sleeping bag, wriggled out of it, and crawled toward the door.

"What are you doing?" Lana whispered urgently.

"Checking out our visitor," Claire replied with every bit of bravery she could muster. Clutching the flashlight with one hand, she unzipped the tent a few inches and peeked into the darkness, ready to jump back should she come face-to-face with a dangerous predator.

Feral eyes reflected the unsteady beam of her flashlight from just inches away.

Claire barely held back a scream.

A ferocious hiss answered.

Okay, maybe not so ferocious. More like a squeak.

Frowning, Claire directed the beam of the flashlight down.

A pair of gleaming cat eyes stared back at her from a bundle of bristled fur.

Oh crap. A mountain lion cub!

Then Claire took a closer look.

It wasn't a mountain lion, not even a tiny one. It was a kitten—a white and gray tabby. Head tilted to the side, it gazed up at her. "Meow?"

Lana flopped back onto the air mattress, laughing. "Oh my God! That's the dangerous creature lurking outside our tent?"

Claire let the beam of the flashlight trail over the campsite and the surrounding trees, searching for the kitten's mother, but other than the rustle of leaves in the breeze, nothing moved out there. "No mama cat."

"Meow!" The kitten snuck through the gap in the door and darted past Claire, flicking its tail as if it owned the place.

"Oh, no, no, no! Catch it! It can't come in here! Cats have fleas. And sharp claws. It'll tear up the tent!" Claire scrambled after it.

But before she could reach it, the tiny cat had climbed into Lana's lap and rolled into a small ball of fluff.

"Right," Lana said with a smirk. "It's clearly evil and destructive." She tilted her head the way the kitten had and looked at Claire. "Aww. Have you ever seen anything so adorable?"

"I have," Claire said. "Every single day." She sighed. "Fine. It can stay. But only until morning." She zipped up the tent and crawled back into their shared sleeping bag, careful not to dislodge the tiny feline.

Both shut off their flashlights, and Claire's heartbeat finally slowed its frantic rhythm.

Something touched her thigh with light pressure. Then another touch came, an inch next to the first spot, followed by another.

Claire reached down to see what was going on and encountered soft fur.

As she smoothed her fingers over it, a surprisingly loud purr filled the tent.

Claire's heart melted against her will. "I think it's kneading my leg."

"Aww. It likes you. Clearly, a kitten with good taste." Lana reached down too, and their fingers brushed as they both petted the cat.

Finally, Lana yawned and sleepily smacked her lips. Her hand stilled against Claire's.

Lana had been right. Some camping surprises might not be so bad after all.

But they still weren't going to keep the cat.

Claire closed her eyes and let the purring and Lana's quiet breathing lull her to sleep.

A cacophony of shrill squawks startled Claire awake.

It sounded like parrots, as if she were in the middle of the Brazilian jungle.

She opened her eyes and looked around, disoriented for a moment before she remembered where she was: in a tent, camping!

The sun was rising, so it had to be around seven. The first light filtered through the orange tent walls, which bathed everything in a warm glow.

Lana was still asleep, only a tangle of dark hair and the top half of her face peeking out from the cocoon of their shared sleeping bag. She looked peaceful, her brow uncreased and her breathing deep and even.

Their uninvited guest was curled up on top of the sleeping bag, nestled between them, as if it had slept like that all night.

Claire lingered for a few moments, not wanting to get up.

She used to be an early bird with an efficient morning routine, but Lana with her just-five-more-minutes koala hugs had destroyed her productive habits.

Claire cuddled close until the uncomfortable pressure in her bladder reminded her that she had to pee.

As quietly and carefully as possible, she crawled out of the sleeping bag.

Apparently, the fresh air made Lana sleep like a log because she didn't even twitch.

Claire managed to get dressed and fold the sweatpants and long-sleeved T-shirt she had slept in into a neat pile without Lana stirring.

The rasp of the tent door zipper sounded awfully loud.

Claire froze and glanced back over her shoulder, but Lana slumbered on.

The kitten, however, had lifted its head and instantly seemed wide-awake.

Claire willed it to stay put as she put on her hiking boots and ducked outside.

Before she could zip up the tent, the kitten shot past her like a furry bullet.

The crisp morning air hit Claire's cheeks, sharp and invigorating. Quickly, she closed the tent flap to keep the warm air in, pulled the zipper of her fleece jacket higher, and tucked her chin into the collar. She stretched and looked around, surprised at how well-rested she felt. After the bear-that-turned-out-to-be-a-kitten incident, she had slept astonishingly well.

Mist clung to the ground, weaving around the old sycamores. The sun broke over the horizon, its light casting a glow over the canyon and making the dew on the grass sparkle.

The kitten took a few comical leaps, apparently not a fan of getting its belly wet. Its antics pulled an involuntary laugh from Claire.

A flock of wild green parakeets flew past, making Claire and the kitten turn their heads in unison as they followed the birds' path.

Claire paused to take it all in until the trickle of a nearby creek reminded her of her more pressing needs.

After a quick glance back at the tent, where Lana was still sleeping, she set out toward the closest restroom.

The kitten ran after her, its little tail curling up.

"Oh no you don't! Go home! Shoo!" She waved her hand at it.

The tabby didn't listen. It meowed plaintively and darted between her legs, nearly sending her sprawling.

Claire put her hands on her hips. "What part of 'shoo' don't you understand?"

By the time she reached the restrooms, the kitten was still hot on her heels.

Claire pointed a finger at it. "You're not coming in with me!"

The kitten sat down next to the restroom door as if it understood.

When Claire emerged a few minutes later, the cat was where she had left it.

As she walked toward their campsite, the fuzzball padded after her.

The camp host passed them in his SUV on one of his rounds through the campground. He slowed, then stopped and rolled down the window. "Looks like you made a camping friend." He gestured at the kitten, which had paused next to Claire.

"It's not mine," Claire said quickly.

"I know. I've seen it around. I think its mama is one of the feral cats that live around here, but it's been around campers a lot, so it's used to people." He grinned at her. "Feel free to take it home with you."

Claire lifted both hands. "Oh, no. No. I'm not a cat person."

The kitten rubbed against her shin.

The camp host laughed. "Good luck convincing the little one of that." He rolled the window back up and continued on his way.

Claire looked down at the kitten. "Don't get any ideas."

"Meow," the kitten replied.

"Good. As long as we understand each other."

The cat trailed after her all the way back to the campsite.

When they reached the tent, Claire peeked inside.

Lana was still cocooned in their sleeping bag, so Claire decided to surprise her with breakfast.

It took her only two tries to get a fire going, and she was very careful to use an oven mitt so she wouldn't repeat the cooking disaster of the previous day.

The kitten watched her every move, letting out a demanding "meow" from time to time.

"Stop it," Claire whispered. "You'll wake Lana!"

When Claire crouched next to the fire ring and stirred the oatmeal, the tabby trotted over and put its front paws on her thigh so it could see what was in the pot.

"It's not for you," Claire said firmly, but then relented and gave it a quick scratch behind one ear.

The kitten pushed up into the touch and purred loudly.

Claire stood to get the last handful of peanut butter cups from the cooler.

The tabby sprinted after her and circled her legs with eager meows.

Claire sighed. "Okay, okay." She rummaged through the cooler and found another package of hot dogs.

Apparently, Lana had bought enough to feed the whole campground.

She pulled one from the package, then hesitated. Were hot dogs safe for cats to eat?

Before she could decide, the kitten pounced and snatched it out of her hand.

"Don't blame me if you get sick." She cleaned her hands with a baby wipe before chopping up the peanut butter cups and sprinkling the chunks over the bowl of oatmeal.

With the bowl in one hand and two metal mugs of coffee in the other, she headed toward the tent.

The tabby bounded after her, and she had to keep it from sticking its nose into the oatmeal as she set the bowl down in the grass so she could free one hand and unzip the tent flap.

When she crawled inside with her offerings, Lana's nose twitched. She opened her eyes and pushed herself up on her elbows, her hair a wild mess around her face. "Morning," she said, her voice gravely with sleep. "What's this?"

"Breakfast in bed. Uh, well, sleeping bag, in this case." Claire managed not to spill anything as she handed over the bowl and one of the mugs.

"Aww. Thank you!" Lana sat up and paused with the spoon inches from her lips. "Want some?"

"No, thanks. It's all yours." Claire never ate breakfast, and while she had broken her no-carbs-after-six rule last night, she wasn't about to ditch another dietary habit just because they were camping. "But be careful—it might still be too hot."

Lana eagerly dug into the peanut butter cup oatmeal, despite Claire's warning. A moan rose up her chest. "Oh my God! Marry me!"

Claire laughed. "I already did." She watched Lana devour her breakfast. "The oatmeal disappeared almost as fast as the hot dog," she commented when the bowl was empty.

"What hot dog?"

"Our uninvited guest decided it was staying for breakfast," Claire said.

They both looked at the kitten, which had been exploring the tent and now came over to get pets from Lana.

"I was hoping it would stick around." Lana lifted the tabby's tail. "*She*. You know, I don't think she's as young as I thought last night. She's probably closer to three months old than two. She's just small, but definitely weaned."

"I didn't know you're a cat expert," Claire said. Camping had revealed a bunch of new talents she hadn't known Lana had.

"I'm not an expert, just a fan. We always had cats when I was growing up. I take it you didn't?"

Claire took a sip of coffee and shook her head. "My mother is allergic."

"We should ask around, find out if she belongs to anyone," Lana said.

"I already did."

Lana's eyes lit up. "You did?"

"I mean, I ran into the camp host, and he mentioned the kitten's mom is a feral who lives around here."

"So we could…?"

"No!"

The kitten flopped down onto Claire's lap and played with the zipper of her fleece jacket.

"No," she said again, to both Lana and the tabby. "Cats are messy. They shed fur everywhere." She pointed at her fleece, which was already covered in cat hair. "They knock things over, have zoomies at 2 am, and their litter boxes smell."

Lana gave her a pleading look. "We can't just leave her here, where the bears might get her."

Claire couldn't help laughing, even as she tried to remain stern. "A trustworthy source tells me there are no bears around here."

"And *my* trustworthy source said there has been a bear sighting in 2023," Lana replied.

Claire reached over and tapped her nose. "I need to be careful what I say around you."

Lana gave her a soft kiss. "No, never."

"Okay, how about this: We take her to LA. Your sister keeps saying she wants to adopt a second cat, so..."

Lana nodded eagerly. "That might work. At least we can visit her every now and then." She bent down toward the cat, which had curled up on Claire's lap. "What do you say? Want to come with us?"

"Meow," the kitten said.

Lana beamed. "That's decided, then."

It turned out Lana's sister had been inspired by their weekend adventure and had gone camping too, so she hadn't been home when Lana had tried to call her.

Reluctantly, Claire had agreed to let the kitten stay with them until they managed to reach Avery.

So far, all of Claire's predictions had come true:

The tabby had left fur all over her work outfits, frenetically darted through the house after midnight, and swatted Claire's uncapped Montblanc pen off her desk, spattering ink all over the floor.

At least the kitten had adapted to the improvised litter box right away, and she had kept her claws off the designer couch...so far.

On Monday evening, Claire was at her computer, researching the best odor-controlling cat litter, when Lana came home from her audition.

"How did it go?" Claire asked as soon as Lana set foot inside her home office.

Lana leaned in the doorway. "Oh, you know the drill: don't call us; we'll call you. But I have a good feeling."

"They'd better give you a callback," Claire said. "Or I'll boycott the movie."

Lana laughed. "I'll let them know. How was your day? And where's the little one?"

Claire turned her office chair around and nodded down at the cat asleep in the cradle of her left arm.

"Aww! That's the cutest thing I've ever seen!"

Claire had to admit it was pretty cute...even though her arm was starting to fall asleep. "She helped me do research but fell asleep halfway through."

Lana walked over and peered at the screen. "Do we have a winner?"

"Not yet. I've narrowed it down to two."

"Then what's in your cart?" Lana pointed at the traitorous icon that indicated one item had been put into the shopping cart.

"Um, a new T-shirt for you."

"Ooh, show me."

Claire hadn't been sure she would actually go through with buying it, but now she had no choice. She clicked on the cart to reveal its content.

Lana leaned closer to read the slogan on the front of the T-shirt. "Cat hair on everything is the new black." She laughed and brushed a few white-and-gray hairs off Claire's shirt. "So true. Not much longer, though. Let me take a quick shower, and I'll call Avery and see if she wants to pick up the kitten tonight."

"Uh, actually... I talked to Renata at work today."

Lana tilted her head. "Does she want to adopt a cat?"

"No. She has three already, so she told me all about the cat distribution system—how cats just wander into your life and make themselves at home when you least expect it. She says messing with it is bad luck." She peeked up at Lana. "So maybe we shouldn't."

"Shouldn't...what?" Lana asked in a breathless whisper.

"Mess with the cat distribution system. Maybe we should keep her." Claire nodded down at the kitten.

A loud squeal from Lana made the cat wake up, and Lana slapped a palm over her own mouth to stifle her excitement. "Really?" she whispered through her fingers.

Claire shrugged. "Cats are messy and chaotic. But they're fun too, and if last weekend taught me one thing, it's that stepping out of my comfort zone every now and then isn't so bad."

"Oh my God, oh my God, oh my God!" Lana rained kisses across Claire's face, then bent to kiss the kitten's head. "We need cat toys and a cat tree! Oh! And we need a name! We can't keep calling her 'kitten.'"

"She came running when I called her Monster earlier," Claire said with a grin.

"We're not calling her"—Lana covered the cat's ears with her hands—"Monster. What about…Bear?"

"Over my dead body." Claire playfully pinched her. No way would she tell that embarrassing story to every guest who met their cat. "There are no bears in LA, remember?"

Lana trailed her fingers over the kitten's fur. Her paws, belly, chest, and part of the face were white, while grayish-brown fur with black stripes covered her back and flanks—except for a thin swirl of white on her back.

It was shaped like a question mark…or maybe a fish hook…or the tail of a seahorse.

Lana patted that spot. "How about…Hippo? Like Hippocampus Stellaris."

Claire shot her a you-can't-be-serious look. "I'm not standing on our front porch, shouting, 'Hippocampus' for all the neighbors to hear."

"Okay, okay."

They glanced at the kitten, then at each other. "Stella," they said at the same time.

It was perfect—short, sweet, and a nod to their camping adventure under the stars.

"It means *star*," Claire told the cat.

"Meow," the kitten replied.

Lana laughed. "Sounds like she approves. I can't believe it! First camping, now cats! What's next—backpacking? Staying at a campground without restrooms?"

A shudder went through Claire. "No, thanks. Besides, we have a cat now. We can't just drop everything and traipse through the wilderness whenever we want." Triumphantly, she cradled Stella to her chest.

"Ooh, I see! She's part of your evil plan to avoid future camping trips!" Lana nudged Claire's shoulder, careful not to jostle the cat. "Come on. Admit that I won you over to the joys of camping."

"You won me over," Claire said, but she wasn't talking about camping. "But maybe our next anniversary could involve a cabin with a plush mattress and a hot tub."

Lana bent to kiss her. "Deal."

If you enjoyed this short story, make sure to read *Just for Show* by Jae, the novel in which overly neat, posh psychologist Claire hires impulsive actress Lana to play the role of her fiancée.

Stalling Out

by Jazz Forrester

"I feel like a gin fizz," Naomi says.

Dani Cooper laughs. While she feels sorry for her friend and future cousin-in-law, Naomi *did* bring this on herself. The moment Dani's cousin Sarah proposed, Naomi said that she wanted a fancy dress fitting at a "proper bridal shop" somewhere outside of small-town Riverwalk, and she's getting it. The full experience, ugly dresses and all.

"What the hell is a gin fizz?" Dani asks from behind a bridal magazine.

"A drink." Naomi twirls in the mirror, the voluminous tulle of her skirt fanning out around her as she frowns at the fluffy material swishing around her legs. "Made of gin, egg whites, and this *fucking* wedding dress."

Dani looks up from her magazine. The white fabric makes a nice contrast against Naomi's dark-brown skin, but that's just about the only positive. The dress practically engulfs her. Sarah will think Naomi is the most gorgeous thing on the planet no matter what she's wearing, but Naomi is clearly unhappy.

"I'm thinking more...merengue," Dani says. "Marshmallow fluff. That thing that happens when you put dish soap in a fountain."

Naomi scowls. "*Very* romantic, thank you."

From Dani's right side, Nora pipes up. "You know, you have a talented seamstress in your wedding party. Mila is already making the bridesmaid dresses. I'm sure she'd help if you asked."

Nora has been fairly quiet through this whole thing, which is a bit of a surprise to Dani—on top of being Naomi's maid of honour, she easily has more experience with shopping in high-end stores than Dani and Naomi combined. During her first few weeks in Riverwalk all those years ago, on her summer trip before she and Dani ever started dating, Nora wore nothing but deeply expensive outfits that made her stand out among the locals. Her style has relaxed a lot, especially since they moved in together, but she still pulls out those fancy dresses for special occasions.

"My beautiful girlfriend has a good point." Dani grins when Naomi rolls her eyes. Everyone is used to Dani's effusive affection for Nora by now, which hasn't dimmed a bit in the four years since they made things official, but they still complain sometimes about how cheesy Dani can be. It's always made Nora smile, though.

"Mila has enough on her plate running the shop. I'm not asking her to make the wedding dress too," Naomi says. Their friend Mila is, in fact, running late to this very fitting, despite being in the wedding party, because she's so busy with her clothing shop and tailoring business. "Doesn't this place have anything that isn't so...pouffy?"

"What is a wedding dress if not ninety percent pouff?" Nora says.

Naomi sighs. She steps behind the privacy fan, and the fabric rustles as she wrestles her way out of the gauzy monstrosity. "I want something *slinky*. Something Sarah will want to rip off."

"Gross. That's my cousin you're talking about," Dani calls out. She folds her ankles together, flicking through the pages of her magazine again. Ball gowns, drop-waists, mermaid cuts—none of them could be considered *slinky*.

Naomi's head pops around the side of the divider. She's recently had her tight curls styled into long braids, and they hang heavily as she sticks her tongue out at Dani. "You didn't have to come to the fitting, you know. You're Sarah's maid of honour, not mine."

"It's really one big wedding party, isn't it?" Dani says. Sarah has always been more like a sister than a cousin to Dani, so there was never any doubt that she'd be Sarah's pick, but since she and Naomi share friends, the party is pretty egalitarian. "Didn't we decide dresses on your side, suits on Sarah's? Since Mila isn't here yet, I'm here to offer my vast fashion knowledge."

When Dani looks up from her magazine, Naomi and Nora are looking at her with raised eyebrows. She glances down at her outfit. It's not like she came straight from work. She's wearing her best jeans—no holes whatsoever and only a faint grass stain on the knees—and a flannel over her cleanest white T-shirt. Sure, there's a bit of dark auto shop crud on her steel-toed boots, but overall, she looks perfectly presentable.

"What? I know fashion stuff. Like...vintage. Bespoke," Dani says, casting around in her memory as she lists her short collection of terms on her fingers. "Oh—couture. That's a fashion thing."

"Darling, I find you unmanageably hot. You know this. But your fashion sense is about as far from *couture* as it's possible to get." Nora twirls her hand through Dani's dark-blonde ponytail. "You've got engine grease on your shirt."

"Hey, that's an old stain," Dani says, plucking at the fabric. "And it's hidden under the flannel. I bleached it, like, twelve times."

The salon door flies open. Dani is saved from the fashion critique when in spills the bundle of tall, vibrant chaos that is Mila, with an annoyed-looking dress consultant trailing behind her. Mila is paying her no mind, carrying a purse and a tote bag over her shoulder with a Bluetooth headphone in one ear and an extra-large coffee in hand.

"Sorry I'm late, I had a fabric shipment coming in, and the truck missed the Riverwalk exit on the highway *twice*. I wasn't sure you'd still be here." Mila drops the bags onto the floor beside the couch and flops down next to Dani, waving away the consultant who seems relieved that Mila is actually with their group and not some random person wandering in from the street. "This place is overpriced, by the way. Where's Naomi?"

Mila, like Nora, actually looks like she belongs in a high-end dress shop. She's in a very fashionable romper that she probably made herself, with her long legs on full display. She settles in comfortably, pinching the fabric of one of Naomi's discarded dresses with a grimace.

"Changing out of the latest disaster," Nora says. "We've been striking out so far. Naomi wants a slinky dress."

"I told you I can make you a slinky dress!" Mila shouts toward the privacy fan.

Naomi groans. She steps out from behind the divider in yet another dress, this one crusted in rhinestones that reflect a blinding light from the window like some kind of nuptial disco ball. "I don't want to put another thing on your list."

"This is your wedding. To *Sarah Cooper*. We've been rooting for you two since you were dancing around each other in high school." Mila sets down her coffee and finishes off Dani's mimosa. "And I'll make dresses for everyone in the wedding party, whenever you people decide to tie the knot."

"Even the boys?" Dani asks, peeking over her magazine. Naomi's younger brother Owen and his boyfriend Ryan are in the party too, acting as brides-man and flower boy respectively, but they had no interest in coming to the dress fitting.

Mila nods, not hesitating for a moment. "Especially the boys. And since nobody else is saying it, Naomi, that dress is ugly as hell."

While Mila goes behind the privacy fan to help Naomi wrestle her way into a new dress, Dani's attention slides to Nora.

Nora is watching the proceedings with a familiar look of subtle affection. It makes her eyes sparkle, and crinkle at the corners—she's become so much more expressive than she was when Dani first met her, when she was all cool and detached. She'd walked into Dani's auto shop four years ago with a broken car and a guarded attitude, intent on staying in town only for the summer; a platonic coffee date and a single night of stargazing later, Dani had been head over heels.

Nora was polished then, uptight and a little snarky, with her pressed outfits and her perfectly silky dark hair, but Dani had seen something underneath it all. Something soft and real. She could feel Nora wanting to open up as they spent the summer getting to know each other, but she could also feel that Nora was always holding herself back from really leaning into it. Nora held herself back when she left town at the end of the summer to go back to her corporate job, and she held herself back when she stayed there for three months before finally deciding to return to Riverwalk for good.

Now, it's Dani holding something back. Specifically, the ring currently hidden in her sock drawer.

It's been there for years at this point, just waiting for the perfect time. It belonged to Dani's mother, handed down when she passed. It's somewhat dated, but it's been cleaned and polished until it looks nice enough to grace Nora's finger. Dani has been close to pulling it out once or twice over the years, but ever since Sarah proposed to Naomi, it's been on the back burner. The last thing she wants is to steal their thunder, and she's not in any rush. After all, she's known since they moved in together that she wants to spend her life with Nora. Since before that, even—since the day Nora climbed into Dani's truck after three months of distance and told her she wanted to stay.

Dani might have dropped down to one knee right then and there if it hadn't been such a massive stereotype. She'd waited a perfectly respectable thirteen months before even suggesting they move in together, thank you very much.

It's easy—as Naomi finally gives up the whole endeavour and stalks back behind the partition to change into her street clothes—to imagine Nora trying on dresses in a shop like this. She probably wouldn't want something slinky or pouffy, but instead simple and tasteful. Something that matches her style. Dani can see it in her mind's eye: Nora's pale skin against a warm, cream-coloured gown, her dark hair in an elegant updo. Or maybe she'd want it curled, spilling over her shoulders as she beams at Dani from the end of an aisle.

Nora is always beautiful, whether she's in sweatpants or a designer blouse, but that particular image makes Dani's heart skip a beat.

"I know Dani will go the suit route like Sarah, but what about you, Nora?" Mila asks, now halfway through Nora's mimosa. "What will you want? Slinky? Ballgown? Miniskirt?"

"I don't think you'll ever get me in a wedding dress," Nora says, chuckling. "Getting married seems exhausting. All the frills and pomp and ceremony. I mean, why do there need to be five separate parties?"

Dani's thoughts skid to a halt.

"Are there really that many?" Mila says, unaware of Dani's mini crisis.

"Engagement party, bridal shower, bachelorette, rehearsal dinner, wedding." Nora counts off on her fingers. "Some people even do luncheons. I don't know how Naomi and Sarah are doing it all. It's a little too much for me."

Dani chews on her lip, bringing the magazine up to cover part of her face.

Fuck.

It's not like they've never talked about the future—Nora has always been consistent in her commitment. They've talked countless times about future plans, vacations, pets, kids, growing old together. They're both in it until the end. It's a total given now.

Why on earth had Dani not thought to ask if Nora ever saw herself getting married?

"Really? So no wedding for you two?" Naomi asks as she re-emerges, pulling her braids into a tie. She looks to Dani.

Dani scrounges up a smile over the magazine, hoping it covers the turmoil inside her head. "Whatever Nora wants."

The conversation moves on. As a group they gather their things while Mila peppers Naomi with questions about her ideal dress design.

Nora slips her hand into Dani's, and Dani holds tight.

A commitment is a commitment. She doesn't need a ceremony to be happy with Nora, as long as they're together. Maybe someday she can even give the ring to Nora as a simple promise ring, without any of the frills of a wedding day. If Nora is happy, so is she.

Well. Dani has always *thought* Nora was happy. But what if she's missed some sign? What if Nora doesn't want to get married not because it's too much fuss but because she's not as settled in Riverwalk as Dani thinks she is? What if Nora now wants something else? Something more? What if she regrets her decision to leave the city and stay in Riverwalk?

The carpool home seems longer than it should be.

The weeks before the wedding pass in a blur of planning and parties. Since the wedding itself is being hosted at Dani and Nora's lake house, Dani is far more involved in the intricate details than she would be normally. Everything from catering to the exact arrival time of the flower arrangements is on her plate as much as it is the brides. She doesn't mind helping—as Sarah's maid of honour, she wants her cousin's wedding to go off without a hitch as much as anyone else—but it does all serve as a stark reminder.

Nora doesn't want to get married, and the thought that the decision could be tied to some unhappiness that Dani is missing is difficult to forget.

The bridal shower passes without incident, nice and simple, but Naomi and Sarah are much more exacting in their planning process for the joint bachelorette party. Their list of requests is long: big-city club, a nice hotel, bottle service, a night of partying that would make Riverwalk proud—which is how they all end up in a limo driving through the streets of Toronto, pre-gaming with tiny complimentary bottles of liquor while they head to a club that only Nora and her old connections in the city could bribe them into.

Nora drops her full name at the door, getting them inside in a way that's surprisingly attractive.

It couldn't be clearer when they get past the bouncer that they don't blend in.

The club is chock-full, but the dance floor is sparse. People are mostly milling about in expensive clothes, sipping expensive drinks. Every man in Dani's field of vision looks like he's itching to explain investment banking to the nearest willing set of ears. There's not a domestic beer or a pool table in sight.

Everyone in their group is dressed the part, at least. Nora and Mila had final say over everyone's outfits. Dani is in brand-new pants and fancy Oxford shoes, with a crisply ironed black shirt that Nora styled with the top few buttons open. Nora herself is dressed to kill in a little black dress to match, with smoky makeup around her grey eyes and her dark hair spilling over bare shoulders. She looks spectacular; Dani can hardly stop looking at her.

The brides-to-be go straight to the dance floor, dragging Dani and Nora with them. Owen and Ryan follow, Ryan complaining all the way about the price of bottle service and taking swigs out of his flask instead. Mila sets herself up near the bar, and in the span of twenty-five minutes, Dani watches her win two separate drinking contests without paying for a single beverage.

Even after years living there, Dani has found that Nora doesn't often indulge in drinking to the level of most Riverwalk locals. She usually turns down anything stronger than a glass of wine. Tonight, she takes Sarah and Naomi's request to heart: She takes shots. She dances without self-consciousness. She leans into Dani, running her hands along Dani's arms as they move to the pulsing music together.

When they first met, Dani had assumed that Nora's frequent staring meant that she was just not used to seeing muscular women, but as soon as they started sleeping together, it was made clear that Nora really likes Dani's strength. She almost wishes she'd worn something sleeveless tonight, to enjoy Nora's touchiness to the fullest extent.

These days, Nora doesn't have to disguise her staring, and Dani doesn't have to hide the fact that she wants to kiss Nora at every possible opportunity. She can just do it. She can do it on the dance floor, enduring the long-suffering groans of their friends. She can do it in the booth while Sarah pours another round. She can do it in the hallway near the bathrooms.

"Before you even suggest it," Nora says, shivering when Dani pushes her harder against the wall and grips her waist, "I am not having sex in a public restroom."

"It's nothing we haven't done before," Dani murmurs. She hadn't really been considering it, but there's nothing she likes better than teasing Nora a little. They're alone in the dim corridor, and it's always fun to get her worked up.

Nora snorts. "That one was a single. It had a lock. I'm not fucking you in a stall."

"Do you think they'd be mad if we got a separate cab tonight, then?" Dani asks, nipping at Nora's earlobe. Her perfume is strongest here, and Dani breathes it in with a pleased hum. The glittering stone of Nora's earring clatters against Dani's teeth. It's oddly satisfying.

Nora arches her neck, giving Dani more access. "No, but I think your cousin would be upset if we had sex in a conjoining room to hers."

"We could be quiet," Dani says. She trails kisses down Nora's neck, biting gently at her collarbone as the lights flicker above them.

Nora chuckles. It's low in her chest, vibrating under Dani's lips. "Have I ever *once* been quiet?"

Dani groans, but when the bathroom door swings open to let out a crowd of very drunk women, she lets Nora lead her inside by the hand for a perfectly G-rated bathroom break. "No. If only I wasn't such a sex savant."

Nora laughs, pushing Dani toward a stall several down from her own. "Your suffering is endless, isn't it?"

When they return to the booth to find that Sarah and Naomi have gone back to the dance floor, Nora seems happy to have the opportunity to sit down. She's never been the first person to get up and dance, usually needing to be cajoled, and she's always liked to people-watch, taking in everything around her like she's going to be given a pop quiz before they leave. Dani, on the other hand, likes to watch Nora.

Nora has changed so much in the last few years. She looks the part right now of who she used to be, how she looked when they first met and Nora strolled into the auto shop in a Prada coat and $1500 shoes, but these days, Dani gets to see a different version back home. A relaxed, happier version, Dani has always thought. The version that grew and thrived that first summer Nora spent in Riverwalk. Now she fits with their little family like a hand in a glove.

Still, the doubts that surfaced at the dress fitting are lingering in Dani's mind.

"You know, it's interesting seeing your old world," Dani says over the music. "Your fancy city circles."

All around them, people jostle and drink; they hover at the edges of the dance floor, watching or searching or waiting. It all strikes Dani as a bit lonely. Everyone here is alone, searching for connection. The bar back home is the opposite—it's a place to meet up with people you already know and love. The mismatched tables and chairs and the ancient pool table there are shabby in comparison to the chic leather couches and pulsing lights of this club, but the River Run is a warmer place. Friendlier. It's one of the many places that Dani started to fall in love with Nora.

She's always thought that Nora felt the same way after officially moving to Riverwalk, but this feels like a perfect time to investigate that theory.

Nora snorts. "Interesting? What makes you say that?"

"Everything about you interests me. Do you miss it here?" Dani aims for casual.

"Not in the least," Nora says shortly. "And this was never my world. I've never been a partier, you know that. My world was work and my apartment."

"You come to all the Riverwalk events," Dani points out.

"That's different."

Dani drums her fingers on the table, watching the surface of her drink vibrate slightly with the club music's bassline. "You've seen everything there is to see about my life before I met you. I guess I'd like to do the same."

"And see what? I assume my old apartment is now occupied. We can't go there, unless you're craving a little breaking and entering," Nora says, arching a brow.

Dani grins, slinging an arm over the back of Nora's seat—Nora's dry sense of humour is one of the many things Dani loves about her. "You still have a pass to get into CromTech. You go to meetings there sometimes, right?"

"Do you think your cousin will appreciate you bailing on her bachelorette party? To go *there*?" Nora shakes her head as she sips her drink. "I know everyone forgave me for being a corporate shill, but that didn't erase their dislike for my old company."

"We could go in the morning."

Nora frowns. She turns more fully toward Dani, shifting in the booth seat. "Why are you so intent on seeing my old workplace?"

Dani bites at her lip. Sarah and Naomi are tearing it up on the dance floor, wrapped up in each other. Normally she would be right there with them, dragging Nora with her, but this conversation feels strangely important.

"I don't know. I feel like there's this big gap where I had no idea what was going on with you," Dani says. "When you went home, after that first summer. Before you came back to Riverwalk. I guess I want to fill in the blanks. See what made you want to come back to us. See the CEO Eleanor Cromwell of yesteryear."

"Riverwalk is home," Nora says. There's a crease between her brows. "I haven't been *Eleanor* in years, and I can fill you in right now on what was going on with me after I left you—I was miserable. My life was exhausting and unfulfilling before we met."

"So you're happier now? You wouldn't want to move back here?"

Nora turns fully toward her now, her brow deeply furrowed. "Of course I'm happy. Have I given you some indication that I'm not?"

"No," Dani says quickly.

Nora tips a finger under Dani's chin, guiding her to meet her eyes. "Dani, is something wrong?"

"I'm fine," Dani mumbles.

"You don't seem—"

All around them, bodies spill back into the booth. The movement jostles Nora's hand, almost spilling Dani's drink, and Dani hides her face in a deep gulp of gin and tonic.

"You guys are not nearly energetic enough," Sarah says. She's pouring shots of tequila from the communal bottle, pushing one toward each person. "I'm the bride. Get on my level."

"You're one of the brides," Naomi says, running a hand through Sarah's short, auburn hair. "But we're in agreement on that. Catch up, bridesmaids." Naomi takes her shot smoothly, accepting a slice of lemon from her fiancée's mouth.

Dani throws a balled-up napkin in their direction, but it doesn't deter them.

"Brides-*man*," Owen corrects before downing his tequila.

"Ooh, shots!" Mila says, making her way over from the bar after her latest free drink, but when she sees the bottle, she wrinkles her nose. "Ugh – tequila. Don't we have anything else?"

Nora scootches over to let her into the booth. "How many drinks have you had already?"

"That's between me and the bartender, my friend."

If only to avoid Nora's abandoned question, Dani takes her shot and allows herself to be pulled out of the booth. A few songs and a few drinks are enough to forget the conversation entirely; Dani pulls Nora close, and she dances the night away.

The only person besides Dani to make it to the hotel's free continental breakfast is Sarah.

"Morning," Sarah grumbles. She's ghostly pale and still in her pyjamas. Her hair is sticking up at the back. She grabs two mugs, filling them both to the brim with coffee.

Dani knows her cousin well enough to understand that neither coffee will be shared.

"How you feeling?" Dani asks, filling her own mug with hot water and snagging a teabag. She only had a few drinks last night, and she's feeling perfectly fine. Sarah had continued the festivities in her hotel room late into the night, playing drinking games with the others, and now looks like she's struggling to stay conscious.

"Violently hungover," Sarah mutters. She takes several long gulps of coffee. "How are you so perky?"

Dani shrugs. "I guess I just have a higher tolerance than you do."

"Or you didn't drink much." Sarah grabs several varieties of pastry but winces as they pass the hot plate full of scrambled eggs. "What was up with you last night? You went to bed early."

"Nothing," Dani says quickly.

Sarah makes an unhappy noise, but Dani drowns it out with the sizzle of batter hitting a hot iron as she makes a complimentary waffle.

After a long pause, Sarah clears her throat.

"Feel like I gotta ask," Sarah says. "Were you and Nora in a fight or something?"

"We weren't in a fight," Dani says. She pulls out her finished waffle, flooding the plate with syrup. "We were in a discussion. Sort of. We never really finished it."

"About?"

"I just…asked her if she was happy."

Sarah trails Dani to the nearest table, sitting heavily and unwrapping her cutlery. "That's an intense question. Why would you ask her that if you're not in a fight?"

Dani cuts her waffle into bits, but she's feeling less hungry by the minute. "I just wanted to make sure. What if she isn't?"

"Then do what you need to do to fix it," Sarah says. She takes a small bite of a croissant but seems to have trouble swallowing. "*Fuck* me, I'm nauseous."

For a while, they eat in silence. Sarah mostly drinks coffee, and Dani pushes her increasingly soggy waffles around on her syrupy plate. Most of the tables around them are empty by the time Dani finally voices her biggest fear.

"What if I can't fix it?" Dani says quietly.

Sarah puts her mug down. Her brow furrows, and she leans forward to brace against the table.

"I see where your brain is going. Nora loves you. She loves you like nobody I've ever seen," Sarah says firmly. "She left her whole life to come back here and be with you. Why would you ever doubt that?"

"That's exactly what's bothering me," Dani says, finally abandoning the last of her breakfast and pushing her plate away. "She left everything. I haven't really thought about it since then, but...what if she regrets it?"

"What's bringing all of this up suddenly?"

Dani heaves a sigh. "At Naomi's dress fitting, she sort of...mentioned she wasn't sure she wanted to get married."

"Oh," Sarah says, her expression softening. "And you've had your mom's ring in your sock drawer for four years."

Dani fiddles with the string of her teabag. "Yeah. I didn't want to do it until after your wedding. Now I'm glad I waited."

Sarah blows a quiet raspberry, leaning back in her chair. "Fuck. I'm sorry, kiddo."

"That's not even what's bothering me, really. It's—I'm fine without a wedding, if she really doesn't want one." Dani rubs her hands together, cracking her knuckles thoughtlessly. "I hope it's as simple as that. But how did I not think to *ask*? What kind of girlfriend am I?"

"It's normal to—"

"And what if the reason she doesn't want a wedding is because she isn't as happy as she could be? Her life was so different in the city. What if, subconsciously. she doesn't want to tie herself to me forever because she might someday get sick of the kind of life I can give her? What if I can't offer her enough?" Dani presses her lips together after the last of her anxious word vomit has settled between them. She's been stewing on this for weeks now, and as good as it feels to say it out loud, it also makes it feel less like a silly panic response and more like a real problem.

Sarah blinks. "Wow. Okay. I am way too hung over for this." She rubs her face. Her words are muffled by her palms. "Dani, you really need to talk to her directly. You're working yourself up without having any idea how she actually feels."

"I know." Dani picks sullenly at a stain on the tablecloth. "I'm going to wait until after the wedding, at least. Things are too crazy right now."

Sarah finishes off her second cup of coffee. "Sure, wait if you want. But I guarantee she's noticed that you're acting weird."

"You think so?"

"*Talk. To. Her,*" Sarah says loudly, clapping her hands between each word for emphasis. She winces at the volume of her own claps, pressing her fingers to her temples. "Ugh. But don't talk to me right now. I think I need to ralph."

Sarah scrambles up and jogs toward the lobby bathrooms.

Dani is left alone with her mushy waffle.

The wedding day dawns with a gorgeous summer sunrise.

Dani hardly gets to enjoy it. The house is a flurry of activity from the get-go—the tent arrived last night, and it's waiting out in the front yard for tables and chairs to be set up. There are flowers to arrange and a bar to stock and linens to steam. It's a simple set-up, but the effort to get everything together by the time the brides walk down the aisle is astronomical.

It's all hands on deck, thankfully, and with a group effort, things sort themselves out as the morning wears on. The catering arrives, and then the DJ. While everyone else is getting their hair and makeup done by Mila, Dani struggles through putting together a wedding arch down on the dock where the vows will be exchanged, stapling flowers to the wood with Owen and Ryan. It takes far longer than it should, and by the time Dani manages to start getting ready, it's fifteen minutes to go-time. She ends up hopping around the house, trying to tie her shoes while Mila chases her with a curling iron.

"You're cutting it close, love," Nora says, floating past Dani in the hallway as she heads toward the stairs to the bedroom. She's fully decked out, her hair cascading in dark curls over the thin straps of her pale-purple bridesmaid's dress, matched perfectly to Dani's tie.

Dani doesn't often see Nora in pastels. She usually likes a jewel tone. Dani stops hopping to take in the full picture; the moment she stills, Mila descends with a can of hairspray.

"*Stop* it." Dani waves away the acrid fumes. She coughs and ducks another spray. "I can't breathe!"

Mila bats her hands away. "Your hair's gotta get done. If you'd been here an hour ago, this would be easier."

"I know! It's not my fault." Dani's tie isn't cooperating, and breathing in hairspray fumes isn't helping. "The caterers needed help carrying everything to the tent, and then the lights weren't working, and *then* Ryan almost dropped the arch into the river. How long do we have?"

"Everyone is seated. Naomi's getting her dress fluffed. Not long," Mila says.

Dani manages to get the tie knotted properly, but when she fishes into her pocket for a tie clip to keep it anchored to her shirt, she comes up empty.

"Shoot—babe?" Dani calls out up the stairs, dodging Mila's hands as she fusses with her already overdone hair. "While you're up there, can you grab my tie clip?"

"Where is it?" Nora calls back.

"In my dresser somewhere?"

Mila has finally proclaimed Dani's hair finished by the time she hears Nora's voice again.

"Dani," Nora shouts from the bedroom, her voice a little high and squeaky, "could you come here for a second?"

Abandoning Mila, Dani darts up the stairs, grabbing a tissue on the way—Nora usually uses that voice when there's a bug that needs to be relocated, and it's best to be prepared. But it's not an insect that she finds when she shoulders open the bedroom door.

It's Nora, standing next to Dani's open sock drawer with a tiny velvet box in her hand. The lid is open; Dani's mother's ring glints incriminatingly in the sunlight streaming through the window.

"Oh, fuck," Dani whispers.

Nora's eyes flick back and forth between Dani and the ring three full times before Dani manages to connect her mouth to her brain.

"I don't want to get married!" Dani shouts.

It seems to echo through the room.

Nora's hand twitches around the box. Dani has no earthly idea what she might be thinking. Nora has one of the most spectacular poker faces Dani has ever known, especially when she's trying to process something. It's like a porcelain mask, with the slight movement of her hand being the only indication that she's feeling anything at all.

"Of course," Nora says after an excruciatingly long pause, though Dani can hardly hear her over her own thundering heartbeat. "That's the logical conclusion."

"I wasn't going to give it to you," Dani says, each word tumbling over the next in her panic. "I know you don't want to get married. I know that."

"You're right," Nora says. Her face is still a mask of calm. "I don't."

Past the roar of panic in Dani's ears, Nora's voice is different. Usually, Nora refrains from speaking until she can get control of it. Now it quivers slightly. Each word is sharp and a little over-enunciated.

Dani likes to think she's known Nora long enough to pick up when she's lying.

"Your tie clip is on the side table," Nora murmurs, brushing past Dani and pressing the ring box into her hand.

The box snaps closed. Dani turns, catching Nora's sleeve. "Wait. I thought—"

Before she can line her words up in the right order, the door is opening. Mila appears and grabs each of their arms to pull them toward the stairs. "*There* you are. Come on, everyone's waiting."

Dani hides the ring box in her fist and stuffs it into her pocket as soon as Mila lets go of her arm.

She accompanies Nora down the aisle without a tie clip.

The wedding is every bit as beautiful as Sarah and Naomi deserve. They exchange vows on the dock, with everyone they love gathered on the grass. Before the thing has even begun, Aunt Carol is right up front with Naomi's parents, already sobbing in joy at the sight of her daughter standing at the altar. Ryan serves as both ring bearer and flower boy, scattering petals from his bedazzled fanny pack down the aisle as he dances his way to hand the rings to the maids of honour. When the occasional riverboat drifts past during the ceremony, they honk and cheer for the happy couple.

Dani passes the ring to Sarah with careful hands while Nora does the same for Naomi. Owen is sniffling to Dani's left; Mila has full-on tears rolling down her cheeks as Naomi slides a wedding band onto Sarah's finger.

Nora has the driest eyes in the bunch. To someone who doesn't know her well, she might seem less affected than everyone else, but Dani is struck more by the look in her eyes than she would ever be by Nora's tears.

Nora is looking at Naomi and Sarah as they finish their vows with an expression so intense that Dani can't look away from it, even to watch the brides' first kiss as a married couple. Nora claps along with everyone else, smiling when Sarah lifts Naomi up into the kiss, but there's something beyond simple happiness in it. Dani can't quite parse it.

When she catches Dani's eye across the aisle, Dani has never been more curious about what's going on in Nora's head. It takes some self-control not to interrupt the hour of picture-taking that follows the registry signing to ask her about it, but Dani manages to rein in the impulse.

It helps that Dani is a bit afraid of the answer.

The reception is classic Riverwalk. After dinner and speeches and the first dance, the party ramps up almost immediately—music blasts from the rented speaker system. The drinks flow, and the drinking leads to dancing. Dani participates a little, joining in a few line dances and taking a couple rounds of shots with the brides, but it's a distraction more than anything. A way to keep her occupied, rather than mulling over the image of Nora standing in their bedroom with the ring in her hand. The ring that's now burning a hole in Dani's pocket.

Nora is predictably sticking to the party's edges, avoiding the dance floor and instead chatting with Aunt Carol. She's been watching Dani closely with that same strange expression since the reception started.

When a slow song comes on and everyone separates into couples, it's a shock to the system when Nora, of her own volition, is the one to find Dani in the crowd. That porcelain expression from earlier is gone, and Nora holds her hand out with a soft smile in a wordless request to dance.

"Are you sure?" Dani asks. Nora's avoidance so far has been pretty clear, and the sudden switch is a surprise. Dani had been expecting to have The Talk tomorrow.

"Always." Nora guides Dani's hand to her waist. Her own arm lands on Dani's shoulder, pulling her close as they sway gently to the music.

Dani clears her throat. "Nice wedding, right?"

Nora's lips quirk. "Beautiful. You did a great job with the arch."

The song is soft, and seems softer with the yellow glow of the fairy lights strung overhead. Through the tent's open sides, the river shimmers with the approaching sunset. All around them, everyone dances in their respective pairs—Naomi and Sarah, Ryan and Owen, Mila and her husband Lucas. Each couple wrapped up in each other, sealed in their own private moments.

"About the ring," Nora says.

Dani's stomach does a funny sort of swoop, aided by the two fuzzy navel shots she took not long ago. Her grip tightens on Nora's waist. She glances around them, but nobody seems to be paying attention. Dani is absolutely sure her ears are red, judging by how hot they feel.

"Is this why you've been asking me once a week lately if I'm happy?" Nora asks. She's looking up at Dani intently, like she's trying to solve one of her thousand-piece puzzles.

"I wasn't going to propose," Dani says quickly.

Nora raises an eyebrow. It says all it needs to say.

"Well—okay, yes. I was originally. But then, at the dress fitting, you said you didn't want to get married, so I put it away and I wasn't going to, I swear." Dani lowers her voice when a few people glance their way. "I wouldn't push you like that. I was going to keep it and give it to you someday as like—I don't know—a promise ring or something. I'm totally fine with not getting—"

"Yes."

Dani stops dead.

Everyone else keeps swaying, leaving them motionless in a sea of swishing dresses. The music plays on.

"Yes, what?" Dani asks.

Somehow, Nora's eyebrow raises higher. "What do you think?"

"But I didn't propose."

"And yet."

Dani shakes her head, letting out a burst of nervous laughter to loosen the tension in her chest as she starts up their swaying again. She's not even sure what song they're dancing to at this point. "Nora, you don't want to get married. I promise I'm okay with that. And, yeah, that's why I've been asking if you're happy," Dani says. "I just have this—this fear that I'm holding you back. That you might someday regret leaving your whole life behind to come back to Riverwalk for me."

"I didn't think you were ever afraid," Nora says. The hand on Dani's shoulder moves to the back of her neck, and Nora scratches gently at the base of her hair. It's something she always does when Dani is upset, to calm her. It works like a charm. "You've been so sure of yourself since we met."

"I'm afraid to lose you," Dani admits, just loud enough to be heard over the crescendo of the song. "People break up over marriage all the time. I don't want that. I just want you, in whatever form that takes."

"Dani," Nora says, more firmly this time, "*yes*."

Dani stops again. Thinking and swaying and talking all at once with two shots in her system is making things too difficult. "The absolute last thing in the world I want is for you to say yes just because you think it's what I want, and then regret it."

"I'm not saying yes just to make you happy," Nora says.

"You literally said a few weeks ago—"

Nora's fingers touch under Dani's chin, cutting her off gently before she builds up too much steam. "I know what I said. Can you listen to me for a second?"

Dani nods silently.

The slow song ends. The dance floor floods with people again as something more upbeat starts to play, and Nora leads Dani by the hand out of the tent and over to the edge of the woods. The sun is setting over the tips of the trees, making Nora's skin glow golden orange.

"Firstly, I never actually said I didn't want to get married. Just that I didn't think it would ever happen," Nora says.

Dani opens her mouth to reply, but all it takes is a tilt of Nora's head to close it again.

"Secondly. Before we met, I thought I'd be alone for the rest of my life." Nora takes both of Dani's hands. They hang between their bodies with Nora's thumbs making little circles. "And I was okay with that. I never really considered marriage as a real option. And then I met you, and the first part of that equation changed. I never thought to re-examine the second."

Nora bites at her lip, slowly wearing away her lipstick. She's clearly heading somewhere with this, and Dani keeps her mouth shut to let her work through it.

"When I found that ring, it was the first time that it struck me that you might actually want that," Nora finally says. "With me. For some reason."

Nora's low self-worth has been an issue since Dani met her; she's always thought negatively of herself, always given herself a high bar that no human being could ever rise to. Only in the last few years has it been getting a bit better. Clearly it still needs some work.

"Of course I do," Dani says. "How many times have I said I want to spend the rest of our lives together?"

"It's one thing to say it. It's another to bind yourself legally to me. My father went through wives like he went through cars: a new model every few years," Nora says. She's been staring somewhere around their feet, but now she raises her gaze to Dani's; they're shiny in the twinkling lights overhead. "That's all marriage ever was to me. But now we're at this beautiful wedding, surrounded by everyone we love, and I started thinking about what it would actually be like to marry you. To *be* married to you."

Dani swallows, hard. "And now it's a yes? Just like that?"

"You've always shown me that my initial assessments can be wrong." Nora drifts closer, squeezing Dani's hands. "The ceremony, the parties, I don't care so much about that. But you're *it* for me. If it isn't you, it's no one. What's a wedding besides a celebration of that?"

"But, what if—"

"You know I didn't come back to Riverwalk just for you, right?" Nora interrupts.

Dani blinks. Nora's brow is raised, but she's smiling—a wry, affectionate sort of look while Dani flounders.

"Does it sound totally self-absorbed to say no?" Dani asks.

Nora laughs. Her head tips forward, her hair spilling over her shoulder to hang like a curtain—it's lost most of its curl now, back to its usual gentle wave. "A lot of it was for you. Because I love you. But I also fell in love with this place. I fell in love with this house and the bar and the woods. I fell in love with our friends. Our *family*. I fell in love with this life, Dani. I don't regret it. I never will."

There's a loud, frenetic country song playing in the tent. When Dani glances over, Ryan is dancing on a folding table while Owen waits to catch him when it inevitably collapses. Sarah and Naomi are wrapped up in each other at the head table, leading everyone in shouting the lyrics. Mila is carrying the empty punch bowl inside—she shoots a finger gun at them as she passes.

This isn't just Dani's home. It's Nora's home too. These are *their* people. Their family. It's their life.

It's only when Dani pulls her attention away from the tent that she realizes Nora has sunk down onto one knee.

Suddenly, Dani's heart is doing something strange in her chest that makes it hard to breathe. Nora is holding up something that glints in the fairy lights—a simple silver band. It's Nora's engineer's ring, earned when she graduated and always worn on her pinky.

"Dani," Nora says, seemingly uncaring that she's getting dirt on her dress, "will you marry me?"

Of all the ways Dani ever imagined a proposal going, this possibility never even entered her mind.

It's perfect. So perfect that it feels like fate. Here in their home, within eyesight of the dock where Dani first opened herself up to Nora entirely, serenaded by the voices of their friends from the tent. It's everything it needs to be.

Dani isn't sure whether to cry or laugh or pull Nora into a kiss. In the end, she does all three.

She's kissed Nora hundreds of times by now. Thousands. Each one has felt special in its way, from the whirlwind exhilaration of their very first to the sweet, simple comfort of four years in. But this one is in another category. It's deep and slow. Intimate. Unhurried. Nora fits against her perfectly, and Dani can feel her smiling into the kiss. It seems to stretch out forever and be over in no time at all.

When Nora pulls back, ending it with a soft kiss to the tip of Dani's nose, Dani is left feeling a bit punch-drunk. She's clinging to Nora's waist—she has no memory of moving her hands there in the first place. She's completely lost track of why they started kissing, lost in the softness of Nora's lips.

"That's. You're..." Dani blinks a few times, letting Nora come back into focus. What's left of Nora's lipstick is smudged. "What were we talking about?"

Nora takes Dani's left hand from her waist, holding it between them again. The engineer's ring touches the very tip of Dani's finger, and it all comes back in a rush of breathless joy.

"May I?" Nora whispers.

Wordlessly, Dani pushes her fingertip through the ring.

It barely goes past the first knuckle.

"Shit," Nora says, grinning when Dani starts to giggle. Their foreheads knock together. "I forget how big your hands are. I'll get you a real one that fits, I promise."

Still laughing, Dani pulls the velvet box out of her suit pocket. Nora holds her left hand up without being asked.

The ring slips perfectly onto her finger. It's small and elegant, a gold band with mostly inset stones; it's what her parents could afford when they got engaged. Nothing like the rock she's sure Nora might have gotten if she'd chosen someone in the city. Someone more on her level.

"This is beautiful," Nora murmurs. She holds it up to the light. "It looks vintage."

A deep, settled sense of calm washes over Dani. Whatever vestiges of fear she might still have had, of that inadequacy that's haunted her for months, are eased by Nora so naturally that it's like they never existed.

"It was my mother's," Dani says.

Nora's eyes widen and then soften. She wraps her hand around Dani's tie, tugging gently until Dani dips down for another kiss. "It's perfect. Absolutely perfect."

Their lips have barely brushed before the tent erupts into noise nearby. It's mostly laughter and some raucous shouting—Ryan's table has finally collapsed, leaving him half-caught by Owen's taller frame. Someone hands him a fresh drink, which he takes a sip of after he's gotten himself comfortable in a bridal carry in his taller boyfriend's arms.

Nora smiles fondly, leaning against Dani to watch the chaos from afar.

Dani dips down ever so slightly to talk low in her ear. "Do you think they'll miss us if we go upstairs right now?"

"Probably," Nora says. Despite it all, she seizes Dani's hand.

It's a mad dash up the deck stairs and through the sliding door to the kitchen, where Mila is busy mixing another batch of punch.

She hardly looks up when they enter. "Hey, guys! Do you have any gin? We ran out of vodka."

"Liquor cabinet, above the microwave," Nora calls out as they pass, dragging Dani up the stairs. "Take whatever you want!"

The bedroom door has hardly slammed behind them before Nora is pulling Dani in by the collar for a hard, messy kiss.

"Mila is *so* going to tell everyone we left the party to bone," Dani mumbles into the kiss. She starts to walk them toward the bed, Nora walking backwards as she works on getting Dani's tie loosened.

"Sarah and Naomi had sex in the bathroom at their own bridal shower," Nora says, low and breathy as she bites down on Dani's lower lip. "They can deal."

Dani can't argue with that.

It's six steps from the door to the bed, but the journey takes longer than usual as Nora pulls Dani's tie free and deftly unbuttons her shirt. She gets as far as unbuckling Dani's belt before her knees hit the mattress, and, with a fist clenched in Dani's shirt, she tries to pull Dani with her as she falls back.

Nora's hair fans out on their white duvet, a familiar contrast of dark against light. Dani stays standing, bent slightly, but resisting the pull of Nora's hands. "Wait."

Nora props herself up on an elbow. Her brow furrows. "What's wrong?"

Dani grins. She sinks down onto one knee at the edge of the bed, slowly parting Nora's legs and pressing a light kiss to her knee. "Just one thing. I never got to actually ask, you know."

Nora's posture relaxes. Her head falls back as she chuckles, lifting her hips when Dani slides quick fingers under her dress to hook around her underwear and ease them down her legs. "Well then, ask away."

"Eleanor Cromwell." Dani tosses the scrap of fabric aside and smooths her hands up Nora's calves. "Will—"

"Yes," Nora says immediately.

"Impatient. You're interrupting my moment," Dani says. She grins, sliding Nora's skirt ever upward as she kisses her way higher and higher. "Will...you..."

"Yes," Nora insists, her smile widening when Dani nuzzles at the faded stretchmarks that grace her inner thighs. She tries to ease a hand into Dani's hair, but the hairspray makes it more difficult than usual; after a moment of giggling, she resorts to gently holding the back of Dani's head. "I'm always going to say—"

The words break off into a squeak when Dani rises, scooping Nora up and manoeuvring her further up the bed. Her back hits the mattress with a breathless sort of sound, which shifts into a whimper when Dani gently pins her hands. Dani hovers there, grinning and just out of reach, as Nora arches up into her.

"Marry me?" Dani whispers.

Nora's eyes twinkle in the last of the bluish dusk filtering through the window. She hooks a leg around Dani's hips, pulling her in until they're pressed close together, even with her hands occupied. Dani can feel the heat of her, pressed against her hip bone.

"Only if you kiss me right now."

It's the easiest wish Dani has ever granted.

The party rages on outside the window an hour later as Dani catches her breath, the music audible even through the closed window. The sheets are bunched up at the foot of the bed, the pillows in disarray—Nora is stretched out beside her, naked and sweaty and gorgeous even in the dark. Neither of them has moved to turn on the bedside lamp.

"Damn. We *are* good at that," Nora says breathlessly.

"Next-level. We could teach a class."

"Do you think they noticed we left?"

"Depends how much liquor Mila put in that punch."

Nora chuckles, wiggling until she's tucked into Dani's shoulder. "Our wedding had better not be anything as big as this one. I don't think I can say my vows in front of this many people."

"Deal." Dani kisses Nora's knuckles over the ring, smiling at the cool metal and stone against her lips. *Our wedding.*

"And can we skip the engagement party? And the bridal shower. It's just too many gifts."

"You got it."

"And I want you there when my dress is fitted," Nora says. "None of that *not before the wedding day* bullshit. And the bachelorette—"

Dani snorts, kissing the top of Nora's head. "Babe. If you wanted to get married alone and naked on the beach, I'd do it. Whatever you want. I just want to be your wife."

Dani can feel Nora's smile against her shoulder.

To keep from hijacking Sarah and Naomi's day, Nora takes the ring off before they go back outside and leaves it in the velvet box on the bedside table, but Dani keeps the engineer's ring on the end of her finger.

The party is rowdier than ever when they re-enter the tent, dressed in their somewhat rumpled clothes. Dani's hair was unsalvageable, the only solution being to throw it into a ponytail, but since she wears it like that every other day of her life, she's hopeful that nobody will notice. Nobody makes a fuss about their presence—the late-night snack table has been set up recently, and everyone is busy building their own poutines—so, to avert suspicion, they part ways at the door with a quick kiss and a shared smile.

Dani has already scarfed two servings of fries when Sarah finds her in the crowd. She's less drunk than Dani thought she'd be by now, though there's a noticeable flush to her cheeks.

"Are you guys good?" Sarah shouts over the music. She piles her own plate high with fries and cheese, pouring an obscene amount of gravy over the whole thing. "Mila said you left in a hurry."

Dani nabs a fry. They agreed to keep a lid on the engagement, but she can't seem to stop smiling. "We're great. Totally perfect."

Sarah's eyes narrow. She looks over to Nora at the other side of the tent—she's dancing with Naomi and Mila, glowing brighter than the fairy lights.

Sarah drops her plate onto the nearest table to seize Dani's hand, staring at the evidence.

Dani wiggles the tip of her ring finger.

"You son of a bitch!" Sarah yells, grinning wide and throwing Dani's arm back at her. "Did she propose to *you*?"

Dani laughs, shrugging helplessly. "We sort of proposed to each other?"

"I don't see her ring?"

"Upstairs, in the box. We didn't want to take the attention away from your big day."

Sarah scoffs, pushing Dani in Nora's direction. "Don't be stupid! Go put it on her. This is the perfect place to announce it."

"Are you sure?"

"*Go*, you dingus."

Thankfully, Nora is enthusiastic about the idea. Dani sprints back to the house and Nora slips the ring back on, accompanying Dani to the front of the tent, where Naomi is shouting for everyone to quiet down.

"We have a big announcement over here!" Naomi says, gesturing them both to the mic. "Dani, Nora, do you have something to tell us?"

"Just a quick thing," Dani says, clearing her throat into the microphone and glancing at Nora. "Um. We're probably gonna have another wedding to plan pretty soon?"

When Nora raises her hand to show off her ring finger, the tent erupts.

The loud cheers drown out the music. Mila starts to shower them with leftover flower petals. Owen and Ryan surge to the stage, grabbing Dani by the waist and lifting her into the air with some difficulty. Aunt Carol pulls Nora into a hug, crying what Dani knows are tears of joy.

Over it all, Dani meets Nora's eyes. She's smiling, genuine, and sparkling in the midst of the life they've built together.

Dani can't wait to keep building.

If you enjoyed this short story, you might also like the novel where these characters first met: *Shifting Gears*.

About the Authors

Liz Arncliffe

Liz Arncliffe has been telling stories big and small since she was a child, spinning yarns about imaginary critters in the Appalachian foothills where she grew up. She's only ever lived in the southeastern United States, though she constantly threatens her wife and family with packing up and moving to parts far and wide. Liz has spent much of her adult life either studying or teaching history, religion, and historic theologies. She loves to travel, grow things, read, and write. She watches far too much tennis and spends any remaining time cursing at the woodpeckers in her backyard as they refuse to respect her boundaries.

Thea Belmont

Thea grew-up in rural Australia, developing her love of reading and writing from a young age. As a young adult, she left for the city, where she had her first brush with kink and fell in love with a world that balanced devotion and discipline.

She currently enjoys life in Sydney with her cat.

Cheyenne Blue

Cheyenne Blue has been hanging around the lesbian erotica world since 1999 writing short lesbian erotica which has appeared in over 90 anthologies. Her stories got longer and longer and more and more romantic, so she went with the flow and switched to writing romance novels. As well as her romance novels available from Ylva Publishing, she's the editor of *Forbidden Fruit: stories of unwise lesbian desire*, a 2015 finalist for both the Lambda Literary Award and Golden Crown Literary Award, and of *First: Sensual Lesbian Stories of New Beginnings*.

Cheyenne loves writing big-hearted romance often set in rural Australia because that's where she lives. She has a small house on a hill with a big deck and bigger view—perfect for morning coffee, evening wine, and anytime writing.

Carrie Byrd

Carrie Byrd is a California native and college professor who lives just outside Philadelphia. She loves hiking and kayaking, burritos, video games, Old Hollywood, Eagles football and Phillies baseball, teaching poetry, talking a mile a minute, and traveling around the world with her wife.

An extrovert who thrives on a stage, Carrie once won first place by crowd vote for her improvised lip sync of "Jessie's Girl" at a packed drag brunch. She considers it one of her life's greatest accomplishments.

Carrie's favorite word is *thistle*. It feels good to say out loud.

Charley Clarke

Charley Clarke writes romance, both contemporary and speculative fiction. She loves baked goods, long walks, and relaxing with a good book and a cup of tea.

Jazz Forrester

Jazz Forrester spends her days getting lost in research rabbit holes over insignificant details. Growing up in rural Ontario, she spent her life constantly reading and creating stories in her head without ever thinking to write them down. Once she started putting pen to paper in 2018, she never looked back. When she's not writing, she spends her time with fandom nonsense, gaming, playing D&D, and trying out new recipes on her partner.

Jazz currently lives in Niagara, Ontario, and enjoys her day job talking to people about history.

Jennifer Giacalone

Jen Giacalone is a neurodivergent queer nerd who has lived many lives and brings with her a wealth of experience to tell high-octane drama, thriller, and mystery stories across books, film, and TV.

After spending her twenties as a rock and roll frontwoman, and her thirties as a graphic designer in boardrooms of Fortune 500 companies, she's currently in what she likes to call her "final form" as a writer.

You can usually find her disappearing down rabbit holes of fascinating research on random subjects that will turn up in one of her books. And, of course, she sprinkles a little glitter on everything she touches.

Quinn Ivins

Quinn Ivins has been addicted to romance since she was a teenager, when she stayed up on school nights to read more X-Files fanfiction.

Now finally done with school after 27 years, she has published three lesbian romance novels. Her second book, Worthy of Love, won the 2022 Goldie award for Contemporary Romance: Mid-Length.

Quinn lives in the United States with her wife and her son.

Jae

Jae grew up amidst the vineyards of southern Germany. She spent her childhood with her nose buried in a book, earning her the nickname "professor." The writing bug bit her at the age of eleven. Since 2006, she has been writing mostly in English.

She used to work as a psychologist but gave up her day job in December 2013 to become a full-time writer and a part-time editor. As far as she's concerned, it's the best job in the world.

When she's not writing, she likes to spend her time reading, indulging her ice cream and office supply addictions, and watching way too many crime shows.

Lola Keeley

Lola Keeley is a writer and coder. After moving to London to pursue her love of theatre, she later wound up living every five-year-old's dream of being a train driver on the London Underground. She has since emerged, blinking into the sunlight, to find herself writing books. She now lives in Edinburgh, Scotland, with her wife and four cats.

E. J. Noyes

E. J. Noyes is an Australian transplanted to New Zealand which may be one of the best things that's happened to her. She lives with her wife and the best cat in the world.

She started writing because she was bored and had "ideas" and thought writing might free up some brain space. It didn't. Now she's addicted and spends much of her free time bashing out words while more new words jostle for attention.

In her scant free time, E. J. scream-swears at computer games, wishes she was skiing, coos at her cat and works the fact she's a best-selling and award-winning author into conversation.

E. J. loves to procrastinate, so feel free to get in contact so she can read that instead of doing work.

Liz Rain

Liz is from sunny Queensland, Australia and grew up doing lots of swimming, cricket and netball. She started a degree in journalism but decided early on she didn't want to be a journalist because she heard the hours were long and the pay was bad. She couldn't think of anything else she wanted to study, however, so decided to get the degree anyway.

After that she taught English in Japan, where she joined a soccer team to meet girls. Luckily the captain was a very nice American who is now her wife.

They live quietly in Logan, Queensland with their two daughters and a cat named Carly-Rae. Liz's interests are women's Australian Rules football (especially the Brisbane Lions) and teaching herself the mandolin off YouTube.

Rachael Sommers

Rachael Sommers was born and raised in the North-West of England, where she began writing at the age of thirteen, and has been unable to stop since. A biology graduate, she currently works in education and constantly dreams of travelling the world. In her spare time, she enjoys horse riding, board games, escape rooms and, of, course, reading.

Tiana Warner

Tiana Warner is a writer and outdoor enthusiast from British Columbia, Canada. She is best known for her critically acclaimed "Mermaids of Eriana Kwai" trilogy and its comic adaptation. Tiana is a lifelong horseback rider, a former programmer with a Computer Science degree, and a dedicated supporter of animal rescue initiatives.

Chris Zett

Chris Zett lives near Berlin, Germany, with her wife. TV inspired her to study medicine, but she found out soon enough that real life in a hospital consists more of working long hours than performing heroic rescues. The part about finding a workplace romance turned out to be true, though.

She uses any opportunity to escape the routine by reading, writing, or traveling. Her favorite destinations include penguin colonies in Patagonia and stone circles in Scotland.

Beyond the Epilogue

Available in paperback and e-book formats.

ISBN (paperback): 978-3-69006-169-8
ISBN (e-book): 978-3-69006-170-4
ISBN (pdf): 978-3-69006-171-1

Published by Ylva Publishing, legal entity of Ylva Verlag, e.Kfr.

Ylva Verlag, e.Kfr.
Owner: Astrid Ohletz
Am Kirschgarten 2
65830 Kriftel
Germany

www.ylva-publishing.com

First edition: 2026

For questions about product safety, please reach out to:
info@ylva-publishing.com

Credits
Edited by Astrid Ohletz, Michelle Aguilar, and Lee Winter

Cover Design and Print Layout by Ylva Publishing

Image rights cover illustration provided by Canva; Graphics provided by Canva

www.ingramcontent.com/pod-product-compliance
Lightning Source LLC
LaVergne TN
LVHW041110080826
845145LV00007B/1751

* 9 7 8 3 6 9 0 0 6 1 6 9 8 *